Asian Contextual Theology for the Third Millennium

Princeton Theological Monograph Series

K. C. Hanson, Series Editor

Recent volumes in the series

Bonnie L. Pattison
Poverty in the Theology of John Calvin

Anette Ejsing
A Theology of Anticipation: A Constructive Study of C. S. Peirce

Michael G. Cartwright
Practices, Politics, and Performance: Toward a Communal Hermeneutic for Christian Ethics

Stephen Finlan and Vladimir Kharlamov, editors
Theōsis: Deification in Christian Theology

David A. Ackerman
Lo, I Tell You a Mystery: Cross, Resurrection, and Paraenesis in the Rhetoric of 1 Corinthians

John A. Vissers
The Neo-Orthodox Theology of W. W. Bryden

Sam Hamstra, editor
The Reformed Pastor by John Williamson Nevin

Byron C. Bangert
Consenting to God and Nature: Toward a Theocentric, Naturalistic, Theological Ethics

Richard Valantasis et al., editors
The Subjective Eye: Essays in Honor of Margaret Miles

Caryn Riswold
Coram Deo: Human Life in the Vision of God

Philip L. Mayo
"Those Who Call Themselves Jews": The Church and Judaism in the Apocalypse of John

Asian Contextual Theology for the Third Millennium

A Theology of Minjung in Fourth-Eye Formation

EDITED BY

Paul S. Chung

Kim Kyoung-Jae

Veli-Matti Kärkkäinen

Korean essays translated by

Paul S. Chung

Pickwick *Publications*

An imprint of *Wipf and Stock Publishers*
199 West 8th Avenue • Eugene OR 97401

ASIAN CONTEXTUAL THEOLOGY FOR THE THIRD MILLENNIUM
A Theology of Minjung in Fourth-Eye Formation
Princeton Theological Monograph Series 70

ISBN 10: 1-55635-044-9
ISBN 13: 978-1-55635-044-3

Cataloging-in-Publication data:

Asian contextual theology for the third millennium: a theology of minjung in fourth-eye formation / edited by Paul S. Chung, Kim Kyoung-Jae, and Veli-Matti Kärkkäinen.

Eugene, Ore.: Pickwick Publications, 2007
Princeton Theological Monograph Series 70

xii + 360 p. ; 23 cm.

Includes bibliography

ISBN 10: 1-55635-044-9
ISBN 13: 978-1-55635-044-3

1. Minjung theology. 2. Christianity—Asia. 3. Theology, Doctrinal—Asia. 4. Christianity—Korea. I. Chung, Paul S. II. Kyoung-Jae, Kim. III. Kärkkäinen, Veli-Matti. IV. Title. V. Series.

BT30 A8 A78 2007

Manufactured in the U.S.A.

Contents

PART II
Asian Contextual Theology and Interfaith Diapraxis

PART III
Asian Contextual Theology in Dialogue with Judaism

Foreword

John B. Cobb, Jr.

BEGINNING in 1973 with the publication of *The Theological Declaration of Korean Christians,* minjung theology grasped the attention of the world. Its authors paid a high price for their commitment to the Korean people and especially to the exploited poor. Some of them were rejected by the Christian churches. Some lost their positions as teachers. Others were imprisoned by the military government.

The interpretation of the Bible by minjung scholars, and especially of the gospel, was impressive as scholarship and gave critical grounds for their work. Although they were part of a worldwide liberation movement, they clearly did their own thinking and carried out their own scholarship. Minjung theology employed sophisticated scholarly methods learned from Western Christians. But it was a fully contextualized form of theology able to enter into discussion with theologians from other countries as an important expression of global Christian thought.

However, by the 1990s developments in Korean theology had dropped out of sight for theologians in other countries. This was partly because of changes we should all celebrate. The improved political and economic climate in South Korea reduced the need for the real world struggle of which minjung theology was a part. The long-exploited workers at last began to benefit from the growing prosperity. Unfortunately, it was also partly because of the short attention span of readers looking for the latest novelties. It did not mean that South Koreans had stopped doing their own thinking, or that they had ceased to do so creatively and well.

It is past time now to revisit Korea and the development of Christian theology there. It is time to acknowledge the creative work of a new generation of Korean theologians. This book reacquaints us with the earlier phases of minjung theology and helps us to see how it has developed in ever changing contexts. It brings Korean voices back into the international conversation.

The heart of the book is made up of the contributions of Korean scholars. However, to add to its international character, the editors have included essays by North American and European theologians as well. Many of us are happy in this way to make any contribution we can to revitalizing discussion between progressive Korean theologians and the West.

Christianity plays a far more important role in Korea than in other nations of Northeast Asia. In Japan it is a rather stable minority with a public voice disproportionate to its membership. This is largely because of the prominence of Christian institutions such as universities. Christianity also provides a basis for some Japanese intellectuals to play a counter-cultural role. Still it remains a minor factor in Japanese society as a whole. In China it has emerged from a time of persecution with considerable vitality and is growing rapidly partly because of the spiritual vacuum left by the end of Maoist teaching. But Christianity is even more marginal in China than in Japan. It has little foothold in influential circles. In Korea, in contrast, it is a dynamic force in the culture and politically and socially important.

It is well to recognize, however, that other religious movements also play an important role in Korea. Unlike Japan and China, and European nations as well, South Korea is a religious country. What happens in the religious communities is important for the people as a whole. That gives a significance to theology there that it lacks in many parts of the world. Most of the theology taught and preached in South Korea is quite conservative and closely follows the teaching of nineteenth-century Western missionaries. Some of it is modeled on contemporary American conservative evangelicals or Fundamentalists. All the more, the work of Korean pioneers in progressive theological work is important for the future of the country.

I rejoice that in this volume there is recognition of the valuable role of Han Shin Seminary and its leader, Kim Kyoung-Jae. He has not only contributed his own creative ideas to the development of Korean theology, but he has also insured that Han Shin would offer a home for frontline thinkers. He is widely appreciated in Korea but too little known elsewhere.

Acknowledgments

In this volume we express our gratitude to contributors. Asian minjung theology implies an important paradigm shift for the Asian church, because now it must take seriously a combination of Jesus and *ochlos*-minjung in favor of Christian social responsibility. Prior to this minjung turn, there was a forerunner, Kim Chai-Choon, who is almost unknown to English-speaking readers. Since minjung theology became popular in the 70s and 80s in South Korea, there have been significant efforts among Asian theologians to develop and deepen its insight and inspiration in an encounter with the wisdom of World Religions on the one hand, and to correct and improve its anti-Jewish strains in terms of Jewish-Christian renewal on the other. The former effort is represented by a leading theologian, Kim Kyoung-Jae, who was a pupil of Kim Chai-Choon, Ahn Byung-Mu and Suh Nam-Dong. He appropriates the hermeneutical-cultural theory of a fusion of horizons for minjung theology. The minjung turn from a political perspective to a cultural one finds its meaning in Kim's attention to religious-cultural minjung in world religions.

We appreciate Moltmann's rejoinder to the minjung theology of Ahn Byung-Mu, his former friend, written in his memory and dedicated to the Han Shin Theological Seminary, the Mecca of Asian contextual minjung theology in South Korea. Special gratitude should be given to the late F.-W. Marquardt at the Free University of Berlin and to Andreas Pangritz at the University of Bonn. For F.-W. Marquardt's theology after Shoa, Judaism is not regarded as one of the world religions, but as a root of Christianity.

Asian contextual theology is open proleptically towards being challenged and renewed by the reality of minjung and the wisdom of World Religions, in which the character of contextuality is to be shaped and dynamically reformulated. As *ecclessia semper reformanda,* so *theologia semper reformanda*. Last, but not least, Kim Kyoung-Jae and Paul S. Chung offer their gratitude to John B. Cobb, Jr. and Hans Küng for their leadership in interreligious dialogue and solidarity with Asian contextual theology and with the church.

Acknowledgment is also given to the following publishers:

1. "Minjung Theology for the Ruling Classes" by Jürgen Moltmann / trans. Margaret Kohl. From *Experiences in Theology* (pp. 249–67) by Jürgen Moltmann, copyright © 2000 Augsburg Fortress. Used with permission.
2. "Warum mich als Christen der Talmud interessiert!" by Friedrich Wilhelm Marquardt / trans. Don McCord. From *Auf Einem Schul-Weg: Kleinere Christlich-Jüdische Lerneinheiten* (pp. 257–76) by Friedrich Wilhelm Marquardt, copyright ©1999 Orient & Okzident. Used with permission.
3. "The Christian Witness to Buddhists" by John B. Cobb, Jr. From *Beyond Dialogue: Toward a Mutual Transformation of Christianity and Buddhism* (pp.121–43) by John B. Cobb, Jr. copyright © 1998 Wipf and Stock Publishers. Used with permission.

Introduction

Asian Contextual Theology of Minjung and Beyond

Paul S. Chung

Asian minjung theology refers to a Korean contextual theology of suffering people that arose out of the Christian response to the South Korean social and political reality in the 70s and 80s. Some Korean theologians started with the particularity of their own situation in solidarity with poor people's attempts to overcome their suffering and in responsibility to their liberating history and culture. A contextual theology of minjung must consider the universal significance of Jesus Christ and its witness to God's reign in this particular East Asian context, which is characterized by relative economic backwardness and by an abundance of multireligious spiritualities. It is these things that constitute Asian contextual theology and ecclesiology.

Asian contextual theology of minjung is aimed at reinventing and transforming itself. This is also its challenge, as it struggles with and approaches a new situation, so that a shift can occur from the "political and populist minjung" of the older frame of reference (in the 70s and 80s) towards a "spiritual and multi-religious minjung" of the new frame of reference (the third millennium). Further, this shift of reference must also take into account the socio-political reality of minjung under economic globalization.

In this volume, we attempt to highlight the genesis, progress, and transformation of Asian contextual theology of minjung, introducing its historical point of departure, its development, and its transformation in light of younger Korean and Korean American scholars' endeavors. In this regard, the new Asian contextual theology, which is emerging, strives to integrate both minjung and the wisdom of World Religions into its own framework and direction, assuming the character of a public theology and remaining humble and open before God's mystery while featuring its association with minjung in a holistic way. Let me delineate the contents and perspectives of Asian contextual theology of minjung.

The Presbyterian Church in the Republic of Korea (PROK) and its Han Shin Seminary developed and championed minjung theology in order to challenge the political dictatorship and economic injustice of the 1970s and onward. Ahn Byung-Mu, together with Suh Nam-Dong, discovered and extended the meaning and significance of the term *ochlos* in the New Testament in relation to the social and political reality of the poor and the oppressed in the Korean context. However, their theological struggle cannot be understood properly without considering the influence of their teacher, Rev. Dr. Kim Chai-Choon (1901–1987), a founding father of the PROK.

In addition to the minjung theology represented by Ahn Byung-Mu and Suh Nam-Dong, there are diverse trends in contextualizing minjung theology from different perspectives in South Korea.[1] However, for the purposes of this study I will trace and analyze the line and direction from Kim Chai-Choon and the multi-religiously fused theory of Christianity by Chung Dai-Wi via the minjung theology of Ahn and Suh towards the hermeneutical theology of religions by Kim Kyoung-Jae. And then I will discuss different perspectives on Asian contextual theology of minjung and others in regards to Judaism and pneumatological-Pentecostal spirituality.

Kim Chai-Choon is widely regarded as the first committed liberal-minded theologian of the Korean Protestant church. As a church leader, he combated the over-influence of Western missionaries and the fundamentalism of Korean Protestantism while emphasizing instead the Christian responsibility for history and society. Moreover, he recognized the importance of other religions already in the 60s.

With his approach "Jesus in History," he attempted to comprehend Jesus' life and ministry concretely in relation to history. Because of his theological orientation, he became the scapegoat of fundamental-conservatives in South Korea. According to Kim, Jesus is the *Logos* who came into human history and became flesh. Jesus did not bypass the reality of human life and social history. His proclamation of God's kingdom aimed at establishing the order of the heavenly kingdom on earth. Finally, Jesus was crucified within this history.

At this juncture, Kim makes it a priority that the real life of Jesus be grounded in history, such that a dualistic understanding of Jesus at the

[1] Cf. Michael Amaladoss, *Life in Freedom: Liberation Theologies from Asia* (Maryknoll: Orbis, 1997) 3–11.

historical level or at the kerygmatic level is sharply critiqued. "History embraces the secular world, which God in Jesus Christ has declared regarding the world."[2] Jesus in history reached his climax when he became the suffering servant of God on the cross. In evaluating this statement, Ahn Byung-Mu characterizes Kim as the first theologian in South Korea who comprehended Christ in the secular world.[3]

Kim claims that God's history in Jesus Christ is "a history that reveals the spiritual and moral dimensions of a historical event, and interprets its new eschatological meaning."[4] In accepting Karl Barth's idea of *Urgeschichte*, Kim seeks the meaning of incarnation in light of Christ's eternal being from a salvific-historical perspective. Therefore, salvation history, according to Kim, can be comprehended only by faith, because it differs completely from natural or secular history.[5]

From his theological concept of God's historical activity in Jesus Christ for the world, Kim argues for the Christian responsibility for political participation and commitment in favor of prophetic liberation. In this regard, Kim endorses Bonhoeffer's ethical formation and direction. Herein, "Christians must always stand on the side of the weaker party, offering fair criticism and presenting constructive suggestions for the best solution."[6] Using the word "revolution" in a more comprehensive way, the most radical revolution for Kim is to restore human nature in accordance with God's way of incarnation.[7]

In addition to his political theology, Kim offers an important cultural dimension for Christian theology. When it comes to non-Christian religions, Kim accentuates God as the Creator of the universe and the Lord of history, so that God shows universal love through the life and death of Jesus Christ not merely to Christians, but also to people of other faiths. Furthermore, he proposes interreligious dialogue in which each dialogue partner can enrich and deepen his or her own teaching and belief system in a fresh and creative way.

For instance, the Confucian teachings of human origin and Heaven's mandate can become more explicit in their ethical development when they

[2] Byung-Mu Ahn, *Draussen vor dem Tor: Kirche und Minjung in Korea*, ed. Winfried Glüer (Göttingen: Vandenhoeck & Ruprecht, 1986) 132.

[3] Ibid.

[4] *The Life and Theology of Changgong, Kim Chai Choon,* ed. Hwang Sung Kyu (Seoul: Han Shin University Press, 2005) 200.

[5] Ibid., 201.

[6] Ibid., 212.

[7] Ibid., 213.

dialogue with the Christian teachings of God the Creator and humans created in God's image. The Korean spiritual matrix, under the influence of Confucianism, Buddhism and Taoism, is a longing for an idyllic life within and a harmonious life with nature. This characteristic, when it engages in conversation with Christianity, can be combined with inner peace and joy of the Holy Spirit.[8]

This interreligious sharing and mutual recognition distinguishes itself in Kim's concept of Christian community in terms of the pan-universal community of love. According to Kim, the Confucian principle of benevolence (human-heartedness) means that "a benevolent person loves principle and takes the mind of universe [heaven] as his or her virtue."[9] This Confucian virtue is compared to "love of giving without expecting compensation."[10] Kim integrates this virtue into Christ's universal love which is "the fountain of life that springs from the heart of a believer."[11] The fountain of love which comes from the Holy Spirit lies in one's own heart. Christian community, seen in light of the pan-universal community of love, should be inclusive, public, and open to worldly issues and people of other faiths.

Kim's legacy of political theology and religio-cultural openness finds an echo first of all in the writings of Chung Dai-Wi (David Chung in American parlance) and in the work of minjung theologians such as Ahn Byung-Mu and Suh Nam-Dong. David Chung (1917–2003) made his valuable study of the religious-cultural complex of Korean Christianity in its initial stage. He evaluates positively the significance of the indigenous religious culture for Korean Christianity and its influence thereupon.[12]

Using a religious-scientific method to explore the religious-cultural relation in continuity and discontinuity with the Christian message and with the pre-Christian religious heritages of Korean society, David Chung reveals significant commonalities between the Korean religious traditions and Christianity. He identifies congenial elements such as their monotheistic concept of God, their longing for salvation, their experience of messianic hope, their ideas of eternal life in the Great Beyond, etc. In fact,

[8] Ibid., 248.

[9] Ibid., 255–56.

[10] Ibid.

[11] Ibid., 257.

[12] Cf. David Chung, *Syncretism: The Religious Context of Christian Beginnings in Korea* (New York: State University of New York, 2001). David Chung completed his doctoral study in the department of Religion, Graduate Studies at Yale University in 1958 under the guidance of his supervisor Prof. H. Richard Niebuhr.

the multi-religious background and heritages in Korea play a constructive role rather than a detrimental role in the rapid progress and growth of Christian mission and evangelism.[13]

In analyzing the universal nature of syncretism, David Chung understands the interreligiously fused nature of relations in Korea and focuses on the meaning of syncretism in a comprehensive context. He does this by using Pinard de la Boullaye; a) Indifferentisme plus ou moins absolue, b) Indifferentisme relative, c) Melange philologique et historique.[14]

At the first level of meaning, tolerance and blending happen between two different cults or religions that contain more or less equivalent elements. When two or more religions come into contact, contextual equivalence articulates the similarities by disregarding the particularities of any belief system on either side of the religions in contact. This aspect can be seen explicitly in Adolf Harnack's interpretation of the early Christian mission. According to Harnack, Christianity was not originally syncretistic itself. However, Jesus' disciples were responsible for the primitive shaping of Christianity. In trying to win the pagan world for the church, Christianity became syncretistic.[15]

At the second level of meaning, regardless of disagreement on other matters, all Christians make consensus on the essential issues. Consensus in a local societal situation refers to the framework of so-called popular belief, although in larger and more complex societies it often assumes a more flexible character and is more difficult to define.

At the third level of meaning, an accidental (historical and philological) combination of the borrowed elements occurs in the reflection of more or less different origins in different cults. The contact and merging of two different religious and cultural configurations leads to a problem of communication. In spite of linguistic limitations, communication occurs as an adventure in producing an open channel toward syncretism.

For instance, Christianity, with its insistence on having a claim to absolute truth, has to make itself universal in diffusion, while at the same time it has to maintain its creed with vigorous exactitude. In other words, the Christian absolute truth claim cannot be a part of bringing about a process of diffusion or enculturation. In favor of evangelism, there should be a hermeneutical necessity of changing and enriching Christian lan-

[13] Ibid., 179.

[14] Ibid., 84.

[15] Cf. Adolf Harnack, *The Mission and Expansion of Christianity in the First Three Centuries*, vol.7, 38. Further see vol. 2. 391, 393–94.

guage. If it lacks expressions for higher concepts, Christianity has to create new vocabularies. And when alternate expressions of these higher concepts are available, it has to adopt or accommodate the native vocabularies.

Given these methodological deliberations, David Chung, who is interested in evaluating both Matteo Ricci's method of accommodation for China and the Nevius method[16] for Korea, attempts to investigate the diffusion and convergence between Christianity and other religions (Confucianism, Buddhism, Taoism and Shamanism) in a more comprehensive religious-cultural and social context.

Like Niebuhr's classic Christ-culture typology,[17] Chung's contribution toward deepening a typological interconnection of Gospel and religions remains a classic, inspiring the imaginations of the next generation in the Korean church and improving Korean intercultural theology. David Chung should be acknowledged as the first theologian to pave a way for a significant contextual theology with regard to the multi-religious complex in South Korea.

Inspired by the political side of Kim Chai-Choon, minjung theology began to concretize and develop a deeper contextual understanding of the Gospel of Jesus Christ from the perspective of the minjung who suffered under the political dictatorship and economic injustice of the 70s.

Ahn Byung-Mu (1922–1996) critiqued Luther's discovery of the righteousness of God in Rom 3:28 during his doctoral study at the University of Heidelberg, Germany. In discovering "the people"—the poor (*ochlos* in Greek) in the Gospel of Mark—Ahn brings to the forefront a reciprocal relation between Jesus and the *ochlos*. From the beginning of his public ministry in Galilee up until the time of his crucifixion, Jesus identified himself with them. Choosing the word "minjung" as a translation of the Greek *ochlos*, Ahn tries to comprehend the reality of minjung from the perspective of those who suffer on the underside of dominant history and society. Although minjung theology does not lose sight of its own cultural-indigenous significance, its primary concern is rather to focus on and contextualize a political theology of suffering people.

Ochlos in Mark's Gospel means neither Israel as God's people (*laos* in Greek), nor the Gentiles (*goyim* in Hebrew). Mark's usage of the word *ochlos* refers to sinners excluded from Jewish society, people without reli-

[16] Nevius' method was represented by John L. Nevius, whose article "Planting and Development of Missionary Churches" influenced American missionaries who arrived in Korea in 1884. Its main tenet lies in self-support, self-government and self-expansion. Cf. David Chung, *Syncretism*, 71.

[17] Cf. H. Richard Niebuhr, *Christ and Culture* (New York: Harper & Row, 1951).

gious identity, people without ethnic coherence, and people without land (*am ha'aretz*) or property. They are despised as the multitude of the lost. However, it is these people with whom Jesus sits and teaches, the *familia dei*. Jesus' mission is not to call the righteous, but the sinners. In terms of the social history of minjung, Ahn conceives of the *ochlos* as the homeless, driven-out, scattered Jews and Christians after the destruction of Jerusalem in 70 CE.[18]

In turning to the side of the *ochlos*, Jesus proclaims the kingdom of God as their future, and fights together with them on the front of God's advent. To the forsaken, oppressed, and marginalized minjung, Jesus appears as a brother or a sister, rather than becoming Christ of the church with his golden crown. Jesus' personality and his movement become meaningful only when they are seen as a life-history in his fellowship and identification with the *ochlos*. God's people (*laos*) became the forsaken people (*ochlos*) under the Roman Empire. Ahn's hermeneutic of discovering and interpreting the story of Jesus' life in the Gospel of Mark in terms of the socio-biography of the *ochlos* provides an exegetical basis for Ahn to contextualize a theology of suffering *ochlos* (minjung) in Korean society.

Coupled with Ahn's exegetical work, Suh Nam-Dong (1918–1984) developed his reflection on minjung in a more constructive and intercultural way. Before turning to minjung theology, he was preoccupied with introducing general trends in Western theology to the theological society in South Korea. Thus he is called "the antenna of the Korean theological circle." In the middle of the 1970s he began to immerse himself in the thought of Dietrich Bonhoeffer and Harvey Cox. Inspired by these two thinkers, Suh attempts to deepen and radicalize the theology of *Missio Dei* in the context of urban mission in industrial factories. This is a context in which several minjung pastors are deeply engaged.

Cox's reflection on the theology of secularization and social change enables Suh to utilize socioeconomics in his minjung theological development. Suh tries to discern the presence of God and Christ in the face of the others, i.e., the suffering minjung (Matt 25:31–46). He then uses this minjung basis to interpret his theology of *Missio Dei*. A radical turn in theological paradigm and orientation thus becomes inevitable for him. According to Suh,

[18] Jürgen Moltmann, "Minjung Theology for the Ruling Classes," in Jürgen Moltmann, *Experiences in Theology*, trans. Margaret Kohl (Minneapolis: Augsburg Fortress, 2000) 254.

> theological activities do not end with the exposition of biblical texts on the salvation or liberation of people by God. In the Bible, the Exodus, the activities of the prophets, and the event of the Cross offer new insights, but these texts ought to be rediscovered and re-interpreted in the context of the human struggle for historical and political liberation today.[19]

For Suh, the Korean concepts of *han* and *dan* become instrumental in formulating his theology of minjung-*han*. He understands *han* to indicate an accumulation of experience that is suppressed and condensed. "*Han* is a dominant feeling of defeat, resignation, and nothingness." Further, it also refers to a feeling of tenacity of will for life, which comes to weaker beings or victims.[20] The first dimension can be seen in a sublimated form of great artistic expressions, while the second can surface in the form of revolutionary or rebellious energy. Against this feeling of *han*, *dan* is self-denial, a cutting of the chain of the circulation of *han*. In other words, *dan* refers to the transformation of secular attachment. In order to cut the vicious circle of revenge, continuous *dan* should overcome accumulated *han*.[21] In using *han*, driven by revenge or self-righteous anger, as the language of minjung, Suh seeks to view the reality of the minjung experience positively in the wider spectrum of *Missio Dei*.

Taking into consideration this understanding of *Missio Dei*, Suh Nam-Dong does not confine himself to only the biblical revelation of salvation. Instead, he expands the relationality between Jesus and minjung as a reference to testify to its convergence with the minjung tradition in Korean history. Suh's method of the converging of different narratives and horizons expresses his recognition of a salvation history not only recorded in the Scriptures, but also in the minjung experience, in a collective and historical sense.

Therefore, Suh affirms God's salvific work within the suffering life and experience of minjung. In doing so, Suh boldly breaks down the qualitative difference between the biblical salvation history and the salvation experience in other religious traditions. The salvation histories come together as tributaries, and form a river. Whether the river is the Jordan, the Mississippi or the Yangtse, there is no qualitative difference between them regarding God's mission.

[19] Suh Nam-Dong, "Towards a Theology of Han," in *Minjung Theology: People as the Subject of History*, ed. Commission on Theological Concerns, Christian Conference of Asia (Maryknoll: Orbis, 1983) 57–58.

[20] Ibid., 58.

[21] Ibid., 65.

Suh radicalizes the theology of *Missio Dei* by accepting worldly occurrences as divine intervention or the work of the Spirit. He encourages others to participate in these worldly events and infuses them with theological language and meaning. Beyond a christological teaching of justification in an individualistic and forensic sense, he tries to actualize the Jesus event *hic et nunc* in an on-going pneumatological manner. Although he wants to read traditional Christology and universal pneumatology in a complementary way, he is more concerned with reading the history of revelation and the minjung tradition in Korean history together, in light of universal pneumatology, which is to say, simultaneously, synchronically, and ideologically, but also critically.[22]

In relation to the religious cultural legacy of Kim Chai-Choon and David Chung on the one hand, and to the political dimension of minjung theology on the other, Kim Kyoung-Jae paves the way toward integrating the religious-cultural matrix of minjung theology into the web of religious pluralism. In appropriating and extending H.-G. Gadamer's theory of fusion of horizons to religious-cultural realms, Kim proposes taking into consideration a model in which the Christian Gospel is engrafted into the Korean cultural soil.

According to Kim Kyoung-Jae, there are four models for understanding the relation between Gospel and culture in speaking of the history of Christian mission in South Korea: a) the sowing model (its representative, Park Hyung-Nong, 1897–1978), b) the yeast model (its representative, Kim Chai-Choon, 1901–1987), c) the converging model (its representative, Suh Nam-Dong, 1918-1984), d) the grafting model (its representative, Ryu Tong-Shik, 1922–).[23]

According to the sowing model (taken from the parable of the sower in Mark 4:1–32), the seed (the Christian message) is presupposed to be something that retains life-giving power in the absolute sense. The seed encounters the soil (the cultural life setting) which is regarded as neutral, barren, and even desolate. A wilderness full of poisonous weeds must be removed in order for good seeds to sprout. The conservative fundamentalist identifies the Christian message of Western missionaries with the Gospel itself without further ado. Fundamentalist theology, which was formed in the American church of 19th century, was accepted as the Gospel. Its cultural ideology plays a judging, normative role in denouncing Korean

[22] Cf. Kim Kyoung-Jae, *Christianity and the Encounter of Asian Religions* (Uitgeverij Boekencentrum: Zoetermeer, 1994) 134.

[23] Ibid., 120–44.

cultural heritages to be inferior, barren, lifeless, and even heretical. This orientation is well articulated in the following statement of Park Hyung-Nong, one of the fathers of Christian fundamentalism in South Korea: "Passing on the true theology to a new generation exactly as we received it from the missionaries 80 years ago."[24]

Against the fundamentalist model of Gospel and culture, Kim Chai-Choon makes a proposal of the yeast model (taken from the parable of the dough in Matt 13:33, Luke 13:20–21). The Gospel functions like yeast which penetrates the dough. The meaning of the Gospel is not exclusive, but particular-universal, because *Missio Dei* in Jesus Christ is not merely confined to the ecclesial sphere. The cultural context is not barren and lifeless, but created and cared for by God, and therefore good. For Kim Chai-Choon, the essence of the Christian Gospel lies in the biblical statement that "the Word became flesh."

Thus the Christian Gospel must be incarnated again, which means that it must assume cultural particularity and universal humanity in different particular contexts in order to genuinely keep the Gospel message relevant. In such a process, the Western interpretation of the Gospel can be renewed and transformed as it encounters intercultural life settings. Therefore, the cultural soil can also be enriched and become more fruitful in terms of the life-giving power of the Gospel itself.

According to the converging model (taken from Jesus' parable of the sheep and goats in the Last Judgment in Matt 25:31–46), Suh Nam-Dong argues that in the context of the Christian Gospel, liberative minjung traditions must be considered equally with God's salvific work as it is recorded in the biblical narratives. Salvation history converges with universal history so that they form a more life-giving concept of God. His pneumatological-synchronic hermeneutic paves a way toward a theology of religious pluralism in which there is no need to separate the unique Christian revelation from the minjung tradition of world history.

Additionally, according to the grafting model (taken from the illustration of grafting trees in Rom 11:17–27), the scion is to the Gospel what the stock is to the non-Christian culture. In the grafting model, the scion could become helpless without the life-giving power of the stock. According to Paul, however, the stock is not compared to Greek or pagan cultural soil, but to the Jewish soil as the root of Christianity. Based on

[24] Park Hyung-Nong, *Dogmatic Theology*, vol.1. Introduction. Cited from Kim Kyoung-Jae, *Christianity and the Encounter of Asian Religions*, 121.

God's faithfulness to Israel, Paul is convinced that God does not cast away God's disobedient people.[25]

However, by twisting Paul's concern, to some extent, Ryu Tong-Shik illustrates his understanding of this image in terms of *Logos* and *Tao*. The Greek *Logos* is not identical with Jesus Christ. Yet, *Logos* offers a horizon for Gentile Christians in Hellenism to understand the Gospel of Jesus Christ. Likewise *Tao* can be appropriated in order for Asian Christians to understand the Gospel, although it does not replace Jesus Christ. As much as the Word of God is understood in the context of Jewish culture, Western theology also represents a cultural understanding of the Gospel that is rooted in the Greco-Roman culture and framework. Likewise, according to Ryu, Koreans have their own cultural angle. Therefore, the Gospel is to be engrafted into Korean soil. What is striking at this point is how Ryu Dong-Sik unconsciously reaffirms the Western propensity toward antisemitism.

In deliberating these four models, Kim Kyoung-Jae corrects, modifies and deepens each model inter-culturally in light of the hermeneutical theory of fusion of horizons. Korean religious tradition functions as the history of effect in which a particular Korean understanding of the Gospel gains its uniqueness in accordance with the Jewish tradition of the Hebrew Bible and the Christian tradition of the Greek Bible. The texts of Scripture work together in shaping the particular interest and horizon of the reader in more comprehensive way. In such a process, parochial Christianity is renewed and expanded, fulfilling and realizing the universal meaning of Jesus Christ. To uphold his universal Christology working among people of non-Christian religions, Kim agrees with John Cobb: "Christ will carry out the authentic Christian mission."[26]

Paul S. Chung is inspired by the social concern of minjung theology and by David Chung's theology of culture and civilization. He makes an attempt to overcome the anti-Jewish residue in Asian minjung theology[27] and to initiate an Asian contextual theology of the other from a postfoundational-hermeneutical perspective, learning critically from the radical

[25] Cf. David J. Bosch, *Transforming Mission: Paradigm Shifts in Theology of Mission* (Maryknoll: Orbis, 2004) 160–65.

[26] John B. Cobb. Jr. *Beyond Dialogue*, 145. Cf. Kyoung-Jae, *Christianity and the Encounter of Asian Religions*, 143.

[27] Wolfgang Kröger takes issue with the anti-Semitic tendencies of Ahn Byung-Mu which his "Declaration of Farewell to Judaism" underlines. Cf. Wolfgang Kröger, *Die Befreiung des Minjung: Das Profil einer Protestantischen Befreiungstheologie für Asien in Ökumenischer Perspektive* (Munich: Chr. Kaiser, 1992) 132.

legacy of Reformation theology and from the wisdom of world religions. Chung's articles in this volume, "Dietrich Bonhoeffer Seen from Asian Minjung Theology and the Fourth Eye of Socially Engaged Buddhism," and "Mission and Inculturation in the Thought of Matteo Ricci," are an expression of his gratitude in loving memory to his respected teachers, the late Ahn Byung-Mu and David Chung. For Paul S. Chung, Jesus' faithfulness to the Torah brings him closer to the *am ha'aretz* and the *ochlos*-minjung. Jesus does not compete with the God of Israel (Mark 12:26). The quest for the historical Jesus in relation to *ochlos* can be uncovered where the Jewishness of Jesus is recognized and highlighted in his teaching, life and ministry.

According to Paul Chung, the Jewish rejection of Jesus needs to be discussed in light of Jesus' faithfulness to the Torah and his embracing forgiveness of the Jews, who became God's enemy for our sake. Israel's rejection is not final (Rom 11). At this point, Chung challenges the biblical method of historical criticism (or redaction criticism), widely practiced in the circles of minjung theology. Instead, he is in favor of becoming socially and ideologically critical of historical criticism in light of a hermeneutics of ideology critique. Historical critiques, including the interpreter, should be more critical, so that postfoundational hermeneutics can uncover social bases and dimensions of the human life setting.

From the perspective of God's mysterious faithfulness to Israel, Chung engages the Buddhist logic of non-duality in a hermeneutical manner for an interreligious encounter in which a positive understanding of the Jewish rejection of Jesus Christ may become a point of departure for his interreligious commitment. St. Paul's solidarity with Israel plays a normative role in Chung's approach to people of other cultures, in which he opposes the expatriation of Israel in minjung theology.

In sum, the first model of minjung theology, as represented by Ahn Byung-Mu and Suh Nam-Dong, is strongly based on an immanentalist model, oriented more toward a social and economic analysis and a political and liberative praxis. The second model, represented by Kim Kyoung-Jae, is more embedded in the intercultural, liberative tradition of World Religions for minjung cultural life.

Because of the contextual character of minjung theology, its task is to overcome its theoretical framework vis-à-vis the ever-changing reality of the poor and their religious spirituality in a society that is both unjust and multiculturally fused. It is at this point that minjung theology is confronted by the mysterious voice of God emerging from the others and from the wisdom of World Religions. Asian contextual theology of minjung must be of "beyond" character before the mystery of God and God's preference for minjung, not because of minjung's poverty, but because of God's mysterious partisanship for them.

From Pentecostal circles, a young Korean-American theologian, Koo D. Yun, contributes his theology of minjung and of religions from a Pentecostal-pneumatological perspective. Influenced by Donald Gelpi at the Graduate Theological Union in Berkeley, California, and by Harvey Cox at Harvard Divinity School, Koo D. Yun attempts to develop the Pentecostal side of minjung in a wider spectrum. According to him, there are two different minjungs: socio-political minjung and Pentecostal minjung. Yun's thesis is provocative; he claims that Pentecostal minjung better represents the reality of minjung. He calls for dialogue between socio-political minjung theology and Pentecostal minjung theology in an ecumenical and global context. Additionally, Choi In-Sik invests a special interest in the prospect of Judaism extending its significance and relevance for Asian contextual theology. He appreciates the perspectives of the Aggadic tradition for enriching biblical narratives and the message of the Gospel in a more Jewish-Christian way.

With the hermeneutical and cultural process of the fusion of horizons taking place in the encounter between Christianity and world religions on the one hand, and with the socio-political reality of minjung on the other, Asian contextual theology of minjung is being renewed and transformed socially, materially, and culturally. This happens in respect to *Deus dixit* (God's speech event) taking place in every direction, and in faithfulness to the reality of God's people who suffer in the world. *Deus dixit,* as an on-going experience in the church as well as in the world, is a postfoundational point of departure to shape and characterize a new direction of an Asian contextual theology.

It is committed to God's covenantal faithfulness to Israel; therefore, it reconstructs Christology without negating and expatriating Israel. Such an approach is ecclesiastically open and politically committed, culturally sensitive in recognizing difference as different, and interreligiously engaged. This approach is dedicated to listening attentively to God's unpredictable and irregular voice which emerges even from the diversity of world religions. In encountering the wisdom of world religions rooted deeply in the historical situation and life-setting of East Asian people, Asian contextual theology tries to understand the Gospel story of Jesus Christ in relation to the cultural, religious and spiritual tradition from which they come. In terms of diapraxis, Asian contextual theologians, rooted in a multireligious tapestry, continually create higher universal horizons that transcend the particularity of the past of minjung theology.

Given this fact, Asian contextual theology is in the process of shifting from socio-political minjung praxis toward an integration of interfaith praxis with the wisdom of world religions, deepening the fourth eye of socially engaged Buddhism, and constructing a theology of multicolored tapestry. In this framework, the third eye (enlightenment and wisdom) is refined and elaborated in terms of the fourth-eye (compassionate praxis in solidarity with suffering humanity, including all finite beings, yet without attachment to them) in a more universal, more ecological and more spiritual way. Therefore, Asian contextual theology is in fourth-eye formation, faced with the reality of minjung and engaged in the wisdom of world religions.

The Good Samaritan of today is summoned to approach the wounded in our society, making them neighbors. The wounded symbolize the least of Christ's sisters and brothers. Our encounter with Christ occurs on our way to the others, especially those who are disfigured, alienated and despoiled, which is to say, those who have no beauty or majesty, nothing in their appearance that we should desire them (Isa 53:2). Conversation with God is embedded in conversation with Christ and his people, from whom we would usually turn away our eyes. God speaks through the lives of today's *ochlos*, minjung, to the world. In solidarity and identification with the world's *ochlos* in the context of the Empire of global capitalism, Asian contextual theology of minjung finds its echo in the ecumenical-global awareness of God's forsaken people, Lazarus-*ochlos*, who suffer from the burden of the sin of the world.

PART I

Asian Contextual Theology and Minjung Praxis

1

Christian Theology and Its Participation in the Social Historical Realm*

Kim Chai-Choon

THE ancient Greeks developed an aristocratic philosophy that tended to conceptualize reality as it appeared. In this manner, they taught and educated themselves. In contrast, the Hebrews sought to discern and know the will of God before they thought about it and obeyed it. For instance, the Ten Commandments deal with the relationship with God first and then with parents and neighbors. In the Decalogue there is no such thing as Socrates' dictum, "know thyself." In addition, Confucianism offered the fundamental teaching of Eastern Asian ethics in terms of human relationships.

The Greeks were interested in metaphysical truth that transcends history, while the Hebrews were concerned with historical events, interested in completing the will of God who acts in history. The Confucianists, however, were concerned with ethical conduct and behavior, such that they developed a system of filial ethics. These ethics were focused on interpersonal ethics among human beings and close relatives and then they were extended to developing the ethics of the ruler and the ruled. Although personal loyalty was a basic virtue in Confucian ethics, the sense of historical consciousness remained ambivalent, since they were less concerned with the social-democratic ethics of justice and equality.

1. When we examine the divine revelations given to Israel, we come to know that God's plan and economy always related to the historical meaning in the life setting of Israel. The creation account is the first example

* Translated from the Korean and edited by Paul S. Chung

of this. God created the heavens and the earth and everything visible and invisible in it, and finally made Adam and Eve in God's image. Then God commanded human beings to subdue the earth and gave a mandate for them to take care of all the creatures. This indicates that nature does not come into existence by itself, but exists in elemental connection with human history.

Human beings are free subjects. Even God does not control or take away their freedom. When freedom is suppressed or destroyed, human beings are dehumanized and degraded to the level of "things." However, humanity attempted to build up human history without God and chose its own way instead of God's way of light, sin instead of righteousness. As a result, nature is subject to futility. Nature still waits, with an eager longing, for the revelation of the children of God and for the liberation that will finally come with the glory of the children of God (Rom 8:19–24).

God desires human beings to freely return to God and gives a plan of salvation for them. Therefore, God's providence is always clearly expressed in terms of historical events. God chose Abel instead of his brother Cain, elected Noah who was descended from Abel, Shem from Noah, Abraham from Shem, and Jacob from Abraham. The twelve tribes of Jacob formed a people, called Israel. God also made a particular revelation in history in God's covenant with them. At this point, the "election" is God's "condensed history," and the covenant is God's activity, which occurs in history, both by grace and through laws.

God's providence was evidently embodied in the Exodus, which was the march and progress of the Hebrew slaves escaping from Egypt to Canaan, the promised land. If history is conceptualized as the gradual progress of human consciousness towards freedom, like G. F. Hegel states, then the Exodus can be the very symbol of human history. However, the main character of the Exodus is God, and God's activity in history. God used natural forces to deliver Israel through the Red Sea and the wilderness. God led the Hebrews by means of a cloud during the day and a pillar of fire during the night.

As a result, the Exodus is not only defined by the history of the Israelites' liberation, but may also function as the model for the liberations of all of history. History moves from A to B, in other words, it escapes from A and marches towards B. The same thing can be said about secular history. History moves, escaping from the primeval earth which was full of plunder, fighting, and revenge among clans, and marching towards the consummation of God's kingdom, which means the end and completion of human history, including the world of nature. Christ acts behind history and is involved in human history in terms of setting in motion a right direction for the future of God. We perceive it in the eyes of faith.

Similarly, the Hebrew prophets proclaimed to the leaders and the people of Israel the word that they received from God. The standard of their prophecy was God's covenant and word in the event of the Exodus. God was the Lord in the history of the Exodus. God was the Lord of Moses and the Israelites. The goal of divine action was the completion of human freedom. For this purpose, God was the Subject who acted in history. The word in the mouths of the Hebrew prophets was the action of God "in, for and with" history. God's word spoke definitely for the poor, the distressed, and the oppressed, and it judged the greedy and spoke against those with power and authority who did not listen to the distressed. The prophets critiqued established religion that looked good in appearance, but had no spiritual or moral essence. A prophet was God's spokesperson who was confronted with the historical and social reality of the world of politics, economics, culture and religion.

2. With the advent of Christ, history moved from A to B. Jesus Christ came from above to below. While on earth he directly participated in human society. He first attempted to preach the good news through the synagogue, but he was rejected. So he went directly to the society of the people in need. In particular, he became a friend of the poor, the sick, the isolated, and the abandoned, and he strove to restore their lost humanity in relation to God's Torah. Thousands of people followed him. At the same time, he was suspected more and more by the religious authorities. The authorities' suspicion initiated a series of events against him.

The most significant event was the crucifixion. Jesus was crucified on the charge of instigating a political revolt against the Roman empire. He was regarded as a member of a sect of Zealots whose aim was to liberate the Jews. He was referred to as the king of the Jews on the cross, which indicated that he was convicted as a political criminal. If he had taught only a conceptual truth apart from historical reality, or if his teaching was concerned only with profound academic philosophy, he would have not been slain on the cross.

Moreover, the authorities didn't leave Jesus alone because he criticized their vices. The expression "historical Jesus or confessional Christ" simply reflects a hermeneutical understanding of Jesus Christ. He himself is both "the historical Jesus and historical Christ." His life cannot be understood merely in terms of a historical explanation of what is mystical or miracle in Jesus Christ; all the events that happened in his life are historical ones.

History is a stage on which God performs in Christ, not only for God's kingdom but also for the secular world. History is an arena where the contemporary and living Christ works. History is arbitrary and faithful. It is of dynamic and christological character. At this juncture, we are reminded of Karl Barth's idea of pre-history (*Urgeschichte*). Barth argues that the original and eternal history of God was established in the life, death, and resurrection of Jesus Christ, and this history became the foundation and hidden meaning for all histories. So God's eternity or pre-history refers to the history of God's gracious election of the world. Therefore, God's eternity includes human temporal history through God's gracious act of election in Jesus Christ for all.[1]

Therefore, we regard history not as fixed but dynamic, moving forward to God's future. One cannot simply connect one historical event with another without hesitation. Some think that history repeats itself or reveals itself, but there is no such thing as the fixed regulation of making history in the pattern of repetition. In fact, Christ in his dynamic act moves secular history in accordance with God's reign. Therefore, we should have eyes to see "the signs of the times" (Matt 16:3). We need to be mindful of recognizing what God is doing and what God aims to do in our present history. Thus as Christ's disciples, we take part in history, taking up the cross of discipleship every day in service of and for the sake of God's purpose of history.

Jesus said to the sick, "Your faith heals you," when he healed the sick by the power of God. Jesus teaches us that healing becomes effective only when one responds to it with faith. Likewise, in the historical process—though Jesus is the Lord of history—healing society is not possible unless human beings respond to Christ with faith. For instance, if war is not a historical necessity, but comes from an eruption of sinful human desire, Christ does not want it. If we ignore a warmonger or an agitator who stirs up international hatred—on the condition that we as Christians have no interest in history or think that we are self-transcendent for heaven –can we say that we are righteous according to the biblical standard? We are summoned to participate in the movement of peace and reconciliation, and show interest in national and international affairs of politics, and take responsibility to challenge provocative and evil activities and to improve good will.

[1] [Editor's note: Cf. Karl Barth, *Church Dogmatics* II/2: The Doctrine of God, eds. G. W. Bromiley and T. F. Torrance (London, New York: T & T Clark, 2004) 33. Borrowing the term *Urgeschichte* from Franz Overbeck, Barth discusses it in the context of God's election of Jesus Christ in a supralapsarian sense.]

When a whole nation is filled with injustice and corruption—but if we remain silent about injustice and the corruption of the people in power—we would remain non-believers who turn away from Christ's on-going work in human history. Economic development becomes possible by an owner's oppression of laborers, such that this situation creates the phenomenon of "the rich getting richer and the poor getting poorer." Economic injustice is not the will of Christ. If we are not moved and stirred by the death of a young laborer burning himself to death, claiming the right application of the labor law, can we say that we are Jesus' disciples? We must respond dynamically with faith to the situation of economic injustice in our current society and make an effort to find a solution to social problems.

3. Love is an absolute commandment of Christ. Paul says that knowledge, faith, and prophecy are useless without love (1 Cor 13). God makes the sun shine on both the evil person and on the good one. God sends rain to fall on both the righteous and the unrighteous (Matt 5: 45). This is God's full love which transcends provisions or human morals. Love is not like sweet talk or advertising. It is a physical and concrete service for neighbors in need. The word 'neighbor' here refers not only to my neighbor but includes all, even enemies. Our neighbors are millions of Korean brothers and sisters. In a broader sense, our neighbors are the human race. We live in relation to our neighbors—near and far.

Politics should be the way of putting this kinship into the actual practice on both the national and international levels. The legislature makes laws; the executive administers the laws; the judiciary judges by the laws. We call these institutions and their actions 'politics'. There is an international politics that protects one's own country from any possible invasion or disadvantage.

If a government lacking political legitimacy rules a nation, the whole nation suffers. It is a problem not for one or two people but for the whole population. Even though a few leaders in the last days of the *Chosun* dynasty turned the country over to Japan for colonial rule, millions of Korean people—because of the politics of a few, suffered terribly from Japanese colonialism. Given this fact, can we still brag that as Christians we are not interested in politics?

Jesus is not involved in every single political event, because his politics is based on the overall plan for 'alpha' and 'omega', the beginning and the end of history. However, since we are limited to time and space, we cannot be responsible for all the phases in the past, present and future.

To the degree that we engage in history through Christian faith, we are going in the right direction and fulfilling Christ's purpose, responding to our historical calling as Christ's disciples. If we exclude our life from the secular world because of its secularity, how can we express our loving commitment to Christ and our neighbors? How can we enter a strong person's house without first tying up the strong person? (Matt 12:29).

Today's social injustice derives from the corruption of the powerful who are supported by the power structure. Individual good deeds are not effective if they do not address and fight the systemic evil. Often good individual morality could be used as a vehicle for serving hypocritical goodness and the purpose of the evil power.

Therefore, Jesus began his mission with his confrontation with the devil. After passing through all the temptations, he confirmed his victory by commanding Satan, "Go away!" The apostles also had the authority to "cast out the devil." Paul also said that he fought against those who held hands with the rulers of power in the heavenly realms (Eph 6:12). This means fighting against the evil forces that have dominion and power, inferior to God but superior to human beings. In short, fighting against the political evil that can enslave a human life is a means of obeying God's commandment to "love your neighbor."

Therefore, Christian political participation is a fundamental and pivotal part of our confession to Christ and faith in him. Christians must practice love through participating in organizations and social institutions in favor of those who are poor, weak and needy. Since the Second World War, the theology of political involvement has been developed in diverse forms such as political theology, the theology of reconciliation, the theology for a responsible society, the theology of revolution, and the theology of liberation, etc.

Whatever this theology is called, it tries to put into practice what Dietrich Bonhoeffer calls "ethics as formation."[2] It signifies that we must make a concrete decision for taking part in making our present world reflect Christ's image and God's reign, in which the real person establishes real and genuine human history before God. After all, to make our faith a living faith, our life itself must become a witness to and a living record of historical events within God's history. It is incumbent upon us to fulfill human 'reformation' through the reformation of history.

[2] [Editor's note: Cf. Dietrich Bonhoeffer, *Ethics* (New York: Touchstone, 1995) 82–86.]

2

Is Dialogue between Buddhism and Christianity Possible?—From a Christian Perspective*

Kim Chai-Choon

It is generally said that a religion is based on the absolute or consists in humanity's relation to the deity. It would be difficult to agree with the argument that everything in the world of religion is relative except for the absolute. In all religions, there is a tendency toward becoming idolatrous, conceiving of themselves as the absolute ones. This is, however, a 'false absoluteness'. For instance, in Christianity, God is the absolute. However, it is also difficult to concede that the Bible, confessions, dogma, ecclesial office, or church are not the absolute per se, regardless of the fact that these elements relate to the absolute God. It is hence worth noting H. R. Niebuhr's insistence on radical monotheism or consistent monotheism.[1]

Generally, the most conservative Christians think that because God is the absolute, Christianity is also absolute. This logic provides the reason why Christianity ought to reject any dialogue with other religions. Before

* Translated and edited by Paul S. Chung. This paper was published in a Korean journal, *Thought World*, in December of 1964. Kim Chai-Choon, a founding father of the liberal Presbyterian Church in South Korea (PROK), was a leading figure who played a prominent role in stressing Christian social responsibility and encouraging the Christian church to have a dialogical attitude toward non-Christian religions. This paper, seen in light of the theological situation of 1964, shows his remarkable approach to a relation between Buddhism and Christianity.

1 Cf. H. Richard Niebuhr, *Radical Monotheism and Western Culture: With Supplementary Essays* (New York: Harper and Row, 1970).

answering whether a dialogue between Buddhism and Christianity is possible, let me first outline a relationship between Christianity and other religions.

The Christian View of Judging Paganism as Heretics

From the ancient church to the promulgation of the Edict of Milan by the great Constantine in the year of 313 CE, the church grew at a rapid tempo. Before this period, normal people despised the church as victims, intellectual philosophers despised it as folly, and Rome despised it as a minority religion, the spawn of Judaism, and a rebellious group. The Christian church on the defensive tried to justify its legitimacy as a religion, responding non-violently to Roman persecution and using the wisdom of pagan philosophy.

However, from 313 until the early 16th century, the church occupied a hierarchical position by becoming the state religion and took an aggressive position against other religions in terms of an exclusivist attitude and direction. As such, any heretical group within the church was ruthlessly rooted out, so that the church became one single religious group, and exercised power and authority. Among Christians, of course, there were some who were in service of the pagans by practicing Christian love. However, such examples were exceptional.

From around 1550 to 1800, Christianity was divided into two factions, Roman Catholicism and Protestantism, and both relationships were pushed to the limit. As a result, the line of demarcation between Roman Catholicism and Protestantism seemed to become more obvious and more hostile than the possible line between the Christian religion and non-Christian religions.

Since the 19th century, Christianity in the West has begun to have more knowledge of other religions with the help of modern civilization and missionaries' work. Instead of remaining hostile toward people of other faiths, Christianity went positively in its movement to missionize them.

If I take a more a concrete example from the scriptures, St Paul, the apostle to the Gentiles, in his letter to Corinth, offers a telling case (2 Cor 6:16–17). All pagans are seen as related to idolatry. Because idolatry was most hated in light of the prophetic tradition in the Hebrew Bible, pagans associated with this cult were an extreme abomination.

It is conceived that Greek philosophers and dramatists were unilaterally regarded as diabolic. A great Christian apologist in the second century gave evidence to this: "What kind of similarity is there between Christians and philosophers? What do disciples of Greek philosophy and disciples of heaven have in common? What relation is there between those who corrupt the truth and those who restore and teach it? The heretic comes out, manipulated by philosophy. Woe to Aristotle! Cunning and refined man, speculating the truth at random! What has Athens to do with Jerusalem?"

This is Tertullian's stubborn rejection of philosophy, despite the fact that he himself was a philosopher, and it was so strong because of his own born-again experience. Regardless of the fact that his expression sounds so harsh to us, the ancient church was for the most part in agreement with his attitude. In the 4th century, Augustine paid tribute to Plato and other great Greek philosophers, but later he turned away from them. The virtue of the pagans was a colorful sin, and the classics of the pagans are a straight road to the hell.

It was not long before the medieval philosophy of Aristotle and theology of scholasticism entered the soil of the church. It was because of Thomas Aquinas' use of Aristotle for his dogmatic framework that Aristotle came to the highest seat in the church. Be that as it may, there was no doubt that there prevailed still a negative attitude against Greek philosophy as a whole.

The Reformer's attitude against the pagans was far more resentful. Particularly Martin Luther said in *The Large Catechism* (1529) that

> all who are outside the Christian church, whether heathen, Turks, or false Christians and hypocrites, even though they believe in and worship only the one, true God, nevertheless do not know what his attitude is toward him. They cannot be confident of his love and blessing. Therefore they remain in eternal wrath and damnation.[2]

The Reformer's hatred of the pagans was much stronger than that of the scholastics. Luther was upset at the authority of Aristotle, which was given credence by the medieval universities, that he argued that the universities became pagan schools and that Aristotle, the master of the pagans, prevailed more than Christ. In fact, according to Luther, Aristotle was sent as a plague by God to punish our sins. Luther and Calvin were more suspicious of this philosophy than of the Roman Catholicism of the Middle

[2] Martin Luther, "The Large Catechism (1529)" in *The Book of Concord: The Confessions of the Evangelical Lutheran Church*, trans. and ed. Theodore G. Tappert (Philadelphia: Fortress, 1959) 419.

Ages. They thought that philosophy was obviously the hidden enemy which could corrupt the Gospel.

In the mission movement of the 19th century, the attitude of Western missionaries was hostile towards indigenous religions of the countries that were introduced to Christianity. According to their judgment, the philosophy of the heathen country is worse than the ignorance itself. Hinduism was denounced to be a terrible perversion, and Islam to be a regressive religion. In short, paganisms were always false.

Conversion or Elimination

Western missionaries, who entered Korea in the 19th century, carried this same exclusivist feeling and attitude. Ancestral cults in Confucianism and statues of Buddha were denounced as idolatry and the product of the devil. Therefore, becoming Christian or receiving Christianity became possible only after renouncing all of one's traditional religious and cultural heritage, essentially after coming into an empty state of mind. A Christian individual's giving alms to a Buddhist monk was regarded as an act of idolatry, so that one became the object of religious punishment or even excommunication. Herein, a strong emphasis was placed on conversion to Christianity; otherwise, there was contradiction or elimination. In this situation, dialogue was impossible. Such a situation typifies what the Christianity meant in the 19th century of Korea.

In the Christian tradition, of course, there was another stream, though not invisible. This was an effort to apply the relation between the Jewish Torah and Christianity to a relation between Christianity and paganism. This effort was grounded in and centered on Christ as the fulfiller of all truths which means the fulfillment according to Matt 5:17: "Do not think that I have come to abolish the law or the prophets: I have come not to abolish but to fulfill."

Justin Martyr and theologians of the Alexandrian school from the second to the third century said that Christ was the eternal Word (Logos), and having spoken already to Abraham and Moses, so he had spoken to Socrates and Plato long before he was incarnated in Jesus of Nazareth.[3] According to Justin, because Christ is the Logos (Reason), every human being is imparted reason through him. People living in accordance

[3] [Editor's note: Of the Logos-sower of St. Justin we read, "In moral philosophy the Stoics have established right principles, and the poets too have expounded such, because the seed of the Word (*sperma tou logou*) was implanted (*emphuton*) in the whole human race." Justin Martyr, *Apologies*, vol. 2, ed. Miroslav Marcovich (New York: De Gruyter, 1984).]

with reason, whether they are called pagans or atheists, are all Christians. Therefore, Socrates, Hercules, and others like these pagans, whether Greek, Barbarian (anyone who was not Greek), together with Abraham or Elijah, belonged to the same category. Stoic poets, prosaic poets, and those who spoke about something good were all those who had received the small seed and spark from the Logos of God. Therefore, those who spoke good words are all truly Christians like us.

Clement and Origen in Alexandria took a similar pattern of thought. Contrary to Roman Catholicism, the Greek Orthodox Church grew up in Greek civilization, so it believed in the ultimate unity of all human lives and thoughts. Furthermore, it believed that this unity was fulfilled in Christ, thus it moved in a consistent direction. Gregory of Nyssa, inheriting the spirit of Origen, contended that the philosophy of the pagan world was the companion and partner of Christian theology, moving in search of higher life and truth. At any rate, it would be a question to what extent such liberal ways of thinking could be reconciled with the present exclusive attitude of the Greek Orthodox Church. There is, however, no denying that a liberal and open tendency toward pagan philosophy has run along with the mainstream of the Greek Orthodox Church. Such a spark has also influenced the Roman Catholic Church, which became successful by including and accommodating many pagan saints, customs, and festivals into Catholic life.

Alfonse Gregorio, who was active as a Jesuit archbishop in the late 16th century, was called one of the greatest Catholic theologians since Thomas Aquinas. According to him, members of the respective Christian denominations, and followers in Judaism and Islamic society, or even non-Christian philosophers, etc., were to be regarded as those who fulfilled and fulfill their salvation, practicing good faith in their respective religious group with the help of God's grace.

They practiced in their religious community the true and good instruction which was originally revealed by God. In defending this position, Baron von Hügel made the following comment: This position does not mean that all are the same, rather indicates that the origin of religious community and wisdom comes from God and each religious community remains incomplete in itself.

A modern Catholic theologian, Jacques Maritain, is liberal and free in speaking of religious others. According to him, the statement that there is no salvation outside the church is not surprising. Because the soul of the church is the truth, it indicates that there is no salvation outside the truth.

Those with good faith, and the righteous who do not contradict the light of Christ, nor reject grace, belong to the soul of the church.

Since the 18th and 19th centuries, such an open and cooperative ideas were also discernible in Protestantism. In liberal theology, the history of the human race was seen in terms of unity, and religion was also investigated in terms of the evolutionary process. Therefore, the earlier aggressive consciousness against religious others was by and large dampened. However, the new consciousness that emerged was too cool and indifferent to engage a positive fellowship or to develop dialogue with religious others. Although a pantheistic feeling of the union between all humanity and the universe was sung and praised in the poetry of William Wordsworth and Alfred Tennyson, it did not find its echo within the church or give impetus to the church for open attitude.

A New Understanding

1. In dealing with the superiority of dogma and confessions, Christianity is convinced of and proclaims its superiority and absoluteness in the sense that it believes in the living personal God of righteousness and love, and in the unity of the human race. Thus God revealed Godself to redeem the human race. Christianity believes that the human race will love God and love each other, and finally good will prevail over evil. In previous eras, Christianity attempted to convert people of other faiths to the Christian church, convinced that Christian dogma was superior to other religions.

However, the human race and the world in the present day have come of age (Dietrich Bonhoeffer). It is impossible to resolve the problem by way of dogmatic dispute in which authentic dialogue cannot be exchanged. Because Buddhism or Confucianism or other religious communities have become mature and grown up, they also put forth their highest interest in defending their independence and truth claims. Despite the fact that Christianity has excellent dogma and confessions, it is no surprise that it cannot overcome religious others through such a conviction. Such an approach aims at a kind of coercion.

In Islamic countries, mission efforts by non-Islamic religions are blocked by legal channels. Although Buddhist countries, such as Malaysia, are neither self-defensive nor hostile toward other religions, the necessary humble and open attitude for dialogue does not come easily. In some countries which have been dominated by a certain religion functioning as the state religion, the state is tied inextricably to the religion. This being the case, the state has to protect the state religion. Such a case may be seen in India. Because there is no state religion in South Korea, all religions are equal and free in their beliefs and mission.

2. It is affirmed that the idea that the rights of other religions can be resolved with external force is totally an illusion. In medieval times, Christian emperors used political force to bring about conversion. Such was seen in case with Islam. An emperor forced conquered countries to choose between "baptism or death." There was no other alternative. Many people chose baptism. There were, however, protestors too. When they complained, the emperor beheaded around 4500 people in just one day.

During the period of the Crusades, Muslims were slaughtered terribly, until their blood rose up to the feet of the Christian crusaders. On the evening after this slaughter, Christian people bowed and rejoiced heartily, being moved to shed tears of joy before the altar, which was located near the tomb of Christ. It is no surprise that Muslims never intended to become Christian. Even in Christian countries, Jews were hated and persecuted terribly. Christian anti-Semitism is the worst case. During the Third Reich, Hitler's "final solution" for the Jews demonstrates what really happened in the notorious Auschwitz. Given this fact, we remember that the Christian attempts at solving the encounter with people of other faiths by using external pressure has failed completely.

3. Granted that each religion is mature in itself, equipped with its subjective independence, this does not necessarily mean that it may justify its own absolutization. Human beings or human achievements remain always relative, no matter how positive they are in relation to God. Therefore, we may not be self-righteous, or divinize our particular religion. As each religion remains humble before its own ultimate divine reality, it also must remain humble before other religions. This does not mean to imply cowardice. On the contrary, spiritual poverty or humility bears witness to its own religion while respecting the uniqueness of other religions at the same time.

Dialogue is Possible

What I have described so far applies to Christianity, as well as to all other religions. There must be a few considerations in this matter. 1) We are not supposed to have the intention to defeat or convert people of other faiths to Christianity. We should not have self-superiority in conversation with people of other faiths. On the other hand, we should not have a suspicious mindset beforehand, because of our fear of defeat or conversion. A cooperative and fraternal attitude is highly recommended, so that dialogue partners, as truth-seekers, complement each other's limitations, learn something about their ignorance, and search for the commonality of the truth together.

It is therefore out of the question to establish a superior attitude that favors dogmatic dispute or presupposes superiority. Furthermore, differences in nationality, status, power and culture, under every circumstance, may not become the driving force for interreligious dialogue. The primary reason for the Western missionary failure in the colonial era was based in their feeling of superiority and their hypocritical attitude that occasioned mistrust and resistance on the part of the indigenous people.

Truthfulness and love are the best attitude. Not only in Christianity, but also in all other religions, the common quest can be seen in the effort to bring about peace, mutual trust, and cooperation for human life and for a just society. Christianity emphasizes uniquely the fact that such interreligious and fraternal cooperation would remain incomplete without taking seriously God's reconciliation with humanity and the world through Jesus Christ.

Regardless of the fact that every religion aims to break down the barrier between humans and the divine, nevertheless, religious people have attempted to rebuild the wall in the name of religion, or under the pretext of the authentic and absolute religion. They refuse to cross over the front line of other religions. In our century, religious war is the most terrible and ruthless example among all wars. We find it absolutizing war in the name of the absolute religion.

If the cross of Christ expresses the most sublime spirit of love, even through it bears the sin and death of all for salvation, how self-contradictory is it that Christianity denounces non-Christians as the enemy and has an antagonistic attitude toward them? If a Buddhist cannot be an object of our Christian love because of Buddhist identity, how do we Christians live up to the following biblical statement: "But God proves his love for us while we still were sinners" (Rom 5:8). Instead of converting Buddhists or people of other faiths, Christians must be converted from our own self-egotism and desire for religious domination towards diakonia and love of people of other faiths. What is at stake is not about dogma, but about love. When love comes first, all obstruction will give way to fraternal dialogue and mutual understanding.

If a Buddhist burns down a Catholic village during the Vietnam War, this act would express crude emotion because the Catholic church is declared to be a enemy. This does not demonstrate a solely religious problem.

If the Vietnamese government in response persecutes Buddhists, it would be a mistake on the part of the government. In South Korea, the natural religious environment includes Confucianism, Buddhism, Christianity, and other religions; however, there has not been a religious conflict, at least so far. Rather, there has been close cooperation among them, especially in case of the March First Movement.[4]

Therefore, regarding what has been suggested above, I wonder whether we are in a better position for a more positive attempt at inter-religious conversation. As is already obvious in the March First Movement, such dialogue may be necessary to improve and expand examples of interreligious partnership and cooperation with regards to social diakonia or some urgent national affairs. As the process of dialogue continues and develops itself in an honest and sincere way, Christianity will be more indigenous and culturally Koreanized, eschewing the residue of Westernized colonial Christianity. Likewise, in the process of interfaith dialogue, Buddhism could be renewed toward the international horizon and beauty that it has. Today I believe that "Won Buddhism" in South Korea refers to a wonderful example in this direction.[5]

[4] [Editor's note: The March First Movement (1911) was a decisive national movement in protest against the Japanese rule of colonization in terms of remarkable cooperation among interreligious communities.]

[5] [Editor's note: "Won Buddhism" was founded by Sot'aesan (born May 5, 1891) whose main concern was related to Buddha as Dharmakaya (the aphophatic dimension of Buddha) rather than as Smbhogakaya (the cataphatic dimension of Buddha). At this point, 'Won' denotes Dharmakaya. Its emphasis was on integrating Buddhist faith, meditation and precepts into unity. His successor, Chongsan, developed Won Buddhism in terms of the Samdong principle that "all doctrines have the same origin."]

3

Jesus and *Ochlos* in the Context of His Galilean Ministry *

Ahn Byung-Mu

JESUS left for Galilee after the arrest of John the Baptist. He began his ministry for God's kingdom in the countryside of Galilee rather than in the city.[1] In attempting to get a closer picture of the historical Jesus, I am interested in this geographical circumstance. Therefore, my quest for the historical Jesus will differ from any metaphysical search within Christology. Major theological works in the West, up to the present, have been primarily concerned with understanding "Jesus Christ" as the object of our faith and worship rather than "Jesus" in a more historical and concrete sense. This theological meaning has dominated Biblical interpretation. Kerygma is related directly to "the theology of God's Word."

However, theology is not a factual reality in itself but only reveals the meaning of facts. It is natural that we should pursue the meaning of facts and events. But if we become locked into a particular interpretation of meaning, we cannot help being held captive by dogma. Theologians of kerygma regard the sermons of the first Christians to be the basic source of the formation of the Gospels. These sermons are perceived as a response to questions regarding who and what Jesus was rather than a reiteration of the life and words of the historical Jesus. Therefore, they approach all theologies merely as a quest for the meaning of Christ.

In so doing, they have pushed the historical Jesus (as a fact) into the periphery of theological endeavors. Since Schmidt's book, *The Framework*

* Translated and edited by Paul S. Chung.

1 G. Theissen, *Soziologie der Jesusbewegung*, 47.

of the Words of Jesus,[2] came out, theologians have come to believe that the events of Jesus in the Gospels would be meaningful only to the extent that they become instrumental in bringing forth the fragmentary words of Jesus. Arguing that this is consistent with the Greek literary form of *apophthegma*, Bultmann supports Schmidt's conclusion and develops it one step further.[3]

As a result, the historical Jesus becomes insignificant and kerygma becomes only the concern of biblical scholars. It would be impossible to identify the events of the historical Jesus, since Jesus is only accessible through the kerygma. Besides, such queries about the historical Jesus are denounced to be an act of disbelief (by Bultmann, for instance). How can we explain this phenomenon? Why is there an insistence on discarding the stories that make up almost all of the Gospels? The answer to these questions is twofold. First, there is a tendency to disregard or depreciate the role of stories in the academic world. There is a working assumption that the intellectual community should not take stories seriously. Secondly, there is the strong influence of philosophical idealism in German intellectual societies that has affected theologians, as well. Against this background, we now seek the historical Jesus.

In order to do this, we must first ask questions about whom Jesus fought for and against. A short cut to understanding one's words and action lies in understanding one's companions and antagonists. Questions regarding whom Jesus addressed and what Jesus spoke can be best answered by discerning and examining the meaning of those words in his life context. Jesus' words are not soliloquies; they are expressed to someone in a particular situation. Determining to whom those words are addressed becomes an indispensable part of understanding what those words mean. Both the speaker and the listener exist within a particular context. Therefore, discerning this context enables us to discover the meaning of the words.

Jesus was not a hermit.[4] Neither was he a mystic whom others could not understand, nor did he speak in a language incomprehensible to others. His words were not philosophical or metaphysical; they sprang forth from the context in which he lived. Therefore, it is important to recognize

[2] Cf. K. L. Schmidt, *Der Rahmen der Geschichte Jesu*, 1919.

[3] R. Bultmann, *Geschichte der synoptischen Tradition*, 8. [Editor's note: Bultmann calls the "Jesuswort" into the short framework of forms of Apothegmata, which are common in Greek literary history.]

[4] This point stands out vividly in comparison to the followers of John the Baptist and the Essenes.

who his companions were. From the beginning, the Gospels introduce Jesus as being together with others.

To this day, however, there has been a tendency to focus solely on the existence of Jesus alone, just as there has been a tendency to mistake his personality as aloof and vain. Even in cases where his companions are noted, they are simply perceived of as secondary background characters who appear in order to support the leading character of Jesus. In this way, the historical character of Jesus' life has been distorted and even lost. In order to understand the historical Jesus, we begin by focusing our attention on those who were with him. These companions were not just with Jesus; they lived together with Jesus. Who were these people? And what happened through Jesus' encounters with them?

Christianity is commonly perceived of as a philanthropic religion. It is said that Jesus loved all people alike. But is this really the case? As the basis of the claim that Jesus is a philanthropist, the following passage is often cited:[5] "Your Father who is in heaven… makes his sun rise on the evil and on the good, and sends rain on the just and on the unjust" (Matt 5:45). If this is the case, how are we to understand the will of God as explained by Jesus through the story of a shepherd who leaves behind ninety-nine sheep in search for one lost sheep (Matt 18:12–14)? What about the story of a woman who searches endlessly for her one lost coin (Luke 15:11–32) or the story of a father who rejoices at the return of his lost son (Luke 15:11–32)? Jesus did not simply convey these stories; he lived them.

Some people assert that the above stories deal not only with the lost, but apply to those who are not lost as well.[6] How, then, can we interpret Jesus' statements, "I came not to call the righteous, but sinners" (Mark 2:17) and "Come to me, all who labor and are heavy laden, and I will give you rest" (Matt 11:28)? These distinctions between the righteous and the sinners, and concern for those who labor and are over-burdened, are found

[5] This is the basis of the commandment to love one's enemy, and is not intended to reveal the fundamental nature of God.

[6] This text should not be interpreted in the light of the teachings in verse 14ff, which teach that none should be lost from the whole. The particular significance of this parable lies in the fact that ninety-nine sheep have been left behind in the search for the one that is lost. The tendency to connect this parable with the one that appears in verse 14ff has been strengthened since Schlatter. Cf. A. Schlatter, *Der Evangelist Matthäus*, 1929, 552f. J. Schniewind does not distinguish the risen from the life of the church. Schniewind claims that the lost sheep refers to the sinners of the church and that the parable teaches that the whole community of the church can only be saved when it receives sinners into its community. J. Schniewind, Das *Evangelium nach Matthäus*, 299f. However, I cannot agree with this interpretation.

throughout the Gospels. For example, they appear in stories that most clearly reveal the will of Jesus through parables, such as the high priest and the Samaritan (Luke 10:25ff), the rich man and the beggar (Luke 16:19ff), the judge and the widow (Luke 18:1ff), the Pharisee and the tax collector (Luke 18:9ff), and the privileged guests and the people of the street (Luke 14:15ff).

It is important for us to note two passages that reveal the life and the form of Jesus. The first is the statement made by Jesus at the beginning of his public ministry, found in Luke 4:18–19, and the second is the response given to the question of whether he is the one who is to come. Regarding the declaration that he came to liberate the poor, the captive, the blind and the oppressed, Jesus contends that his life is the concrete realization of the Gospel, and that he is the one who will heal the blind, the crippled, the leper, and the deaf, and the one who lives among the poor and brings resurrection to the dead.

Slight differences exist between the two passages, but nevertheless both of them reveal that he did not come for the righteous, the law-abiding, the truth-seeking, or any of the otherwise recognized models of the upper-class society of his time.[7] For whom, then, did Jesus come? In sociological terms, those for whom Jesus came are called *ochlos* (the poor crowd; in Korean terminology, minjung). Who were they? To answer this question, the primary thing is to reveal the origin of *ochlos*-minjung within the traditions of Jewish society.

The *Ochlos*-Minjung of Jewish Society

The Hebrew word *am-ha'aretz* means "people of the land." Originally, this word is used to denote landlords. In Israel, the blessing of God is closely associated with the land, and therefore land owners are considered to be blessed by God.[8] But the concept changed when the Babylonians invaded the land of Israel and captured members of the upper-class society, including its rulers and landlords. They redistributed the land previously owned by Israel to the remaining lower-class population of Israel and to foreigners who had been subject to the immigration policy. From then on,

[7] This fact is stressed by Luke, who argues for the importance of the co-existence of the poor and the wealthy.

[8] Land is a consistent promise in the Old Testament. The Land of Canaan was believed to have been acquired through the blessing of God. This tradition was transmitted to Mark, in which the acquisition of land appears as one of the beatitudes (Matt 5:5).

the Israelite ruling class, taken as prisoners by Babylon, used the term *am-ha'aretz* to denote the people who had settled on their land as an expression of anger and contempt.

This term appears in both Ezra 10:1[9] and Neh 10:31 to denote people of the lower class who are contrasted first to the Hasidaeans and then later to the Pharisees.[10] Thus, the meaning of the word *am-ha'aretz* is transformed. In Korean, the word *sang min* would be its equivalent. The term *am-ha'aretz* is used to refer to the peasants, the ignorant,[11] and those who did not know about the law.[12] They were treated like pagans and considered to be unworthy even of sharing the same table.[13]

The word *am-ha'aretz* was again redefined in later Judaism—in rabbinic Judaism when the Pharisees were in control. The religion of the rabbis was dominated by the law. The reason for inserting the law into all spheres of life stemmed from a desire to equip the people of Israel with the law and prevent Israelite identity from crumbling.[14] These motives were well-intended but resulted in two fatal outcomes. First, this system restricted the freedom of the people and was immensely oppressive to the poor.

Poor people were forced to work throughout the week to prepare for the upcoming Sabbath. Because of strict enforcement of the law of cleanliness, they were restricted in their choice of jobs. Secondly, it brought

[9] H. Kreissig, *Die soziale Zusammenbau des Jüdischen Reges*, 1970. 34. According to Kreissig, the *Am-ha'aretz* have been objects of contempt since the post-rabbinic times.

[10] J. Jeremias, *Jerusalem zur Zeit Jesu*, 294, 302ff. Rabbi Akiva commented. "When I was 'Am HaAretz' I said: "give me a 'Talmid Chacham' (a rat student) and I shall bite him like a donkey." Cf. H. Kreissig, *Die Soziale Zussamembau des Jüdischen Reges*, 85.

[11] D. W. Bousett, *Die Religion des Judentums im Späthellenistischen Zeitalter*, 187. A Pharisee made the comment in John 7:49: "Those ignorant of the Laws are cursed."

[12] J. Jeremias, *Jerusalem zur Zeit Jesu*, 303.

[13] Cf. Mark 2:16.

[14] This type of activity dates back as far as the time of Hasidim. During the Maccabean War, those in the Assembly of Hasidim were those who took part in the struggle for the preservation of the Jewish faith. These persons were loyal followers of the law and known conservative nationalists. Cf. M. Hengel, *Judentum und Hellenismus* (Tübingen: J. C. B. Mohr, 1969) Bd.2. 319, 324ff. Both the Pharisees and the Essenes locate their origins in this group of people. However, a separate sect was formed among those followers of the law who advanced the position that the Torah was sufficient. They then gradually came to hold full right and authority over the laws, and thorough fulfillment of the commandments became the center of all activity. Discussions concerning the commandments were activated and expanded in order to ensure that the life of the faithful was in unity with the teaching of the Torah. These were precisely the characteristics which distinguished the rabbinic Jews from the others. M. Hengel, *Judentum und Hellenismus*, 314f.

about the division of the Israelites between people inside and outside the system. Those within the system were those who fulfilled all of the requirements of the law and were therefore "true Israelites" and "righteous," while those outside the system were ostracized as "sinners." The people who were forced out of the system are precisely those known as *am-ha'aretz*. The reason that they were forced out will be discussed in more detail later. At this point, suffice it to say that it has to do with the temple system itself.

The structure of the Jewish temple of the rabbis was passed down through a book known as Mishna.[15] This book contains detailed laws governing all aspects of life, including laws and regulations concerning farming, observation of festivals, spouse-relationships, worship, dining, and cleanliness. An examination of the Sabbath law is sufficient for us to understand the importance of this system. The content of the Sabbath law will be scrutinized in detail at another time, but what concerns me is the question of who was able to observe these laws.

If we reflect on this law, we realize immediately that the only ones capable of observing the Sabbath are those who, at the very least, are certain of their next day's provisions. People who, by occupation, are forced to obtain food through daily wages in terms of working as shepherds, boat workers or prostitutes, or peasants confronted with drought, could not possibly observe the laws of the Sabbath. The same principle applies to Jewish slaves of Gentiles and men employed in the army. Since they could not obey the Sabbath laws, they were alienated from the system and were branded "sinners." These people were the *am-ha'aretz*.

The same applies to the law of cleanliness. People who worked in unclean jobs could not comply with this law. Those who were constantly tainted with the smell of muck from cleaning the sewers could not attend worship at the temple. According to certain records, the occupations of donkey herdsman, camel herdsman, boat worker, cart pusher, shepherd, peddler, medical healer (quack doctor), and butcher were all considered to be vulgar. Other documents add rag picker, copper-smith and leather maker to the list of "unclean" occupations.[16] Thus these people, although they were Israelites, were alienated from the Jewish community. These were the *am-ha'aretz*, the minjung of that time.

[15] The rabbis claim that the Mishnah dates back to Moses. The Mishnah is a collection of interpretations of the Old Testament. However, it came to play an even more significant role than the Old Testament as a systematic text.

[16] J. Jeremias, *Jerusalem zur Zeit Jesu*, 365.

The People with whom Jesus was Associated

The Gospel of Mark, from the beginning, repeatedly states that many people followed Jesus.[17] Everywhere he went, a crowd of people followed. Who was the crowd? The first to be recognized were the sick. Stories about Jesus' healing appear most frequently in the Gospels,[18] an indication of the importance of this activity in the life of Jesus. It is, in fact, very integral to his life. Therefore, in his answer to John the Baptist's disciples, he says, "Go and tell John what you hear and see: the blind receive their sight and the lame walk, lepers are cleansed and the deaf hear, and the dead are raised up, and the poor have good news preached to them" (Matt 11:4–5).

Jesus' proclamation at the beginning of his public ministry is similar in Luke 4:18–19. Jesus did not merely heal the diseases of those who followed him; he regarded this healing as a part of his movement to drive out Satan. From the perspective of the sick who were alienated and persecuted by the system, Jesus' willingness to listen to their wishes by healing was a sign of his battle against demons.

There were many women around Jesus.[19] Considering the nature of patriarchal society and the customs of Jesus' time that considered women as "private property with minds," we may regard the records of Jesus' association with women to be based on historical fact. In fact, it would be most likely that there were many more stories about Jesus with women in addition to those recorded in the Gospels since such stories would have been condensed or disregarded by the men who handled them. Those women who appeared around Jesus followed him to the very end and were witnesses to his crucifixion along with many other people. This issue also will be treated separately elsewhere.[20]

Fishermen were at the core of Jesus' movement. Fishermen were not necessarily symbols of poverty. Recalling that James and John owned a boat and had hired men to help them, they could not be considered poor. However, the occupation of fishery was one of the vulgar jobs. The reason was, from a moral position, that fishermen tricked fish into their nets. But more importantly, they were unable to comply with the Sabbath law.[21] It

[17] Cf. Ahn Byung-Mu, "Jesus and Ochlos", in Ahn Byung-Mu, *Minjung and Korean Theology* (Seoul: Hankuk Theology Institute, 1982).

[18] Chapter on "Struggle with Satan," cf. Ahn Byung-Mu, "Jesus of Galilee," in ibid., 132–55.

[19] Chapter on "Jesus and Women," ibid., 156–84.

[20] Ibid.

[21] J. Jeremias, *Jerusalem zur Zeit Jesu*, 345.

was impossible and overburdening for fishermen to return ashore to observe the Sabbath on time.

It is also remarkable that a tax collector was one of Jesus' disciples. What is more remarkable is that there was a Zealot among Jesus' disciples when Zealots were generally known to be enemies of tax collectors. In Jewish society, tax collectors were equated with robbers and treated with contempt and disdain. In fact, even offerings from tax collectors were turned away. They were regarded as enemies of the Zealots. Although tax collectors were not poor, they were treated as less than human in Jewish society.

The Gospels definitely specify that Simon was a member of the Zealot party. Likewise, it is a strong probability that Judas Iscariot was one of the Zealots, particularly when we recall that he was referred to as Judas Sicarier. The term *sicarier* denotes "one who carries a sword in his breast" and was used to identify the assassins of the Zealot party.[22] Similarly, Peter was also under suspicion of being a Zealot since he was also known as "Simon Bar-Jona" (Matt 16:17), which in Aramaic can be interpreted as "terrorist."[23]

Furthermore, if the record of the two robbers who were crucified along with Jesus is historically true, it is without doubt that they were also Zealots. At the time, Zealots were referred to as "bandits," at least by Josephus. Since this was a term used by those in Roman authority, if Zealots were simply "robbers," they would not have hung on the cross.[24] This being the case, it implies that Jesus was closely associated with Zealots.[25] These so-called 'robbers' were members of the Zealot party who were fighting for the liberation of Israel. If at least one of Jesus' disciples was a Zealot, it would be hard to deny that Jesus was intimately connected with the Zealot party. The center of the Zealot party was Galilee. Economically, most of them in Galilee were impoverished. Socially, they bore a close resemblance

[22] Hengel, who makes an analysis of the Sikarii and the Zealots, claims that they are two separate sects sharing a common ideology. Cf. M. Hengel, *Die Zeloten*, 387. Such a distinction is not very meaningful.

[23] R. Eisler, *Die messianische Untergang Jakobus der Gerechten nach der neuerschlossenen Eroberung von Jerusalem des Flavius Josephus und der Christlichen Quellen dargestellt*, Bd.2, 67f.

[24] G. Baumbach, *Jesus von Nazareth im Lichte der Jüdischen Gruppenbildung*, 24f.

[25] Josephus claimed that they were a new breed of bandits known as Sikarii. Hengel has no doubt that Jesus was a member of the Zealots; see M. Hengel, *Die Zeloten*, 30.

to the crowd which followed Jesus. As a result, there are some scholars who seek to understand Jesus in relation to the Zealots.[26]

What is certain, however, is that the crowd and the Zealots who followed Jesus can commonly be defined as *ochlos*-minjung. In the stories of Jesus, we also see that many of his followers were of low social status—peasants, workers, the poverty-stricken, the unemployed. It is reported that at times as many as four or five thousand of these people (though excluding women and children) gathered around Jesus. If we had to choose a common word to describe the minjung, it would be "poor." How poor were they? Let's look at some specific examples. At that time, a day's wage was one denari. One denari could buy thirteen liters of grain. With this income, people lived on about six scoops of grain per day, depending on the size of the family, and thus could barely maintain subsistence.

The Gospels tell a story about a widow who give all her life possessions as offering in the amount of one lepta. Two leptas equal about half a denari and thus, all the possessions this widow owns in the world could buy no more than half a scoop of grain. In the Bible, widows are the symbol of the minjung.

When it comes to the Gospel report of the four thousand people who followed Jesus (Matt 15:38), this crowd had not eaten anything for four days, and the cost to feed them would have been about 200 denari. This calculation was based on an average of 1/4 scoop of grain per person. These estimates roughly reflected the market price of that time. Of course, if we were to add the women and children to this figure, the amount of grain allocated to each person would be far smaller. From this, we can imagine the degree of their poverty.

As noted earlier, fishermen are not necessarily a symbol of poverty. In the Bible they are said to own some property (a boat or some nets). Similarly, tax collectors by occupation came in contact with money and thereby amassed great property, depending on their position. The story of Levi, who becomes one of Jesus' disciples and gives a huge feast (Mark 2:15),[27] and the somewhat fairy tale-like story of Zacchaeus allude to the fact that tax collectors were men with some means. Nevertheless, they were not wealthy, since they served mostly as errand boys for the wealthy.[28]

[26] S. F. G. Brandon, *Jesus and the Zealots* (Manchester: Manchester University Press, 1967) 322f.

[27] The Gospel of Luke reports that Levi had given a large banquet for Jesus (5:29).

[28] Jewish tax collectors were not government officials. Like Roman levy contractors, they paid taxes to the Roman government on behalf of the Jewish people, and later collected this in the form of a levy from their people. They were accountable to the chief tax col-

All of these people were the lowly and the outcasts of society. Jesus did not even approach the cities of the wealthy,[29] nor did he associate with even one person of reputation.[30] Mark groups the followers of Jesus into one category and refers to them as the *ochlos*.

Ochlos

The Gospels reveal a great interest in the crowd that followed Jesus. The earliest of the Gospels, Mark, notes the crowd that gathered around Jesus in his description of Jesus' entrance into public ministry. In chapter 1, Mark describes the crowd with the word 'people,' 'many' and 'all,' but in chapter 2 (verse 4), as if he were revealing their identity. Mark refers to them as *ochlos*.

In Greek, the words *laos* and *ochlos* refer to 'the masses'. The term *laos*, as a word that denoted a collective of people who gathered around some organic commonality, was generally used to mean 'the people of God' or 'people of Israel'. 'National people' would be its equivalent in today's language. The term 'citizen' is almost consistently translated as *laos*. Compared to this, the word *ochlos* is used rather infrequently and only to refer to 'slaves', 'soldiers of the employed army', or 'conscripted soldiers'.[31]

Literally translated, the word *ochlos* means 'a disorderly mob.' It refers to a group of people whose assembling is not based on any power, duty, or any other relationship in Jewish society. The term 'crowd' is strictly distinguished from the term 'national people' or 'citizens.' Citizens, as members of a national society, have rights and duties in that society which, in turn, provides for their safety and welfare. But those of the 'crowd' have no such rights or duties, nor do they receive protection from the society.

---

lector and formed an association centered around him. According to Schurer, because the amount of the levy was not predetermined, there was always the possibility of corruption on the part of the tax collector. E. Schurer, *Geschichte des judischen Volkes im Zeitalter Jesu Christi*, 475.

29 Jesus had no exchanges with them, even in Jerusalem.

30 Joseph of Arimathea was said to be "a respected member of the council" (Mark 15:43). According to Gnilka, he was a member of the Council of Arimathea and a wealthy landlord. Cf. J. Gnilka, *Markus, II*, 332f. Although he is portrayed as a devout Jew who awaited the coming of the kingdom of God and was sympathetic to the Jesus movement, he was not one of Jesus' disciples.

31 Meyer and Katz, "Ochlos," in *Theologisches Wörterbuch zum Neuen Testament*, Bd. V. 583ff.

In any case, the editor of the Gospel of Mark chose the word *ochlos* over the word *laos* in referring to Jesus' crowd. In other words, the followers of Jesus were *ochlos*, not *laos*. Could it be that Mark was not familiar with the term *laos*? By no means! In fact, he uses the word *laos* on two different occasions: once in 7:6, which quotes a passage from the Old Testament, and then again in 14:2, when he cites the words of a scribe. Juxtaposed with this, the word *ochlos* appears no fewer than thirty-six times. The case is somewhat different in Matthew and Luke. Matthew uses the term *ochlos* fifty-one times and the term *laos* thirteen times; Luke uses *ochlos* forty times and *laos* thirty-five times.

Nevertheless, the basic position in both Matthew and Luke has been passed down by Mark and the word *ochlos* in these two Gospels continues to possess particular significance. A number of times, the word *ochlos* is replaced with *laos*, but in those cases the meaning does not differ greatly.[32] Luke substitutes *laos* for *ochlos* in describing the members of the community of Christ,[33] but this does not detract from the fact that these people were the forsaken, the persecuted, and the economically and politically alienated.

What is actually meant by *ochlos*? We can begin to discern its meaning by examining the context of Mark 2:13–17. Verse 13 reads: "… and all the crowd (*ochlos*) gathered about him (Jesus)…" Following this verse, we are told of Jesus' meal with tax collectors and sinners at the house of Levi. Thus the meaning of *ochlos* as signifying "tax collectors and sinners" is suggested.

These were the people who followed Jesus. Upon seeing Jesus share the same table with these unrighteous people, the Pharisees and scribes would not eat. To this Jesus replied, "Those who are well have no need of a physician, but those who are sick; I came not to call the righteous but sinners" (2:17). We can now assert the position that Jesus came to call the minjung, who—like the tax collectors and sinners—are precisely the *ochlos*.

The particular characteristics of the *ochlos* can be categorized as follows. First, everywhere Jesus went, the minjung (*ochlos*) followed (2:4–13; 3:9–20, 32; 4:1; 5:21–24, 31; 8:1; 10:1). It would be impossible to envision Jesus of Galilee without the minjung and likewise it would be difficult

[32] For example, Mark 11:32 and 12:12 state that Jesus' enemies were afraid of the *ochlos*. Luke replaces *ochlos* with *laos*, but the meaning remains unchanged.

[33] Unlike Mark, who reports that it was the *ochlos* who shouted for Barabbas' release (15:11; 15:15), Luke uses a denominative pronoun to depict the crowds. Prior to doing so, however, he assumes that the *ochlos* is *laos*.

to think about the minjung of the Gospels without Jesus. The minjung are not those who appear in the background in order to reveal who Jesus was. It is the reverse of the typical subject-object. That is, Jesus was nothing but a mirror that reflected the minjung!

Therefore, Jesus of the Gospels was not alone; he was a 'being together' with the minjung. We cannot say that there were two separate stories: Jesus and then the minjung; rather, there is only one story of *uri* (us).[34] There are the stories of Jesus living among and together with the minjung. Therefore, we must admit that the gospels are not the personal or individual biography of Jesus[35] but the history of Jesus' minjung movement. The Gospels are stories about the development of Jesus' movement. This is a point that differs fundamentally from Paul's representation of Christ. This fact serves as a consistent basis for the illumination of Jesus' life and attitude.

Second, Jesus shared the same table with the minjung (Mark 2:13–17). The nature of this act is most clearly conveyed to us in the Q source in Luke (7:33–34). " 'For John the Baptist has come eating no bread and drinking no wine; and you say, 'He has a demon.' The Son of man has come eating and drinking; and you say, 'Behold, a glutton and a drunkard, a friend of tax collectors and sinners!" Two facts can be noted from this passage. The first is that Jesus ate and drank with sinners and tax collectors. The second is the concrete fact that Jesus was their friend. These were precisely the characteristics that separated Jesus from John the Baptist.

Although John preached to the minjung, he isolated himself from them. That is, the minjung were no more than the object of his mission, those with whom he 'communicated'. Unlike John the Baptist, Jesus ate and drank with them—acts that disclosed the intimacy of their relationship. These acts were not a demonstration for or of anything; they were simply a natural part of Jesus' life. But they were acts that shattered the value system of the upper class of that time and the structures that defined the minjung as 'sinners'.

[34] [Editor's note: Uri is 'we' in Korean. Ahn is engaged in endless effort to overcome Western individualism (or 'I' centrism) based on the subject-object schemata. In using the Korean term for 'We', Ahn uncovers a collective sense of Jesus in relation to the *ochlos-minjung*.]

[35] Innumerable stories about Jesus were written before it was proven that the gospels were not written with the intention of givinga biography of Jesus' life. With the discovery of the true character of the gospels, such attempts were suspended. For a discourse on the nature of the gospels, see G. Bornkam, *Jesus von Nazareth*.

Third, by placing the *ochlos* at odds with the rulers in Jerusalem of that period, the author alludes to a relationship of solidarity between Jesus and the *ochlos* against the Jerusalem citizen (Mark 2:4–6; 3:2–6, 22–35; 7:1–2; 8:11; 11:18, 27–33). The minjung of Galilee were intimately associated with Jesus. In the words of Renan, this made for the continuation of the 'Spring of Galilee'. The Galilean minjung were close to Jesus, but occasionally Jesus was in conflict with the Pharisees and scribes who came down from Jerusalem.

Jerusalem was precisely the place where Jesus was crucified. The fact that the minjung of Jerusalem cried out in approval of the crucifixion of Jesus does not necessitate an anti-minjung diatribe here and now; neither do the Gospels attempt to beautify their description of the Galilean minjung. Therefore, there is no need to vindicate the acts of the minjung who had been infected with the disease of avarice for money. The Jerusalem citizens were just as much to blame for the minjung's avarice as they were for stigmatizing them as 'sinners' and treating them inhumanely.

Fourth, the *ochlos* were a threat to the powerful ruling classes (Mark 11:18–32; 12:2). This fact could have been included in the third characterization, but I choose to distinguish it from the rest simply because it deserves special emphasis. Why did the ruling class fear them? It was due not only to the injustice they had committed against the minjung but also to the fact that the minjung were united under Jesus. This union meant great strength for the opposition. This is precisely why the Pharisees and the Herodians[36] (who should have been like fire and water) from the beginning were in collusion to try to kill Jesus (Mark 3:6) and also why Romans, Pharisees and Herodians remained united until the death of Jesus. Thus, the identity of the anti-minjung forces was exposed. They were the enemies of the minjung and it was they who collaborated in the plot to execute Jesus.

Fifth, Jesus perceived of the *ochlos* as "sheep without a shepherd." This expression embodies two different ideas. The first is the idea of a people who have degenerated and are subjects of punishment (Zech 13:7).

[36] It is difficult to make any conclusive statements about the members of the Herodians. It is said that the appearance of the minjung, loyal to Herod, is related to the event of Herod's tribute of 109 head of bulls to the temple at the time of Augustus' sending of Markus Agrippa to Jerusalem, which greatly increased the wealth of the temple. Cf. Bo Reicke, *Neutestamentliche Zeitgeschichte*, 78. These would be the same people who played an active role as the members of the Herodians during the time of Herod Agripa. They would also be the ones who took part in Herod's plot to kill Jesus. It is speculated that they belonged to the upper class of Galileans who were loyal to the Roman rulers. J. Gnilka, *Markus, I*. 129.

The other is the idea of people who are suffering because of a ruler (class) who has fallen into decadence.

King Ahab—for the purpose of preserving his throne—mobilized his people to war. Micah said to him, "I saw all Israel scattered upon the mountain, like sheep without a shepherd....These have no master; let each return to his home in peace" (1 Kgs 22:17). These words were in denunciation of the tyranny of King Ahab and referred to the situation in which the sheep had been scattered because their self-appointed ruler, instead of keeping watch over them, had pursued them like a hunter (Ezek 34:5). This was a censure against the tyrannical rulers of Israel. Thus, Jesus' usage of the phrase "sheep without a shepherd" was indubitably a reference to this latter idea. It was certain that the Pharisees and Herodians thought of themselves as "good shepherds," yet Jesus denounced them. This revealed Jesus' stand with the minjung and his perception that they have been alienated by their religious and political rulers.

Sixth, Jesus declared that the *ochlos* were "my brother, and sister and mother" (Mark 3:31–35). It is extraordinary that Jesus should refer to the minjung so indiscriminately as his closest family members. This is a display of the highest relationship of solidarity, surpassing even family blood relations. It is even more exceptional that Jesus should refer to his minjung as 'my mother' as well as 'brother' and 'sister.' The latter can be used to symbolize a certain relationship within a community (as the Essenes and Pharisees used it at the time)[37] or even as an expression of nationalist comradeship, but the term "mother" cannot. As the highest metaphor used to express deep affection and love, the term "mother" is a difficult word for even later editors of the gospels to accept. As a result, Matthew restricts the use of this word to refer to the disciples, and Luke omits its usage altogether from the beginning.

Seventh, and most important, is the fact that Jesus did not make any ethical or religious judgments against the *ochlos*. As has already been mentioned, Jesus did not hesitate to severely criticize and reproach the so-called ruling class, including the Pharisees.[38] However, he did not say one chastising word against the *ochlos,* the so-called 'sinners' of society. Jesus did not demand that these 'sinners' cleanse their past or make new resolutions in either his meetings with them or in his parables.[39] Without mak-

[37] They used the title 'comrade' to refer to one another. D. W. Bousset, *Die Religion des Judentums im späthellenistischen Zeitalter*, 165, 187.

[38] Matt 23:1–36, Luke 12:1–3.

[39] Luke 15:11–32, Mark 2:13–17, Luke 19:1–10.

ing any demands, he defended them unconditionally. But neither did he try to make them seem more perfect than they actually were. He accepted them just as they were and opened himself up to them. It was through this openness that they became his mother, brother and sister.

The above examination of Jesus' *association* with the minjung is based on the Gospel of Mark, but fundamental differences cannot be discerned in the Q portions of either Matthew or Luke. For whatever reason, Jesus stood on the side of the minjung—the suffering, the hungry, the crying, the thirsty, and the oppressed crowds—and gave himself to them. Jesus asked no questions about the powerlessness of the minjung—whether it was the product of political tyranny, exploitation by the wealthy, or their own weakness. At least, such questions were not expressed. With this, we conclude our examination of Jesus' relationship with his minjung and return to the fundamental question that has already been raised; that is, the problem of how we can be free from this subject-object schemata.

It is easy for us to state that Jesus came for the minjung, to call them, cure their sickness, and liberate them. Was this really the case? Jesus certainly went to Galilee, but their relationship was not that of host and guests where Jesus was simply the subject and the minjung were simply the invited guests.

First, it is reported that everywhere Jesus went, the minjung followed. Did Jesus call them or did they come of their own accord? There are many stories of Jesus healing diseases. Did Jesus set up a plan and then methodically begin to carry it out? How did the minjung bring Jesus to heal them through their pleas? If we combine these, they form the question of whether the minjung came because Jesus was present, or whether Jesus came because the minjung were present. This kind of question about the process and activities of Jesus already places us outside the 'host-guest' schemata.

The narratives of the gospels do not state one way or the other what motivated the works of Jesus. Jesus was simply with the minjung everywhere he went. Because the sick were in a state of pain, they sought out Jesus and begged to be cured. Jesus complied and said that their faith had made them well. These narratives of healing are certainly not presented as if Jesus had made a tour to heal the sick like some magician. Jesus was also present in the midst of 4000 people.

If Jesus had been recognized to possess the power to work miracles, then the crowd of 4000 would not have starved for four days. Moreover, Jesus would not have regarded them with sympathy. The minjung of Jesus write this narrative in such a way as to make us understand that the miracle of feeding 4000 people occurred through Jesus' contact with the starving crowd. In order to reveal the fact that Jesus did not perform the miracle alone, the event is based on the fact that someone gave him two fish and five loaves of bread.

The Gospels provide us with a one-sided presentation of Jesus unilaterally teaching the minjung. But was Jesus simply conveying some perfect and systematic logic that he had knowledge of, or did his words represent the longings of his minjung? We must be absolutely sure not to separate these two aspects. Although Jesus and the minjung are made distinct in the narratives of his teachings, this is not, in fact, the case. If we concede that, to a certain extent, Jesus led the minjung, we must also acknowledge the fact that he was surrounded by the minjung whose will he followed through his actions and words, and that it was they who determined his final destiny. Therefore, it is only when we overcome the tendency to perceive Jesus as the host and the minjung as guests that we will be able to accurately understand Jesus' minjung movement. This is the subject of the following discussion.

The Kingdom of God and the Minjung

In the last chapter, we affirmed that the coming of the kingdom of God was central to Jesus' proclamation. Therefore, we have surveyed the facts of 'Jesus together with the minjung' as the most important characteristic defining the life of Jesus. Thus we cannot avoid asking about the relationship between these two most important facts. The life of Jesus, according to Mark, is understood under the great premise of the imminence of the coming of the kingdom of God. We argue that the kingdom of God should not be understood as an object of meditation but as something that is realized within praxis. In that case, did Jesus ever present the direction of this struggle to his minjung?

The majority of the minjung in the gospels appear as the powerless and alienated people of society. The impression we have of Jesus, who lived among them, is that of someone who helped the poor and sick in response to their pleas. This explains why for so long the idea of following Jesus (*imitatio Christi*) has been dominated by a belief in the importance of doing works of charity. However, if we perceive the minjung in relation to the proclamation of the coming of the kingdom of God, we cannot regard them as objects of our charity.

Although this is not clearly presented to us in the gospels, we need to examine the Galilean minjung within the tradition of the minjung of

Israel. For the *hapiru* people, who formed the ancient Israelite tribal alliance, the concept of nationalism indicated a particular social status. The *hapiru* fled from their enslavement under the monarchs and formed their own autonomous alliance. The most critical factor in preserving this alliance was a denunciation of the monarchical system.

This developed into a simple and staunch belief in "only Yahweh" (mono Yahwehism). That is, no authority or sovereignty other than Yahweh would be recognized. A society ruled "only by Yahweh" was the yearning of the *hapiru* people. This ancient Israelite system, which was maintained for nearly two hundred years, was the object of envy even after it was transformed into a monarchy.[40]

It is important to note that Galilee was geographically part of the domain of this ancient Israelite nation, but the people of Galilee were disdained by the Jewish people for their impurity. From the very beginning, the cities of Galilee were built for the purpose of flattering foreign rulers, and this was particularly so during the era of the Roman rule. Therefore, the cities were Greco-Roman societies built by the labor of slaves while the rural areas were societies based on a quasi-Asiatic mode of production. These societies actually were not very different from the ancient Israelite system.

The residents of the countryside were poor peasants, despite the fact that they lived on fertile land. It is impossible for us to believe that Jesus had no specific purpose in mind when he acted and lived among them. Or conversely, it is easily imaginable that the countless minjung who unconditionally followed Jesus were no more than weak people who expected salvation from him. They were people who were being exploited as colonial subjects under the Roman Empire and oppressed by Rome's puppets—the Herodians and the religious elite who colluded with the invading forces so that they could preserve their right to receive tributes from the people. How was Jesus' proclamation of the coming of God's kingdom understood by these people who were the victims of a system of dual and triple exploitation? What did they expect from Jesus that they followed him so faithfully?

As mentioned above, it is often believed that the reason Jesus did not specifically explain what the kingdom of God referred to was either be-

40 [Editor's note: According to Ahn Byung-Mu, the Hebrews, after their liberation from Egypt and settlement in Canaan, sought cooperation with the *Hapiru* slaves who had been exploited under many monarchs, and formed an alliance of Israelite tribes. In this context, Ahn follows "the social revolution hypothesis" (G.E. Mendenhall, N. K. Gottwald), yet with some reservation.]

cause of the mystical nature of the kingdom which eludes human language or because of the situation of Jesus' time which prevented him from elucidating on the facts of the kingdom. I believe that, rather than these two explanations, we would be more justified in believing that it was because the kingdom needed no explanation for the minjung. They understood clearly what "kingdom of God" meant.

4

Missio Dei and Two Stories in Coalescence *

Suh Nam-Dong

KIM Chi-Ha, a well-known poet in South Korea, speaks of minjung in the following way: "In Genesis, God said to human beings, 'Be fruitful and multiply, and fill the earth and subdue it.'" This statement refers to what minjung means. Minjung is to subdue the earth by becoming fruitful, so that it transforms the world and organizes society. In so doing, it appears as a universal physical agent, which propels history. It is constituted by the substantial context of human life, in contrast to the human spirit. Minjung is a social and historical concrete concept in terms of self-labor: cultivating the earth, building houses, and producing.

The concept of minjung is opposite to the concept of power and different from the middle class intelligent strata. In fact, political power originates from minjung. As political power becomes institutionalized, it changes into the oppression of minjung. In the process of history, minjung rebelled against this power by returning it to its original place and restoring public righteousness. Kim Chi-Ha argues that when the powerful betray justice and become anti-minjung, it is righteous to take the side of the minjung and unrighteous to take the side of the powerful.

Kim Chi-Ha also answers the question of why the lowly in the city appear as the featured people in his writings. Insofar as the Gospel of Jesus aims primarily at saving the lowly at the bottom, the church needs to gain

* Translated and edited by Paul S. Chung. Prof. Suh Nam-Dong published this article in 1979, when the military dictatorship forced him to resign his teaching position. His lengthy discourse can be found in his article on "Historical References for a Theology of Minjung" in *Minjung Theology: People as the Subjects of History*, ed. CTC-CCA (Maryknoll: Orbis, 1981) 155–82.

explosive vitality among them. They become the subject of Christian salvation. The reason Kim Chi-Ha features the lowly and the poor in his writings is to highlight the possibility of salvation through their protest and victory. Kim Chi-Ha argues that Jesus the Messiah, whom we Christians adore and to whom we pray, does not come from the privileged group, but from the lowly and the oppressed. The coming of the Messiah who has come from the bottom is at the center of Kim's writings.

Given what Kim Chi-Ha has depicted, I believe that he defines well the essence of minjung, its historical trajectory, and its path to salvation. Minjung was, from the beginning, the covenant partner of God so that it subdues the earth, produces material life, transforms the world and propels history. However, it ends up becoming sinful and lowly because of how they have been isolated and oppressed by the ruling power. The task of minjung is to return the power to its original place and to reinstate the righteousness of God for salvation.

This salvation, in my view, is propelled by God's work and founded especially in the example of Jesus Christ who is the basis for minjung salvation. Though in this context the Genesis narrative is used as grounds for reinstating God's righteousness, the narrative should be understood in a proleptic-eschatological sense rather than in a retrospective-archaic way. In other words, the beginning, the place of origin of Genesis, does not reside in the past (memory-idealism), but in the future (anticipation-action).[1]

According to Kim Chi-Ha, the church is supposed to bring about the unity of God and revolution, refining the tradition of the minjung movement in Korea through the perspective of liberation theology. Thus the church would become a sign of the progression of the human rights movement. I believe that a theology of *Missio Dei* needs to be deepened and radicalized by a Christian response to such challenges.[2]

[1] If I sum up Kim Chi-Ha's definition of minjung, minjung is God's covenant partner, the bearer or agent of God's righteousness in the course of history. It is important to more fully explain these twofold dimensions. The first aspect refers to the fact that minjung is a subjective agent in the area of labor and production. However, this aspect corresponds also to the biblical outlook of the covenant between God and minjung. Taking this a further step, there is a special attention to those who are trodden by political power—the sinner, the poor, the strangers, the crippled, and the thief, the so called Lumpen proletariat—in the biblical context. Insofar as the suffering of minjung functions as an index indicating God's historical economy, a theological understanding of minjung does, in no way, keep company with the socialistic understanding of minjung as a class in the economic sense.

[2] At this juncture, I think of "God ahead of us." *Missio Dei* is, in our current context, to be carried out as the forefront of urban ministry and mission. My theology is to reflect on this mission praxis and ground urban and industrial mission activity biblically and

To precipitate *Missio Dei* for the sake of the human rights movement and social justice, a biblical-theological framework is necessary. For this framework, I include the Exodus event, the event of the crucifixion, and church history, which inherit this liberation tradition, as well as the tradition of the minjung movement in Korean history. References that I mention at this point contradict biblical revelation, which is the theological norm in a traditional sense. Revelation is a religious category while reference is a socio-historical one. I also mention the paradigm or archetypes of historical-theological frameworks. Social mission in the current situation, which I try to interpret by fusing *Missio Dei* with historical references, is related to the embodied historical paradigm of emancipation.

For this task, I attempt to utilize the socio-economic or political-economic method through which the social and political condition of minjung can be better analyzed and more clearly presented. As the history of minjung is revealed in this regard, the social biography of minjung will facilitate our understanding of the collective soul of minjung, their consciousness and desires. At this point, I want to bring Bonhoeffer's idea of the secular interpretation of the Bible to these agenda in order to update its meaning for social diaconal mission and ministry in the midst of a secular city.[3]

The method of theology, which is operated within the framework of hermeneutics, includes the horizon or perspective of the theologian. As Augustinian theology assumed Platonism to be its hermeneutical framework, so Thomism employed the philosophy of Aristotle. Likewise, the philosophy of Kant functioned in the liberal theology of the Protestant church in nineteenth century Germany. The philosophy of existentialism offered an interpretative framework for the theology of Rudolf Bultmann and Paul Tillich. In recent theological trends, I sense that the socioeconomic method or social scientific method is gaining more and more prominence.

Paul Tillich proposes a correlative method in terms of question and answer to deal with a relation between kerygma and the human existential situation. This method seems to be unilateral, losing sight of the socio-economic cultural complex that can influence and condition the human

---

systematically.

[3] [Editor's note: Suh Nam-Dong began to preoccupy himself with relating Bonhoeffer and Harvey Cox to develop his theology of minjung. Norman Gottwald's book *The Tribes of Yahweh* helped him to understand the Israelite faith in relation to the political system of the Canaanite tribes, and the symbol of cross in relation to the political nature of the crucifixion.]

life setting. Political theology in Germany, represented by Moltmann and Metz, and also liberation theology in Latin America call into question what has shaped and conditioned human life socially, politically, and economically.

These theologies take into consideration the social conditions by highlighting the political and economic factors whose dimensions have been neglected in dogmatic theology or existential theology. The debate between the primacy of human being versus consciousness, or social basis versus infrastructure, cannot be properly understood without this dialectical interaction. Be that as it may, political theology or liberation theology tends to prioritize and emphasize socioeconomic or political components and factors as they deal with the relation between God and human responsibility. For instance, social group – race, status, class, sex, age, and, inter-class relations, among other things – plays an important role in constituting the society and propelling history.

Biblical References

1. The Exodus event in the Hebrew Bible is the paradigmatic event in minjung theology. This historical event, together with the crucifixion of Jesus, is the core event of God's salvation for minjung. The biblical narratives can be seen and interpreted in terms of these two events, the Exodus and Christ's crucifixion. In these narratives, God's revelation is manifest as a historical event rather than a religious mystic experience. God's speech came to a historical event. The Exodus event was a political event taking place in the socioeconomic realm.

Under the dominion of Pharaoh Ramset II in the thirteenth century of Egypt BCE, the Hebrews became enslaved and were forced to labor. The Exodus event tells a socioeconomic story of slave emancipation or rebellion according to which the enslaved Hebrew people (*hapiru*) protested the oppressive system of domination and escaped from Pharaoh's rule. If God's involvement in history takes place in the socioeconomic realm, it should not be diluted or reduced to a religious symbol. God's historical involvement is also taking place constantly in today's socioeconomic domains.

2. There are several differences between the Exodus event and the event of the cross, though both of them function as archetypal events of points of reference in minjung theology. In relation to minjung, Moses was a heroic liberator while Jesus was a resisting companion with and for the minjung.

The prophets were the spokespersons of the minjung. The Exodus was a one-time liberation while the event of the cross seems to point toward permanent revolution. In the Exodus the minjung are the object of salvation (salvation model based on the other power) while in the permanent revolution of the cross, the minjung becomes more an agent of salvation (salvation model with emphasis on self-power and practice). Moses was one who responded to the voice (desire) of the minjung while Jesus himself was the embodiment of minjung per se. In this sense, Jesus was of minjung (not merely an individual in support of minjung), the very personification and symbol of minjung.

According to the Q source and the Gospel of Mark, Jesus' teaching is characterized as having religious authority, unlike the scribes and Pharisees. The overarching characteristic is that Jesus was a friend of sinners and tax collectors. In Jesus' life, many people followed him without reservation. The crowd that was around Jesus was not the abstract environment around Jesus but the shadow of Jesus. It formed a living reality with Jesus in an historical sense.

Although there were many people around John the Baptist, they were different from the crowd which followed Jesus. The crowd of Jesus was by and large the poor, the sick, the handicapped, the women, the tax collectors, and the prostitutes, in short, the forsaken who were lowly, and at the bottom of society. These were the *am-ha'arez* (people of land), the public sinners, as they were called by the established Jewish religion. Jesus' mission related to this crowd. This aspect of his ministry challenges us to reflect on the real meaning of *Missio Dei* in the present day situation.

In Mark 3:32–34, *ochlos* is the concept related to the brother, sister, and mother of Jesus. Jesus is the one who embodies the relation between God's will and the *ochlos*-minjung. There is no separation of Jesus from minjung. First of all, from the perspective of redaction criticism, the theological subject of Mark's Gospel is *ochlos* rather than Jesus. Second, *ochlos*, beyond its general meaning, a mass of people, entails the meaning of those who are oppressed and alienated by the ruling class. The goal of today's minjung theology is to reinstate and understand the unique locus of the *ochlos* in relation to Jesus so that Jesus can become an invitation for us to go with *ochlos*. If traditional or christocentric theology focuses on Jesus as Christ without considering his relationship with the *ochlos*, my approach is more concerned with seeing the minjung through Jesus and Jesus through the minjung.

To clarify the linguistic definition and meaning of *ochlos*, I argue that *ochlos* is different from *laos:* it is close to the meaning of "the poor" in the

Scriptures. At this point, *ochlos* cannot be translated as people, *Volk* or crowd. The Korean term minjung better corresponds to Mark's word *ochlos*. Jesus was a friend of tax collectors and public sinners.

In other words, he was a friend of the minjung. In Jesus' parables, we read that Jesus is involved in the lives of the minjung and knows their familiar narratives. Jesus was not only a companion and friend of the minjung, but he also treated them as people, with equality and dignity. Jesus, unlike the scribes in positions of authority, is anchored in this social situation. Jesus teaches the Torah and God in his own language. In this regard, he was *vere homo* and *vere Deus*. At Jesus' time, the law of God became the language of the ruling class in the established religious community. The law took the form of an ideology for oppressing minjung. Jesus' attitude toward the Torah and public sinners was surprising and provocative to the established religion, and as such it is a reference for minjung theology.

Jesus, as a resisting companion of the minjung, ended up with crucifixion. He took the side of the minjung. His public title of friend of tax collectors and sinners functioned as a rebellious action against the ruling system. Jesus' critique of the Sabbath reached its height in his attitude toward the law of Judaism. According to Jesus, the Sabbath is made for people, not the people for it. His challenge to the Temple system in Jerusalem became the primary reason for convicting him, and as a result, he was crucified as a political criminal.

Although historical records about Jesus are obscure in many ways, the obvious thing is that Jesus' crucifixion was the execution of a political rebel. The crucifixion was not accidental but inevitable for Jesus in the midst of his life as a resisting companion. The crucifixion was the inevitable climax for the minjung in the struggle to be in control of their historical fate and future. Minjung salvation begins in the socio-political realm.

In the course of church history, however, this dimension was left behind. The crucifixion of Jesus changed and was sublimated into the religious symbol of the cross. The political implications of the Messiah image were transformed, unilaterally into a distorted religious image of Christ in heaven. In so doing, the event of salvation lost its historical and concrete content. As such, the cross as a religious symbol has no power to transform history. Minjung theology takes seriously the crucifixion of Jesus which is taking place in today's political arena.

In order to reinstate this historical core content, I find a socioeconomic interpretation of Scripture to be pivotal. Jesus after the resurrection promised that he would meet his disciples in Galilee. This is the first testimony about Jesus' resurrection. Galilee, in the context of Mark's Gospel, is the home of minjung, while Jerusalem is the seat of the ruling class. Jesus' promise to go to Galilee after the resurrection means that the resurrected Jesus is present in an on-going way as the Messiah among the minjung who is oppressed and alienated in the socioeconomic realm. This aspect articulates minjung theology's understanding of faith in Jesus' presence among the minjung.

Although I focus on the Exodus event and the Jesus event as the two paradigmatic points of reference for minjung theology, I do not ignore the Torah's concern about minjung (Ex 20–22), wherein God cares for the poor, the sojourner, the orphan, the widow, and the slave. The original meaning of God's Torah is also a core biblical point of reference for minjung theology. Besides the Jesus' event, it is of significance to integrate the social concerns of the ancient church in the New Testament into a minjung theological direction. I propose the following as referential backgrounds of the minjung paradigm: the tradition of liberation in Exodus, the original Israelite community in the pre-monarchical period, the poor (*anawim*) in the prophetic writings, the suffering servant of God, Jesus' mission, and the diaspora sojourners in the ancient church of the New Testament.

References in Church History

As Judaism complied the Tanak, so the church complied the New Testament. In the process of canonization, a de-politicization occurred in regards to the historical nucleus of the Scriptures, namely the liberation message of God for the minjung. I mention here two cultural and historical moments that resulted in this process. One reason can be found in the transition from the historical-apocalyptic horizon of Hebrew culture to the cosmic and metaphysical horizon of the Greek culture.

In the apocalyptic horizon, the day of Yahweh is anticipated as a day of the future in which current injustices will disappear, while on the metaphysical horizon the pure Idea is sought, which purifies and removes false consciousness at the sensible and phenomenological level. The coming of the Messiah, the one who will redeem the suffering minjung, has been depoliticized into the image of a heavenly Christ who sanctions the ruling order on earth. To the degree that the Messiah is depoliticized and reduced to the symbolic image of Christ, the political dimension of the crucifixion is diluted and reduced to the religious dimension of the cross.

The second reason came after Emperor Constantine sanctioned the Christian church as the state religion. Having been elevated from an underground to the upper class, Christianity changed its character from the religion of the oppressed into that of the ruler and the king. Therefore, the apocalyptic and revolutionary potential power of Christianity and faith, which embraced the outcry and protest of the oppressed, was accommodated into the ruling culture of the Roman Empire.

In this, the religion deviated and was transformed to the ideology of the ruler. The original nucleus of Christianity, which was no less than the liberation of the oppressed and the vision of justice, was projected into the heavenly world, namely the realm of transcendence, which has nothing to do with history or the future. It ends up in a timeless eternal paradise that lies beyond history. Religion functions as opium. The Marxist critique of religions is valid in this regard. Nevertheless, religion cannot be displaced as the ruling ideology as long as it remains an outcry of the oppressed and a protest against the oppressor.

The writers of the Gospels sum up the message of Jesus in the following statement: "The kingdom of God comes near." This statement can be seen as a way of deepening the meaning of the day of Yahweh, which the prophets in the Hebrew Bible proclaimed passionately. God's kingdom is also surely more than political revolution. In Constantine Christianity, the kingdom of God was depoliticized, and thus the outcry of the minjung began to relate to the symbol of history-transformational millennialism rather than God's paradise beyond this worldly realm.

God's kingdom is otherworldly and a symbol of the ultimate, while millennialism is historical, this-worldly, and a symbol of the penultimate. God's kingdom is where people will enter after death while the thousand-years-kingdom aims at transforming history and society in the present. God's kingdom guarantees the salvation of the individual thus grounding salvation in the other power, while the thousand-years-kingdom guarantees the salvation of social and collective humanity, emphasizing human praxis and cooperation in it. Therefore, God's kingdom has served as an ideology of the ruling class while millennialism has been the symbol of the minjung desire. In the ancient church of the first century, faith in the thousand-years-kingdom was the orthodox teaching at its center. However, historical Christianity, since Emperor Constantine, has denounced such faith in millennialism and its orientation to the future as heretical.

Augustine established a theology of the church by identifying the era of the church with the era of the thousands-years-kingdom, thereby absolutizing the church. Utopianism began to be adopted as a symbol in the course of the development of Western thought as faith in millennialism diminished. However, utopianism in the Western context was portrayed by elites as an ideal place, apart from the absurd reality of present-day society. This utopia is, by and large, constructed by elect elites, namely the bourgeoisie. In contrast, faith in the thousands-years-kingdom refers to the minjung desire for renewing society as a whole. God's kingdom (Christian eschatology) is otherworldly while faith in the thousand-years-kingdom (chiliasm) is apocalyptic and fanatic.

We need to put in balance the coexistence of Christian eschatology and biblical-apocalyptic chiliasm through complementarity. The symbol of chiliasm can be utilized as an interpretive paradigm in an approach to the entire history of the church. The resurrection, seen from the perspective of chiliasm, has apocalyptic and reality-transforming implications. When faith in the resurrection is separated from faith in the chiliasm, it is depoliticized.[4]

1. Faith in chiliasm, though gone since Constantine, emerged again with Joachim of Flores in the 12th century. He talked about the third period of the Holy Spirit, in which he understood the Trinitarian relationship and history in terms of successive stages of historical-economic developments among the Father, the Son and the Spirit. This runs in a different direction from the traditional and ontological understanding of the Trinity as three modes of being. He developed a theology of Trinitarian history explicitly.

In the age of the Father, the human being remains in the status of the servant under the law. In the age of the Son, he/she remains in the status of a son or daughter under the Gospel. Finally, in the age of the Spirit, he/she becomes the friend under the freedom of the Spirit. In the third age of the Holy Spirit, the human race will be filled with wisdom and joy and will establish, beyond ecclesial barriers and beyond the Scriptures, a mysterious democratic minjung community in which there will be no fear, class, monopolizing of wealth, or domination by the powerful.

Augustine prioritized the grace of the church, the protector of God's truth and blessings, while Joachim viewed truth itself as growing and developing from a bud to a stem and then to flowers and fruits, in accordance with the development of history. In contrast to Augustine, Joachim

[4] Cooperative salvation points to the way of the Holy Spirit who, as the mode of divine existence, awakens, renews and energizes our mind and body. The Spirit works for the salvation of regeneration and vivification. Theology, which stresses salvation merely in a forensic sense, is centered on atonement, meaning of Jesus' blood in a spiritual and automatic way. This magical tendency can be discernable in revivalist and Pentecostal circles in South Korea. Overemphasis on Jesus' blood without connection to discipleship reduces Christianity to a sort magical religion. Semi-pelagianism in Church history does not need to be entirely excluded but is purified and replaced by the ideas of partnership, covenant and participation regarding a relation between autonomy and theonomy.

contemplated both the Old and the New Testaments and believed that God is immanent in the internal power of the process of humanization in history. Therefore God drives the historical process toward a process of humanization, which he speaks of in terms of incarnation, development, and consummation through God's self-evolving movement.

In his "The Divinity of the Holy Spirit," R. P. Hanson argues that the protagonist of the Old Testament is the Holy Father, and the Holy Son is not clearly present there. The Spirit in the Old Testament is merely God's supernatural power. In the New Testament, the protagonist is the Holy Son. The Holy Father withdraws and the Holy Spirit has no real, personal, and independent recognition as the third member of the Trinity. However, the divine status of the Holy Spirit was appreciated and recognized in the writings of Basil of Caesarea in the fourth century. The Holy Spirit will be poured out over all the people at the end. This understanding of pneumatology is a point of reference for minjung theology.

2. In Germany in the 16th century, Thomas Müntzer appeared as a theologian of revolution. If Luther received his inspiration for the Reformation from his inner struggle with God's righteousness, Müntzer took the side of the peasants and radicalized the consequences of Luther's Reformation principle of social revolution. In Müntzer's radical reformation, we see that God's justice and righteousness are connected with the life of poor peasants. Müntzer argued that the chosen people for the revolution would come from among the urban poor and the peasants. According to him, all members of society must have the power of the sword. The minjung would become free and God would remain the Lord of the minjung. Müntzer pushed for a social reformation by means of the power of the sword. This was for him the inevitable means of salvation for the individual as well as for society.

According to Müntzer, individual purification (internal reformation) and social reformation (external reformation) are not sequentially related. Rather, the struggle for social reformation is an inevitable process for an individual's internal purification. Without the accompanying revolutionary action, religious salvation for the individual cannot be realized. Salvation for the individual as a process runs essentially into transcending and overcoming the external condition of the sin, the ruling order, namely through social praxis. One's concept of God could be distorted in an oppressed situation such that it is impossible to talk about God in a proper and righteous way.

In this assumption, Müntzer is different from many other founders of Christian sects in the sixteenth century. He stands for the universal church of the Holy Spirit. He may be understood as a pioneer of the theology of secularization and of the contemporary theology of minjung. I believe that the Holy Spirit is the principle and the power through which we can interpret the Scriptures correctly and profoundly. Such an interpretation opens a new possibility for understanding revelation. Luther's dependence on the Scriptures alone and his understanding of justification in a forensic sense made the minjung wait passively for God's reign.

Furthermore, Müntzer's movement for radical reformation failed in the peasant wars. He was executed by the allied forces of the princes and governors. Some socialist historians agree that he failed because the appropriate time had not yet come and the self-consciousness of the minjung had not fully matured in order to change society. When the minjung are awakened, there will be an authentic revolution.

3. The theologies arising out of today's secular world are based on hope, revolution, liberation, politics, the minjung, and the Holy Spirit. These are the theologies of the post-Christian era. These theological attempts speak out against the tradition that divorced the Gospel from its original life setting and thus de-politicized it for the sake of serving the ideology of the ruling class. Therefore, the theological movement for revolution, for the messianic future, and for the universal reign of the Spirit was usually branded as heterodoxy and heresy and thus banned from church history. In turn, the institutionalized church advocated an otherworldly heaven by denouncing messianic hope for social change.

Christendom in the West has begun to be challenged deeply through the French revolution and the Enlightenment, and Christianity has entered into ecumenical partnership since the formation of the World Council of Churches and Second Vatican Council. The post-Christian era has begun especially in the third world.

In the post-Christian era, minjung theology has attempted to take into account the purification of the person (the realm of human freedom) and the humanization of the social structure (the realm of necessity) which implies, in other words, the unification of God and revolution. It will come into being neither as an accident, nor as a supernatural event falling from heaven. It will not be brought about by heroes or by elites through their ideology. Rather, this unification of God and revolution will be started by and implemented in the formation of the minjung community by their wisdom, conviction, and courage.

Points of Reference in the Minjung Movement in Korean History

The emergence of minjung history in Korean history begins as a result of socioeconomic study. As I have mentioned previously, socio-economics makes a great contribution to the comprehension of the external dimensions of minjung, and socio-literary studies facilitate an understanding of the subjective and corporate soul of minjung. Korean minjung theology takes seriously paradigmatic references from the Korean liberative tradition in which the minjung appear as the subjects and the central figures of history.

With regard to historical developments in Korea, minjung had been the object of dominion by the ruling class for centuries. Through rebellion and protest, minjung has expressed a resistant spirituality and provided a moment of historical change instead of being subordinated to the ruling class. Finally, in this historical process, minjung has paved the way toward becoming a dominant force. Possibly by means of historical materialism, a focus can be placed on the change in the productive relation to explain the change in the social infrastructure. Herein, productive forces tend to influence, shape, and regulate the social basis, namely productive relations, in major ways. However, the content of this historical development can also imply and include the process of human consciousness, which is the process of humanization and culture.

It is fitting and meaningful for minjung theology to understand a process of humanization in which the minjung was instrumental in liberating itself from domination and oppression toward self-conscious and dominance in history. Minjung theology aims at witnessing and attesting to minjung's life decisions and conscience through which minjung has overcome the external oppressive conditions and become self-determining subject in regards to society and its historical fate.

In today's minjung and human rights movement, we take as paradigmatic historical references to liberation, for instance, the *Donghak* revolution, the Independence Association Movement, the March First Movement (1919), and the April 1960 Revolution from Korean history. The historical consciousness of these liberations needs to be rearticulated in terms of its corresponding manifestation and realization of a political consciousness for our present-day situation.

In minjung literature, we find the rudeness, bawdiness, and vulgarities of the minjung to be objectionable and hard to accept. However, looking deeply, we can see that these elements reflect on our distorted lives and function as a protest against the ideology of the ruling class. We find such protests in the *Pansori* (Korean traditional opera) and the *Talchum* (mask dance). These art forms are to be understood as the aesthetic manifestation of the repressed feelings (*han*) of minjung so that they retain the function of critiquing the morality, power, and pretensions of the powerful.

The mask dance reflects the awakening of minjung consciousness. *Pansori* and *Talchum* may be considered vehicles in expressing the liberative potentials of the minjung and in finding minjung's own identity and corporate soul. The problem, however, arises out of the powerful's attempt to accommodate and reduce minjung art forms to forms of entertainment for themselves. In this process of ideologization, minjung arts, such as *Pansori* and *Talchum*, became degraded into a means of entertaining the powerful and even militate, as opium, against the minjung. This is the most insidious kind of exploitation. Harvey Cox calls this phenomenon "the seduction of the spirit" in which minjung religion, its ceremony of resistance and yearning for liberation are reduced to becoming a mere object of entertaining the desires and need of the powerful.

Another way of looking at the liberative tradition of minjung relates to its belief in Maitreya. Historically, belief in the Maitreya arose among minjung, while the rulers regarded this belief to be dangerous and suppressed it as heretical. Maitreya was one of Siddhartha's disciples who died before Siddhartha. Maitreya was a popular minjung Buddha whose character and practice are future-oriented. The stone statue of Maitreya, carved with an axe, stands on the levee of a rice field and represents minjung will and anticipation of the apocalyptic coming of the future Buddha. However, a goldplated statue of a Buddha in a temple represents salvation from the nobility's perspective.

According to Buddhist cosmology, there are several kalpas (aeons) from the beginning of the cosmos to its end. During each kalpa, there will appear a Buddha. The first was Kuryuson Buddha, the second was Kunahammuni Buddha, the third was Kapasa Buddha, the fourth was Siddharta, and the fifth was Maitreya. Siddhartha Buddha is of the present samsaric world while Maitreya is the Buddha of the future.

If we make supplication to Amida Buddha, we will enter the Buddhist pure land in the West after death. If we, however, make supplication to Maitreya, we will realize and fulfill the future world on earth, changing and renewing the present world. Herein we find a tension between faith in Amida and faith in Maitreya. Belief in Amida is the promise of paradise after death. It does not articulate hope to those who are living lives of slavery and experiencing poverty, violence, and oppression on earth. The

Buddhism of the ruling class (Amida) is used to teach people the doctrines of renunciation and of the transitory nature of all forms in material existence.

However, belief in the Maitreya Buddha became the countervailing view of the people. They believed that the Maitreya Buddha would come soon. Regardless of the fact that he was supposed to come some billion years later, minjung's belief in Maitreya and thirst for the coming of the Buddha ignited many resistance messianic movements in Korean history. In fact, Maitreya Buddhism has contributed to the shaping of revolutionary praxis and belief on the part of the minjung.

Different from Amida Buddhism, Maitreya Buddhism stresses minjung's participation in renewing and transforming the present world. Even now, belief in Maitreya is spread still among the Korean minjung. Eujin Miruk, the largest stone statute of Buddha in Korea, is called Maitreya, even though it is actually Kwaneum, the bodhisattva of mercy. Belief in the messianic figure of Maitreya is embedded in the corporate spirit of the minjung.

Belief in Amida and belief in Maitreya conflict with each other, both in dogma and in their historical appearances. In China and Japan, Amida Buddhism flourished while Maitreya Buddhism disappeared. However, in Korea Maitreya Buddhism is still alive together with Amida Buddhism. This fact bears witness to the survival of the oppressed minjung throughout history – its resistance, its yearning for the coming of the new world, and its refusal to accept the promise of an otherworldly paradise. According to Hatata Takasi,[5] a Japanese scholar in the field of Mahayana Buddhism, Korean people have been able to resist powerful foreign invasion due to their belief in Buddha Maitreya.

Two Narratives in Coalescence

The task of minjung theology consists in witnessing to the *Missio Dei* to which the minjung tradition in Korea is integrated and fused. It is of special significance to interpret our current events in the secular realm theologically and hermeneutically, in terms of God's relation to history, the Spirit's work, and the liberating message of the Exodus, and of Jesus Christ. Participation in God's liberation event is the result of the liberative tradition of the Scriptures and from Korean history as well. I call this theological task a pneumatological-syncronic interpretation, contrasting it with a Christological-diachronic interpretation in a dogmatic sense.

[5] Cf. Hatada Takashi, *The History of Korea* (Tokyo: Iwanimi Shoten, 1951).

In the Christological interpretation, Jesus Christ is understood unilaterally to be the one who atones only for me and in my stead whereas, in the pneumatological interpretation, the Jesus event takes place again and again in our present social context. Thus, believers of Jesus Christ are summoned to represent the life of Jesus in terms of diaconal and prophetic discipleship. These two interpretations are not mutually exclusive, but complement each other.

Let me introduce some points from Kim Chi-Ha's story *Chang Il-Dam*, by means of which I want to articulate the characteristics and direction of my minjung theology.

1. According to the story, *Chang Il-Dam* is a preacher of liberation not only for the Korean minjung but also for the Christian *ochlos* tradition. As the point of departure, his mission coincides with people at the bottom. This has implications for spiritual enlightenment. Kim Chi-Ha calls this awakening experience "complete conformity with the *han* of abyss." This refers to the experience of becoming one with those who are cursed and expelled by society, such as robbers, murderers, defrauders, etc.

According to Kim Chi-Ha, such a transgression can be understood as the internally reversed expression of *han* which is caused by oppression. However, *Chang Il-Dam* demonstrates an incarnational aspect of God who assumes and takes up dehumanized humanity into the divine life. When reversing this situation, heaven becomes the location from where the minjung-messiah emerges. At this juncture, Kim Chi-Ha argues for *Donghak*'s principle, namely "the identity between humanity and heaven."

In the story of *Chang Il-Dam*, we read about his spiritual awakening. He sees a prostitute laboring with a child in a brothel. In spite of her mental and physical situation, *Chang Il-Dam* arrives at the deep realization of the truth of life; new life (God) comes into the filthy cesspools of humanity. God's companionship with those at the bottom offers a basis for minjung theology to take seriously the idea that the lowest of the low are the heirs of the Messiah's kingdom, and not confined as workers or peasants in a Marxist sense.

2. The ground thesis in *Chang Il-Dam* is "the unification of God and revolution." In this thesis, we encounter the unification of *Donghak* and Christianity, the unification of the spiritual renewal of humanity and the revolution of the social structure, the unification of theory and praxis, the unification of lowliness and heaven, and the unification of rice (earthly food) and freedom (heavenly food). Kim Chi-Ha attempts to seek this unity through his heuristic understanding of Roman Catholicism, rather than of Communism.

3. Unification between God and revolution is the Great Revolution, higher than any social revolution. Kim Chi-Ha calls it "permanent revolution," the pilgrimage, the way. "My paradise is not in this land. It is a single white road which is like a wind moved by time, passing Seoul towards the world, universe and sky. This road is paradise; and I am a wayfarer who follows the road." According to Kim Chi-Ha, the task of *Chang Il-Dam* is to travel against the flow of the stream which drives the minjung's degradation: farmer to urban immigrant to worker to unemployment to life in the slums to a complete loss of humanity and morality to theft to crime to prison.

4. The theology of *Chang Il-Dam* is that of *han*. Kim Chi-Ha understands himself as propagating the idea of a priest of *han* compared to Solzhenitsyn. Both of them reveal the *han* of the oppressed and address truth as the contradiction. Kim's task is to represent *han* among the third world minjung who is oppressed under the imperialistic system of violence, division, and manipulation. Minjung in the third world is filled with the miserable ghosts of people who have been sacrificed as innocent victims. The world has experienced the historical limitations of communism. Contrary to Communism, Kim understands himself as a humorous optimist. But he thinks that he and Solzhenitsyn are in agreement in that they are priests of *han*.

The accumulation of Minjung's *han* should be changed and activated into revolutionary energy through the cutting or sublimating (*dan*) of *han*. This act of cutting fundamentally takes away secular attachment for the sake of the transformation of secularism! There is a dialectical interplay between accumulated *han* and the continuous act of *dan*. On the one hand, there is *han*'s accumulation, in things like genocide, endless revenge, destruction and unlimited hatred; on the other hand, there is a need for *dan* in an on-going way to transcend the explosion of the vicious cycle of *han*, therein sublimating it to a higher spiritual power.

5. Minjung ecclesiology is found in the role of comforting and resolving minjung's *han*, breaking the vicious cycle of violence caused by *han* so that it can be a sanctuary for radicals, embracing all progressive thoughts and social protestors. Theology of *han* is different from Marxism and also from the traditional theology of atonement. The dialectical interconnection between *han* and *dan* prevents minjung theology from lapsing into a communist revolution. Western theology of atonement over-emphasizes the role of the church, calling for the consciousness of guilt and for the penance of the individual, while minjung theology talks more about the church, whose task is to resolve and console minjung's *han* by stressing the pastor as the priest of *han*. Luther's universal priesthood finds its echo in minjung ecclesiology when it speaks of service, discipleship, and solidarity with minjung.

6. In *Chang Il-Dam*, Kim Chi-Ha develops his understanding of Jesus as minjung in the apocalyptic and revolutionary manner. For the task of indigenization, the glad tidings of God's liberation in Jesus Christ need to be contextualized in Asian life settings. Historical sources and discourses need to be culturally and contextually combined with the Gospel of Jesus Christ toward constructing a theology of minjung, whose ecclesiology is to represent the church of *han* and *dan*. In this regard, minjung theology actualizes the social biography of minjung in South Korea, represents suffering humanity in the Third World, and exists as an agent for God's mission, speaking out against the reality of human life surrounded by the *han* of the wretched of the earth.

5

Minjung Theology for the Ruling Classes

Jürgen Moltmann

Personal Encounters in Korea

I went to Korea for the first time in March 1975, and at the Hankuk Theological Seminary in Seoul met Professor Ahn Byung-Mu. I had prepared a lecture on 'Hope in the Struggle of the People' for an Urban Industrial Mission Conference in Tokyo, and in this lecture I linked my personal experiences as a member of a defeated people in three year's captivity as prisoner of war (1945 to 1948) with the hopes of the new political theology which Johann Baptist Metz and I had developed in the Christian-Marxist dialogues of the 1960s.[1] But it was the New Testament scholar Ahn Byung-Mu whose Heidelberg dissertation on 'Jesus and the *Ochlos* in the Gospel of Mark' stimulated us to think about the church and the people of Christ. When I arrived in Seoul, I was greeted by Professor Park Pong-Nang, whom I already knew, and in the Yonsei University guest house met Suh Nam-Dong, one of the founders of Korean minjung theology. I gave my lecture first at Hankuk Seminary and then at other seminaries and universities, and was shadowed in unfriendly fashion by the Korean secret service.

At that time Korea was ruled by the military dictatorship of General Park Chung-Hee. Protesting workers and students were thrown into prison and ill-treated. Mothers wearing black scarves protested in front of Seoul Cathedral. Among my listeners at the Hankuk Seminary were many

[1] See Jürgen Moltmann, "Hope in the Struggle of the People," in *The Open Church*, trans. M. Douglas Meeks, London 1978 (= *The passion for Life: A Messianic Lifestyle* [Philadelphia: Fortress, 1978]).

students with shaved heads. They had just been let out of prison. A photo shows sitting next to me the unhappy student who was condemned to death for alleged espionage for North Korea, and who had appealed in court to my *Theology of Hope.* I intervened several times on his behalf with the Korean courts, but achieved nothing. In May 1975 eleven professors were dismissed from the university without notice, eight Christians and four theologians. At that time the writer Kim Chi-Ha, whose poems passed from hand to hand, was confined in the condemned cell. Kim Dae-Jung—today the President of South Korea—was also in prison. At that time we had his letters from prison translated and published in Germany.

Ahn Byung-Mu and I quickly came to understand each other at a deeper level. I always visited him whenever I went to Korea in the years that followed, and he often came to Tübingen for medical treatment. Today our joint student Dr Park Jong-Wha is Secretary General of the PROK. In 1984, together with Günter Baum, I edited a book with relevant texts from the new minjung theology.[2] Divided Korea and divided Germany had much in common. But minjung theology is the first liberation theology to come from Asia, with critical questions put to the First World, and questions too challenging the modernization of South Korea according to Western standards. In 1975 South Korea was still a Third World development country with stringent exploitation of the working people; today it is a high–tech state with horrific debts. It is true that today the minjung drives a car, as my friend David Suh ironically remarked; but the suicide rate is appallingly high.

It seldom happens that an exegetical discovery in the New Testament leads to a new congregational movement and a new theology. Hardly anything of the kind has happened again since Luther's discovery of the righteousness of God in Rom 3.28, which set on foot the reform movement in church and society. But during his studies in Heidelberg, Ahn Byung-Mu made an exegetical discovery, and it had theological and practical consequences for the minjung movement in Korea.[3]

He discovered that in the Gospel of Mark 'the people'—the poor (*ochlos* in Greek)—do not just have subordinate walk-on parts for Christ and his messianic work, as academic exegesis had always maintained, but that there was a highly intimate mutual relationship between Jesus and the

[2] Jürgen Moltmann, ed., *Minjung: Theologie des Volkes Gottes in Süd-korea* (Neukirchen-Vluyn: Neukirchner, 1984). On the political ideas cf. Kim Dae-Jung, *Korea and Asia. A Collection of Essays, Speeches and Discussions* (Seoul: 1994).

[3] Ahn Byung-Mu, *Draussen vor der Tür. Kirche und Minjung in Korea*, ed. W. Glüer (Göttingen : Vandenhoeck & Ruprecht, 1986).

ochlos, from the time when he began his public ministry in Galilee until his crucifixion by the Roman occupying power in Jerusalem. He identified himself with them, and they were his 'family.' Ahn Byung-Mu introduced this insight into the Korean Urban Industrial Mission, which took to the streets and went to prison on behalf of the human rights of the underpaid, exploited workers.

The 1960s were the years of the military 'development dictatorship' in Korea. The Urban Industrial Mission was the first church organization to penetrate this society.[4] The purpose of the Christian protests was to build up the people's own organizations in co-operatives, trade unions and support groups. During these years Ahn Byung-Mu and his friends founded the famous Galilee Congregation, a congregation of workers and critical intellectuals, who were continually under the surveillance of the police and the secret service, and were often enough physically attacked. Ahn Byung-Mu himself had to stand trial (Bishop Scharf of the Protestant church in Germany appeared as a witness in the proceedings) and was condemned to two years' imprisonment. Founding the Galilee congregation was a practical step based on the thesis of the New Testament scholar Ernst Lohmeyer about 'Galilee against Jerusalem', a contrast which is reflected in the story of Jesus' life. So the Galilee congregation was to represent Jesus' people, contrary to the all-dominating and modernizing city of Seoul. Ahn chose the word "minjung" as the Korean translation for the Greek *ochlos*. It is not a word for the Korean nation, or for the proletariat either (this is called *In Min*). The minjung is the whole suffering underside of the dominant society. For centuries it has developed traditions of resistance. It has again and again been the source of rebellion when the pain and anger (*Han*) became unendurable, for example in the *Donghak* revolt of 1890.

The Korean minjung theology links Jesus' gospel of the poor (*ochlos*) with these native popular and resistance traditions in the same original way as the Minjung congregations do in the poor districts of Seoul. Minjung theology is not a theology that has been made culturally indigenous, like 'yellow theology' before it. It is a contextual theology of the suffering people in Korea, and is therefore open for people all over the world, the people of God's kingdom whom Jesus called blessed. Minjung theology is also the first political theology to exist in Korea, inasmuch as it is bound up with

[4] On the history and profile of minjung theology, see Wolfgang Kröger, *Die Befreiung des Minjung. Das Profil einer protestantischen Befreiungstheologie für Asien in ökumenischer Perspektive*, Ökumenische Existenz Heute 10 (Munich: Kaiser, 1992). Kröger lived in Korea for four years and worked with Ahn Byung-Mu.

the struggle for human and civil rights, and turns Christians from being a 'people of the church' into 'the congregation of the people.'

Jesus and the People (*Ochlos*) in the Gospel of Mark

Form-critical exegesis always paid a degree of attention to the people round Jesus according to the Gospel of Mark, but hardly any account has been taken of their social character. Liberal hermeneutics was aligned towards historical persons and 'desocialized' Jesus' sayings and acts, so to speak, so that Jesus, 'the man and his work,' stood by themselves and could be applied to other individual persons. But the form-critical method is an exegesis that has to do with social history, and with its help the stories about Jesus appear in a different light. From the very beginning, Mark talks about 'the crowd', 'the many', 'the people'; these were the men and women who gathered round Jesus, the people he lived with and addressed, the people whose sufferings he healed, and to whom he knew himself to be sent by God. Generally they are only called 'the nameless background for Jesus' ministry',[5] a 'background choir' for the appearances of the star, as if Jesus performed his ministry to everyone else, only not to these. But for the New Testament scholar Ahn Byung-Mu this 'crowd', these 'many', this '*ochlos*' are the main reason for Jesus' coming and ministry.

In Mark 1:22, 'they'– the crowd—are mentioned, and at the beginning are referred to in the plural, later in the Greek text through the singular *ochlos* (2:4). The word *ochlos* occurs thirty-six times in the Gospel, not including the plural compounds. That betrays a certain intention. In the Septuagint 'the people' are usually called *laos*. But this word is used for Israel as people of God. The other people are called *goyim* in Hebrew, *ethne* in Greek. In Mark's Gospel, *ochlos* means neither Israel as God's people nor the people of the Gentiles. It is a 'people' without religious identity and without ethnic coherence. So who are the people as *ochlos*?

Mark always uses the word *ochlos* for the people who gather round Jesus and follow him. The 'crowd' consists of 'sinners', that is, those excluded from Jewish society. They are the impoverished country people, people of the land (am ha'aretz), without property, as John 7 and 12 show, people who are not economically in a position to keep the Law of Israel, and are hence looked upon by the Pharisees as *massa perditionis*, the multitude of the lost: 'Cursed are the rabble who do not know the Law' (cf. John 7:49). It is about these people that the Gospel now has the following to say:

[5] See the article '*Ochlos*' in *TDNT*.

Jesus teaches the people (Mark 7:14; 8:34; 5:10);
Jesus has mercy on the people (Mark 6:34);
Jesus heals the sick among the people (1: 34ff.; 6:56);
Jesus feeds the people (Mark 8);
Jesus preaches to the people from the ship (3:7ff.);
Jesus proclaims to the people the kingdom of God in parables (4:2ff.); according to Matthew 5, the Sermon on the Mount is addressed to 'the people';
Jesus calls 'the people together with his disciples' to the discipleship of the way of the cross (8:34ff.).
The people among whom he sits and teaches are his 'true family', he has told his mother and his brothers when they are outside, looking for him. These people are not 'the disciples' (as Luther interpolated, because he was unable to believe what he read in Mark 3:34).
Jesus' own mission is directed towards these people: 'The Son of man came to serve, and to give his life for the many' (Mark 10:45).
His blood, the cup of the new covenant, is shed for 'the many' (Mark 14:24). At Easter he appears to the poor women in Jerusalem and the disciples 'in Galilee' (16:7). Jesus knows that he is not sent 'to call the righteous, but sinners' (2:16f). 'Call' (*kalein*) is the same word that is used at the call of the disciples (1:20), and elsewhere in the New Testament it has the sense of choosing.

Conclusion: the *ochlos* is the addressee of Jesus' mission; he came on behalf of the people, his messianic kingdom is meant for the poor, his love for the many.

Consequently:

1. Jesus 'teaches' the people. He does not teach the people the Torah. He teaches them the Gospel of the kingdom, the messianic beatitudes and the discipleship ethic of the Sermon on the Mount;
2. It is 'the nameless crowd' who are Jesus' people and family, not his own family physically speaking, and not Israel, his 'physically' own people either;
3. *Ochlos* is 'God's people,' the people of God's kingdom, the people of the poor who are 'called' and therefore chosen.

4. The healing miracles of God's kingdom and Jesus' table-fellowship with 'sinners and tax-collectors' take place among these people.
5. When he goes to Jerusalem he calls these people to the discipleship of the cross.
6. He sheds his blood and gives his life for these people.

Who, in terms of social history, were the *ochlos* at the time of the Gospel of Mark? Ahn thinks that Mark was writing after the destruction of Jerusalem in A.D. 70 and was describing the homeless, driven-out, scattered people of his time who had been deprived of their rights, Jews and Christians. They share the fate of the poorest of the poor, the homeless and the displaced persons in the Roman empire.

Where is God? The first destruction of Jerusalem and the Babylonian exile was followed by the growth of Shekinah theology. According to this, God too forsook his dwelling on Zion in order to go into exile with his people. Applied to the expulsion after the year 70, this means that the choosing and liberating God is present among his people, suffering with them. In the poor, homeless people who have been displaced and are therefore lost, God's suffering and accompanying Shekinah is present, a homeless, displaced, poor and scattered God, who wanders with the poor through the dust of the streets. The crucified Christ and the divine Shekinah who suffers in the poor belong together.

Ahn sums this up as follows:

1. *Ochlos* is not the term for a social class. It is a relational term—a rulers' term for the subjugated and dominated. The poor are *ochlos* in relation to the rich. Tax-collectors belong to the excluded rabble, in relation to the Jewish establishment. 'Consequently the term cannot be invested with a particular value or used for an idealization.'[6]
2. The *ochlos* are certainly feared by the unjust and powerful, but they are not organized and therefore cannot be reckoned with as a power faction. The *ochlos* are not the Zealots, who fight against Rome for the nation of Israel. They are the poor, not of much use either for building a state or for a revolution.
3. Jesus is unconditionally on the side of the *ochlos*. He quite evidently has no intention of turning the *ochlos* into an anti-Roman fighting force, but he proclaims to them the kingdom of God as

[6] Ahn Byung-Mu, in Moltmann, ed., *Minjung*, 121 note 116.

their future, the future which already belongs to them here and now, and he fills this people with new hope and with the vision of a way that can be their own. 'Jesus fights together with the suffering minjung (*ochlos*) on the front of this Advent [of God's].'[7]

Messiah and Minjung

According to the model in Mark's Gospel, minjung theologians bring Jesus and 'the people' so intimately close that the transitions are fluid, and the characteristics are even interchangeable. We shall therefore first try to discover who Jesus is in the eyes of the *ochlos*-minjung, and shall then see what the *ochlos*-minjung, together with Jesus, become for the world.

In the eyes of the forsaken, scattered and sick minjung, Jesus is not the remote 'Christ of the church with his golden crown'. He is the brother in need, who understands them because he experiences their fate himself. As their brother he is related to the poor, not set over them as their lord and master. This makes a practical hermeneutical 'realization' of Jesus possible in the minjung's own experiences of suffering; 'Jesus in our midst' became the gospel of the minjung pastors. "Jesus is present when an innocent student under torture refuses to reveal the names of the friends who are 'wanted', and is therefore killed; or when a young worker sacrifices his life for his mates. The cross of Jesus is a present reality, and people, baptized and unbaptized alike, take the way of the cross together with Jesus."[8] This is not metaphorical language. It is one and the same reality, described there with the name of Jesus, here with the name minjung. That only sounds strange and disconcerting to modern Western ears because by personal names we mean individuals existing exclusively for themselves. But if the name 'Jesus' does not mean just a person in himself, but also a life and a life-history in community with the social history of his 'people', the transitions from the Jesus of the minjung to the minjung Jesus become more understandable.

Minjung christology is not the exclusive 'representation' christology of the Reformation's *solus Christus*. It is the inclusive solidarity christology of the divine brother, who suffers with us and who identifies himself with

[7] Ibid., 132.

[8] Kröger, *Befreiung des Minjung*, note 118. This is expounded in more detail by Kim Yong-Bock in *Messiah and Minjung: Christ's Solidarity with the people for New Life* (Howloon, Hong Kong: Christian Conference of Asia, Urban Rural Mission, 1992) 16–18. Cf. also Kim Yong-Bock, *Minjung Theology. People as the Subjects of History*, (Singapore: Commission on Theological Concerns, Christian Conference of Asia, 1981), and Noh Jong-Sun, *Liberating God for Minjung* (Seoul: Hanul, 1994).

'the least' among the people. "As you did it to the least of these my brethren, you did it to me (Matt 25:40). So the least of the minjung belong to his community and represent his presence." Without Jesus' solidarity with the people, Jesus' representation for the people is not conceivable either.[9] All representation christology is based on a christology of solidarity. That is true of Jesus' life and ministry among the people, but it is truest of all of his suffering and death on the cross. The minjung understand him in his suffering because they feel that they are understood by the suffering and dying Jesus. In the daily suffering and sacrifice of the people, the image of the crucified Jesus acquires a wholly different meaning from the meaning it has in the lives of rich people in the First World, which, even if painless, are often empty of meaning. Third World theology, as I have shown, is everywhere at heart a theology of the cross. In Korea, the picture of the crucified Jesus speaks to the Christian and the non-Christian minjung because it gives a different answer to the question of suffering from the Buddhism that is dominant there.

If Jesus is identified with the fate of the minjung in this way, is the minjung then identified with Jesus and his mission so that they acquire messianic feature? If the Messiah belongs to the minjung, do the minjung then become the Messiah?[10] In divided Korea there is in fact a kind of popular messianism, which goes back to the *Donghak* revolt. The widespread Maitreya Buddhism also has messianic features in the 'awakening Buddha' of 'the future' world. The North Korean 'Kim Il Songism', with its Juche ideology, was, and still is, definitely a messianism designed for domination. Kim Il Song certainly claimed to be a Marxist, but he was the self-styled religious savior and father of the people. Contrary to this political messianism, the South Korean minjung theologians have set the true messianism of the minjung, in order to distinguish 'messianic politics' from 'political messianism'.[11]

If we look at the biblical model for the minjung in the *ochlos* in Galilee, the impression is not so uplifting. There the people are not idealized. They are shown as equivocal, and easily led astray. They left Jesus alone on the cross. But that too is part of the poverty of the people, and is

[9] Jürgen Moltmann, *Jesus Christ for Today's World*, trans. Margaret Kohl (Minneapolis: Fortress, 1994) 38–40.

[10] Kröger, *Befreiung des Minjung*, 143 note 118.

[11] Kim Yong-Bock has gone into this question (see note 8 above). Since the end of the Korean war, the *Han* (pain) of divided Korea has thrown up a number of messianic sects, the best known of them the Mun sect.

not something for moral and theological criticism. The minjung are only romanticized by people who do not belong to them.

Worth discussing, on the other hand, is the messianic elevation of the minjung's struggle for freedom and their human rights. According to biblical traditions, the messianic liberation leads to redemption in God's new world. The necessary liberation of the minjung makes these people the subject of their own history. In this historical liberation, the people catch sight of their future in the kingdom of God, but they are not yet there; for how they will shape their history after they have won their liberty is an open question. The hoped-for reunification of Korea is not yet the resurrection into the life of the world to come, but it corresponds to that and points towards it, whereas the painful division of a people and its families contradicts the kingdom of God as harshly as possible. To put it more directly and dialectically: The final must be identified with the provisional so as to set free energies for what is final; but the two must also be differentiated, if there are not to be bitter disappointment. The 'today-here-us' on which every liberation theology must insist includes this double presence of the final in the provisional and the provisional in the final; otherwise its presentative eschatology is not a realistic eschatology.

Who is 'the Suffering Servant of God'?

It somewhat took my breath away when, during a discussion in David Suh's house, Ahn Byung-Mu answered this question by pointing to the minjung. Who, then, must bear the sins of the First World? The Third World. Who must endure the exploitation and violence of those in power? The minjung, the poor, forsaken people. When we sing 'Thou who bearest the sins of the world', we must in a realistic sense think of minjung.

But does this involuntary, reluctant, passive endurance of oppression and exploitation by the poor have any redemptive meaning, such as we mean when we talk about the 'bearing' and 'taking away' of sin through the vicarious and representative suffering of the Servant of God according to Isaiah 53, and the narratives of Christ's passion which were shaped according to the pattern of that image? If the minjung are not merely the suffering people but are also the people of God which through its suffering redeems humanity, then this puts a question to the christology, and also raises the question about an excessive burden laid on the people. At that time I asked Ahn: if the minjung is to redeem the world, like the suffering servant of God, who then redeems the minjung? And if the minjung redeem through their suffering, how can they struggle so as at long last to overcome this suffering? Who, then, has asked the minjung whether it wants to suffer for the redemption of the world? His answer was the one he had already given in writing: 'In Hebrew thinking we find no clear distinction between individual and community. For example, is the suffering servant in Isaiah 53 an individual, or Israel? Western theologians continually try to understand him as an individual. That is not justified by the facts. It is the attempt to identify him with Jesus as an individual. . . . In Asia there is no word for 'personality'. When we say 'human being' it means something collective. . . . Buddha, for example, is not restricted to the individual person Sidharta but is universal—that is to say, from the social aspect a collective."[12]

Ahn has therefore always interpreted the story of Jesus' life as told in the Gospels as a 'socio-biography' of the *ochlos*. The narrative of the passion is a 'condensation of the minjung's suffering destiny'. 'Drawing on the history of Jesus' passion, Mark is telling the suffering history of the minjung of his own time. And conversely, Jesus' suffering is 'actualized' in the fate of the minjung at the time when Mark was writing.[13] But does this apt exegetical insight mean that 'Jesus' is a 'symbol for the minjung,' as Suh Nam Dong said?

I do not believe that this reduction is felicitous phraseology. The suffering servant in Isaiah 53 does not seem to me to mean the people of Israel collectively. He is a 'servant of God' like Moses, who does not just represent his people before God, but represents God to his people too. I believe that the image of the 'suffering servant' 'through whose wounds we are healed' (53:5) is a divine figure. He is not an 'individual' in the modern sense, nor is he a self-contained 'personality'; he is a person from God, who is there 'out of the people, with the people and for the people'. This is already evident from the comparison 'we-he': "All we like sheep have gone astray…but the Lord laid all our iniquity on him (53:6)." The righteous one who "makes many righteous because he hears their iniquities" (53:11) is a name for God himself. Only God can atone by 'bearing' the sins of the people and taking away the burden of them. If we see the suffering servant of God as a figurative embodiment of the 'suffering God', then the alternative between an individual and a collective interpretation of Isaiah 53 and the history of Jesus becomes superfluous. It is replaced by the relation between solidarity and representation. Solidarity and representation are so interwoven, or dovetailed, that solidarity in existence-with-others offers

[12] Ahn Byung-Mu in J. Moltmann (ed.), *Minjung* (n.116), 163 n.110.

[13] Ibid., 167.

the presupposition for representation in existence—for others. However, mere solidarity without representation does not overcome any suffering but merely increases the pain.

Bonhoeffer's insight into 'the suffering of God' which he wrote down in the Gestapo cell come closest to the theology of the cross worked out by the minjung theologians: "The Bible points people to God's helplessness and suffering: only the suffering God can help." "The human being is called to suffer with the suffering of God from the godless world." "Christians stand beside God in his suffering."[14]

The minjung theologians have localized this 'suffering of God from the Godless world' in the oppressed and exploited minjung. If the minjung congregations stand beside the minjung in their pain, they stand "beside God in his suffering." But they do not stand there in order to bear sins for the reconciliation of the world, but so as to rise up with the minjung into the liberty of a just world, in which the pain of the people no longer exists. So it is after all useful to distinguish between atoning suffering, which is solely God's affair, and the suffering of the people, which has to be overcome. The distinction must be made in the interests of the minjung "as they really exist."[15]

Another question put to minjung theology arises from the Christian-Jewish dialogue in Germany. This dialogue has made Christian theologians sensitive to conscious or unconscious anti-Judaism and to unreflected transferences of Israel's experiences of God to the people of Christ.[16] In this dialogue we have learnt to read the stories about Jesus in the synoptic Gospels as a social history of Israel. The history of Jesus is shaped according to the pattern of Israel's history with God—the flight into Egypt and return home from Egypt, the forty days in the wilderness, and, not least, Jesus' exile experience between Gethsemane and Golgotha. According to Daniel 7, "the people of the Most High" also belongs to Jesus' title as Son of man. Whether this 'people' is the people of Israel remains an open question, if 'the Son of man' is a universal divine figure who overthrows empires and fulfils the hopes of humanity. Is the minjung in Korea now

14 Bonhoeffer, *Letters and Papers from Prison* (n.42), letters of 16 and 18 July 1944; poem 'Christians and Pagans.'

15 This is a reference to the distinction made between socialism as an ideal and theoretical form of government and the 'socialism as it really exists' of East Germany and the Eastern bloc in general, before its disintegration.

16 Kröger has taken up this question; see *Die Befreiung des Minjung* (n.118), 130–6: 'Zur Problematik der "Enteignung Israels" in der AT-Rezeption der Minjung-Theologen (Überlegungen aus dem jüdisch-christlichen Dialog).'

taking Israel's place as 'the new Israel', as German critics—in typically German fashion—have mistrustfully conjectured? The same question was also critically raised in opposition to the proclamation of a Korean Year of Jubilee for reunification and social justice.[17]

I think that both suspicions are wrong. There has never been any anti-Semitism in Korea, because there were no Jews there. 'Auschwitz' took place in Germany, not in world-wide Christendom. The charges of anti-semitism thrown out at large by German theologians are nothing other than transparent attempts to hide the burden of one's own guilt in the alleged collective guilt of Christians as a whole. In his interpretation of Mark's Gospel, Ahn Byung-Mu stated very clearly that, in his view, Mark means by the *ochlos* the inhabitants of Palestine who after the destruction of Jerusalem in the year 70 were homeless and without rights—the Jews first of all, then Christians and Gentiles too. In the Roman empire the people of God, *laos*, is made the homeless people, *ochlos*. If Jesus belongs to this *ochlos*, he lives with Jews and Gentiles, and is therefore for them both. For the Christian church to take up 'years of jubilee' is not an 'expropriation' of what is Israel's; it is a grateful endorsement of Israel's insight into God's Sabbath. The same may be said about the archetypal history of the Exodus.

Fundamentally speaking, we have to say here that all the traditions of all the people become universal, and are directed to everyone once they have been committed to writing. How else could we in Europe learn from Lao Tzu, Confucius, and Buddha? How otherwise could Asians read Kant and Hegel? Israel's holy scripture is directed to all nations, since it was for this that Israel was chosen. The holy scripture of Christians belongs to all human beings, because it was written for them all. In my view, therefore, the debate pursued by Jews and Christians about the 'possession' of the Bible is not merely out of keeping with the facts; it is godless, if it really is a matter of the Word of God in these writings.

'We are the People' in Democracy and Church

The Korean word minjung can hardly be adequately translated into German or English because we cannot reproduce the same linguistic and historical connotations, and even if we could, it would not help us to discover the people (*ochlos*) for ourselves in our own situation. We can therefore only allow ourselves to be stimulated to parallel action. For this,

[17] Thus A. Hoffmann-Richter, *Ahn Byung-Mu als Minjung-Theologe* (PhD diss, Heidelberg, 1988, Erlangen, 1990) 159.

the events of 1989 which led to the reunification of divided Germany give occasion enough. "*We are the people,*" cried the demonstrators in Leipzig in November 1989, in protest against the police and military forces of the socialist GDR dictatorship, and thereby initiated the first non-violent revolution in Germany. "*We are one people,*" they cried soon afterwards, and united the divided nation.

What is the difference between the two slogans? In the first case, the oppressed people became aware that they were the nationals of the German 'Democratic' Republic, and that according to the constitution 'all power proceeds from the people'. In the second case, Germans demanded the German national state. In the first case, the dominated people rose up against a dominating party clique; in the second case, Germans demanded that they be allowed to live together with other Germans in a single state. In the first case, it was a matter of democracy, in the second, a matter of the nations; in the first case, a question of civil rights (which correspond to universal human rights), in the second, a question of German citizenship according to inherited nationality, the *jus sanguinis*. In their cry, the Leipzig demonstrators were appealing to two different concepts of 'people'.

The ancient democratic idea has its roots in Greece, and the new democratic idea which was the fruit of the Enlightenment, both made the people the subject of their own political history. All political power emanates from the people, says the doctrine of popular sovereignty. The political groups and parties merely help to form the will of the people, claims the constitution or Basic Law of the German Federal Republic; they act *with* the people, not *for* the people.

Apart from the renaissance of the classical Greek idea, the modern democratic concept has a Christian root too. We find this in the Protestant Reformed tradition of federal (or covenant) theology and federal, or covenant, politics.[18] The idea of popular sovereignty was biblically justified by the Huguenot monarchomachists, and they used it for a new formulation of the right to resistance. According to the *Vindiciae contra tyrannos* of 1579 (generally thought to have been written by Philipp Duplessis Mornay), Christian states are built up on the pattern of the *politia Moisi*, the state or constitution of Moses: God made his eternal covenant with the people, in which he promised "You shall be my people and I will be your God." It follows from this that the people make a contract of rule with their ruler, and hand over to him part of their liberty so that he may act in

[18] J. Moltmann, 'Covenant or Leviathan? Political Theology at the Beginning of Modern Times,' in *God for a secular Society* (n.25), I. 2, 24–45.

the people's stead and in their name. If a ruler breaks this contract, then the people through their other representatives are empowered to resist, so as to force the ruler to remain true to the contract. But if the ruler breaks the people's covenant with God, he is a blasphemer and must be removed. "At the beginning the people had no king other than God." "Consequently kings should always remember that they indeed reign by God's grace, but through the people and for the people." If the people's covenant with God (to which the contract of rule is subordinate) is broken, then the people are freed from all obligations toward the ruler (*Populus jure omni obligatione solutus*).[19]

In the American Declaration of Independence the covenant with God was called *constitution*. The Basic Law (the *Grundgesetz*) of the German Federal Republic entirely accords with this when it says in the Preamble that it was resolved upon in our "responsibility before God and the people." Consequently for the people to avail themselves of the right to resist any breach of the constitution is the test case of democracy.

According to this theological justification of popular sovereignty *vis-à-vis* the ruler (that it springs from the people's covenant with God), 'the people' means everyone who lives within the sphere of the covenant, everyone who enters into it and keeps it, irrespective of his or her race, class, or ethnic affiliation. It is not the nation which makes the people sovereign; it is the constitution. The constitutional republic bases the fundamental rights of its citizens on universal human rights, not on the 'national ties conferred by inheritance', as in the German *jus sanguinis*. This is the 'open public'. Its ultimate goal is a universal republican order in which human rights everywhere become the basic rights of its citizens, so that the people everywhere are the subjects of their own political history, and are nowhere treated as the object of tyranny any longer.

The roots of tyranny can be detected in the inherent difficulties of representative institutions. Representative rule rests on deputization. Deputization is a normal form of shared human life. But deputization or representation 'for others' always involves the danger of the estrangement of the others. Political estrangements develop if the political representatives get on top of the people they are only supposed to represent, and if the people bow down to their own government. What then develops is a separate and remote 'political class' on the one hand and a growing political apathy among the people on the other. Participation democracy then

[19] L. Wyss (ed.), *Wider die Tyrannen*, Basel 1946, 67. That is the precise opposite to Jean Bodin's absolutist principle: *Princepts legibus solutus* - the prince is the dissolution of the law.

becomes an absentee democracy, in which the politicians are left to do what they like as long as they leave the people in peace. This political estrangement is the beginning of political dictatorship and political idolatry. It can only be avoided through active participation by the people in political life, and through factors of direct democracy. Democracy is "a government of the people, by the people, for the people," as Abraham Lincoln impressively proclaimed in his famous Gettysburg address. A government *for* the people only comes third, and presupposes the government *of* the people and *by* the people.

The Christian idea of the people which, according to the Gospel of Mark, is defined by Jesus' relationship to them (the *ochlos*) was not merely left unimplemented in the history of hierarchical church; it was actually suppressed. We shall only rediscover it if we rise up with the cry of a popular protest—this time on the part of the church's people—claming: "We are the church." This is what has happened since 1994 in Catholic congregations in Europe. Ever since the early Christian development of the monarchical episcopate, we have known the church as a hierarchy 'from above' which delegates the universal episcopate of the pope 'downwards', and demotes the people of Christ to the status of 'the faithful', or 'the people in the pews'. The distinction between clergy and laity has split the people of God into two. The word 'lay' originally meant a member of the *laos*, the people of God; but because the clerics were set apart from the people, the word came to mean the ignorant and incompetent, those with no jurisdiction. A 'complete layman' means someone who doesn't understand what something is about. In the hierarchical perspective, 'the people' are only there as the object of 'holy rule', of creative care and guidance by their 'shepherd'. For centuries, people in the church have reacted to this godless and un-Christian deprival of their responsibility with growing apathy and with silence. Since they are no longer 'forced' to go to church, they leave the church altogether. The result is people without a church and a church without people. This is a silent falling away from the church which the church itself has brought about. It is only if this 'church for the people' becomes a 'church of the people and by the people', and if the hierarchical church for looking after people becomes a congregational church, with many different kinds of participation, that the ancient schism between church and people will be overcome.

What applies to the Roman Catholic hierarchy in its estrangement from the people can also be said about the Protestant pastoral aristocracy, or its somewhat more modern variation in the form of a theological and pastoral expertocracy. Ideas about a blanket church-management which will cover the religious needs of the people are not enough to create what in Germany is called a *Volkskirche*, a church intended to meet the needs of the whole population. Even the strenuously promoted programs 'church for the people', 'church for others', or 'church for the world' do not reach the people, because the word *for* cuts the church off from the people and makes the people an object- something to be cared *for*. A people's church which accords with Jesus and the people can grow up only through a congregational renewal that springs from the people and is implemented through the people. For this, the Catholic base communities in Latin America, and the free church, Pentecostal congregations are examples and models.

But there is another picture still for the relationship between the church and the people of Christ, and this leads to an expanded concept of the church.[20] According to the Gospels, there is the *manifest* church of believers and followers of Jesus, and the *latent* church of the poor and those who wait for Jesus. The manifest community of believers lives in the apostolate of Christ: "He who hears you hears me" (Luke 10:16); "As the Father has sent me, even so I send you" (John 20:21). In these sayings Christ—the risen Christ, according to the Gospel of John—promises his real presence in the apostolate of the community of his people, who follows his messianic mission to the world; so we proclaim the invitation to be reconciled with God "in Christ's stead" (2 Cor 5:20). Real presence by virtue of Christ's identification with the community of his people fills the proclamation, the sacraments, the fellowship, and the *diakonia* of his congregation with authority. It is an active identification.

We find a similar-sounding but passively meant group of promises of Christ's real presence in others among the poor, hungry, thirsty and imprisoned—in short the *ochlos*. "He who visits them visit me." "As you did it to one of the least of these my brethren, you did it to me" (Matt 25:40). That is also true of the children: "Whoever receives one such child in my name received me" (Matt18:5) Jesus calls the poor and the children blessed because the kingdom of heaven already belongs to them.

If we absorb this latent fellowship of Christ with the poor and the children of the people into ecclesiology, the result is a tremendous tension which 'the church as it really exists' must bridge: *ubi Christus ibi ecclesia*—where Christ is, there is the church. The true church of Christ is at the place where the fellowship of Christ is. The whole Christ is pres-

[20] I have gone into this in more detail in *The Church in the Power of the Spirit*, note 82, III.7: "The Place of the Church in the Presence of Christ," 121–32.

ent in the manifest community of believers, and in the latent community of the poor—and therefore in the community of believers and the poor, the community of the lovers of the people and the children of the people. Christ's apostolate says *what* the church is; 'the least' say *where* the church belongs. The *hidden* Christ awaits those who are his in the poor and the children of the people. The *manifest* Christ comes to them with those who are his. In the apostolate the risen, coming Christ is present; in the poor the suffering, crucified Christ looks at us and waits for us.

6

Minjung and Asian Pentecostals

Koo D. Yun

Some people simply presume that *minjung* is a Korean word and only applicable to the particular Korean Christians who experienced political oppression in the 1970s. I argue, however, in this chapter that *minjung* in a broad sense has existed long before the emergence of *minjung theology* of the 1970s. Theologically, *minjung* means oppressed, alienated, exploited, and despised "people of God."[1] Thus, any group of people, even non-Koreans, can become a *minjung* vis-à-vis unjust and contemptuous treatments. During the 1970s in South Korea, there have been at least two kinds of *minjung*: (1) socio-political, and (2) Pentecostal. It is apparent from a contemporary study of Korean history that God has utilized both kinds of *minjung* in order to heal the Korean nation.

Understanding Minjung in a Narrow Sense

Who are minjung? Minjung is a Korean word that derives etymologically from two Chinese characters. *Min* means "people," and *jung* signifies "the mass." Hence, minjung literally means "the mass of people."[2] But this understanding of minjung is grounded on Chinese etymology. Suk-Hon Ham has sought to find an original Korean equivalent before the infiltration and domination of Chinese language into the Korean culture. He

[1] The word *minjung* is a collective noun. Throughout this chapter, I use the word as singular when the word underscores the group as a unit, and I also regard it as plural when it highlights individual members of the group.

[2] The Commission on Theological Concerns of the Christian Conference of Asia (*CTC-CCA*), *Minjung Theology: People as the Subject of History* (Maryknoll: Orbis, 1981) 16; Boo-woong Yoo, *Korean Pentecostalism: Its History and Theology* (New York: Peter Lang, 1988) 197–98. See also Paul S. Chung, *Martin Luther and Buddhism: Aesthetics of Suffering* (Eugene, OR: Wipf and Stock, 2002) 109–110.

comes up with the native Korean word *ssi-al,* literally meaning 'seed'.[3] Figuratively speaking, minjung, as the seed of the Korean soil, signifies the propagative source of living things such as humans, animals, plants, and so forth.

A theological translation of *minjung* refers to *the people of God* who do not possess political power, economic wealth, social status, and advanced education in contrast to the wealthy and dominant class.[4] This word, however, does not remain *static*; rather, it stays *dynamic* as well as *multifaceted.* Thus, one cannot pin down this word with a precise definition.

Byung-Mu Ahn, a prominent minjung theologian from South Korea, finds a prototype (*ochlos*) of minjung in the Gospel of Mark. First, he introduces the two Markan words used to designate "the people" who followed Jesus in the first century: (1) *ochlos* (ὄχλος), and (2) *laos* (λαός). In the Gospel of Mark, the word *ochlos* was consistently employed in order to describe the people who gathered around Jesus. On the contrary, Mark does not make use of the term *laos,* except for the two instances in 7:6 (quoting directly from the Old Testament) and 14:2 (referring to the chief priests and lawyers). Furthermore, Paul in his Epistles never employs this word.[5]

According to Ahn, Mark was the first one who started using the term *ochlos* in the New Testament, and it referred to the people who were labeled as 'sinners' and 'tax collectors'. These *ochlos* were alienated and persecuted by the ruling class. Jesus Christ expressed a special compassion toward them because they were like sheep devoid of a shepherd (Mark 6:34). Jesus called the *ochlos* "his mother and his brothers" (Mark 3:34–35). These *ochlos* in Mark represented the "minjung" of Galilee.[6] In Mark, Jesus stood and befriended the *ochlos,* a minjung, as well as promised the future of God to them.[7]

Many people understand the word *minjung* with a narrow definition that only refers to the oppressed South Koreans who participated in the socio-political Christian movement during the 1970s. Furthermore,

[3] Suk-Hon Ham, "*Tsi-al-ui Cham-theut*" ("The True Meaning of Seed), in *Minjung and Korean Theology,* ed. Committee of Theological Study of KNCC (Seoul: Korea Theological Study Institute, 1982) 9–13. This book is written in Korean.

[4] Yong-Hak Hyun, "*Minjung Sok-e Sung-yuk-sin-hae-ya*" ("To Be Incarnated among Minjung"), in *Minjung and Korean Theology,* 15.

[5] Byung-Mu Ahn, "Jesus and the Minjung in the Gospel of Mark," in *Minjung Theology,* 138–40.

[6] Ibid., 141.

[7] Ibid., 151.

minjung theology is delimited to a Korean theology which arose from the Christian experiences of being politically oppressed by Jung-Hee Park's regime.[8] Also, minjung theology carries exclusively Korean stories of oppression and persecution. Although *minjung theology* remains a branch of 'Korean theology', *minjung* as 'the people of God' have existed long before the emergence of *minjung theology* in the 1970s and even go beyond the Korean national boundary. Furthermore, *minjung* exemplifies a universal term that applies to a community of people who undergo alienation, oppression, discrimination, or exploitation.

Universalization of Minjung in a Broader Sense

The word *minjung* does not designate a fixed concept but a relational and fluid notion.[9] Minjung does not merely consist of a group of Koreans; in the truest sense, minjung transcends ethnic, racial, and national boundaries.[10] Boo-woong Yoo posits that *minjung emerge when common people undergo socio-cultural alienation, economic exploitation, or political oppression.* For instance, a group of women become a minjung when they are dominated by other men or a socio-cultural structure. An ethnic minority group becomes a minjung when they face political and economic discrimination by another dominant ethnic group. A particular group of race becomes a minjung when they experience discrimination by another ruling race. Factory workers and farmers become a minjung as they are exploited by evil and selfish employers.[11]

Some of the Korean Christian minjung who had been marginalized and oppressed by the ruling class in the 1970s later became an upper-middle class or members of the ruling political party of South Korea in the 1980s and 1990s. These people who used to be the minjung in the 1970s were being accused by others as 'oppressors' as they have been organized and acquired socio-political power. In other words, once they were a minjung does not mean that they will remain always a minjung; some members of the minjung in the 1970s can become oppressors of other

[8] Kwang-Sun David Suh, "A Biographical Sketch of an Asian Theological Consultation," in *Minjung Theology*, 16.

[9] Ahn, "Jesus," 150.

[10] See Paul Chung, *Martin Luther and Buddhism*, 170–72. Chung elaborates on many forms of minjung in the Old Testament and New Testament times, such as the Jews in the Exodus, another group of Jews after the destruction of Jerusalem in A.D. 70, and later oppressed groups of Christians and Gentiles.

[11] Boo-Woong Yoo, *Korean Pentecostalism: Its History and Theology* (New York: Peter Lang, 1988) 205.

minjung in the later stages, especially when a social or political revolution becomes successful.

Black Minjung in America

Twentieth-century American Pentecostalism finds its real beginning in the Great Azusa Street Revival in 1906, which was led by the black preacher William Seymour. From a Korean minjung perspective, the Azusa Revival can be construed as a *black minjung movement*. These African Americans at the beginning of the 20th century exemplified a minjung, who had to undergo racial discrimination and economic exploitation by the ruling classes. The Azusa Revival started in the poorer quarters of Los Angeles with the black people who were marginalized and oppressed.[12]

In January of 1906, William Seymour, an African-American student of Charles Parham, arrived in Los Angeles with a burning desire to preach the Gospel. After having some initial hardships, Seymour experienced one of the most vigorous revivals in church history. Soon, the Azusa Street revival arrested the media's attention. As a result, thousands of people came to visit the Azusa Street mission, and they went back to their home churches to report the excitement of what they had witnessed.[13]

About fifty years later, another mighty wind, *ruah*, of the Holy Spirit started to blow within mainline churches in the United States. Later, this wind came to be known as the 'Charismatic' or 'Neo-Pentecostal' movement. First, this 'Charismatic' movement occurred within mainline Protestant churches (i.e., Presbyterian, Lutheran, and Anglican) and in 1967, spread to Roman Catholic churches.

Today, no fewer than five hundred million Christians belong to the Pentecostal-Charismatic movement, one of the largest Christian movements in church history.[14] This movement became a major force in twen-

[12] Robert Owens, *Speak to the Rock: The Azusa Street Revival* (Lanham: University Press of America, 1998) 64.

[13] Koo Dong Yun, *Baptism in the Holy Spirit: An Ecumenical Theology of Spirit Baptism* (Lanham: University Press of America, 2003) 13–16. See Edith Blumhofer, *Restoring the Faith* (Chicago: University of Illinois Press, 1993) 55–62.

[14] David Barrett, George Kurian, and Todd Johnson, *World Christian Encyclopedia: A Comparative Survey of Churches and Religions in the Modern World*, 2d ed., (New York: Oxford University Press, 2001). According to this Encyclopedia, the combined number of both Pentecostals and Charismatics in 2000 is about 523,777,004. For more information, see Table 1–1 in the *Encyclopedia*. For the estimated figures of previous years, see Vinson Synan, "Pentecostalism: Varieties and Contributions," *PNEUMA: The Journal of the Society for Pentecostal Studies* (Fall 1986): 43–44; Daniel Albrecht, *Rites in the Spirit: A Ritual Approach to Pentecostal/Charismatic Spirituality* (Sheffield: Sheffield Academic, 1999) 27–28;

tieth-century Christianity. Hence, theologians pay greater attention to this movement and critically examine its essential nature and purpose more closely. Out of a number of intriguing characteristics related to the Pentecostal-Charismatic movement, "Baptism in the Holy Spirit"[15] (also known as "Spirit baptism") represents the most distinctive doctrine of this movement.

The Great Azusa Street Revival in 1906, the benchmark of 20th century Pentecostalism in America, represents a black minjung movement.[16] In actuality, the Revival spawned in the house of Asberry located on 214 North Bonnie Brae Street, where "Negro washwomen" constituted the primary audience.[17] The crowds became bigger and bigger to be handled in a single house so that they had to meet in the abandoned building at 312 Azusa Street.[18] Undoubtedly, in the beginning, the Revival began with lower-working-class blacks, later joined by other ethnic groups. According to Harvey Cox, the main constituencies of the early stage of the Pentecostal movement were the poor, outcast, and despised people.[19]

The African-American participants of the Azusa Revival typified a minjung in America who possessed a suppressed *Han,* a salient word of minjung theology which denotes a deep feeling of grudge or despair.[20] The Azusa Street Mission provided a setting in which the frustrated African-Americans were able to eject the suppressed emotions, such as fear, anger,

---

Harvey Cox, "Pentecostalism and the Future of Christianity," *TIKKUN* 9, no. 6 (Nov/Dec 1994): 43; David B. Barrett, "Annual Statistical Table on Global Mission: 1997," in *International Bulletin of Missionary Research* 21.1, 24–25; C. Peter Wagner, "Church Growth," in *Dictionary of Pentecostal and Charismatic Movements*, 180–95.

15 The two terms (i.e., "baptism in the Holy Spirit" and "Spirit baptism") are regarded as synonyms.

16 For more information on black origins of Pentecostalism, see Walter Hollenweger, "A Black Pentecostal Concept: A Forgotten Chapter of Black History: The Black Pentecostals," *Concept* 30 (June 1970); Ithiel Clemmons, "True Koinonia: Pentecostal Hopes and Historical Studies," *Pneuma: The Journal of the Society for Pentecostal Studies* 4 (Spring 1982); Walter Hollenweger, *Pentecost between Black and White* (Belfast: Christian Journals Limited, 1972).

17 Robert Anderson, *Vision of the Disinherited: The Making of American Pentecostalism* (New York: Oxford University Press, 1979) 65.

18 Edith Blumhofer, *Restoring the Faith*, 56.

19 Harvey Cox, *Fire from Heaven: The Rise of Pentecostal Spirituality and the Reshaping of Religion in the Twenty-first Century* (Reading, MA: Addison-Wesley, 1995) 67.

20 Kwang-Sun Suh, "The Korean Pentecostal Movement and Its Theological Understanding," in *A Study on the Pentecostal Movement in Korea* (Seoul: Korean Christian Academy, 1982) 47–65.

and shame by means of shouting-out and ejaculatory prayers.[21] This releasing of the negative emotion was categorized as *Han-pul-yi* by minjung theologians.[22]

The Socio-Political Minjung

In *Korean Pentecostalism: Its History and Theology*, Boo-woong Yoo introduces two kinds of minjung: (1) socio-political and (2) Pentecostal.[23] The socio-political minjung primarily fought for social and political justice, whereas the Pentecostal minjung mostly worked on spiritual healing of the nation. Indubitably, both kinds of minjung were needed in order to liberate the Korean nation. In the face of the political oppression and economic deprivation in the 1970s, the socio-political minjung in South Korea arose in order to bring political liberation and appropriate distribution of revenues to companies. The participants of this minjung movement often had to undergo house-arrests, torture in prison cells, and even loss of life.[24]

Minjung theology in Korea emerged in the context of the political oppression of the dictator Jung-Hee Park and the economic deprivation of city workers and rural peasants. During the 1970s, the demise of South Vietnam to the hands of the Vietnamese communists, and North Korean threats of invading South Korea helped Park increase his dictatorial measures. With the excuse of maintaining the national security of South Korea, he often manipulated the crowds and eliminated his political opposition.[25]

Modern industrialization in South Korea truly took off in the 1970s through modernization and urbanization. At that time, South Korea did not possess natural resources, capital, and technology that were essentials for economic growth, but she had a relatively well-educated, industrious work-force.[26]

Park's regime borrowed capital from wealthy foreign countries and distributed arbitrarily by choosing the entrepreneurs who would support his dictatorship. Park's regime solely focused on economic growth and at

[21] Robert Owens, *Speak to the Rock: The Azusa Street Revival* (Lanham: University Press of America, 1998) 74.

[22] See Donald Gelpi, *The Conversion Experience* (New York: Paulist, 1998) 34–37. *Han-pul-yi* can be understood as part of affective conversion in Gelpi's categories.

[23] Yoo, *Korean Pentecostalism*, 220.

[24] Kwang-Sun David Suh, "A Biographical Sketch," 16.

[25] Yoo, *Korean Pentecostalism*, 191.

[26] Ibid.

the same time severely undermined the welfare of workers. This eventually engendered protest movements in South Korea.[27] Under these circumstances a group of theologians and Christian ministers issued "The Declaration of Korean Christians 1972," which urged people to fight for the poor and suffering minjung.

During the second half of the 1970s, clearly many people endeavored to delineate minjung theology. Several articles were published in multifarious journals, and soon minjung theology grabbed attention of many Koreans as well as Christians outside Korea.[28] The Commission on Theological Concerns of the Christian Conference of Asia and the Korean National Council of Churches sponsored the Asian Theological Consultation, held in October of 1979.[29] This setting afforded international, interdenominational, and interdisciplinary dialogues among its participants, and as a result minjung theology became known globally.

Without any doubt, most socio-political minjung belonged to the powerless, oppressed, uneducated and underprivileged groups, but many point out the fact that *minjung theologians* did not. One main criticism toward these minjung theologians is that they were not "subjects" of the minjung movement; rather, they remained the "objective observers" who wrote and sold the minjung biographies for their own benefits and credits. It is visible that some minjung theologians reflected the elite class who were highly educated and the socially-upper class. On the contrary, the real subjects of the political minjung did not receive any due credits, and often died without any social and medical helps. One may still argue that "minjung theology" does not represent the authentic socio-political minjung; rather, it is an aristocratic, objective reflection on the suffering of the minjung.

The Pentecostal Minjung and Affective Conversion

In *The Conversion Experience*, Donald Gelpi elaborates upon five forms of conversion. In addition to Bernard Lonergan's three kinds of conversion (namely, intellectual, moral, and religious), Gelpi supplements two more kinds: affective and socio-political conversions. The five kinds or forms of conversion remain distinct and interrelated. The five forms resemble one

[27] Ibid., 192.

[28] Kwang-Sun David Suh, "Korean Theological Development in the 1970s," in *Minjung Theology: People as the Subject of History*, ed. Commission on Theological Concerns, Christian Conference of Asia (Maryknoll: Orbis, 1983) 41.

[29] Ibid.

another in two ways: (1) Each form engages "a turning from" and "a turning to." (2) Each converts from the irresponsible living to the responsible life. Out of the five forms of conversion, all five, except for religious conversion, can transpire in secular and natural settings. A human can initiate these four kinds of conversion, but in religious conversion only God can initiate this.[30]

The first conversion which Gelpi addresses is *moral conversion*. In the realm of morality, there are two sub-categories: 1) *personal moral* and 2) *socio-political.* Out of the two, Gelpi experienced a *personal moral conversion* first. Reared in the Deep South, Louisiana, Gelpi grew up with a racial prejudice. He believed at the time that African Americans were essentially inferior to white people. This racial bias represented the conventional morality in the Deep South, and Gelpi bought into this attitude. An initial moral conversion took place while attending a high school, where Jesuits incessantly condemned racism. Eventually, he conceded and renounced it in his heart. Gelpi points out that in many cases, one needs to break away from 'traditional' and "conventional' morality, which comes with both virtue and vice. Hence, a mature adult conscience must go beyond conventional morality into 'autonomous' morality, constituted by examined, self-critical beliefs. Simply having a noetic admission is not good enough; one should act upon it responsibly.[31]

The second form of conversion refers to *socio-political conversion,* which deals with larger, social institutions such as government, the economy, class structure, and ecclesiastical structure. Whereas personal moral conversion mainly focuses on personal rights and duties, socio-political conversion pays attention to the universal, common good. Several years after renouncing racial bigotry, Gelpi became actively involved with the political and social fight against racism—this could have been counted as his initial socio-political conversion. Fighting against world hunger, nuclear disarmament and environmental preservation exemplify acts of socio-political conversion.[32]

The third form of conversion is *intellectual conversion*. When one takes personal responsibility for the truth and falsity of one's beliefs and for the adequacy or inadequacy of the frames of reference, an intellectual conversion occurs. Many modern scientific studies have been presented

[30] Donald Gelpi, *The Conversion Experience: A Reflective Process for RCIA Participants and Others* (New York: Paulist, 1998) 24–25.

[31] Ibid., 29–30.

[32] Ibid., 31.

with inadequate frames of reference. These reductionistic frames of reference allow neither the asking nor answering of necessary questions. For instance, Newtonian physics does not possess a frame of reference to aptly explain genuine human free will.[33]

Truth can be grasped *rationally* and *imaginatively*. Rational truth is derived by logical and inferential thinking, whereas imaginative truth is available through art, poetry, and literature. By unduly focusing on rational truth, modern sciences tend to undermine the realm of imaginative truth. Hence, intellectual conversion also takes place when one realizes one's inadequate frame of reference.[34]

When human beings are young, we usually follow the teachings of our parents or pastors devoid of serious critical reflection because we simply trust them. In other words, we simply follow their conventional wisdom. Many young people neither have courage nor maturity to go beyond conventional beliefs. A person converts intellectually when one decries some aspects of prejudice or error in his or her conventional belief system. Every communal horizon has some truths and some unverifiable prejudices. Intellectual conversion signifies that a person cannot simply accept everything taught by reliable people including even parents and pastors. They are also fallible beings although we should respect their mature wisdom and opinion, but even theirs are not exempt from error or falsity. Acquiring truth involves more than mere memorization and confessing creeds; it requires an active mind with a critical analysis.[35]

The fourth kind of conversion is described as *affective conversion*, which promotes *personal emotional* health. Empirical and clinical studies of human emotion reveal that suppressed negative emotions tend to bring forth psychological problems. Negative emotions include shame, fear, anger, and guilt, whereas positive emotions embrace sympathy, affection, friendship, love, and forgiveness. Nonetheless, the systemic suppression of negative emotions engenders a variety of personality dysfunction. Nervousness exemplifies the first level of dysfunction. Emotional rigidity, antisocial behavior, self-hatred, and suicide are the other examples of the severe suppression of negative emotions.[36]

Religious conversion exemplifies the fifth form of conversion. In contrast to the other four kinds of conversion, God alone initiates this religious

[33] Ibid., 33.

[34] Ibid., 34.

[35] Ibid.

[36] Ibid., 34–35.

conversion, to which humans respond. In the realm of faith, religious conversion transpires. Religious conversion assumes an authentic encounter with God or a transcendental reality. The reality of God has been revealed through the incarnation of the Son and the action of the Holy Spirit.[37]

In Gelpi's terminology, the Pentecostal minjung for the most part worked on affective conversion. The solid labors of the working class were exploited systematically by owners and employers, so many hard working people were struggling to pay for their basic necessities such as house rent and groceries. In addition, people could not express their feelings of political repression by Park's dictatorship. These conditions of the working class created a great frustration among various minjung. The negative feelings of frustration were vented in many Pentecostal/Charismatic churches. As a result, minjung experienced *affective conversion*.

The Korean Pentecostal Minjung

The groundbreaking book of minjung theology entitled *Minjungkwa Hankuksinhak* (*Minjung and Korean Theology*) was first published in 1982. In this Korean book, Kwang-Sun Suh endeavored to find *minjung* as well as a particular theology done by real *minjung*. Surprisingly, he found other minjung in the Pentecostal-Charismatic movement.[38] Suh remarked, "Recently, I visited various places of the 'Spirit Movement' [Pentecostal-Charismatic movement], which was also creating some controversy among Korean Christians, and I saw an incredible growth of these churches with healing and glossolalia ['speaking in tongues'] of the Holy Spirit. In this movement, I found and met *minjung*."[39] Suh detected the other side of minjung in non-denominational and Pentecostal-Charismatic churches. Numerous members of the Korean minjung found encouragement, consolation, and spiritual healing from the Pentecostal fellowship of Yoido Full Gospel Church in Seoul, the largest Christian church in the world in terms of numbers. Boo-woong Yoo labeled these Korean participants the "Pentecostal minjung."[40]

[37] Ibid., 37–39.

[38] The Koran phrase translated by the author as the "Pentecostal-Charismatic movement" literally means "Spirit Movement." This movement stayed interdenominational and ecumenical insofar as many Presbyterian, Methodist, Holiness, and Baptist churches participated in it.

[39] Kwang-Sun Suh, "*Minjungkwa Sunglyung*" ("Minjung and Holy Spirit") in *Minjung and Korean Theology* (Seoul: Korea Theological Study Institute, 1985) 303. The author translated these sentences from Korean to English.

[40] Yoo, *Korean Pentecostalism*, 205–6.

Suh argues further that these Pentecostal minjung rediscovered the importance of pneumatology and gifts of the Holy Spirit such as healing and mystical experiences. They have been allured by the Spirit's power and hypnotized by propaganda and powerful manifestations in their Pentecostal-Charismatic churches. Suh more or less construes the Korean Spirit/Pentecostal Movement as a rebellion against the traditional Confucian hegemony. The major problems in this movement, however, arose when it became more and more shamanistic and material-success oriented instead of participating actively in the suffering of the oppressed, alienated minjung.[41]

Unlike the Pentecostal movement in America, whose adherents left the mainline denominational churches and created their own churches and denominations, most participants of the Spirit/Pentecostal Movement in Korea stayed in their traditional denominational congregations and worked on revival and renewal of their churches. As a matter of fact, many Korean mainstream denominations including Presbyterian and Methodist carry "Pentecostal" elements in their spirituality. Therefore, in order to comprehend the reality of the Pentecostal minjung, one should include not only Pentecostal-denomination churches (e.g., the Korean Assemblies of God) but also the mainstream Christians who robustly engaged in the Spirit/Pentecostal Movement in Korea.

During the 1970s in South Korea, political oppression, economic exploitation, and dehumanization elicited numerous negative emotions among the Korean minjung. These negative emotions needed to be released in various forms of catharses. The systemic suppression of negative emotions gradually brought fourth *Han*. Many public demonstration movements took place in the 1970s—such as marching on streets and throwing pieces of rock and glass bottles imbued with fuel in their fight against puppets of the dictator Park—which helped the Korean socio-political minjung release their negative emotions. This was a method of *Han-pul-yi* (catharsis) by the socio-political minjung.

The Pentecostal minjung in the 1970s, in contrast, sought for a different cathartic means, such as revival meetings and Pentecostal/Charismatic worship services. In August of 1974, a national, ecumenical revival crusade, titled "EXPLO '74," was held in Seoul. This crusade was led by the Pentecostals Yong-Gi Cho and Joon-Gon Kim. On the first night, more than a million people attended the meeting. The author, having attended

[41] Suh, *Minjungkwa Sunglyung*, 310–16. Harvey Cox also notices the success- and quantity-oriented tendency of Korean Pentecostalism. See Harvey Cox, *Fire from Heaven*, 234.

the crusade, detected emotional release of people's frustration by means of *Tong-sung-ki-do* (shouting-out, ejaculatory prayer), clapping, crying, as well as speaking in tongues. This crusade not only provided a setting for religious conversion (personal evangelism), but it also brought forth a place for affective conversion (emotional healing). The Korean minjung underwent emotional, affective healing by venting their *Han*.

In the past, many mainline Christians in South Korea (e.g., Roman Catholics, Presbyterians, and Methodists) accused the Pentecostal minjung of not participating in the socio-political aspect of the gospel. This criticism finds some warrant, but the Pentecostal minjung still engaged in various forms of socio-political conversion, albeit they chose to do that in a more subtle way. They endeavored to implement the teaching of Matt 6:3, "But when you give to the needy, do not let your left hand know what your right hand is doing." So their activities were not as visible as those of the socio-political minjung, who were marching on many streets against Jung-Hee Park's regime and creating labor unions. As a result, these socio-political minjung received the attention of the media both domestically and internationally. In contrast, the Pentecostal minjung engaged in social action quietly by providing essential items such as rice for starving families (known as *ku-je-sa-up*), and prayed for political progress in Korea as well as encouraged people to vote. Surely, they did not endorse revolutionary theology, but promoted the principles of democracy. But more importantly, Charismatic/Pentecostal churches provided the places where these wounded and oppressed minjung could find rest and emotional healing. At the same time, the socio-political minjung also did not forget to bestow practical needy items on the poor. In that sense, God utilized the whole Korean minjung, both the socio-political and Pentecostal, in order to liberate Koreans from the bondage of sin.

The Indigenous/Shamanic Aspect of the Pentecostal Minjung

The Harvard theologian Harvey Cox recently published a pivotal book on Pentecostalism entitled *Fire from Heaven*. In chapter seven, Cox delineates two essential elements of fast-growing religions in today's world. First, they should be able to include and transform many aspects of pre-existing religions. Second, they should be able to equip their congregants to live in societies that undergo rapid changes. The fast growth of Korean Pentecostalism became possible because it afforded these two elements.[42] The Korean Pentecostal churches absorbed and transformed pre-Christian religious practices, namely, those of shamanism, Buddhism, and Confucianism. In accordance with Cox, Yoido Full Gospel Church of Seoul incorporated some shamanic practices into its worship. The Korean Pentecostal churches produced a setting where thousands of people, who might have been too embarrassed to exercise the rituals of the old-time shamanistic rituals, could do it in a more generous situation with the label of Christianity.[43] Furthermore, Cox does not have a problem with interpreting Apostle Paul as a Jewish shaman.

I have been deeply impressed by Cox's acute and poignant analyses of Korean Pentecostalism as well as other Asian Pentecostal groups. I also believe that Cox is correct that many Asian Pentecostals integrated certain rituals of their indigenous religions, but I insist they did it most likely without clear intention. I am certain that Cox does not employ the term *shaman* in a negative and derogatory term, but most Christians in South Korea do. Here, Cox, being an "outsider," tends to overlook derogatory connotations of the Korean word *moodang* (shaman). Historically and traditionally, many Koreans use the word in order to obviate their political opponents and persecute the low-class people. This word has such a pejorative meaning that most Koreans reject any type of association. As Cox tells in his book, most Korean Pentecostals vehemently refute the shamanic elements in their rituals. In fact, when Korean Pentecostal Christianity was expanding like a rapid fire, some of the mainline Protestant Christians used the term in order to damage the legitimacy and orthodoxy of the Pentecostal churches, calling them "heretics."[44] As a result, Korean Pentecostals had to fight vigorously against that idea by distancing themselves from shamanistic practices. Therefore, most Korean Pentecostals inculcate that some key elements of Pentecostalism such as healing, exorcism, and glossolalia unequivocally stem from the biblical writings, not from shamanism.

Conclusion

At least two kinds of minjung subsisted in South Korea in the 1970s, namely, the socio-political and Pentecostal minjung. In some ways, the

[42] Harvey Cox, *Fire*, 219.

[43] Ibid., 225–26.

[44] See Ig-Jin Kim, *History and Theology of Korean Pentecostalism: Sunbogeum (Pure Gospel) Pentecostalism* (Zoetermeer, The Netherlands: Uitgeverij Boekencentrum, 2003). This book contains the official report of the *Tonghap* Presbyterian denomination on David Younggi Cho's "Pseudo-Christianity" (1994) that impugned the credibility of Cho and Yoido Full Gospel Church.

Pentecostal minjung better represented the reality of minjung. One could find more people on the bottom who were socio-economically poor and powerless from Korean Pentecostal congregants than Presbyterian and Methodist churches. Moreover, most leaders of the socio-political minjung in the 1970s consisted of the elite who were highly educated, whereas most leaders of the Pentecostal minjung such as David Yonggi Cho did not come with advanced university degrees. Many members of the Pentecostal minjung, experiencing contemptuous treatment due to their lack of advanced education and ignorance of Western sciences, were able to become pastors by the instant charismata of the Holy Spirit. The socio-political minjung with many of their members educated abroad, were able to share their ideology and theology in English; consequently, they received the global recognition. On the contrary, the Pentecostal minjung, except for a few leaders, were unable to share their discourses in English because most of them never received opportunities to learn foreign languages in college. Only recently, some publications are coming out regarding the Pentecostal minjung. As Pentecostalism has globally established itself as a major force in Christianity, Pentecostalism in Korea deserves more respect and global acceptance.

PART II

Asian Contextual Theology and Interfaith Diapraxis

7

A Mapping of Asian Liberative Theology in Quest for the Mystery of God amidst the Minjung Reality and World Religions

Veli-Matti Kärkkäinen

The Critical Asian Principle

> There is a quiet determination among Asian Christians that their commitment to Jesus Christ and their words about Jesus Christ must be responsible to the life they live in Asia today. Such theology is called a living theology. . . . Asian theology seeks to take the encounter between life in Asia and the Word of God seriously.[1]

WITH these words Kosuke Koyama, one of the most well-known Asian theologians from Japan, introduces an anthology of essays focusing on the themes of emerging Asian theologies. The continent in which more than half of the world's population lives currently is not easy to divide in manageable units with regard to theological centers. However, for heuristic reasons that kind of classification might be helpful. Theologically, perhaps the most fertile soil has been India and Sri Lanka with the strong Hindu (and to some extent, Buddhist) influence. Because of the long tradition of English-speaking education, these countries have contributed significantly to the emerging international theologizing. Another center of theological thinking is rising, namely Korea, with its phenomenal church growth. There is a strong proliferation of Korean theology between, on

[1] Kosuke Koyama, "Foreword by an Asian Theologian," in *Asian Christian Theology: Emerging Themes*, ed. Douglas J. Elwood (Philadelphia: Westminster, 1980) 13.

the one hand, fairly conservative Evangelical theology that cuts across denominational boundaries and, on the other hand, a more liberal strand of Asian pluralism and *minjung*. Then there is yet another cluster of Asian countries in which Buddhism has played a major role. Countries such as China, Taiwan, Thailand, and Japan belong to this group. Some Japanese theologians, such as Kosuke Koyama, have made gateways into the international theological academy, so also the Taiwanese C. S. Song and some others. The predominantly Catholic Philippines stands in its own category, so also Indonesia, which is strongly influenced by Islam but also in some areas by Hinduism and Buddhism.[2]

While Asia is the cradle of most major religions in the world, with regard to Christian theology it was not until the last part of the twentieth century that major contributions began to emerge on a larger scale. What is distinctive about the Asian context is the continuous correlation between Christian theology and the pluralism of Asian religiosity. Recently, many Asian churches have been on the forefront of ecumenism both with regard to other churches and other religions. The groundbreaking work of the Ecumenical Association of Third World Theologians (EATWOT), founded in 1976, has especially fostered both interreligious and ecumenical activities.

During the years I lived and taught in Bangkok, Thailand, I used to go jogging early in the morning to avoid the deadly heat of the sun. Most often the route I took passed three different worship centers: first a huge Thai Buddhist temple, then an Islamic mosque, and finally a little bit further down the street, a Catholic Church. The Buddhist monks were collecting morning offerings from grandparents from the houses along the street, and the owners of small businesses who set up their markets around 5 a.m. went first to burn incense to the spirits. As devoted Buddhists they knew that spirits or gods do not exist, but for a pluralistically-oriented Asian, paying homage to powers like that did not pose a problem. Their attitude toward me, a theologian and teacher of foreign religion, was always friendly and affirming: promoting religion, most any religion, contributes to the well-being and safety of the community.

[2] See further George Gispert-Sauch, S.J., "Asian Theology," in *The Modern Theologians: An Introduction to Christian Theology in the Twentieth Century*, 2nd ed., ed. David Ford (Cambridge: Blackwell, 1997) 455.

Pluralism and Poverty as the Context for Theology

The words of the Sri Lankan Roman Catholic Liberationist Aloysius Pieris are often quoted to set the stage for theologizing in that continent: "The Asian context can be described as a blend of a profound religiosity (which is perhaps Asia's greatest wealth) and an overwhelming poverty."[3]

In any Asian country, Christians live in a minority position. This fact has implications for Asian theologies when compared to European and U.S. theologies, which are often written from the standpoint of Christianity being a major force in the society. The thrust of Asian theology is to inquire into the identity of Christianity vis-à-vis other religious confessions. Kosuke Koyama aptly notes the various forces that shape Asian Christianity as Asians are addressing the question, "but who do you say that I am?" (Matt 16:15).

This question comes to Asian Christians, who live in a world of great religious traditions, modernization impacts, ideologies of the left and right, international conflicts, hunger, poverty, militarism, and racism. Within these confusing and brutal realities of history the question comes to them. Here the depth of soul of the East is challenged to engage in a serious dialogue with the Word of God. Jesus refuses to be treated superficially.[4]

Poverty and injustice are not peculiar to the Asian continent: Latin Americans and Africans, among others, suffer from the exploitation as well. Yet, the amount of poverty—if not for other reasons than for the huge population—in the East is overwhelming and breathtaking. Most Asian countries are poor, with the exception of Japan, Taiwan, and South Korea. From the Western viewpoint, it is painful to acknowledge the fact that one—if not *the*—major reason for poverty in too many Asian countries is the tragic history of colonialization. This historical fact should make Western preachers of Christ aware of the difficulty with which many Asians hear their message, the message of the former masters.

For many Asian Christian theologians, then, struggle for liberation and justice are key themes. One of the most noted of those champions is M. M. Thomas, a layperson of the Mar Thoma Church of southern India who also held leadership role in the World Council of Churches. His gateway to theology was the emergence of political and social consciousness, coming as he was from Marxist philosophy. The title of his main book, *Salvation and Humanization,* reveals the central orientation of his

[3] Aloysius Pieris, "Western Christianity and Asian Buddhism," in *Dialogue* 7 (May–August 1980) 61–62.

[4] Koyama, "Foreword by an Asian Theologian," 14.

thinking. For Thomas, the validity of Christian theology is based less on its doctrinal orthodoxy than on its contribution to the human quest for a better quality of life and for social justice.

Aloysius Pieris, among others, has joined in this fight against poverty and oppression. In his Christology, this Roman Catholic theologian links Asia's poverty and spirituality to Jesus' "double baptism" in "the Jordan of Asian religions and the Calvary of Asian poverty." This is Jesus' immersion in the Asian context and life. Jesus pointed to the ascetic John as the archetype of the true spirituality of the kingdom of God and denounced the striving for the accumulation of wealth and trust in mammon. Jesus' radical social program, in Pieris's analysis, led him finally to the cross, executed by the power elite. The powerful crucified him at "a cross that the money-polluted religiosity of his day planted on Calvary with the aid of a colonial power (Luke 23:1–23). This is where the journey, begun at Jordan, ended."[5]

Theology as Story

Asian Christian theology is still emerging and distinguishing itself in various Asian forms after a long hegemony of Western influence;[6] understandably there have been various criticisms by Asian theologians concerning the limitations of traditional and Western theology.[7] How would a *Theology from the Womb of Asia*, to cite the title of the book by the Taiwanese Choan-Seng Song,[8] look like?

[5] Aloysius Pieris, *An Asian Theology of Liberation* (Maryknoll, NY: Orbis, 1988) 49.

[6] A helpful discussion is offered by Merrill Morse, *Kosuke Koyama: A Model for Intercultural Theology* (Frankfurt am Main: Peter Lang, 1991) ch. 5.

[7] Tissa Balasuriya of Sri Lanka laments that Western theology for Asians is ethnocentric, ecclesiocentric, clerical, patriarchal, pro-capitalistic, devoid of socioeconomic analysis, and nonpractical. Asian Liberation theologians, with the leadership of Aloysius Pieris, another Sri Lankan, have complained about the lack of relevance of Western approaches to the social and political context of Asia. Choan-Seng Song faults Western theology for rationalism and lack of imagination. J.Y. Lee similarly decries the Western approach for being captive to Aristotelian logic of the excluded middle, which is in opposition to an inclusive *yin-yang* thinking of Asia See further, Tissa Balasuriya, "Toward the Liberation of Theology in Asia," *Asia's Struggle for Full Humanity: Toward a Relevant Theology*, ed. Virginia Fabella (Maryknoll, NY: Orbis 1980); Balasuriya, *Planetary Theology* (Maryknoll, NY: Orbis, 1984) 2–10 especially. Aloysius Pieris, *An Asian Theology of Liberation* (Maryknoll, NY: Orbis, 1988) 81–83 especially. Choan-Seng Song, *Third-Eye Theology*, rev. ed. (Maryknoll, NY: Orbis, 1990) 19–23. Jung Young Lee, *Marginality: The Key to Multicultural Theology* (Minneapolis: Fortress, 1995) 64–70; *Trinity in Asian Perspective* (Nashville: Abingdon, 1996) chs. 2 and 3.

[8] Choan-Seng Song, *Theology from the Womb of Asia* (Maryknoll, NY: Orbis, 1986).

According to the Korean born theologian Jung Young Lee, the "cultural and historical context of the West is so very distinct from that of the East that they seem opposite to each other." However, he adds, "their difference should be regarded not as a source of conflict but as a basis for mutual fulfillment. Their contextual difference will enrich a holistic understanding of the Christian faith."[9] Lee's own biography is typical of so many non-Western theologians. Having conducted his theological studies in the West focusing on Euro-American male theologians' writings, only slowly he began to reclaim his own Asian tradition. In the course of two decades of teaching Asian religions and philosophy in the USA, he became not only an expert in that religiosity but was also able to attempt a fruitful dialogue between traditional Western and his own Korean-Chinese-East Asian background.[10]

Authentic Asian theology, while anchored of course in Scripture and traditions, [11] relates to the realities of Asian life, pluralism and poverty. The billions of Asian people themselves with their daily "stories of joy and suffering, hope and despair, love and hatred, freedom and oppression" form one of the sources. According to the Vietnamese Peter C. Phan, this collective memory includes the women's stories, voicing women's marginalization and oppression that is often even greater than that of men. Furthermore, the sacred texts and ethical and spiritual practices of Asian religion and philosophy serve as sources as the Trinitarian theologies of Panikkar and Lee illustrate.[12] Yet another distinctive feature of Asian theological (re)sources, already alluded to above, is the rich tradition of cultural tools such as myths, folklore, symbols, poetry, stories, songs, visual art, and dance.[13] In that kind of environment, theology embraces other methods than—and sometimes prefers them over—discursive analysis, especially narrative and story telling. For C.S. Song

[9] Jung Young Lee, *The Trinity in Asian Perspective* (Nashville: Abingdon, 1996) 17.

[10] Lee, *The Trinity in Asian*, 21–23.

[11] Peter C. Phan, "Introduction: An Asian-American Theology: Believing and Thinking at the Boundaries," in *Journeys at the Margin: Toward an Autobiographical Theology in American-Asian Perspective,* ed. Peter C. Phan and Jung Young Lee (Collegeville, MN: Liturgical, 1999) xv (italics in the text). See further, R. S. Sugirtharajah, ed., *Voices from the Margin: Interpreting the Bible in the Third World* (Maryknoll, NY: Orbis, 1991).

[12] See further Peter C. Phan, "The Christ of Asia: An Essay on Jesus and the Eldest Son and Ancestor," *Missionalia* 45 (1996) 25–55.

[13] Phan, "Introduction," xii–xviii, quotation p. xvi; I have modified Phan's categorization.

> . . . theology is like storytelling. The story unfolds itself as you tell it. It moves in all directions. It may even stray into byways. But this is the excitement of telling stories. A story grows and expands. It leads to new terrains and depicts new scenes. If this is what our storytelling is like, how much more so is God's storytelling! The story of creation—who are we to define it and restrict it—God's activity in the world—how are we to predict it and dictate it? God's ultimate goal for humanity and for the entire creation—how on earth are we to set a time-frame to it?[14]

In his delightful classic work *Waterbuffalo Theology,* the Japanese Kosuke Koyama, who has worked in Thailand speaks of the need for a narrative, concrete approach to divinity among Thai farmers who are not concerned about metaphysical problems related to God, but they are interested in hearing that the "monsoon rain cannot make God wet! God is the Lord of monsoon rain. He sends his monsoon for his purpose."[15] Koyama also wondered what would happen if we used kitchen imagery such as "pepper" and "salt" instead of dry philosophical categories of the West totally unrelated to the Asian context.[16] Koyama also reminds us in *Three Mile an Hour God,* that God in no hurry, a God better suited for the Thai context with the mentality of *maiphenrai* (meaning something like "It does not matter" or "It is okay").[17]

Theology as biography based on narrative and (personal) story—along with poems, myths, and folklore—honors the preferred vehicles of communication of religion and theology in Asia; in the words of David Ng of China, "one's life story becomes a lifestory, a way of relating the events to providence."[18] A book compiled by Asian and Asian-American

[14] Choan-Seng Song, "Five Stages Toward Christian Theology in the Multicultural World," in *Journeys at the Margin,* 2. See also Choan-Seng Song, *The Believing Heart: An Invitation to Story Theology* (Minneapolis: Fortress, 1999).

[15] Kosuke Koyama, *Waterbuffalo Theology* (Maryknoll, NY: Orbis 1974) 41.

[16] Koyama, *Waterbuffalo Theology,* 79–83.

[17] Kosuke Koyama, *Three Mile an Hour God: Biblical Reflections* (Maryknoll, NY: Orbis, 1979).

[18] David Ng, "A Path of Concentric Circles: Toward an Autobiographical Theology of Community," in *Journeys at the Margin: Toward an Autobiographical Theology in American-Asian Perspective,* ed. Peter C. Phan and Jung Young Lee (Collegeville, Minn.: Liturgical Press, 1999) 82. So also Paul F.Knitter, *No Other Name? A Critical Survey of Christian Attitudes Toward the World Religions* (Maryknoll, NY: Orbis Books, 1985) xiii: "All theology, we are told, is rooted in biography." The first major monograph on the topic of biographical theology was offered by the late James McClendon, Jr., *Biography as Theology: How Life Stories Can Remake Today's Theology* (Nashville: Abingdon, 1974). For important methodological considerations from an Asian perspective, see also Anselm K. Min, "From

theologians on a theological method titled *Journeys at the Margin: Toward an Autobiographical Theology in Asian-American Perspective* illustrates this approach. In a most delightful way Masao Takenaka of Japan paints a picture of doing theology in a mood so different from typical modern Western discursive analysis, compatible with ancient cultures of his own context. In his book *God Is Rice,* he calls this an "Ah-hah!" method, a dynamic way of doing theology much closer to the Bible, in which people did not come to know God by discussion or argument but by experiencing him. We "must awaken in ourselves the appreciation of the living reality who is God. In the Bible we have many surprising acknowledgements. . . . 'Ah-hah! In this way, God is working in our world, in a way I did not know.'"[19] This is an alternative to the typical Western *ya-ya* method based on analysis and debate.[20]

The Chinese C.S. Song's *Third-Eye Theology*[21] is another example of a uniquely Asian way of doing theology. "Third-eye" refers to the Buddhist master who opens our eyes to see areas that have been unknown before. The goal of that kind of authentic Asian theology is "the freedom to encounter Jesus the savior in the depth of the spirituality that sustains Asians in their long march of suffering and hope."[22]

In the remainder of the essay, to make my discussion more particular—and so resist the modernist universalist orientation, too prevalent in all Western theologies—I would like to carry on a critical dialogue with a leading Asian theologian who has spoken to the issue of the mystery of God from an Asian perspective, namely Stanley J. Samartha. An Indian clergyman, ordained in the Church of South India and involved in theological teaching in his earlier years, Samartha has exercised considerable influence through his post as Director of the WCC Dialogue Programme, which he initiated. Throughout his life, Samartha has advocated dialogue among world religions as the demand of our age. He has also been vocal about social justice and equality. There are many reasons why Samartha serves as a wonderful dialogue partner, not only because he represents a moderate, mainline pluralistic approach but also because of his extensive

---

Autobiography to Fellowship of Others: Reflections on Doing Ethnic Theology Today," in *Journeys at the Margin,* 135–60.

19 Masao Takenaka, *God Is Rice: Asian Cultures and Christian Faith* (Geneva: World Council of Churches, 1986) 9.

20 Takenaka, *God is Rice*, 8.

21 Choan-Seng Song *Third-Eye Theology: Theology in Formation in Asian Settings,* rev. ed. (Maryknoll, NY: Orbis, 1979).

22 Song, *Theology from the Womb of Asia,* 3.

ecumenical activities, his ideas are well known and widely debated. For Samartha, the drive behind the interreligious dialogue is not only the common search for truth but also the changed situation in the world in which religions have found themselves caught up in a worldwide struggle against injustice. Interreligious dialogue must seek after truth not only for its own sake but also in order to promote justice, peace, and equality. There can be no lasting justice, Samartha envisions, unless rooted in divine truth, and there is no authentic divine truth that does not produce the fruit of social justice.

"The Unbound Christ"

Samartha claims that Christ is larger than any church or religion. Samartha has become more and more weary of the widespread hostile attitude of Christianity to other religions: "Although most Christians today are unwilling to take a totally negative attitude toward neighbors of other faiths, there seems to be a good deal of hesitation on the part of many to reexamine the basis of their exclusive claims on behalf of Christ. The place of Christ in a multireligious society becomes, therefore, an important issue in the search for a new theology of religions."[23]

In his later main work *One Christ–Many Religions: Toward a Revised Christology*,[24] Samartha argues that christocentrism is applicable only to Christians, whereas it can never be considered as the only way to the mystery of the divine. Christocentrism cannot then be the norm by which the various religious traditions are valued. All various approaches to the divine have their validity.

The Christ acknowledged by Hinduism is often a churchless Christ. For that matter, the Christ acknowledged by Hinduism is often a Christ delivered from the encumbrances of numerous "bonds" with which he is laden by traditional Christianity—whether it be a matter of applauding his message while rejecting the Christian claim to his person, or of receiving from him as one divine manifestation among others in a catalog of divine descents (*avatara*) as varied as it is extensive.[25]

[23] Stanley J. Samartha, "The Cross and the Rainbow: Christ in a Multireligious Culture," in *Asian Faces of Jesus*, ed. R. S. Sugirtharajah (Maryknoll, NY: Orbis, 1995) 104.

[24] Samartha, *One Christ—Many Religions: Toward a Revised Christology* (Maryknoll, NY: Orbis, 1991).

[25] Jacques Dupuis, *Jesus Christ at the Encounter of World Religions* (Maryknoll, NY: Orbis, 1991) 15.

Samartha observes that a process of rejecting exclusive claims and seeking new ways of understanding the relationship of Jesus Christ to God and humanity is already underway. There is a shift from the "normative exclusiveness" of Christ to what he calls the "relational distinctiveness" of Christ. The term "relational" refers to the fact that Christ does not remain unrelated to neighbors of other faiths, while "distinctive" denotes the recognition of the distinctiveness of the great religious traditions as different responses to the Mystery of God.

This Asian theologian argues that the Hindu and the Christian have their own particularly distinctive contributions to make to the common quest for truth. The problem of religious exclusivism (according to which only those who believe in Christ will be saved), is that it cannot explain why a God whose love and justice are universal would reveal the way of salvation only through one savior, one people, and one book. Samartha wonders why the authority of one book should be thought binding for other faith communities with their own books, some of them even older than the New Testament. It is rather the limited view of Christians that argue for that kind of limitation in God's dealing with humankind, he believes. The claim for the exclusive truth in Christianity means putting religion in the prison of history. According to Samartha, genuine pluralism does not relativize the truth; the only thing that can make the truth relative is the different responses by different people. The truth is no one's privilege. The goal of ecumenism and interreligious dialogue is to create a "truly universal community" that will cut across boundaries of nations and religions.

The Sense of Mystery

In the context of India and many other Asian countries, with the growing sense of religious tolerance but increased and intensified political and social intolerance, there is a need for a Christology that is based on something other than clearly defined doctrinal formulations, Samartha contends. And he adds that in order for Christology to take root in Asian soil, the specific nature of the Asian mindset has to be taken into consideration. This is where the concept of "Mystery" is introduced into his theological discourse. Any attempt to formulate such a Christology should take into account at least two factors that have emerged out of Asia's long history of multireligious life. One is the acceptance of a sense of Mystery and the other the rejection of an exclusive attitude where ultimate matters are concerned. However, when it comes to the conception of mystery in Asian thought, it has to be noted that it does not denote something that fills the gaps in rational knowledge. Rather, Mystery provides the ontological basis for tolerance, which would otherwise run the risk of becoming uncritical friendliness.

This Mystery, the Truth of the Truth (*Satyasya Satyam*), *is* the transcendent Center that remains always beyond and greater than apprehensions of it even in the sum total of those apprehensions. It is beyond cognitive knowledge (*tarka*) but it is open to vision (*dristi*) and intuition (*anubhava*). It is near yet far, knowable yet unknowable, intimate yet ultimate and, according to one particular Hindu view, cannot even be described as "one." It is "not-two" (*advaita*), indicating thereby that diversity is within the heart of Being itself and therefore may be intrinsic to human nature as well.[26]

The emphasis on Mystery is not meant as an escape from the need for rational inquiry, but it insists that the rational is not the only way to do theology. The mystical and the aesthetic also have their necessary contributions to theology. Samartha believes that Mystery lies beyond the dichotomy of theistic versus nontheistic. "Mystery is an ontological status to be accepted, not an epistemological problem to be solved. Without a sense of Mystery, *Theos* cannot remain *Theos*, nor *Sat* remain *Sat*, nor can Ultimate Reality remain ultimate."[27]

Western thinking is founded on the dualistic principle of the excluded middle. Sentence can only be true or false, not both-and. Asian way of thinking resists that kind of either-or distinction. It is expressed in various ways, two of which are most well known outside, namely *yin-yang* and *advaita*. The Korean theologian Jung Young Lee builds his vision of the Trinity on *yin-yang* and Panikkar's "cosmotheandric" Trinitarian vision is based on the concept of *advaita*. [28] The pair *yin-yang* includes contradictions and opposites, yet inclusions, it is "both-and" rather than "either-or."[29] The Hindu notion of *advaita* means "non-duality" (literally, not-two), applied to Trinity it means in the words of Panikkar that there

[26] Samartha, "Cross and the Rainbow," 110–11.

[27] Ibid., 111. Jung Young Lee, "The Yin-Yang Way of Thinking," in *Asian Christian Theology: Emerging Themes*, ed. Douglas J. Elwood (Philadelphia: Westminster, 1980) 87.

[28] And by many other well-known Asian theologians such as Samartha, "Cross and the Rainbow," 110–11.

[29] Jung Young Lee, *The Theology of Change. A Christian Concept of God in an Eastern Perspective* (Maryknoll, NY: Orbis, 1979), 3–9; Lee, J. Y. Lee, *Patterns of Inner Process* (Secaucus, N.J.: Citadel, 1976), 193–205, ch. 2 (explaining the basis of *yin-yang* in *I Ching*, the foundational Chinese text); Lee, *Trinity in Asian Perspective*, ch. 2.

"are not two realities: God and man (or the world), as outright atheists and outright theists are dialectically driven to maintain. Reality is theandric; it is our way of looking that causes reality to appear to us sometimes under one aspect and sometimes under another because our vision shares in both."[30] Applied to the ancient problem of unity and diversity in the Trinitarian God, the advaitic principle implies that Father and Son are not two, but they are not one either; the Spirit unites and distinguishes them.[31] Says Lee:

> Jesus as the Christ, as both God and man, cannot really be understood in terms of either/or. How can man also be God? In the West we have to speak in terms of paradox or mystery in order to justify the reality of Christ. However, in *yin-yang* terms, he can be thought of as both God and man at the same time. In him God is not separated from man nor man from God. They are in complementary relationship. He is God because of man: he is man because of God.[32]

One strand of Hinduism has described this Mystery as *sat-cit-ananda*, "truth-consciousness-bliss." This is one way of responding to Mystery in a particular setting that differs from that of the early Christian centuries. The Christian doctrine of the Trinity with Jesus Christ as the self-revelation of God is a way of approaching the Mystery in a particular historical context. The terms *Sat* and *Theos* could be regarded as two responses to the same Mystery in two cultural settings, Samartha concludes.

The nature of Mystery is such that any claim on the part of one religious community to have exclusive or unique knowledge becomes inadmissible. Samartha strongly believes that exclusive attitude erects a fence around the Mystery. Exclusiveness also creates dichotomies between different religious communities and leaves little room for the nonrational elements in religious life, such as the mystical, the aesthetic, meditation, and rituals. Furthermore, exclusive claims isolate the community of faith from neighbors of other faiths, creating tensions and disturbing relationships

[30] Raimundo Panikkar, *The Trinity and the Religious Experience of Man: Icon-Person-Mystery* (Maryknoll, NY: Orbis Books/London: Darton, Longman & Todd, 1973) 75. So crucial is the concept of *advaita* in Panikkar that a recent commentator Ewert H. Cousins, has coined a term—"Panikkar's Advaitic Trinitarianism" (in *The Intercultural Challenge of Raimon Panikkar,* ed. Joseph Prabhu [Maryknoll, NY: Orbis, 1996] 119–30; for a helpful explanation of the term *advaitic,* see especially p. 120).

[31] Panikkar, *The Trinity and the Religious Experience of Man,* 62.

[32] Jung Young Lee, "The Yin-Yang Way of Thinking," in *Asian Christian Theology: Emerging Themes*, ed. Douglas J. Elwood (Philadelphia: Westminster, 1980) 87.

within the larger community. But when the distinctiveness of a particular faith is stated in a manner that avoids open or hidden exclusiveness, then meaningful relationships between different communities becomes possible. As a consequence, Christianity in Asia need not be in competition with the whole range of Asian religions, but can instead foster cooperation in the common quest for fullness of life. The central effort of theology for Samartha is to acknowledge the mystery of Christ and explain the meaning of the person and work of Jesus Christ for theology and the church. Out of this commitment arises his theocentric pluralistic view of Christ.

Theocentric Pluralism

Samartha is a more moderate theologian of religion than many other pluralists. Like many of his colleagues Samartha began with the view according to which the "cosmic Christ" is acknowledged by all religions of various kinds. Later in his theological and ecumenical career, however, he moved in the direction of Raimundo Panikkar and others. The Indian theologian Raymond (Raimundo) Panikkar, a Catholic priest from India, whose father was Hindu, spoke of *The Unknown Christ of Hinduism*.[33] In his earlier works, Panikkar still argued that in the historical Jesus the fullness of revelation had occurred even though not in an exclusive way. But in his revised version of *The Unknown Christ of Hinduism* in 1981, he had moved definitely towards a pluralistic version of Christology. In that book he rejects all notions of the superiority or fulfillment of other religions in Christianity.[34] The reason is simply that the world and our subjective experience of the world have radically changed since the Christian doctrine concerning Christ was first formulated. Along with the change of our experience of the world, our understanding should also be modified. Another noted Asian theologian, the Chinese Choan-Seng Song from Taiwan, one of the leading Asian theologians, has attempted to establish bridges between Buddhist and Christian religions. The key to his theology in general is the term "transposition": it is a transposition from the Israel-centered view of history to the view that regards other nations as constructive parts of God's design of history. In that view, Israel's role as the "people of God" was symbolic, illustrating the way God would also deal redemptively with

[33] Raimundo Panikkar, *The Unknown Christ of Hinduism* (London: Darton, Longman & Todd, 1973).

[34] For an exposition and a critical dialogue with Panikkar, see Veli-Matti Kärkkäinen, *Trinity and Religious Pluralism. The Doctrine of the Trinity in Christian Theology of Religions* (Aldershot, Hampshire, UK: Ashgate, 2004) ch. 8.

other nations. Asian nations have their own specific moments of salvation history parallel to Israel's exodus, giving of the law, captivity, and so on. Furthermore, the savior figures of Asian religions parallel the savior figure of the Christian faith, Jesus Christ:

> the expression of Buddha's compassion for the masses in his vows and the way he toiled unselfishly for their emancipation from pain and suffering are not without redemptive significance. Can we not say that Buddha's way is also a part of the drama of salvation which God has acted out fully in the person and work of Jesus Christ?[35]

Consequently, the task of the proclamation of Christ on Asian soil is not so much one of conversion but of growing with Asians in the knowledge and experience of God's saving work in the world. The contribution of Christian mission is to inform the Asian spirituality shaped by Asian cultures and religions with the love of God in Jesus Christ. This helps to change Asian society towards freedom, justice, and love.

With many other pluralists, Samartha became dissatisfied with the idea of "anonymous Christianity" of Karl Rahner and similar ideas that still betray an assumption of the normativity of Christianity over other religions. Samartha has come to question the absolute finality and universal normativity of Christ. The reason for the shift in his thinking is his theocentric approach to theology in general and Christology in particular: before the total mystery of God, no religious figure or no single religion can call itself the final and full word. Samartha's reluctance to name Jesus Christ the final revelation is, interestingly enough, based on his understanding of God, and this makes his pluralism distinctive:

> The Other [God as the Mysterious Other] relativizes everything else. In fact, the willingness to accept such relativization is probably the only real guarantee that one has encountered the Other as ultimately real.[36]

In other words, those who recognize God alone as Absolute will recognize all religions as relative. Clearly, for the mature Samartha, the incarnation is a symbol of the divine rather than a normative historical happening. Also, the death and resurrection of Christ, even though they are revelations of who God is, are not to be treated as a universally valid paradigm. Samartha

[35] Choan-Seng Song, "From Israel to Asia: A Theological Leap," in *Mission Trends,* vol. 3, ed. Gerald H. Anderson and Thomas F. Stransky (New York: Paulist, 1976) 212.

[36] Samartha, *Courage for Dialogue: Ecumenical Issues in Inter-Religious Relationships* (Maryknoll, NY: Orbis, 1982) 151.

has no problem in affirming the humanity and divinity of Jesus Christ, but he is not willing to affirm the orthodox teaching that Christ is God. The reason is simply that "an ontological equation of Jesus Christ and God would scarcely allow any serious discussion with neighbors of other faiths or with secular humanism."[37]

Samartha is also following Panikkar in that even though he relativizes all particular religious expressions and forms in history, the incarnation of Christ included, he is not willing to deny their necessity. The Mysterious Other must confront us through particular mediations. Therefore, Samartha is not naively assuming the equality of all religions. But what he claims is that each and every religion and its figures are limited:

> A particular religion can claim to be decisive for some people, and some people can claim that a particular religion is decisive for them, but no religion is justified in claiming that it is decisive for all.[38]

For Samartha, classical theology runs the danger of "christomonism" in its insistence on the absolute finality of Jesus Christ. It turns Jesus into a kind of "cult figure" over against other religious figures. Instead of christomonistic approach to other religions, Samartha advocates a theocentric approach, which is more consistent with the God-centered message of Jesus of Nazareth. He tries to hold a dynamic between the normative significance of Christ as the revelation of God and the need for openness in relation to other faiths.[39]

No one could have anticipated in advance the presence of God in the life and death of Jesus of Nazareth. There is an incomprehensible dimension to it. That Jesus is the Christ of God is a confession of faith by the Christian community. It does indeed remain normative to Christians everywhere, but to make it "absolutely singular" and to maintain that the meaning of the Mystery is disclosed *only* in one particular person at one particular point, and nowhere else, is to ignore one's neighbors of other faiths who have other points of reference. To make exclusive claims for our particular tradition is not the best way to love our neighbors as ourselves.

This kind of non-normative Christology, in Samartha's view, gives Christians an opportunity to hold their personal commitment to Christ and even their belief in his universal meaning even though not in an exclusive way. For Christians, Christ represents the fulfillment of God's

[37] Samartha, "Cross and the Rainbow," 111.

[38] Samartha, *Courage for Dialogue*, 153.

[39] Samartha, "Cross and the Rainbow," 112.

promises. "But such an announcement will be an enthusiastic *witness* to their own revealer, *not* a denigrating *judgment* about other revealers."[40] Consequently, "whether it is in the attempts to redefine the goals of life or in the effort to meet human needs in the dust and heat of the plains, wherever two or three Hindus and Christians are gathered together in his name, there one need not doubt the presence of the living Christ in the midst of them."[41]

Buddha, *Rama*, and *Krishna*

As already mentioned, one of the main theological works of Samartha is the one in which he studied the interpretations of Christ in the Hindu Renaissance. He himself shows a clear preference for the *advaita* philosophy of *Shankara*. In an interesting analysis, he regards the *Upanishads* as Protestant movements within Hinduism, seeking to liberate the essence of religion from the authority of the church and old-fashioned modes and practices. Samartha sees a parallel to this in what happened with the early church as it struggled its way through the challenge of expressing the gospel in Greek thought forms. By the adoption of the categories of *advaita* in its classical and modern interpretations in the Hindu Renaissance, "Samartha wants to make room for faith in Jesus Christ in Indian pluralism and overcome the traditional claim of Christianity to absoluteness . . . christology and advaita are to be mutual correctives."[42]

In the Indian context, Samartha sees no way to avoid the comparison of Jesus Christ with the other savior figures of Hinduism and other religions of the area. Samartha cites Buddha, *Rama*, and *Krishna* as examples and argues that no credible Christology can be constructed in an Asian context without relating Christ and these figures to each other. Many things unite these three saviors with Christ. In the life and work of each of them, revelation and liberation stand in a direct connection. Each of these savior figures experienced—according to their followers' interpretation—a development from original humanity to later deity.

Rama and *Krishna* are household words in India and are at the center of theistic *bhakti* (devotional religion), at times merging into the larger

[40] Knitter, *No Other Name?*, 159 (italics in the text).

[41] Samartha, "Unbound Christ: Towards Christology in India Today," in *Asian Christian Theology: Emerging Themes*, ed. Douglas J. Elwood (Philadelphia: Westminster, 1980) 146.

[42] Volker Küster, *The Many Faces of Jesus Christ: Intercultural Christology* (Maryknoll, NY: Orbis, 2001) 89.

horizon of *advaita*. The question of the historicity of Rama and Krishna has always been a complex question, but Samartha does not want to give too much attention to that since the quest for the historical foundations of the founder of any religion is a recent phenomenon. The quest of the historical Jesus did not arise until the emergence of the Enlightenment in the eighteenth century; before that the historicity of Jesus of Nazareth was taken for granted.

Samartha believes that it is easier to talk about the Buddha and Christ together, partly because the case for the historicity of each is strong, and partly because both Buddhism and Christianity have transcended their particularities and become universal in the sense that they have found themselves at home in different counties and cultures. For Samartha, the key to the similarities between Buddha and Christ lies in their role as the liberators. During the past few centuries the life and work of Jesus of Nazareth has provided both an inspiration and an example for reformers working for the liberation of the poor and oppressed in Asian society. In more recent years, it is the Buddha who has provided both a shelter (*saranam*) and dynamic source of power to missions of *Dalits* (the lowest class of people, the "class-less"). Millions of *Dalits* have adopted the religion of Buddhism in India and rebelled against the ruling Hindu caste system. Christ can be an inspiration for the followers of Buddha, Samartha argues, but a "Christology of domination" is not good news for Buddhists. In this context, Samartha quotes with approval Pieris, who has argued that an Asian theology of liberation evolves into a Christology that does not compete with Buddhology but complements it by acknowledging that the "one path of liberation of which Christians join Buddhists in their *Gnostic detachment* (or the practice of voluntary poverty) and Buddhists join Christians in their *agapaeic involvement* in the struggle against forced poverty. . . . It is only at the end of the path, as at Emmaus, that the path itself will be recognized by name (Luke 24:31)."[43]

With regard to his consideration of these four different savior figures—Buddha, Krishna, Rama, and Christ—Samartha argues that the theory of multiple *avatara* (Hindu term for incarnated gods or other significant persons) seems to be theologically the most accommodating attitude in a pluralistic setting, one that permits recognizing both the Mystery of God and the freedom of people to respond to divine initiatives in different ways at different times.

[43] Samartha, *One Christ—Many Religions*, 126.

A Western Interlocutor Enters the Dialogue

One of the most exciting developments in current globalizing theological reflection is the desire to approach the mystery of Christ from different angles and viewpoints. There is a need to encounter the Other in a mutually honoring and learning dialogue. The present book represents that kind of dialogue between Korean and other Asian theologians as well as several Western theologians. I am a Western male theologian and as such limited to and defined by my own context. The fact that I have lived and taught in Asia and am fluent in one of the Asian languages does not make me an insider. Yet I can do much about helping myself overcome some of the built-in limitations and barriers by opening up myself to a dialogue. I find the approach of one of the contributors to this volume, Jürgen Moltmann very helpful. In his *Trinity and the Kingdom of God*, Moltmann freely "recognizes the conditions and limitations of his own position, and the relativity of his own particular environment."[44] This acknowledgment, however, is an asset rather than an obstacle for doing a more inclusive theology. Speaking of himself in the third person, Moltmann remarks: "For him this means a critical dissolution of naïve, self-centered thinking. Of course he is a European, but European theology no longer has to be Euro*centric*. Of course, he is a man, but theology no longer has to be *androcentric*. Of course he is living in the 'first world,' but the theology which he is developing does have to reflect the ideas of the dominating nations."[45] Acknowledging the situatedness and particularity of one's own approach to doing theology, in this case Trinitarian theology, frees the theologian to enter a dialogue. Moltmann, thus, claims that "…truth is to be found in unhindered dialogue." [46]

The remark by Miroslav Volf, Moltmann's student, who comes from the war-stricken Balkans and has developed a politically sensitive Social Trinity to help negotiate our fear of and rejection of the Other, is worth hearing:[47]

44 Jürgen Moltmann, *The Trinity and the Kingdom of God: The Doctrine of God*, trans. Margaret Kohl (San Francisco: Harper & Row, 1981) xii.

45 Ibid., xii (emphases in the original).

46 Ibid., xiii.

47 Miroslav Volf, "When Gospel and Culture Intersect: Notes on the Nature of Christian Difference," in *Pentecostalism in Context: Essays in Honor of William W. Menzies*, ed. Wonsuk Ma and Robert P. Menzies (Sheffield: Sheffield Academic, 1997) 233. According to Volf, liberal accomodationism, postliberal traditionalism, or sectarian retreat are all unsatisfactory ways of accounting for the cultural challenge. See 233–36.

> Christian difference is always a complex and flexible network of small and large refusals, divergences, subversions, and more or less radical alternative proposals, surrounded by the acceptance of many cultural givens. There is no single correct way to relate to a given culture as a whole, or even to its dominant thrust; there are only numerous ways of accepting, transforming, or replacing various aspects of a given culture from within.

With these insights in mind, let me join the conversation with Stanley Samartha and some other Asian theologians mentioned above and suggest respectfully some challenges and corrections. Samartha has done a service to Christian theology and missiology by challenging its traditional exclusivism. He has both taken notice of the changing, more tolerant atmosphere of the contemporary world and the pressing need of religions to find a peaceful co-existence in a rapidly globalizing world. Through his extensive writings and wide ecumenical engagement he has contributed significantly to the emergence of the discussion about plurality to the forefront of theology and religious studies. In a most helpful way, he has made theology speak to social and political issues such as poverty and injustice. This is all good.

However, there are also challenges and problems in a pluralistic Christology such as his. It seems like this kind of pluralistic Christology emerged out of practical encounters with other religions rather than an extensive theological reflection. In response to the pluralistic Christology championed by Samartha and others, I will present theses for a Christian theology of Christ and religions in the pluralistic context of Asia that I think are conducive towards developing a culturally and theologically sensitive approaches:

First, the truth question of religion cannot be compromised for the purposes of pluralism. It seems to me Samartha and many other Asian theologians too easily resort to the *advaita* or *yin-yang* principle to push to the margins the necessity to pursue the question of truth of theological statements. No other contemporary theologian has argued more clearly for the necessity of the claim for truth in religions in general and Christology in particular than Wolfhart Pannenberg.[48]

According to him, in all religions, beginning from the ancient religions and culminating in the plurality of contemporary religions, the dominant theme is the search for universal truth. Pannenberg rejects the older approach to the study of religions in which there was a search for a

[48] See Wolfhart Pannenberg, "Religious Pluralism and Conflicting Truth Claims," in *Christian Uniqueness Reconsidered*, ed. Gavin D'Costa (Maryknoll, NY: Orbis, 1990) 96–116.

"common essence." For example, John Hick's view of a new, "pluralistic" religion that shares several elements from existing religions and at the same time cannot be identified with any of them is foreign to Pannenberg.[49]

Instead, for Pannenberg, religions represent rival conceptions of the ultimate truth. In this sense, his method takes the risk of placing all theological principles on the open market of public accountability.[50]

> For a "truth" that would be simply my truth and would not at least claim to be universal and valid for every human being could not remain true even for me. This consideration explains why Christians cannot but try to defend the claim of their faith to be true.[51]

Denying the universal truth of religions' claims to truth would finally lead to the very denial of religions. It is the recent consensus among researchers of religion(s) that the essence of religions is to postulate some sort of absolute truth claim. Religion by its very nature deals with the ultimate issues of life and death and it might not be meaningful to talk about religion without such claims.[52]

> Without [this] element of truth claim, the teachings of religions would not make sense, since the question of the truth is an essential aspect of religions. If a religion does not talk about the ultimate things, but rather talks about the more superficial, that religion most probably cannot be regarded as a genuine religion. From the perspective of metatheology, the conceptions of religions concerning the truth vary significantly, but still the right to present a truth claim is an irrevocable right for any religion.[53]

[49] For an assessment of Hick's pluralistic proposal in light of the Asian context, see V.-M. Kärkkäinen, "'Universe of Faiths': Theological Challenges of John Hick's pluralism," Dharma Deepika [Delhi, India] (January–June, 2003) 5–16.

[50] Carl E. Braaten, "The Place of Christianity Among the World Religions: Wolfhart Pannenberg's Theology of Religion and the History of Religions," in *The Theology of Wolfhart Pannenberg: Twelve American Critiques with an Autobiographical Response*, ed. Carl E. Braaten and Philip Clayton (Minneapolis: Augsburg, 1988) 287–312, esp. 294.

[51] Wolfhart Pannenberg, *Anthropology in Theological Perspective* (Philadelphia: Westminster, 1985) 15.

[52] See further Wolfhart Pannenberg, *Systematic Theology*, vol. 1 (Grand Rapids: Eerdmans, 1991) chs. 2 and 3 especially; see also Charles Taliaferro, *Contemporary Philosophy of Religion* (Malden, MA: Blackwell, 1998) 206, 236.

[53] Matti T. Amnell, *Uskontojen Universumi: John Hickin uskonnollisen pluralismin haaste ja siitä käyty keskustelu*, Suomalaisen Teologisen Kirjallisuusseuran Julkaisuja 217 (Helsinki: STK, 1999) 64–65, my translation.

To argue with Samartha that the truth claim for Christ only applies to those inside the Christian household is a self-contradictory notion: truth cannot be true only to some people. It either is true or is not. It is a disservice to Christian mission vis-à-vis other religions to try to soften the encounter by a reference to a "partial" truth. At the same time I acknowledge the approach of Pannenberg and his followers smacks of both modernist foundationalism and typical Western rationalism.[54] Acknowledging that does not of course make his theology invalid, it just helps us put it into a proper context. What would happen if these two traditions, a strongly rationalistic approach such as that of Pannenberg and a pluralistically oriented approach of Samartha and likes would engage in a critical dialogue. Those encounters are yet to happen in a new theological context of the third millennium.

Even several Asian religions, such as Buddhism and Hinduism, while they have been more tolerant and pluralistic than Christianity and Islam, still regard themselves as the true religions.[55] The mystical nature of many Eastern religions does not translate into an indifference to the truth question as pluralistic Christologies imply. Tolerance and denial of the truth claims of one's religion are not identical questions, but pluralism does not make a clear distinction between these two. Even though tolerance is a highly respected characteristic, there is no neutrality in religious claims. To deny the right to absolute truth claims would mean changing the concept of religions as they are understood currently, and that most probably will not happen.

Second, the biblical testimony of Jesus' claim for a unique relationship to the Father and the coming of the kingdom has to be affirmed differently than does pluralism. The theocentric Christology of Samartha claims that Jesus of Nazareth shied away from accepting any claim for his uniqueness in his desire to serve God's kingdom. This is an old claim going back to Classical Liberalism's quest of the historical Jesus; it makes Jesus an honorable servant of God, but less than the unique savior. The problem is that theologically it makes the whole idea of the coming of God's kingdom dubious: in the New Testament, the coming of the kingdom is dependent

[54] I don't think Pannenberg is necessarily a foundationalist even though he calls for a rationalist approach to theology. A helpful discussion can be found in F. Leron Shults, *The Postfoundationalist Task of Theology: Wolfhart Pannenberg and the New Theological Rationality* (Grand Rapids: Eerdmans, 1999).

[55] For an insightful study focusing on contemporary neo-Hinduism and Tibetan Buddhism, by a leading Roman Catholic theologian of religions, see Gavin D'Costa, *The Meeting of Religions and the Trinity* (Maryknoll, NY: Orbis, 2000) chs. 2, 3.

on the person and work of Jesus of Nazareth. Jesus not only accepted the claim for a unique relationship to his Father; that claim finally led to his rejection by the religious authorities of his day. To eliminate this central teaching of the New Testament "demythologizes" the early Christian message into an ethical teaching without a claim to universal truth and saving force.[56]

Third, while there are notable similarities between the savior figures of various religions, as Samartha and other Asian theologians have highlighted, it is not fair either with regard to Asian religions or Christianity to relativize their claims for uniqueness. Apparent similarities on the surface level do not necessarily validate the claim of the "common essence" of all religions that Arnold Toynbee and others have held in the past. One could argue either way: Either that regardless of apparent differences on the surface level, the deep structure of religions is still the same ("common essence") or that while on the surface religions seem to be similar (e.g., they have similar types of prayers) the deep structures do differ considerably. A merely phenomenological survey of religions does not give us a definite answer here. The lesson is clear: the role of the savior figure in religions, for example Jesus Christ in Christianity, cannot be determined on the basis of apparent similarities or differences but on the basis of the theological structure of each religion. The claim of biblical and orthodox Christianity for the absolute uniqueness of Jesus Christ cannot be judged on the basis of phenomenological similarities between various savior figures.

Fourth, what one believes about Jesus Christ determines to a large extent one's beliefs about God. Classical Christianity argues for the knowledge of the Father only in the person and work of Jesus Christ. If one argues for a pluralistic Christology, as does for example John Hick, who moved from God-centered Christology finally to "Reality-centered pluralism" (according to which no God as such exists; what we call "god[s]" is the "Ultimate Reality"), one is left with a vague view of God. In Christian theology, access to the conception of God is in and through Jesus Christ. Pluralistic Christology sooner or later deprives us of the concept of God in the classical sense of the term or it leaves us with a merely formal concept of God as in the latest writings of Hick (the only thing you can say about "G/god" is that "G/god is," but you cannot identify any divine attributes

[56] For a fuller argumentation, see Kärkkäinen, *Trinity and Religious Pluralism*, esp. 169–74.

or substance); when that development is taken to its extreme, one wonders if it still makes any sense to talk about "religion."[57]

Fifth, the concept of dialogue as used in pluralistic approaches needs a more nuanced definition. Dialogue does not necessarily mean giving up one's truth claims, nor should it. An honest dialogue with a predetermined idea of denying one's own and the counterpart's truth claim is not presuppositionless as is often believed. Here again Pannenberg's approach seems more relevant. Pannenberg comes to the dialogue table with the adherents of other religions with a set of commitments, the most important of which is that there is one, unified, coherent truth to be searched for. Also, he contends that the Christian view of God is superior to the views of not only ancient religions but also of the living faiths of our day. Unpromising as this kind of attitude might sound to most pluralists of our age, Pannenberg's theology of religion in fact does carry a lot of potential for a sustained dialogue. The purpose of the dialogue is not meant to soften the differences of religions and consequently to blur the importance of the search for a unified truth. That religion which has the potential of offering an explanation of the experience of the world in the most satisfactory way will most probably prevail or at least offer itself as the most viable religion. As Pannenberg has insisted, the history of religions is the arena in which competing truth claims finally show to what extent they are able to illumine our experience of the world. The religion that finally is judged as able to cast light on the whole experience of human life and world history most probably will prevail. In the final analysis, "dialogue" and "mission" are not contradictory: genuine mission is always a dialogue, but a dialogue with certain convictions. Its aim is to present a truth claim for the consideration and affirmation of the other party. It cannot be, and it never is, without a certain agenda and presuppositions. Christian mission from the beginning has always survived best in the marketplace of competing religions as the person and work of Jesus Christ has been offered as the Way, the Truth, and the Life for all men and women. Again, one needs to be reminded of an overly optimistic and somewhat naïve approach of Pannenberg. While researchers of religions may approach the dialogue table with mindset of his, few, if any, followers of religions would be mainly interested in or primarily focused on a "neutral" quest for the truth.

Sixth—and I think this is crucial to the agenda of *minjung* theologies—the perennial question of the relationship between particularity and

[57] Some theologians of religion, for example Wilfred C. Smith, have in fact argued for the "end of religion"; instead of talking any more about "God," they prefer the term "Reality." This is a logical and unavoidable conclusion of extreme liberalism.

universality (whatever those terms may mean in a postmodern setting) needs to be defined in a more nuanced way than has been done in the theology of religions in general and in many Asian theologies of religions in particular. According to Vinoth Ramachandra, a Sri Lankan theologian, the particularity of Christ is "a particularity that God takes seriously in his dealings with his creatures." God chose a nation to be the bearer of the cosmic history to the rest, and one mediator to include all. Thus, incarnation is geared toward universality. Particularity is for the purpose of universality, not exclusion. Therefore, Christian faith has always been a missionary faith. Missionary urgency flows from the very logic of the incarnation, death and resurrection of the Messiah of all peoples.[58] As an Asian theologian, Ramachandra further argues that the normativeness of Jesus, inherent in the Christian trinitarian faith, rather than being something foreign imposed on Asian religions, in fact, "safeguards some of the legitimate concerns of contemporary Asian theologians."[59] He claims that better than the major Asian religions, Christianity takes seriously the cause of the poor, fully endorses the equality of all persons created in the image of God, and celebrates humility and self-sacrificial life and service, among other things. The "gospel humanity" results in the creation of a new human community that celebrates plurality under one God. Continuing dialogue is needed and badly to clarify these issues.

Even when some critical theological remarks should be offered, we need to affirm the basic intention of Samartha, Panikkar, many *minjung* and other Asian theologian to attempt to transplant the person and work of Jesus Christ in Asian soil. Otherwise, we can never even come close to "the freedom to encounter Jesus the savior in the depth of the spirituality that sustains Asians in their long march of suffering and hope."[60]

Asia's struggle for humanization faces enormous challenges. Any authentic and genuine Asian Christology cannot help but delve deeply into the suffering and wounds of Asian people. Chi-Ha Kim, a Korean poet, wrote a play titled *The Gold-Crowned Jesus*. The scene is set in front of a Catholic Church, where there is a statue of Jesus, made of cement. Christ is wearing a golden crown. Below the statue, on a cold winter day, beggars are lying. Looking at the gold-crowned Jesus, one of them wonders what might be the relevance of such a savior figure for a beggar with no place to

[58] Vinoth Ramachandra, *The Recovery of Mission* (Eugene, OR: Wipf and Stock, 2002) ch. 7, quotation on 233.

[59] Ibid., 216.

[60] Song, *Theology from the Womb of Asia*, 3.

go. And after all, how can a Jesus made of cement speak or feel anything? In the midst of his anguish, the beggar feels something wet, like small drops falling on his head. When he looks up, he sees the cement Jesus weeping. Noticing that the golden crown might be of value, the beggar is about to take it for himself, when he hears the voice of Jesus: "Take it, please! For too long a time have I been imprisoned in this cement. Eventually you have come and made me open my mouth. You have saved me."

8

Dietrich Bonhoeffer Seen from Asian Minjung Theology and the Fourth Eye of Socially Engaged Buddhism

Paul S. Chung

ASIAN contextual theology was born out of an experience of faith in the midst of political and religious worldviews. In this contextual theology, Christian theology is reformulated and contextualized in an encounter with socio-political injustice, as well as with the religious-cultural spirituality of the world religions. Minjung theology in South Korea was inspired by and finds its echo in the theology of Dietrich Bonhoeffer.

Ahn Byung-Mu (1922–1996), the founding father of minjung theology, updated and radicalized Bonhoeffer's theological direction with respect to the poor and marginalized in the Korean context. Bonhoeffer left an indelible imprint upon the development of minjung theology, which is interested in recognizing the ungodly as a theological locus and in reinterpreting the underside of history in light of those who suffer.

Furthermore, there are many eminent figures in Buddhism who contribute their own spirituality and wisdom toward the transformation of the human consciousness and of society. For example, Thich Nhat Hanh, a Buddhist monk from Vietnam, championed the peace movement. His teaching of mindfulness is not a flight from the world into an individualistic practice of meditation, but an effort to live consciously in the present.

According to him, "if you are awake you cannot do otherwise than act compassionately to help relieve suffering you see around you. So Buddhism must be engaged in the world. If it is not engaged it is not Buddhism."[1] Buddhist soteriology and ethics can be reoriented and re-

[1] Ken Jones, *The New Social Face of Buddhism: A Call to Action* (Boston: Wisdom, 2003)

interpreted to address the comprehensive reality of *dukkha* (suffering) in social, political and economic injustice and violence, as well as in ecological and environmental degradation.

Socially engaged Buddhism extends the spiritual awakening of third-eye of enlightenment toward a fourth-eye of praxis in compassion in a socio-existential manner. It extends its public engagement in caring for the needy, protesting structural social injustice and the exploitation of environment, and envisioning a socially just and ecologically sustainable society.

In this regard, Asian minjung theology and engaged Buddhism, together, protest against the discrimination of the oppressed, and share solidarity with them. The *prajna* (wisdom) and compassion of the Bodhisattva does not contradict the way of Jesus in company with the Jewish poor (*ochlos*).

In this paper I shall attempt to analyze Bonhoeffer's inspiration of Ahn Byung-Mu, and construct possible learning points between Asian minjung theology and engaged Buddhism in which Bonhoeffer's insight is appreciated and contextualized. Let me first deal with Bonhoeffer's influence upon the development of an Asian theological reflection on Jesus and the *ochlos*-minjung.

Dietrich Bonhoeffer and a Theology for the Others

Bonhoeffer's uniqueness lies in his christocentric inclusivity, in terms of connecting to those who stand outside the Christian church. Bonhoeffer claims that the world has come of age through Jesus Christ (LPP. 342).[2] On the basis of the Gospel and in light of Christ we are supposed to affirm the world's coming of age. From a christological perspective, the godlessness of the world is full of promise, even in its stance against religion and the church. The godless of the world is closer to Christ than to the hopeless godlessness in religious and Christian clothing (E. 104).

This thought became more explicit in his statement from prison: "The world that has come of age is more godless, and perhaps for that very reason nearer to God, than the world before its coming of age" (LPP. 362). Therefore, the church's service to the world consists in being there

179.

[2] LPP refers to Dietrich Bonhoeffer, *Letters & Papers from Prison*, ed. Eberhard Bethge (New York: Macmillan, 1971). E refers to Dietrich Bonhoeffer, *Ethics*, trans. Neville Horton Smith (New York: Macmillan, 1955).

for others as Jesus is there for others. "The church is the church only when it exists for others" (LPP. 382).

Bonhoeffer's solidarity christology remains deeply connected to others who do not confess the name of Christ. Christianity's particular confession to Jesus Christ is, in fact, connected with Christ's inclusivism. The claim to exclusiveness apart from Christ's universalism leads to fanaticism, while the claim to universalism apart from Christ's particularity leads to the secularization of the church of Jesus Christ, argues Bonhoeffer. He supports those who suffer for the sake of a righteous cause, even if this cause has little to do with the confession of Christ's name (E. 62).

Bonhoeffer's non-religious interpretation of Bible speaks out against people in their excessive attachment to the power of God in the world. Herein, God is understood as the *deus ex machina.* In some ancient Greek dramas, an insoluble crisis is solved by the intervention of God, which is often brought about on stage by an elaborate piece of equipment. This god, from a machine, is literally translated as *deux machina.*

However, according to the Bible, people in distress are related to the powerlessness and suffering of God. Bonhoeffer's foundational thesis reads:

> Only the suffering God can help. To that extent we may say that the development towards the world's coming of age . . . has done away with a false conception of God, opens up a way of seeing the God of the Bible, who wins power and space in the world by his weakness. This will probably be the starting-point for our 'secular interpretation' (LPP. 361).

The secular and worldly interpretation, which aims at demythologizing the power of the God of religion, offers a basis to support and recognize human maturity and autonomy. God calls us to this recognition. The reality of our coming of age leads us to live without God. The God with us is the One who abandons us (Mark 15:34). The God before whom we stand is the One who does not need our working hypothesis of God. Before God, and with God, we live without God. God allows Godself to be driven out of the world on to the cross. God is powerless and weak in the world. And Christ helps us not by means of his omnipotence, but by means of his weakness and suffering. Therefore, "we have to live in the world *etsi deus non daretur*" (LPP. 360).

Bonhoeffer's *theologia crucis* assumes a religionless form and shows the remarkable solidarity of Jesus with the working class:

> [T]he working class may distinguish between Jesus and his Church; he is not the guilty party. Jesus, yes; Christ, no! Jesus can then become the idealist, the socialist. What does it mean when the proletarian says, in his world of distrust: 'Jesus was a good man?' It means that nobody needs to mistrust him. The proletarian does not say, 'Jesus is God'. But when he says, 'Jesus is a good man', he is saying more than the bourgeois says when he repeats, 'Jesus is God'.[3]

What is at stake is for Bonhoeffer to protest against bourgeois self-satisfaction, or "a convenient reversal of the Gospel" (E. 64). At the same time, Bonhoeffer's idea of arcane discipline prevents this-worldliness from dissolving the Christian Gospel into secularity. His idea of arcane discipline, which takes a silent and hidden form of being Christian, finds its expression explicitly in the prayer and righteous praxis of the core community of minjung.

Jesus and Ochlos-Minjung in Light of the Social Biography

Bonhoeffer's view from below, i.e., "from the perspective of the outcast, the suspects, the maltreated, the powerless, the oppressed, the reviled—in short, from the perspective of those who suffer" (LPP. 17) fired the theological imagination of Ahn Byung-Mu to such an extent that he critically took issue with Western Christology in terms of Jesus' identification with the *minjung* (*min* meaning *the poor* and *jung* meaning *mass*). Furthermore, Bonhoeffer's Christology in solidarity with the working class motivate Ahn to develop a Christology in company with the *ochlos* from the standpoint of the social biography of Jesus.

Ahn Byung-Mu, in his study of the Gospel of Mark, points to a special category of people called the *ochlos*. The *ochlos* were not just "people" (that would have been *laos*), but the unorganized crowd that was constantly around Jesus. They were differentiated from the disciples and the ruling class. Like the despised tax collectors or those considered sinners, they were engaged in occupations that were not approved of in civil life. Furthermore, they were sick in various ways, and sickness was considered to be a consequence of sin. Jesus accepted them, however, without reservation. Ahn interprets the biblical term *ochlos* as the Korean word minjung.

Because of his solidarity with the *ochlos* and his purification of the Temple, Jesus was eliminated by being put to death. Minjung appear in

[3] Dietrich Bonhoeffer, *Christ The Center* (New York: Harper & Row, 1978) 35.

various forms in biblical texts. The minjung are the oppressed people of Egypt, whose liberation is narrated in the story of the Exodus. The Hebrew word *am ha' aretz* (people of the land) first denoted the landlord blessed by God. Since the Babylonian invasion the meaning of the term changed, and it became associated with people of the lower class. Later in rabbinic Judaism, the word *am ha' aretz* was redefined as the sinners who stand outside the system of the law. These people were alienated from the Jewish community even though they were Israelites. In Rabbinic Judaism *am ha' aretz* is referred to as "the poor and the powerless class which was despised and marginalized."[4]

In the Gospel of Mark, the word *ochlos* is used to refer to the crowd around Jesus rather than the word *laos,* which usually denotes the people of God, or people of Israel. Tax collectors and sinners at the house of Levi (Mark 2:13) gathered around Jesus. The crowd of the religiously forsaken, the economically alienated, and the politically oppressed were the *ochlos* who followed Jesus. Jesus demonstrated a friendly attitude toward the *ochlos* by accepting and supporting them without reservation. He promised the Kingdom of God to them as their future.[5] Jesus is portrayed as one of them—sharing their same fate and destiny. This is the true meaning of Christ's kenosis and suffering. What is at issue for Ahn is the suffering God, which requires God in human form. This God contradicts the all-mighty God as *deus ex machina.*[6]

At this juncture, there is a parallel between Ahn's reflection on God in human form and that of Bonhoeffer. According to the latter, God as a working hypothesis or as a stop-gap becomes superfluous in respect to the maturity of religionless people. The encounter with Jesus Christ, which is the basis for the transformation of all human life, becomes meaningful in that Jesus is for others.

This being for others is, according to Bonhoeffer, characterized by God's omnipotence, omniscience, and omnipresence. Christian faith is understood as a participation in the being of Jesus for others (in the incarnation, the cross, and the resurrection). The authentic meaning of God's transcendence must be found in God in human form, the one for others,

4 Byung-Mu Ahn, "Jesus and the Minjung in the Gospel of Mark," in *Minjung Theology: People as the Subject of History*, ed. Commission on Theological Concerns, Christian Conference of Asia (Maryknoll: Orbis, 1983) 150.

5 Ibid., 142.

6 Byung-Mu Ahn, *Draussen vor dem Tor: Kirche und Minjung in Korea,* ed. Winfried Glur (Goettingen: Vandenhoeck & Ruprecht, 1986) 14.

which is to say, "the Crucified, the man who lives out of the transcendent" (LPP. 382).

Ahn Byung-Mu quoted Bonhoeffer's insight approvingly in order to expand the existence for others toward the life of the oppressed and the poor.[7] Inspired by Bonhoeffer's statement that "the transcendental is not infinite and unattainable tasks, but the neighbor who is within reach in any given situation" (LPP. 381),[8] Ahn continues,

> We, the Christians and non-Christians in South-Korea live like Bonhoeffer at his time in the same situation. We experience suffering in hope, which is directed toward the future. Thereby the door is open for the 'transcendental'. As Bonhoeffer states, 'we suffer without God, but we live before God without knowing'.[9]

From this perspective, Ahn draws a consequence from his christological proposal. Regarding the dialectical unity of fulfillment (*pleroma,* John 1:14 or Luke 2:40) and emptiness (*kenosis,* Phil 2:7), Ahn places emphasis on the latter, contending that "identification or being for the others is identical with the word 'self-emptying'."[10] This self-emptying existence for others is compared to the nothingness of Taoism or the *sunyata* of Buddhism. The Buddhist or Taoist idea of nothingness is evaluated from the Christian perspective only in a negative sense. But Ahn retorts,

> although there is negation within Buddhism or Taoism, in reality it moves toward the positive. What is at issue is the attitude of total commitment for the others in order to fulfill a total expectation and readiness, and to make oneself fulfilled through others.[11]

Ahn's interest in Buddhism is based on its understanding of personhood and community. For Ahn, Jesus is a representative of the social history of the *ochlos*, rather than merely an individual person. Ahn's christology is an inclusive identity christology in which Jesus identifies himself with the least among the people (Matt 25:40). Ahn's provocative thesis title, "Jesus and the *Ochlos* in Galilee," is based on his profound reflection on the minjung who bear the sins of the powers that be. Jesus is involved in their life and destiny as a participant. When we sing "Thou Who Bearest the Sins of

[7] Ibid., 37.

[8] Ibid.

[9] Ibid., 37–8

[10] Ibid., 38.

[11] Ibid., 39.

the World," we are reminded of the vicarious and representative suffering of the servant of God (Isaiah 53).

In updating the Hebrew manner of expressing relationality between the individual and the community, Ahn appropriates the Buddhist principle of relationality between the individual person, Siddharta, and the universal, Buddha, from the perspective of the socio-biography of the *ochlos*. This implies a non-dual relationship between Jesus and the minjung, and avoids falling into monistic identification. This non-dual notion underlines and distinguishes Ahn's minjung epistemology from a Western notion of personhood. Given this fact, Jesus can be conceived of only in his relationship first with the Jewish *ochlos* and then with Christians and Gentiles (in other words, the inhabitants of Palestine, without home or rights in 70 C.E., after the destruction of Jerusalem).[12]

Thich Nhat Hanh and Engaged Buddhism

In sharing Ahn's interest in Jesus and the minjung, the Buddhist-Christian relationship can be explored and developed within minjung theology toward cooperation with the engaged Buddhists for social justice, the peace movement, and ecological pro-existence. Some scholars are committed to actualizing the liberative dimension of S_n (Zen in Korean) with respect to the life of the minjung.

What underlies Thich Nhat Hanh's core vision is the *Heart Sutra*. The *Heart Sutra* is one of the early Prajnaparamita sutras. The fundamental principle of this sutra is that all things inter-are. To be means to inter-be. Inspired by the Bodhisattva Avalokita (*Kwan Yin* in Chinese, *Quan Am* in Vietnamese, *Kannon* in Japanese, *Kwanum* in Korean), who says that "form is emptiness, emptiness is form," or "form does not differ from emptiness, emptiness does not differ from form,"[13] Thich Nhat Hanh interprets the principle of inter-being in a way that reveals emptiness as being empty of something. Inter-being is to be empty of a separate substance, which, in turn, is full of everything.

In *The Awakening of Faith*, which is one of the important classics of Chinese Hua-yen Buddhism, the non-dual principle of form and emptiness is likened to the totality of water and wave:

[12] Jürgen Moltmann, *Experiences in Theology: Ways and Forms of Christian Theology*, trans. Margaret Kohl (Minneapolis: Fortress, 2000) 258–59.

[13] Thich Nhat Hanh, *The Heart of Understanding: Commentaries on the Prajnaparamita Heart Sutra*, ed. Peter Levitt (Berkeley: Parallax, 1988) 1.

> This may be illustrated by [the simile of] the water and the waves which are stirred up in the ocean. Here the water can be said to be identical [in one sense] and not-identical [in another sense] with the waves. The waves are stirred up by the wind, but the water remains the same. When the wind ceases, the motion of the waves subsides; but the water remains the same.[14]

Form (Wave) does not differ from emptiness (water), as emptiness does not differ from form. This insight leads Thich Nhat Hanh to take seriously a dimension which is full of everything, full of life, instead of presupposing absolute nothingness. This is in contrast to Masao Abe, at the Kyoto school in Japan,[15] who thinks about the reality of *sunyata*.

This radical sense of interdependence and interpenetration is rooted in the earliest Mahayana sutras and reached its climax in later Hua-yen Buddhism in China. This principle becomes the foundation for Thich Nhat Hanh's whole vision and practice regarding world occurrences. The Buddhist principle of dependent co-arising is socially appropriated and practically actualized with respect to the affairs of the world in which we live. Insight into emptiness leads to the overcoming of all discrimination.

The Principle of Inter-being and the Social System

In applying the principle of inter-being to social systems, it can be understood how a poor girl is pressured to become a prostitute because of the entire structure, which supports wealthy families at the cost of the poor. "Wealth is made of non-wealth elements, and poverty is made by non-poverty elements."[16] In light of the principle of inter-being, we are challenged to see the prostitute in the non-prostitute people and the non-prostitute people in the prostitute. Observing the life of the young prostitute includes penetrating the reality of the non-prostitute people. Affluent society exists in interdependence with the society that is deprived of everything.[17]

To eliminate one side or the other would lead one to spurn suffering by violating both sides. However, genuine breakthroughs in politics or social justice demand a more inclusive, non-dual framework that does justice

[14] Asvaghosa, *The Awakening of Faith: The Classic Exposition of Mahayana Buddhism*, trans. Teitaro Suzuki (Mineola: Dover, 2003) 67.

[15] Cf. Masao Abe, *Zen and Western Thought*, ed. William R. Lafleur (Honolulu: University of Hawaii Press, 1985) 158.

[16] Hanh, *Heart of Understanding*, 33.

[17] Ibid., 32–3.

to both sides. For Thich Nhat Hanh, the transformation of our consciousness becomes the indispensable basis for our engagement for peace and social justice in the world.

Emancipation comes from the transformation of the poor people's consciousness by penetrating into the nature of inter-being. Through this transformation, the poor will know that they bear the pain of the whole world. This is the principle of interpenetration, which reveals that everything contains everything else.[18] The overcoming of a discriminating consciousness prepares people for perfect freedom and peace. The nature of inter-being—co-existence, or mutual interdependence—is implied in each word of the insight that the *Diamond Sutra* offers. Like Jesus' teaching—"But when you give alms, do not let your left hand know what your right hand is doing" (Matt 6:3)—this principle wisely instructs that the right hand help the left hand in a formless way.[19]

With the principle of inter-being in mind, the Sutra concludes with a mantra encouraging and challenging us to go to the other shore from the world of suffering to perfect freedom and liberation. In chanting the mantra, one travels the path which leads to liberation and brings about liberation for all beings. "Gone, gone, gone all the way over, everyone gone over to the other shore, enlightenment, svaha! [like "Welcome!" or "Hallelujah!"]"[20]

Buddhism and Christianity in a Mutual Learning Process

Let me compare and explore minjung theology and engaged Buddhism for mutual learning. What is at issue in minjung theology is how to transform the consciousness of society in respect to the massive suffering of the poor and their spiritual significance. The false consciousness of the dominant economic and political system must be eliminated so that we can appraise the actual situation in the world. Learning to see history from the reality of the sufferer, Bonhoeffer inspires minjung theology to take issue with the ideological apparatus that presents the *status quo* as reasonable and acceptable. Therefore the critique of ideology is the first step on the road to liberation in accordance with the transformation of consciousness for minjung theology.

[18] Ibid., 39.

[19] Thich Nhat Hanh, *The Diamond That Cuts Through Illusion: Commentaries on the Prajnaparamita Diamond Sutra* (Berkeley: Parallax, 1992) 37.

[20] Hanh, *Heart of Understanding*, 50.

In the Buddhist tradition, the principle of becoming aware of suffering and ideology flows from the First Noble Truth of the Buddha and the Buddhist principle of non-attachment. Meditation helps us to cope with suffering, leading to a realization of the First Noble Truth. The principle of inter-being functions as a critique of ideology, challenging the absolutization of any doctrine or perspective, including a Buddhist one. At this juncture, minjung theology needs to consider the Buddhist insight of non-discrimination and non-attachment, which helps distance minjung theology from any tendency to romanticize itself, and precludes any type of apocalyptic fanaticism, so called "minjung messianism."

According to minjung hermeneutics, the Bible does not provide the answer; rather, the answer depends on the reader's question. The hermeneutics of minjung do not endorse Christian doctrine or a third eye of non-commitment, but encourage a co-participation of the reader in the biblical witness to God's event in the world. At this juncture, there is a parallel between a minjung hermeneutic and a Buddhist hermeneutic. As Thich Nhat Hanh states,

> as reality can only be lived and experienced, Buddhist doctrine would never have as an aim the description of reality; the doctrine serves only as a method, as a guide, to the practitioner in his experience of this reality.[21]

In the vision of inter-being, according to Thich Nhat Hanh, all discrimination is to be overcome. In light of dependent co-arising, the Buddhist nondiscriminatory acceptance of good and evil alike exposes a limitation in minjung theology that is more partisan, oriented toward class struggle and social progress. However, Jesus' sensitivity to the criminals and the others is remarkable. According to Bonhoeffer, in Jesus Christ there is no God without the world, or world without God. In Christ's reconciliation, "the abyss of the love of God encompasses even the most abysmal godlessness of the world (E. 72)." Nevertheless, the reality of evil will not be solved until God's final and universal redemption. God's prolepsis would be a counter-thesis to the present-centrism of Buddhism.

For minjung theology, a protest is made against colonized consciousness and the powers and principalities which dominate contemporary society. This praxis of transformation is rooted in the vision of Christ among the poor as presented in the parable of the Last Judgment in Matthew 25 or in the parable of the Good Samaritan. The Good Samaritan is not

[21] Thich Nhat Hanh, *Zen Keys*, trans. Albert and Jean Low (Garden City: Anchor, 1974) 47.

exemplified as the symbolic representative of Jesus Christ, but reversely the robbed one in the street represents where Jesus Christ is present. The robbed, when seen as the lowest of the low in the context of the Last Judgment in Matthew 25, is identified with Jesus Christ. This standpoint expands the horizon of *theologia crucis* in regards to the reality of suffering, taking serious Jesus' statement: "The publicans and the harlots go into the kingdom of heaven before you (Matt 21:31)" (E. 62).

For Thich Nhat Hanh, the transformation is rooted in the vision of oneself in all beings and of all beings in oneself. Similar to the story of the Last Judgment in Matthew 25, Thich Nhat Hanh articulates the presence of the Buddha among the lowest of the low in light of the *Diamond Sutra*. In the absence of form, appearance, or images we look for the Buddha "in stagnant water and in beggars who have leprosy."[22]

The vision of inter-being does not intend to dilute the aspect of resistance, but rather to block self-glorification and righteousness on the part of the resistant.[23] The poor girl in Manila who becomes a prostitute out of desperation is intimately related to the lifestyle of the wealthy family who contributes to the poor girl's desperation and choice of lifestyle.

> Only by seeing with the eyes of inter-being can that young girl be freed from her suffering. Only then will she understand that she is bearing the burden of the whole world.[24]

"Bearing the burden of the whole world" (John 1:29) is a key phrase to the vision of minjung theology in that it takes seriously Jesus' calling of himself into question among his disciples. "But you, who do you say I am?" (Mark 8:29). Bonhoeffer understands the Lamb of God, who bears the burden of the whole world, in terms of "the messianic sufferings of God in Jesus Christ" (LPP. 362). In the horizon of Isaiah 53, Bonhoeffer conceptualizes *theologia crucis* in solidarity with Jewish suffering and people who suffer outside the walls of Christianity. There is a connection between Jewish suffering, cross of Christ and Isaiah 53. This insight upholds solidarity of participation in the reality of the powerlessness of God in the world. God became a real man, and in this man God is reconciled with the cosmic reality. In the man Jesus Christ, judgment is passed on all of humanity, in which the whole hope of the world is comprised. To offer the hungry and

22 Hahn, *Diamond*, 103.

23 Daniel Berrigan and Thich Nhat Hanh, *The Raft Is Not the Shore* (Boston: Beacon, 1975) 102.

24 Hahn, *Heart of Understanding*, 38.

the thirsty bread and drink is to prepare the way of the coming of Christ (E. 136).

Ahn, in pursuing the prophetic, liberating line and direction of Jesus Christ, understands the poor, the captives, the blind, and the oppressed as the *ochlos* of God who representatively bear the burden of the superpowers of the world. However, for Thich Naht Hanh, the Buddhist principle of inter-being helps the poor bear the sin of the world without attachment to it. This insight radicalizes the protest against injustice and violence rather than diluting it, such that it takes up partisanship with the poor for the sake of liberation on both sides.

Reading Critically and Complementarily: Minjung Theology in Terms of Asian Postfoundational Hermeneutics

To overcome some limitations of minjung theology, and yet maintain its socio-political concern, I propose a postfoundational Asian hermeneutics of relationality (by appropriating and updating the Lutheran idea of God's mystery in relation to Bonhoeffer's idea of recognition of the others) to God's covenantal event with minjung in a wider global context. For the most part, Asian minjung theology takes its point of departure from the minjung experience of suffering, self-transcendence, and liberation from an unjust society. At this juncture, a theological negation of the Jews and Judaism occurs for the sake of the prophetic tradition. Jesus would be portrayed merely as the Great Liberator who breaks completely with the established Jewish religion.

My approach to Asian contextual theology of minjung is, however, concerned primarily with God's faithfulness to Israel and the Jewish self-understanding of God. God's mystery can be articulated well, in that God has not cast away God's people whom God foreknew (Rom 11:2). Moreover, God's mystery is related to God's faithfulness to God's people in spite of their disobedience.

According to Bonhoeffer, "The Jew keeps open the question of Christ (E. 89)." From this insight, I understand that Bonhoeffer retains in his Christology a positive significance of the Jewish 'No' for Christianity. For Bonhoeffer, Israel could testify to the eschatological proviso in the self of God, resisting the Christian pathos of the finality of time. However, this God is not God beyond God, nor the hidden God. Rather Israel's witness is evidence of the freedom of God from Godself, which is not annulled even in the sending of Jesus Christ.[25]

In terms of the Gospel, the Jews become God's enemies for our sake (Rom 11:28). Such an approach does not signal the removal of Israel and Judaism. Instead, it brings into focus a need for their hermeneutical retrieval. Taking into consideration Israel as the biological-covenant environment of Jesus, my postfoundational approach calls attention to God's speech event which is taking place in each and every direction. I take seriously the Jewish "No," and recognize along with it the "No" of atheistic humanism and other religions to Christian claims for exclusiveness and finality. With Israel's 'No' in mind, it is important to retain the eschatological reservation of God, despite Christ, because Jesus Christ does not compete with the God of Israel.

Regarding the particular-universal relationship between God and *hapiru* (or *am ha'aretz* or *ochlos*), I integrate into the discourse of Asian contextual theology God's faithfulness to minjung and its self-understanding of God.[26] Interreligiously, my approach assumes a hermeneutical-liberative character encountered with the Buddhist insight of *sunyata* and universal compassion, in favor of social justice. It is inclusive in its embrace of the other, without discrimination, and it features postfoundational sensitivity in recognition of the different as different.

A positive understanding of the Jewish rejection of Jesus Christ may become the basis for interreligious dialogue. God's solidarity with those who suffer outside Christianity should be, first of all, found in the significance of Israel's "No" to Jesus as the Messiah, and then the in maturity of the world in its godlessness. Every serious atheist, as well as the spiritually mature of other faiths, may find their biblical justification along with the Jewish "No" to Jesus and Israel's faithful act to the Torah. Given this fact, F.-W. Marquardt's statement is appropriate: "In Jewish self-understanding, saying No to Jesus Christ is an act of faithfulness to the Torah."[27]

In his interpretation of the Gospel of Mark, Ahn Byung-Mu states that Mark means, by the *ochlos*, the inhabitants of Palestine, who, after the

[25] Friedrich-Wilhelm Marquardt, "'Feinde um unsretwillen,' Das jüdische Nein und die christliche Theologie," in Friedrich-Wilhelm Marquardt, *Verwegenheiten. Theologische Stücke aus Berlin* (Munich: Chr. Kaiser, 1981) 335. Cf. Andreas Pangritz, *Karl Barth in the Theology of Bonhoeffer*, trans. Barbara and Martin Rumscheidt (Grand Rapids: Eerdmans, 1989) 128.

[26] Cf. David Chung, *Syncretism: the Religious Context of Christian Beginnings in Korea*, ed. Kang-nam Oh (Albany, NY: State University of New York Press, 2001) 155–78.

[27] Marquardt, "'Feinde um unsretwillen,'" 315.

destruction of Jerusalem in the year 70 C.E., were homeless and without rights—the Jews, first of all, and then Christians and Gentiles.[28] During the Roman occupation, the people of God, *laos*, became the homeless people, *ochlos*. To the degree that Jesus belongs to this *ochlos*, he lived with Jews and Gentiles. In this regard, minjung theology may pay special attention to the non-dual relationship between Jesus and his people, the *ochlos*, rather than falling into the expropriation of what is Israel's. The writer of Mark affirms the Hebrew Scriptures, and he converses with scribes, Pharisees, and Sadducees over issues in Torah while attacking the corruption of the temple, which economically dominated Jerusalem.[29]

In the Gospel of Matthew, Jesus invited the crowd (*ochlos*), as the recipients of his ministry, even encouraging them to hear the teaching of the scribes and the Pharisees who sit on Moses' seat. Yet their practice should not be imitated. "Therefore do whatever they say to you and follow/keep it; but do not do as they do, for they do not practice what they preach (Matt 23:2–3)."

Their sitting on Moses' seat and the reference to doing whatever they say indicates their teaching role in the interpreting of the scriptures. Their teaching and interpretation of the Torah should be listened to, while their failure to practice, according to what they preach, should be rejected. In this context, Jesus instructed the crowd of people (*ochlos*) and his disciples to learn the Torah from the teachers of the oral tradition and live it, as developed and taught in the Mishna and the Talmud. At this juncture, Jesus invites the *ochlos* to the heart of the Rabbinic Judaism of his day.[30]

In the political situation of the first century C.E., the rulers from Herod's family faced strong opposition from the Pharisees, the Sadducees, and other Hellenized Jewish groups under Roman occupation. *Am ha'aretz*, the people of the land, were disdained and hated.[31] We know that two schools, Beit Shamai and Beit Hillel, were inside the Pharisaic tradition and held different beliefs regarding the *am ha'aretz*. The house of Shamai

[28] Those who date the Gospel of Mark after 70 C.E. argue that Mark tries to justify the Christian community's break with the Jewish cult. Against this dating, Ched Meyers holds a pre-70 dating of the Gospel of Mark. Cf. Ched Meyers, *Binding the Strong Man: A Political Reading of Mark's Story of Jesus* (Maryknoll, NY: Orbis, 1988) 41.

[29] Cf. Meyers, *Binding the Strong Man*, 78–79.

[30] See Friedrich-Wilhelm Marquardt, "Why the Talmud Interests Me as a Christian" in this volume.

[31] Cf. Hillel: "There is no uneducated person who fears sin and no 'Am HaAretz' is God-fearing" (Talmud, Avot ch. 2). In B. Talmud Pesh, "One should not give witness in court on their behalf. . . . One should not appoint them as caretakers of orphans or charity boxes."

disdained *am ha'aretz*, but did not hate them. In contrast, the house of Hillel hated the *am ha'aretz*, but did not disdain them.[32] Unlike the literalistic and legalistic interpretation of the Torah in the house of Shamai, the house of Hillel moved in missionary spirit, interested in gaining *am ha'aretz* (including the Gentiles) for the Torah.[33]

For the house of Hillel, what the Torah did not forbid explicitly was allowed, while for the house of Shamai, what the Torah did not permit explicitly was forbidden. It was the Pharisees from the house of Shamai who came to harass Jesus' movement and to complain about his disciples' behavior.

In Matt 15:3 (cf. Mark 7:1–8) we read:

> Then some *Perushim* and *Torah*-teachers from Yerushalayim came to Yeshua and asked him, (2) 'Why is it that your *talmidim* break the Tradition of the Elders? They don't do *netilat yadayim* before they eat!' (3) He answered, 'Indeed, why do you break the command of God by your tradition? (4) For God said, 'Honor your father and mother, 'and' Anyone who curses his father or mother must be put to death.' (5) But you say, 'If anyone says to his father or mother, 'I have promised to give to God what I might have used to help you,' (6) then he is rid of his duty to honor his father or mother. 'Thus by your tradition you make null and void the word of God! (7) You hypocrites![34]

Jesus' answer to the Pharisees and Torah-teachers in this context stands foundationally in the Word of the Torah. The commandments of the Torah take precedence over the traditions of the elders. In addition, Jesus confesses Israel's *shema* as the foremost commandment of all (Mark 12: 29–30; cf. Deut 6:4–5):

> Hear, O Israel! The Lord our God is one Lord. The foremost is: "Love the Lord your God with all your heart, and with all your soul, and with all your mind, and with all your strength." The

[32] Joseph Shulam, "Jewish Sects & Messianic Rumors in the First Century in the Land of Israel," 3. (http://www.neivyah.org.il).

[33] Y. Hagar, *Tests of History* (Tel-Aviv: Devir, 1951) 11.

[34] *The Jewish New Testament : A Translation of the New Testament that Expresses its Jewishness*, trans. David H. Stern (Clarksville: Jewish New Testament Publications, 1996). We read in Mishna Nedarim 64, "The Rabbis concur with Rabbi Eliezar on issues that come between him and his father or him and his mother. They open the 'argument' by showing honor or with his mother or with His father. . . . If the person said 'korban' that which you can use (from the status of the property) and repeats that this only is what is useable, than the Rabbis release that man from his vow."

> second is: "You shall love your neighbor as yourself." To Jesus the scribe responds, "Right, Teacher, you have truly stated that He is One; and there is no one else beside him. And to love him with all the heart and with all the understanding and with all the strength, and to love one's neighbor as himself is much more than all burnt offerings and sacrifices.

Jesus proclaimed to the scribe that he is not far from the kingdom of God. Jesus' attitude toward the priority of the Torah brought him closer to the *am ha'aretz* and *ochlos*-masses. So the Jesus movement within the Pharisaic tradition appealed to the *ochlos*-masses and to the *am ha'aretz* and called them under Roman occupation to live in accordance with the Torah and the liberative message of the prophets. So Jesus was not ashamed to be called "a friend of tax collectors and sinners" (Luke 7:34).

As a matter of fact, Jesus did not bring a different God than the God of Israel (Mark 12:26). The quest of a historical Jesus can be accomplished only through inclusion of all that can be recognized as Jewish in the life and in the teaching of Jesus Christ. The Jewish "No" to Jesus needs to be discussed, therefore, in terms of Jesus' faithfulness to the Torah. Luke 4:15 records that Jesus taught in the synagogue and everyone praised him. Jesus was, in fact, an observant Jew who ministered almost exclusively to Jews living within the land of Israel. The New Testament does not demonstrate that the Jewish people, as a whole, reject Jesus. Given this fact, Ruether's thesis that anti-Judaism is "the left hand of Christology"[35] needs to be corrected and transformed to the point where the left hand of christology should be found only in the Jewishness of Jesus and his faithfulness to the Torah.

Integrating F.-W. Marquardt's theology of Jewish self-understanding, I speak out against theological, hermeneutical, and methodological anti-Judaism in minjung theology, yet takes seriously the relationship between Jesus and his Jewish people, the *ochlos*-minjung. Historical criticism, which is appropriated in the minjung exegetical work of Ahn Byung-Mu and Suh Nam-Dong, must be more critical. In other words, Asian postfoundational hermeneutics can be articulated and contoured by being socially and ideologically critical of historical criticism.[36]

35 Rosemary Ruether, "Anti-Semitism and Christian Theology," in *Auschwitz: Beginning of a New Era? Reflections on the Holocaust*, ed. Eva Fleischner (New York: Ktav, 1977) 79.

36 Friedrich-Wilhelm Marquardt, "Exegese und Dogmatik in Karl Barths Theologie. Was meint: Kritischer müssten mir die Historisch-kritischen sein?" in Marquardt, *Verwegenheiten*, 402.

As long as Jesus is understood as the Liberator from established Judaism, Asian minjung theology is bound to repeat, unconsciously, the anti-Jewish overtone that originates from the Western theological tradition. In the framework of Asian minjung theology, the Law of Moses has lost its meaning in favor of the event of Jesus, and Judaism is reduced to a pharisaic religion in contrast to Jesus as the Liberator. Jesus appears as a destroyer of the Jewish religion. However, contrary to this direction, it is not the removal of Jesus' Jewishness but the hermeneutical retrieval of Jesus as a born Jew (Martin Luther) that remains at the center of my post-foundational approach to Asian minjung theology.

At this point, Bonhoeffer's openness to the Jewish people is of special significance.

> Western history is, by God's will, indissolubly linked with the people of Israel, not only genetically but also in a genuine uninterrupted encounter. . . . An expulsion of the Jews from the West must necessarily bring with it the expulsion of Christ. For Jesus Christ was a Jew (E. 90–91).

Therefore, the Christian encounter with Israel leaves christology open and proleptic. Bonhoeffer's insight into the reality of the sufferer is well articulated: "Jesus is one whose only concern is for others." He is "the human for others." By deepening and actualizing Bonhoeffer's insight of the world come of age and its religionlessness in regards to a church on the defensive, I am prepared to take risks for the minjung and to view religious others as full of God's promise.

In the face of the mass suffering of the poor and with their spirituality rooted in a multi-religious reality, God can speak in a completely different way. A strange, even uncomfortable voice of God serves as the inspiration for setting Asian Christianity free from captivity to parochialism, and leads to humility and openness toward God's reconciliation in Jesus Christ with the world. As Bonhoeffer argues,

> the Church confesses that she has witnessed the lawless application of brutal force, the physical and spiritual suffering of countless innocent people, oppression, hatred and murder, and that she has not raised her voice on behalf of the victims and has not found ways to hasten to their aid. She is guilty of the deaths of the weakest and most defenseless brothers of Jesus Christ (E. 114).

Against the positivism of revelation in Barth's thought[37] Bonhoeffer paved the way toward renewing arcane discipline, as well as retrieving biblical worldliness wherein Christ becomes the Lord even of the religionless world (LPP. 280). According to Bonhoeffer, the world should not be left to its own devices. Since "in, with and under" the proclamation of Jesus Christ as the crucified Reconciler, the godless world bears the mark of reconciliation as the ordinance of God. God has overcome tension and conflict between the Christian and secular elements (E. 292). In this light we hear the provocative statement of Bonhoeffer, which he attributed to Martin Luther: "the curses of the godless sometimes sound better in God's ear than the hallelujahs of the pious."[38]

An Asian postfoundational minjung approach, based on God's mystery in love and freedom, appropriates the Buddhist principle of non-discrimination, and it does not necessarily lead to a pluralistic theology of religions with total relativism. God does not, in fact, stand in opposition to pluralism itself, because God is the one who accepts the world's pluralism and integrates all its variety through God's inclusive grace in Jesus Christ for God's future.

The Buddhist language of *sunyata* does not claim an ultimate and absolute truth, even in the Buddhist doctrinal system. From the Buddhist perspective, human language will always be a limited tool, not unequivocally identical with the Truth, nor dissimilarly distanced from it. In this regard, I find the following Buddhist remark meaningful: "Do not look at the finger! If you do, you will miss the moon. Look at the moon through the finger!"[39]

Against a dualistic way of thinking, Buddhist hermeneutics of the middle way, or non-attachment, maintain the indescribable and ineffable nature of all things. Reality is constantly in a flowing stream, such that it is hard to contain or conceptualize a living reality by means of a rigid linguistic conceptual framework. In fact, there is a distance between human words or concepts and that which is to be described.[40] Buddhist language is, therefore, analogical, metaphorical, and hermeneutical.

In light of dependent co-arising, the dialectics of *prajnaparamita*, which looks, for instance, at a rose, yet is not attached to it, transcend

[37] Cf. Pangritz, *Karl Barth in the Theology of Dietrich Bonhoeffer*.

[38] Dietrich Bonhoeffer, *Act and Being: Transcendental Philosophy and Ontology*, trans. H. Martin Rumscheidt (Minneapolis: Fortress, 1996) 160.

[39] Hanh, *Diamond that Cuts Through Illusion*, 80.

[40] Ibid., 95, 109.

the sword of human conceptualization.[41] "Buddhas are called Buddhas because they are free of ideas."[42] The bodhisattva's great vow, in which all beings must be lead to the ultimate nirvana to attain liberation, lies in a spirit of formlessness, without an idea of helping. Because Buddhadharma is made up of non-Buddhadharmic elements, it cannot be found outside of non-Buddhadharma. In looking deeply into the reality of suffering, we find the answers. A true question already contains the answer to it. As Thich Nhat Hanh says, "the beautiful lotus grows out of the mud. Without afflictions and suffering, we cannot make a Buddha."[43]

In Jesus Christ, God becomes the victim. As God's speech goes out in every direction, we become aware of God's on-going challenge to the rational and memetic desires that would produce violence and cause craving and suffering. Jesus Christ remains a stumbling block still today. "Why do you call me good? No one is good except God alone" (Mark 10:18). Rather, he delivers a challenge to the complacent self-righteousness and the satisfaction with the *status quo*. He represents the divine compassion for the minjung in the foolish and kenotic way in which he bore the sin of the world for all. So the stone rejected by the builders has become the cornerstone (Mark 12:10). As Bonheoffer says,

> it means that nothing is lost, that everything is taken up in Christ, although it is transformed, made transparent, clear, made free from the anguish of selfish desire. Christ restores all this as God originally intended it to be (LPP. 170).

41 Ibid., 47, 59.

42 Ibid., 75.

43 Ibid., 105.

9

Christianity and Culture

*A Hermeneutic of Mission Theology in an East Asian Context**

Kim Kyoung-Jae

My focus in this presentation is on a religio-cultural theology in order to make Christian mission more available and accessible in the East Asian cultural soil. Because of this, I am interested in pursuing a paradigm shift from a traditional Western theology of mission toward a more hermeneutical and experiential theology of mission in respect to our global context.

The term East "Asian cultural soil" refers geographically to Chinese-speaking countries, specifically countries, such as China, South-Korea, Japan and Vietnam. These are cultural communities which are composed of multi-religious societies and share the great religious cultural legacies of Buddhism, Confucianism, Taoism and indigenous religions for over 2000 thousand years. In this particular human civilization there have existed various cultural and religious expressions which breathe freshly, in that each culture has flowered its unique bloom as the core substance of cultures. Seen from the perspective of a typology of religion, it is by and large agreed that there have been three great streams existing until today.[1]

The first stream is Semite, prophetic religions, which emerged out of the Middle East. This stream is the Abrahamic religions such as Judaism, Christianity, and Islam; a stream whose matrix is based on nomadic life in the Middle East. What is common in these Semitic religions is pietistic

* Translated and edited by Paul S. Chung.

[1] Cf. Hans Küng and Julia Ching, *Christentum und Chenesische Religion* (Munich: R. Piper, 1988).

faith, prophetic faith, faith in a transcendental creator, consciousness of time and history, and justice-based community.

The second stream is a genealogy of mystic religion that emerged out of India. This is the Veda religion of Brahmanism that is articulated in Upanisad and includes Jainism (initiated by Mahavira), Buddhism, and Hinduism. These Hindu religions are called mystic because of their emphasis on the ontological identity between the ultimate reality of the universe and human nature. Furthermore, these religions have in common a validation of the original unity between the universe and the self by means of meditation and spiritual exercise.

The third stream is a religion of wisdom that is essentially oriented toward sagehood. It emerged out of China. The nature of sagehood religion encourages the potentiality of humanity, emphasizing the way of means and fostering human life in harmony and unity with nature such that neither the prophet nor the mystic but sagacity is honored as the goal of the ideal human individual in this religious culture.

However, the characteristics of East Asian culture, especially religious culture in Korea—except for national folk religions such as indigenous Shamanism and *Donghak*—consist in the fact that Korea is the final stage for incorporating these three streams of the world religions described above. In fact, the three world religious cultures reached their climax and blossomed in Korea. For instance, Buddhism, Confucianism, and Christianity, as the representative religions of each stream have profoundly influenced the world view of Koreans, impacting their *Gestalt* of the moral value system, their artistic consciousness of the beautiful, their view of life and death, their consciousness of social ethics, and their political culture, among other things.

What is theologically important in such a multi-religious civilized society is first of all to establish a right relation between Christianity and other religions. Furthermore, it is important to clarify theologically, a basic relation between the gospel and East Asian culture vis-à-vis the mission process of the Christian gospel. Colleagues from Europe and Brazil who are now present at this conference grew up by and large over years in the Christian tradition of faith and its religious cultural heritage. However, in East Asia, particularly in South Korea, there is a relatively short mission history of Christianity. To seek a theological paradigm shift is not an easy task; and yet, it is a very urgent and meaningful task, because it is a "hot potato" for theologians of today and for lay people who are concerned with this issue.

What is obvious is that the gospel cannot become the bread of life or the living water unless there is a process of it being re-embodied into the concrete and particular cultural life and spirit.[2] By being re-embodied into various languages of culture, art, and tradition, not only does the gospel creatively transforms the culture by assessing and illumining it, but according to the principle of the hermeneutical circle, the culture can also illumine the gospel as having various colors in human life. In so doing, the gospel can be interpreted anew and freshly enriched in its new cultural context.

This is why culture is not like clothing that the human community simply puts on, but like the flesh, blood and soul of the shaping of the community. It is very naïve thinking of spreading the gospel by negating a living and breathing culture as a whole, and implanting Christianity culturally into the indigenous society without hesitation. And it is also one-dimensional for us to regard culture superficially like a simple clothing on the Gospel. My interest in this presentation is, therefore, to reinterpret the relationship between gospel and culture honestly and boldly and then face without fear what is really happening in this inter-religious encounter. In fact, it is religion as the core essence of culture that makes culture into a *living* culture of human life.

The Process of the Hermeneutical Fusion of Horizons and Human Cultural Life as a Complementary Weaving of Textiles

Human life proceeds, individually and corporately, in terms of the most basic three movements. The first is a self-integrating movement of life that holds onto self-identity. The second is a self-creating movement of life that creates something new and enjoys it and brings it forward. The third is a self-transcending movement of life that transcends finitude and limitation, and finally improves upon them.[3] To a certain extent these three basic movements of life bloom at the phenomenological level of human life in a creative and emerging manner. At the highest level of such movements,

2 *Report of the World Alliance of Reformed Churches 23rd General Council,* Debrechen, Hungary, 8–20 August 1997. See the Study Texts: Sections and Subsections, 17–20.

3 Cf. Paul Tillich, *Systematic Theology*, vol.3. (Chicago: University of Chicago Press, 1963) 32–106. See "1. The Self-integration of Life and Its Ambiguities, 2. The Self-creativity of Life and Its Ambiguities, 3.The Self-transcendence of Life and Its Ambiguities."

there occurs the phenomenon of personality-experience, the phenomenon of culture-creation, and the religious phenomenon.

The phenomenon of moral personality appears to the degree that the self-integrating movement of life arises as the highest stage. Culture, in this regard, can be explained as a communal phenomenon that dynamically denies repeating the same thing, like in the system of instinct. Furthermore, the self-creating movement of life appears at the level of human consciousness and free will wherein something new is being continuously created. Religion is not only of progressive creative character at the horizontal level, but it also deals with a phenomenon of life-experience that can emerge at the vertical-transcendental level as well. This movement is in pursuit of something higher, namely, holiness and immortality.

Considering retrospectively the history of the human race, however, we must remember that a higher personal moral consciousness, the blooming of cultural evolution, and the emergence of a spiritual and cosmic universal religion became possible through a self-sublimating process explicitly visible in the interaction and competition between civilizations. As the development of a species through the breeding of close kinship is not desirable biologically, so a self-closed civilization and religion becomes more and more degenerate, when it loses its openness toward and interaction with other cultures and religions. Finally, it is not capable of carrying out its persistent creative power. As a result, it perishes, or is left behind as a hardened, reified religious culture.

By the way, in spreading the Christian gospel in the multi-religious society of the non-Christian world, Western missiology warned against and tried to avoid syncretism vigorously. This warning is apropos. However, it is, first of all, more important to clarify and define syncretism. It is clear that without a consensus or a definition of syncretism, Christian fundamentalists and anti-intellectual dogmatists in the Korean church are prone to denounce, as collaboration or syncretistic sympathy, any serious theological efforts to pursue and explore Christian mission in multi-religious cultural contexts. Such an attitude must be resisted and surmounted.

In the religious history of the West, the term syncretism has been used pejoratively. What the term syncretism refers to, at this juncture, is idea that the essence of the Christian gospel, when exposed to indigenous religion and culture, is diluted or lost, particularly in the history of Christian mission, such that Christian self-identity is severely threatened.

Instead, missionaries set up their fixed form of theological dogma. In other words, they created normative Christian paradigms of theology in regard to a certain historical period of Christianity. As they forced indigenous culture and religion into their own constructions, cultural conflict and pain occurred, inevitably and indescribably, in the indigenous society. By and large, Western missionaries were not able to distinguish from the gospel a historical form of Christendom that was formed and interpreted in a certain historical condition. Without eschatological reservation, they absolutized their conception of Christianity forming its specific historical form and thereby forced indigenous people to convert and denounced their subjective and independent faith as an idolatrous form of syncretism.

For instance, at the time of Roman Catholic mission (1784), when the Vatican declared the Confucian cult of ancestral rites in Korea to be idolatrous, around ten thousand Korean Catholic Christians were martyred as a result.[4] In addition, in the 18th and 19th centuries, Western Christian civilization entered Asian countries in collaboration with a wave of colonial politics and Western imperialism. Western theology, as seen from the perspective of the sociology of knowledge or in terms of an ideological critique, was not aware of its own missiological paradigm under the impact of cultural imperialism. Western theology was generally associated with the Hegelian dialectical understanding of history or a historical view of progress. This idea itself was the result of the emergence of Western greed and self-interest.

Since the Vatican Council II (1962–1965) there has been a fresh and provocative theological paradigm shift in the Korean Catholic church, which seems to be almost revolutionary in the history of the Korean church. The Korean Protestant church, from its perspective of fundamentalism, denounces as theological syncretism the Catholic attempt, for instance, at forming a Korean indigenous theology, integrating toleration of traditional family rites, such as the ancestral rites, and developing a Korean theology of culture and religions, among others.

In this presentation, I propose a technical tern to avoid the pejorative term, syncretism, coupled with the profound misunderstandings of its meaning. For this purpose I'd rather use "a fusion of horizons" of the life-experience (Hans-Georg Gadamer), because this term is discussed and used as the subject-matter of modern human sciences in the field of philosophical hermeneutics. Furthermore I have coined the metaphor "complementary weaving of textiles."

[4] Yu Hong Yul, *History of the Korean Catholic Church*, vol.1 (Seoul: Catholic, 1962) 97–430.

As Wilhelm Dilthey correctly described, human life consists of the creative process of experiencing unique and inherent value and meaning (experience). It is related to the human act of expressing what is experienced (expression). Further-more, this act of expression culminates in the process of understanding what is expressed (interpretation).

I accept this triadic process as a hermeneutical life; it refers specifically to human life as successive movement. In this we can experience the inner quality of life, express its moving and effect, and understand the expressed art for the sake of interpreting it. Human beings are, at this juncture, hermeneutical beings, thus historical and cultural beings. As a hermeneutical being, the human being, whether consciously or unconsciously, lives with a certain "horizon of understanding."

In terms of the hermeneutical process of understanding, human beings are in a position to experience, extend and deepen continuously their life understanding and their ontological-cultural horizons in on-going way. For this reason, Gadamer characterizes this hermeneutical reality metaphorically in terms of the life-experience and the fusion of horizons.[5]

What constitutes the human horizons of understanding is, in fact, diverse. As for the metaphysical constitutive component, I take the transcendental self-communication of God (as described by Karl Rahner), or the humanity of God (as described by Karl Barth),[6] as examples in which truth is accepted and understood as truth. Therefore, in pursuing something meaningful, valuable, beautiful and new in the context of human life, a transcendental experience can become possible. In addition to the transcendental aspect of God's grace, we may discuss the ontological capacity of pre-understanding in an historical sense, that is, the constituting component of the existing horizons of understanding.

In other words, we may discuss a worldview that originates from several things, including tradition, structures of language, geographical climates, distribution systems of production, religious rituals, myths, and systems of symbols. The hermeneutical perspectives, inseparably intercon-

[5] For life reality of human beings as hermeneutical being, see Hans-Georg Gadamer, *Truth and Method*, trans. Garret Braden and John Cumming (New York: Crossroad, 1982). Richard E. Palmer, *Hermeneutics: Interpretation Theory in Schleiermacher, Dilthey, Heideggar and Gadamer* (Evanston: Northwestern University Press, 1969).

[6] To avoid a misunderstanding of Barth and Rahner, it is important to understand their respective approaches: Rahner was concerned with the ontological aspect of human beings in receiving the grace of God's self-communication while Barth emphasizes the inclusive and universal horizon of God's act in the assumption of human flesh in respect to cultural and religious realms outside the churchly sphere.

nected with one other, make it possible for human beings to have a living self-consciousness, understanding the self and the world.

"Understanding of horizon" is a metaphor used in Greek philosophy. When a new religion such as Christianity began to impact Korean life in the 18th and 19th centuries, the eyes of Koreans were open wide by the gospel to the horizon of understanding of a new truth. In fact, my conversion to Christianity means—no matter how the process of the faith-decision occurred—that the horizon of truth, seen through the Bible, became more extended, enlarged, and explicit, so that the Gospel could bring this decisive change to my life.

However, Gadamer's concept of fusion of horizons is not enough to account for or to resolve the conflict or the complexity in respect to the human life-experience, the experience of cultural diversity, or the encounter of different worldviews. From the start, East Asians were well aware of this problem. The metaphor of the fusion of horizons becomes adequate and proper when sharing the experience of encountering diverse life horizons rooted in a pluralistic culture.

Additionally, it is generally recognized that religions with different paradigms or world-views are not easily fused into the life of a Korean Christian who has been formed by the history of Buddhist culture, Confucian culture, Christian culture, Taoist culture, and indigenous folk religions, Rather, it becomes more explicit that the difference appears as different and the distance as distant in such a process. In this case, people, as a rule, first choose between two different positions, one of which is chosen unilaterally and excludes others (exclusivism). The other approach takes Christianity as the highest religion of fulfillment, conceiving of the uniqueness of diverse religions, and integrating the good elements from other religions into Christianity by means of critical process and choice (inclusivism).

Furthermore, the third position is generally called pluralism. It occurs when diverse cultures and religions meet and converse with one other. Rather than using the term "pluralism," I would rather use the metaphorical phrase a "complementary weaving of textiles," comparing it with the truth experience or the "engrafting process" between trees.[7] This metaphor

[7] As in East Asian culture of religion, I understand the encountering of religions, mission, and the process of inculturation in Korean society in a way similar to other societies influenced by religious pluralism—as an engrafting process in terms of a biological metaphor. Cf. Kim, Kyoung-Jae, *Christianity and the Encounter of Asian Religions: Method of Correlation, Fusion of Horizons, and Paradigm Shifts in the Korean Grafting Process* (Zoetermer: Boekencentrum, 1994).

originates from the refining process of weaving textiles or the process of engrafting the trees.

Take, for example, a carpet from Turkey, the Native American art of weaving textiles, the diverse colors of a shoulder bags of Tibetan Buddhists, or a silk clothing patterned beautifully in the Chinese or Korean tradition. Material for clothing is made with a diverse array of colors, patterns and materials in which the difference appears as different and reveals, through the color contrast of unification, harmony and complementarity, the aesthetical sense which arrives at a much higher level.

The truth-experience points to, fundamentally, the aesthetic feeling of beauty. The experience of beauty reveals a more perfect beauty, as a whole, by arranging contrasting and even unharmonious objects in opposition into the proper framework, instead of arranging the homogenous unilaterally. This principle can also be applied to music. In a macrocosmic way, East Asian culture has little to do with monotony, like the weaving of various textiles into a single color.

East Asian culture can be understood as the history of an on-going process in which a "complementary weaving process" of truth experience has occurred. As a matter of fact, this culture has never been experienced in Western cultural spheres. East Asian history of culture must be understood as an integrating of the world's religions, such as Confucianism, Buddhism, Taoism, Islam, and Christianity, which creates, in turn, beautiful religious patterns and figures in the heart of the Asian minjung (the poor) and weaves the clothing of life.

Oftentimes, the dominant political power appropriated territory, used the newly adopted religion as the new ruling ideology, and replaced the former religion that dominated the previous era. However, those who created and absorbed culture substantially (for instance, the crowd, the minjung, grass roots people, and ordinary people) have integrated and fused by a creative process the previous history into their mindset, so that this spiritual penetration and fusion remains basically the soil, or at the heart of minjung like an organic fertilizer, creating culture.

I have previously proposed three models by categorizing a theological perspective that accounts for the mission process.[8] "The sowing model" is a parable in which culture and the human heart in the indigenous country is likened to the soil, where the gospel, like seed, falls down, spreads, germinates, and grows. This model is adequate in speaking of the gospel-seed's power of life. However, herein the function of the soil would be almost ig-

8 Ibid., 120–40.

nored, such that the pure seed's germination and growth becomes possible only in relation to the cultural soil. Therefore, it ends up a disintegrating living organism in co-existence with the soil. The result is a theology of mission that aims at conquering indigenous culture and finally at adopting exclusivism as it encounters religious others.

"The yeast model" refers to a metaphor in which yeast penetrates inside the dough and transforms it. Richard Niebuhr's model "Christ the Transformer of culture" is an example of this type of model.[9] Herein the cultural-historical reality of a country is regarded positively as the recipient of the Gospel. However, it is not accepted as the subjective place of changing. The creative agent of change is the Gospel, or Christianity, according to which every reality of life in the recipient country is defined as a passive object to be changed in accordance with the Gospel.

Therefore, this model contradicts the hermeneutical principle of fusion of horizons. Because such a yeast model overcomes exclusivism and supports inclusivism, the position of fulfillment, it makes mission possible by eradicating conflict with other religions or causes of religious war in a multi-religious society. As a rule, the Catholic theology of mission since the Second Vatican Council or the progressive Protestant theology of mission in South Korea (for instance, Kim Chai-Choon) belongs to this school.

The third model is a metaphor that looks at the mission process as a grafting process between two living trees. Using the metaphor of the grafting process, East Asian civilization is likened to a living tree of life. In the process of receiving and changing the Gospel, which can be seen as inserting a shoot or a branch into the stock, the indigenous culture and the gospel become mutual subjects along with the role of the Gospel. Thereby, the mission process is not meant to be like a process of implantation, in which a foreign tree growing in Western soil is rooted up, then inserted completely into the indigenous soil. Rather, the indigenous reality of culture is likened to the stock, and the Gospel is understood as a shoot or branch that is inserted into it.

This being the case, the world historical process of the culture of religions, including Christianity, will become, after all, a process of screening and refining the truth and beauty of a certain religion. This process entails the "self-witnessing power of the truth," so that each religion revives and enriches itself. The diverse truth experiences of religions go through the higher process of the fusion of horizons, retaining their unity in more

[9] Cf. H. R. Niebuhr, *Christ and Culture* (New York: Harper & Row, 1951) 190–96.

beautiful and diverse development, such that this process can be spoken of as the weaving of textiles in dedication to the ultimate reality of truth.

In other words, the history of religion is not the history of distinction between lower religion and higher religion, as scholars of the history of religion school have judged imprudently. Rather it means looking deeply at what kind of religion, by overcoming ambiguity and the idolatrous character of religions more explicitly, "worships in spirit and truth," and "revives life and enriches it" so that grain and weed could be judged even before the last day. According to Tillich, in the triadic logic of theonomy—autonomy—heteronomy, or with a sacramental—mystic—prophetic basis for the history of religions, the religion of the concrete spirit acts as the *telos* of eschatology.

From this perspective, the uniqueness of the revelation in Jesus Christ appears as a bearer of the universal power of salvation in terms of a fusion of horizons, or a weaving process or a grafting process of truth-experience, no matter what the terms are. Does this revelatory uniqueness retain a meaning for those of other cultures whose salvation paradigm and unique character are different? Seen in the light of the universal activity of creation and salvation of the Holy Spirit, what relation and meaning does the message of the Gospel itself have and speak for non-Christian religions and cultures in an East Asian context? Is there a certain religious spirituality in a historical community that originally determines this community? What, if any, relation does this have to the mission process of Christianity?

Typological Character of a Salvation Paradigm and a Question of Interpretation Regarding the Uniqueness of Jesus Christ

Korean culture, which is geographically located at a central place in the East Asian cultural world, is a small country in respect to politics, economy, military power, and sports. However, in view of its religious cultural aspects, it is a community that possesses boundless possibility and potentiality in an unprecedented way. As mentioned already, it represents three cultures of the world's religions; namely, the Buddhist culture, the Confucian culture and the Christian culture, and it retains the majority of the constituting components of the religious culture. Furthermore, there is an inherent indigenous spirituality that is capable of fusing the horizons of these religions or mediating them as complementary in an extraordinary weaving process.

In an inter-religious context, Paul Tillich once proposed a typological approach. In the 60s he came to Japan, understanding deeply the East Asian Buddhist culture, and he became a pioneer of theology of culture. I confess that my theological perspective still remains profoundly influenced by Tillich's orientation, which I have an affinity for, although I critically move beyond his limitations at some points.

According to him, the truth-experience of all the world's great religions is rooted in the revelatory epiphany of truth originating from the Holy itself. The typological character that makes all religious cultures possible must be respected because of its Holy character, which is not circumscribed by time and space. In this regard Tillich takes a step beyond the fulfilled superiority of Christianity or superficial and simple inclusivism.

Let me first of all examine all typological characteristics of Christianity and Buddhism through the lens of Tillich's approach. He characterizes the most profound symbol of what constitutes Christianity in terms of the kingdom of God. Likewise, the symbol of Buddhism corresponding to it is Nirvana. The former symbol is more political, social and personal, while the latter symbol is more ontological.[10] Because of the two different typological characteristics, these two great world religions reveal an essential difference, which speaks of the non-sameness. Nevertheless at the same time, there exists an open communication which enables dialogue.

Why would a Christian—living in an East Asian cultural world, yet practicing a Christian faith intellectually and practically—struggle with a religious-cultural task? Western Christians do not adequately understand the reason. To better understand this problem it seems important to contrast the Buddhist salvation paradigm with Christianity's by following Tillich's typological approach. By using the Greek philosophical term *telos,* Tillich defines the two religions' *telos* formula in what follows:

> In Christianity the telos of *everyone* and everything is united in the kingdom of God; in Buddhism the telos of *everything* and everyone is fulfilled in the Nirvana.[11]

In this statement, Tillich distinguishes between the two religions and their typological characteristics by emphasizing not only the different order of everyone and everything, but also two different words in italics. Above all, Christianity draws its ultimate reality from a personal symbol, while

[10] Paul Tillich, *Christianity and the Encounter of the World Religions* (New York: Columbia University Press, 1963) 64.

[11] Ibid.

Buddhism draws its reality from an impersonal or transpersonal symbol, the absolute nothingness or *sunyata*.

As is typical of this sort of salvific paradigm, Christianity's principle of participation is compelling. In it, the following becomes manifest: personal responsibility and a responding participation of the individual, realization of community through the individual's preservation of value and participation, an emphasis on justice and divine command, faith in the resurrection of the body, a process of history and a historical consciousness with a future orientation, a reform-resistance spirit in thirst of justice, and agapeic love.

In contrast, Buddhism, on the basis of the principle of identification, states that everything is the creative basis of being itself ontologically and exists as the middle way in an emergence of being in dependent co-arising. Therefore, ontologically speaking, being is identified with the reality of suchness, or *sunyata*, which is no less than being itself. The enlightened is characterized in the following way: fullness, freedom, non-attachment, transcendence of life and death, the middle way, disinterestedness, identification-consciousness with everything and everybody, and unconditional *mahakaruna* (great mercy) for all sentient beings in ignorance.

This being the case, is it difficult for two religions to communicate with each other because of their heterogeneous differences? According to Tillich, for communality between Christianity and Buddhism, we may illustrate the mystic tradition in Christianity, namely, the tradition of apophatic theology, and the consciousness of social ethics in Mahayana Buddhism. A Buddhist takes refuge in the universal merit of Amida Buddha and the like. Typological characteristics of the two religions would be incompatible in a theoretical framework of scholars, but it is experienced, to those who live a living faith experientially, as a more complete extension of horizons of truth-experience by becoming more complementary to each other.

If we understand the history of the introduction of Buddhist culture to China, the process of translating the Buddhist sutras (canons), and the process of enculturating Mahayana Buddhism, to some degree, we realize that Chinese Buddhism—since the introduction of Hindu Buddhism to China—is re-embodied, accepted and more culturally and socially deepened in Chinese culture and society. The translating of Buddhist sutras written in the Sanskrit or Pali language into Chinese language is an indicator of the indigenization of Hindu Buddhism into Chinese Buddhism.

Furthermore, Buddhism could not establish its roots in China without the concepts and spirituality of Taoism such as non-action, non-being, the middle way, fullness and emptiness, non-desire, and the natural way, etc. Features of Chinese Buddhism, such as T'ien T'ai, Hua-yen, and Ch'an, could bloom their flowers as features of East Asian Mahayana Buddhism, which is rooted only in this Taoist soil.

As Buddhism and other more ontological and cosmic religions came into China, the thinking-horizon of Chinese thought was extended and deepened in its encounter with them. Externally speaking, although Buddhism, Taoism, and Confucianism fought against each other and were in competition for ruling Chinese society ideologically, yet materially speaking, Neo-Confucianism as such could not be established without Buddhism or Taoist philosophy.

Especially, consider the example of "the heart principle," which is the core theory in the school of idealism in Neo-Confucianism (for instance, Wang Yang Ming) or consider the example of "fostering the existence and the nature of the heart." These are the core principles of the Confucian exercise of spirituality in which the human experience, with immanent transcendence, is articulated and emphasized. This idea functions the role of mediating of Buddhism, Taoism, and Christianity from the perspective of Neo-Confucianism.[12]

Seen from a religious cultural perspective, the Korean process of accepting other religious cultures is very unique, and worthy of intensive investigation in light of a theology of mission. Ryu Dong-Sik, a Korean theologian of culture and mission, makes a pioneering contribution to this field.[13] According to him, what remains in the collective consciousness of the Han nation is *Pyung Ru Do*, as stated by Choi Chi-Won, a great Buddhist scholar in the Silla period of Korea, mentioned.[14] This refers to an archetype of spirituality inherent to the Korean mindset, with which Koreans are capable of integrating foreign religions such as Buddhism, Confucianism, Taoism, and Christianity into the heart of Korean people by way of *Pyung Ru Do*.

In order for any foreign religions to be enculturated into the life of the people's religion, they carried out self-development by adhering to the

[12] Neo-Confucianism is a so called synthesizing Confucianism with respect to Taoism and Buddhism. Cf. Youlan Feng, *A Short History of Chinese Philosophy*, ed. Derk Bodde (New York: Macmillan, 1948).

[13] Ryu Dong Sik, *Pyung Ru Do and Religious Thought in Korea* (Seoul: Yun Sei University Press, 1997)

[14] "Han nation" means the Korean people as a nation in an etymological way. The Sila period in Korean history declared Buddhism its state religion. Choi Chi Won was an important scholar during the late period of Sila.

spirituality of *Pyung Ru Do*. Conversely, the spirituality of *Pyung Ru Do* concretizes the content of the foreign religions within it—with the mediation of it—and enriches and develops Korean religious culture more colorfully. It is what Ryu proposes as a hermeneutical theory of mission theology.

Pyung Ru Do can be called the archetype or matrix of the religious mindset of the Korean people (I borrow this concept of archetype from Carl Jung's theory of archetype.) The archetype represents various conditions that occur at the base of the human spirit, with a capacity of emitting indefinite energy rather than being an intellectual concept. It is a transcendental condition of enabling the act-pattern of community to repeat itself constantly, and the morphological element of self-emptying.[15] Considering this in a hermeneutical way, I find the model of engrafting to be similar to Ryu's theology of mission.

The introduction of Christianity and its process of indigenization in Korean culture mean that the gospel comes down and is accepted into the cultural religious soil which was already fertilized by Buddhism, Confucianism, Shamanism, and indigenous folk religion. When Christian mission began, Korea was in the beginning stages of opening its doors to Western culture in a cultural-sociological sense.

At this time, people could not expect from Korean religions, such as Buddhism, Confucianism, or Shamanism, any creative energy that could be able to initiate a process of modernization. Those religions had already lost their dynamic force of life. This was not only because of the loss of moral leadership of traditional religions but also the hardening of spiritual power.

Materially speaking, the modernization of Asian society was meant to be a strengthening, controlling, and developing of society and nature on the basis of modern scientific civilization. The periodization of the world as the process of secularization and transition of personal relationships are based on blood kinship and local community. In addition, structure of the social contract is based on the social personality, and the process of humanization is in accompaniment of engineering technology and medical progress.

Because all these processes—modernization, secularization, historization, technological advancement, socialization and the like—worked more effective in a world-view that finds its matrix in Christianity, Korean

[15] Cf. Lee Byu -Young, *Analytical Psychology: C. J. Jung's Theory of Human Mind* (Seoul: IL Jo Gak, 1984) 89–91.

society accepted Christianity very positively as the mediator of openness toward Western civilization.

Above all, it would be fair to say that the truth of the Gospel as a spiritual religion, which was transmitted through the Bible, caused a response of correspondence mutually communicated by *Pyung Ru Do*'s temperament of the Korean religious archetype. Christianity was given a chance. So the Bible was translated into Korean and spiritual energy was poured into the heart and mind of the minjung. Their spiritual eyes were awakened and changed in the power of truth that set them free. In Korea a new era of Christian mission was open, and then a new horizon was extended and deepened. There can be many explanations at various levels to clarify why Christian mission took a dynamic form and became successful only in Korea among many countries of East Asia. However, we must not overlook that the religious-cultural-theological explication is one of the most important ones.

We cannot apply a relation between the process of modernization in Korea and Christianity extensively to East Asia as a whole. Most Asian countries, except for Japan and Korea, were subjected to the colonial rule of Christian civilization and its countries. Because they experienced devastation of Asian culture and religion in the meantime, they can only reject Christianity, unconsciously and consciously. They made a critique of Christianity in its historical religious form. Christianity was denounced as being in collaboration with the Western imperialistic policy of exploitation by sanctioning and agreeing with it.

In our era of globalization, in which cultural information is transparently open, it would be out of the question to speak of the conquering of religious culture, as in the theory of "East-Way and West-technology,"[16] or the theory of inclusivist fulfillment. This was the faith system of mission theology in the 19th and 20th centuries which is, however, regarded today as undesirable and unacceptable. On what theological theory and basis can Christian mission be offered in a religiously pluralistic society of awakened East Asians?

Let me quote once again an insight from Paul Tillich:

> In the depth of every living religion there is a point at which the religion itself loses its importance, and that to which it points break through its particularity, elevating it to spiritual freedom and with it, a vision of the spiritual presence in other expressions of the ul-

[16] This parole says that Eastern Asian culture is based on philosophical metaphysics, but Christian West on scientific world view.

> timate meaning of man's existence. This is what Christianity must see in the present encounter of the world religions.[17]

From this statement, Tillich intends to emphasize that Christianity must overcome its temptation as a historical religion to become idolized by absolutizing its finite value. Again, through self-transcending, Christianity as a spiritual religion must retain absolute freedom and a transcendence-experience in itself. In other words, to the degree that Jesus as a historical existential person was capable of emptying himself without hesitation, he was exalted as the Messiah and recognized as God's beloved son.

Likewise, if Christianity as a historical religion has the spiritual capacity of denying itself, paradoxically, without losing its identity, it can keep the absoluteness of the Gospel and the uniqueness of salvific power in Jesus Christ. This is the paradoxical meaning of the Christian faith in the cross and the resurrection.

Given this fact, we must warn against religious syncretism in Christian and non-Christian encounters in the context of East Asia. At the same time, with the Protestant principle in mind, we must also thoroughly warn against the idolization of relativity, because this is the theological system and dogma which have been formed in the historical process. As Tillich says, a point of existence in the depth of all living religions is the very sanctuary of God who is present there as the spirit of the truth, and God as the God the mystery makes the sun to shine and gives rain to the good and the bad as well (Matt 5:45). Now it is time to come back to the Protestant principle, namely the basic spirit of the Reformers whose primary emphasis becomes explicit in Luther's formulation, "Let God be God." This spirit refers to a prophetic critical spirit against the temptation to idolize all relatives and to live out what monotheistic faith means.

Epilogue

In conclusion, I summarize a hermeneutical theology of mission with a view to what has been portrayed and discussed. First, in East Asian culture, especially in the history of religious culture in Korea, which is based on the religious legacy inherent to Korean people, the three streams of world religions plunged together into its multi-religious society, forming and developing religious fusion and exchange among them.

Second, in examining carefully the mission process, we see that as a cultural community accepts the Gospel and is changed by it, it goes

[17] Paul Tillich, *Christianity and Encounter of World Religions*, 62.

through a hermeneutical process. The hermeneutical process is to accept and understand the Gospel as the truth and, as a confessional process of acceptance, it goes through the fusion of horizons, and the weaving process or grafting process.

Third, the Gospel that is not engrafted into an indigenous culture does not reveal the authentic power of life. In speaking of a relation between Gospel and culture, the former illumines and criticizes the latter, while the latter illumes the former, and also reinterprets it, enriching, and making it diverse.

Fourth, the essence of the Gospel in mission is the meaning and power of new being as it is revealed in Christ. This refers to agapeic absolute love. Therefore, God's righteousness and God's kingdom are manifest in the event of the cross and the resurrection.

Fifth, the theological system, dogma, and symbolic ritual system in Christianity as a historical religion are precious when they manifest their typological characteristics. In so doing, they must be preserved, but not absolutized. We learn to confess that the salvific economy of God and the work of the Spirit as the Spirit of life have been effective among the world's religions. Therefore, in terms of understanding the typological characteristics of the world religions and grasping their complementary relation, we must warn against exclusivism and syncretism.

Sixth, a history of religious culture in Korea is a history of the world religions, which have developed themselves by concretely embodying the religious spirituality inherent to Korea, the so-called *Pyung Ru Do*. The uniqueness of *Pyung Ru Do* spirituality lies in its inclusive character in orientation toward wholeness. In other words, this refers to the character of freedom in orientation toward being moved by the Spirit, wind and art. This means the character of life in affirmation of the concrete life. The indigenizaton of Christianity into the religious cultural history of Korea needs to develop itself in regard to a correlation between Gospel and *Pyung Ru Do*.

Seventh, the absoluteness of the truth revealed in Jesus Christ and the uniqueness of the salvation revelation become paradoxically effective only in the power of unreserved self-denial rather than in a formulated system of dogma. This becomes valid in the worshiper, in spirit and truth (John 4: 23), not in this mountain or in that mountain. Furthermore, it holds truth through orthopraxis in commitment to what revives life and enriches it (John 10:10). This is everlasting *koan* (an incomprehensible and mysterious statement) for the Christian faith, which is evidenced by orthopraxis as well.

10

Pneumatological Perspectives on World Religions

The Cosmic Spirit and Ch'i

Koo D. Yun

In the past, a Christological perspective on world religions brought forth division, dispute, and derogation of other faiths. In contrast, recent pneumatological perspectives help eschew unnecessary arguments and hostility between religions by underscoring the ubiquity of the cosmic Spirit.[1] In this article, I will first analyze pneumatologies of two premier scholars today, namely Jürgen Moltmann from Germany and Stanley Samartha from India. Second, I will look at the implications of their works in the Asian context that is religiously plural. Both Moltmann and Samartha support the idea that the Holy Spirit is present in people of other faiths. Moltmann particularly points out that Yahweh's *ruach* (Spirit) is present in every thing. This understanding of the Spirit is very similar to the Taoistic understanding of *ch'i* (*qi* or *ki*) that is the power of life interpenetrating all entities including both animate and inanimate objects. Furthermore, both pneumatologies of Moltmann and Taoists underscore continuity between the Holy Spirit (the primordial *ch'i*) and human spirit (substantial *ch'i*).

[1] See Veli-Matti Kärkkäinen, *An Introduction to the Theology of Religions: Biblical, Historical and Contemporary Perspectives* (Downers Grove, IL: InterVarsity, 2003). This book provides an excellent overview of theology of religions. Kärkkäinen also introduces theologians who employ pneumatological approaches, such as Jacques Dupuis, Gavin D'Costa, and Amos Yong.

Jürgen Moltmann

The Spirit of Father and the Spirit of Christ

In his groundbreaking book, *The Spirit of Life*, Jürgen Moltmann avers that the Holy Spirit is both "the Spirit of the Father" and "the Spirit of Christ." The work of creation is generally assigned to the Father, so the Spirit of the Father refers to *the Spirit of creation*. This creative Spirit, Yahweh's *ruach*, animates and gives life to all God's creation. As the divine energy of life, the creative Spirit interpenetrates all living things according to the Hebrew Scriptures.[2] Moltmann writes, "There [in the Old Testament], God's Spirit is the life-force of created things and the living apace in which they can grow and develop their potentialities."[3] The creative Spirit not only stays inside the church, but also stays outside the church. Furthermore, this creative Spirit remains universal.[4]

On the other hand, "the Spirit of Christ" alludes to *the Spirit of redemption* since the work of redemption is generally ascribed to Christ. The redemptive Spirit works on salvation, which not only involves one's soul but also the resurrection of the body and the new creation of all things. Gnostics taught the false idea that salvation was simply to escape from the evil body, but in the biblical sense, God's whole creation, which consists of both material and immaterial things, is longing for salvation.[5]

God's creative Spirit and redemptive Spirit stay one and the same. In this sense, both one's experience in the Christian faith and experience of social love lead to the same Holy Spirit, who is also present in nature, plants, animals, and the ecosystem of the earth. In other words, both the creative and redemptive aspects of the Holy Spirit belong to the one, same Spirit.[6]

I concur with Moltmann insofar as there are at least two aspects of the Holy Spirit, namely creative and redemptive. Most Evangelical and Pentecostal churches in America as well as most churches in South Korea refute the cosmic, ubiquitous aspect of the Spirit and solely accept the redemptive work of the Spirit. In this regard, the Spirit is present only in

[2] Jürgen Moltmann, *The Spirit of Life: A Universal Affirmation*, trans. Margaret Kohl (Minneapolis: Fortress, 1992) 8.

[3] Ibid., 84.

[4] Ibid., 8.

[5] Ibid., 9.

[6] Ibid., 9–10.

the church. On the contrary, Moltmann argues that the Holy Spirit as the life-force (vitality) and the living space is present in all creatures.

Is God an Object of Human Experience?

"No" has been the answer of most modern European thinkers according to Moltmann inasmuch as their constitution of reason inculcated that God as an object could neither be known nor experienced.[7] Immanuel Kant insisted that God as an object was hidden and unknowable. In human objectivity, God does not exist. God cannot be perceived in objectivity, but God can only be experienced in subjectivity. Descartes endeavored to prove God's existence in the human subject's certainty of herself, and Schleiermacher did similarly in "immediate self-consciousness." God is experienced subjectively in one's self-consciousness as "transcendental" condition, which is categorized as "self-transcendence" by Karl Rahner and "ecstatic self-transcendence" by Wolfhart Pannenberg.[8]

Moltmann contends that the modern European concept of experience is too narrow to embrace real and potential experiences. The modern concept of experience solely deals with consciousness in active terms. Moreover, it has a homogeneous and uniform structure. Therefore, one needs to expand this modern European constitution of experience in order that experience of God is not limited to "self-consciousness" or the human subject's experience of self.[9]

God can be also experienced objectively in the experience of others, nature, and sociality, as the Wisdom of Solomon 1:7 states, "God's spirit fills the world and he who holds all things together knows every sound." Wisdom 12:1 also says, "Thy immortal Spirit is in all things." One can experience God *in, with, and beneath* everyday experiences of the world because God is in all things and all things are in God.[10] The notion that God is in all things find its further basis from several passages in the Hebrew Bible. Job 33:4 says, "The Spirit of God has made me and the breath of the Almighty gives me life." Psalm 104:29–30 remarks, "When you hide your face, they are dismayed; when you take away their breath, they die and return to their dust. When you send forth your spirit [breath], they are created; and you renew the face of the ground." On the basis of these verses in the Hebrew Scriptures, one can conclude that the Spirit not only

7 Ibid., 31.

8 Ibid., 31–32.

9 Ibid., 34.

10 Ibid.

dwells in human beings as their breath, but she is also present in all things. Therefore, a person can experience the Spirit of God both in the "spiritual" realm and in the realm of everyday, sensuous events.

Ruach *and Spirit in Other Religions*

It is very difficult to translate the Hebrew word *ruach* into English. Although the Greek *pneuma*, the Latin *spiritus*, and the German *Geist* are antithetical to matter and body, *ruach* should not be understood in this dualistic context. In the Hebrew Bible, *ruach* can be perceived as a storm or force in body and soul. Therefore, *ruach Yahweh* can be best understood as "the divine energetic force or presence." Furthermore, Yahweh's *ruach* has two sides, namely, transcendent and immanent. In terms of the immanent side, the *ruach* correspond with *the power of life or power to live in all the living. Ruach* may be found in everything, and she keeps all things in being and in life.[11]

If one follows Moltmann's understanding of the Holy Spirit as the life-force or vitality of all created things, she or he cannot certainly deny the presence of the Spirit in other faiths. There is a life in other religions! Indubitably, people of other faiths have a robust desire for life and good living like Christians in the church. They are breathing because of the Spirit of life in them. These people of other faiths also long for love, joy, peace, patience, kindness, generosity, faithfulness, gentleness, and self-control (Gal 5:22). Therefore, we cannot doubt the Spirit's presence in other faiths. Rather, we are to question the degree and purity of the Spirit, but these criteria at the same time apply to the Spirit in the church as well.

Stanley J. Samartha (1920–2001)

Introduction

Stanley Samartha, one of the premier theologians in Asia, was born in India in 1920. He was the son of a pastor of the Basel Evangelical Mission and grew up in the South of India. He received theological education both in India and abroad. At Union Theological Seminary in New York, he studied with Paul Tillich and Reinhold Niebuhr and completed his doctorate degree at Hartford Seminary. He also studied under Karl Barth in Basel, Switzerland before his return to India in 1952. In 1968, he joined the staff of the World Council of Churches as an Associate Secretary in the Department of Studies in Mission and Evangelism. In his life, he devoted

[11] Ibid., 40–42.

his energy to ecumenical and interreligious dialogue. He passed away on July 22, 2001.[12]

The Reasons Preventing the Question about the Holy Spirit in People of Other Faiths

Before World War II, people of other religions were mostly treated as objects of Christian mission, but this situation has been drastically rectified after the war because more and more Christians started living with people of other faiths and ideological convictions. Christians today live in a religiously plural world. Often in this plural context, people raise the question concerning the presence of the Holy Spirit in other religions.[13]

There have been two main reasons which have stalled the debate about God's concern for people of other faiths. The first reason exemplifies syncretism that is defined as "an uncritical mixture of elements from other religions without center or integrating principle."[14] Despite such initial fear of syncretism during the 1970s and 1980s, no attempt in various interreligious dialogues was made to bring forth such a mixture of religions. Instead, interreligious dialogue usually pointed out difference. Hence, the fear of syncretism was proven to be unnecessary.[15]

The second reason stalling the debate deals with relativism, which accepts many absolutes so that truth is relative to each culture and religion. Many people feared that any recognition of the presence of God or the Spirit in other faiths would lead to the peril of relativism. During the past century, the study of religion in the West more or less taught are to perceive an other's strange thought and behavior in view of what is absolute for him or her.[16] In order to become aware of one's "self-absolutization," one first needs to change his or her attitude toward other religions and cultures.

Samartha demarcates pluralism from relativism. The plurality of religions and cultures does not necessarily lead to relativism. Human the-

[12] Konrad Raiser, "Tribute to Dr. Stanley J. Samartha," The World Council of Churches; available from Http://wcc-coe.org/wcc/what/interreligious/cd38–02.html; Internet; accessed 20 January 2006.

[13] Stanley Samartha, "The Holy Spirit and People of Other Faiths," *Ecumenical Review* 42 (2004) 250–52.

[14] Ibid., 252.

[15] Ibid.

[16] Jean Jacques Waardenburg, *Classical Approaches to the Study of Religion: Aims, Methods and Theories of Research* (The Hague: Mouton, 1973) 75, quoted in Stanley Samartha, "The Holy Spirit and People of Other Faiths," 253.

ologies and concepts about God exemplify human *responses* to Truth that are conditioned and diluted by history, and they are fallible and tainted. Hence, although Truth can be absolute, the human statements about the Truth cannot be absolute.[17] Samartha insists on relativity of human concepts of God, not relativity of God.

Deeper Factors Precluding the Interreligious Debate on the Spirit

Samartha expatiates upon other sensitive and deeper factors that have precluded the discussion about the relation of the Holy Spirit to people belonging to other faiths. The first factor is the equivocality and vagueness of the Holy Spirit in the Trinitarian context. In order to have a dialogue with people of other faiths, Christians ought to have a better comprehension of the person of the Spirit. But the christological or even christomonistic orientation of Western theologies in the past did not provide much clarification regarding the person of the Spirit, and she[18] was treated as an addendum. Not much theological reflection and clarification on the Spirit took place before the 4th century. Even the Nicea-Constantinople Creed of 381 did not unequivocally state the full divinity of the Spirit by not endorsing the *homoousios* of the Spirit.[19]

The second remains the question of *filioque*, namely, does the Spirit proceed from the Father alone or the Father and the Son? The Nicene Creed (A.D. 325) simply says, "And [we believe] in the Holy Spirit, and the Nicea-Constantinople Creed (A.D. 381) elaborates this further by stating, "I believe...in the Holy Spirit, the Lord, the Giver of Life, *who proceeds from the Father,* who with the Father and Son together is worshipped and together glorified."[20] The Latin Western Church added the *filioque* phrase (and the Son) later.[21] According to Samartha, this phrase has significant

[17] Samartha, "Other Faiths," 253.

[18] The feminine pronoun *she* is used here because the Hebrew word *ruach* exemplifies a feminine noun, and also I want to underscore the feminine qualities of the Holy Spirit. For more information on this, see Donald Gelpi, *The Divine Mother: A Trinitarian Theology of the Holy Spirit* (New York: University Press of America, 1984) 11.

[19] Samartha, "Other Faiths," 254.

[20] *Italics* are mine.

[21] For more information on the *filioque* controversy, see Karl Barth, *Church Dogmatics,* vol. I/1, trans. G. W. Bromiley (Edinburgh: T&T Clark, 1975) 479–87; Wolfhart Pannenberg, *Systematic Theology*, vol. I, trans. G. W. Bromiley (Grand Rapids: Eerdmans, 1991) 317–19. Karl Barth defends the *filioque* phrase, whereas both Pannenberg and Moltmann refute the *filioque.*

implication in terms of the presence and work of the Spirit in other faiths. The double procession of the Spirit, which accepts the filioque, may bring forth the limitation of the Spirit's activity because the Holy Spirit is available almost exclusively through the christological channel. In contrast, the single procession of the Spirit in the Eastern Church allows a bigger space for the Spirit to breathe more freely through the whole creation, not limited to Christians in the church.[22]

The third factor that prevents the interreligious debate on the Spirit's presence has to do with the link between the outpouring of the Spirit in Acts 2 and the works of the Spirit before Pentecost. The very fact that the Spirit spoke through various prophets of Israel in the Hebrew Bible might suggest some possibility of the Spirit's activity on prophets of other faiths.[23]

The fourth factor that averts further debate on the presence of the Spirit in other faiths is elicited by the relation between *baptism* and *gifts* of the Spirit. In the Acts of Apostles, especially chapter 10 and 19, the Holy Spirit was bestowed prior to the act of water baptism—for many Roman Catholics, this sacrament of (water) baptism brings a person into the church of Jesus Christ. Moreover, Samartha refers to a Hindu who receives many blessings from the Hindu divine *Sakti* (power or energy) by attending Christian charismatic services.[24] Samartha illustrates the presence and activity of the Holy Spirit outside the Christian church.

Discerning the Works of the Holy Spirit

Samartha provides four criteria in response to the question, "How do we discern the marks or works of the Holy Spirit according to the Bible?" The first criterion is freedom. The work of the Holy Spirit is so spontaneous and unpredictable that no one can clearly tell where the Spirit is heading. Second, the Spirit as "wind" stays boundless in such a way that she often transcends one's theological system and conventional wisdom. Creating new relationships is the third criterion insofar as the Spirit engenders reconciliation between two hostile groups and religions. Samartha presents examples of religious reconciliation in this article. The fourth criterion deals with new communities. When the genuine Spirit works, it brings

[22] Samartha, "Other Faiths," 255.

[23] Ibid., 256.

[24] Ibid.

forth new and peaceful communities. The new communities are imbued with acts of compassion, service, humility, and sacrifice.[25]

Samartha postulates that the most obvious way of discerning the works of the Spirit outside Christianity is found in Gal 5:22–23, "By contrast, the fruit of the Spirit is love, joy, peace, patience, kindness, generosity, faithfulness, gentleness, and self-control. There is no law against such things." These fruits of the Holy Spirit remain genuine signs of the works of the Spirit so that they do not necessitate any further theological investigations.[26]

Besides ethical dimensions, Samartha speaks of "inward" or "interior" dimensions of the Spirit's presence. These are less visible and not readily recognizable qualities. A person can procure these by being rooted in the Spirit or abiding in the depths of God, which leads one to serenity, restfulness, and inner peace. Inwardness or interiority underscores *being* in God, rather than *doing* something for God and other people. The Hindu and Buddhist traditions best emphasize this inwardness of the Spirit's presence.[27]

The major thrusts of Samartha's article are twofold: First, he concedes the presence of the Holy Spirit in people of other faiths. Second, the presence of the Spirit is somewhat discernable. In addition, according to the Hebrew Scriptures and the New Testament, Christians are not called to *restrict* the presence and work of the Holy Spirit, but called to *discern* them. Therefore, Christians cannot monopolize the presence of the Holy Spirit.

The Holy Spirit and Ch'i

One can readily find some similarities between Moltmann's construal of the Holy Spirit and *ch'i* insofar as both Yahweh's *ruach* (Spirit) and *ch'i* are understood as the power of life that interpenetrates all existing things. In accordance with Jürgen Moltmann, Yahweh's *ruach* possesses both transcendental and immanent aspects. As the immanent efficacy, the Holy Spirit is "the power of life in all the living."[28] Moltmann writes, "When we think about the *ruach*, we have to say that God is in all things, and all things are in God—though this does not mean making God the same as

25 Ibid., 258–59. See also Stanley Samartha, "The Holy Spirit and People of Various Faiths, Cultures, and Ideologies," in *The Holy Spirit,* ed. Dow Kilpatrick (Nashville: Tidings, 1974) 33. Here, Samartha elaborates on two more criteria, namely, life and order.

26 Ibid., 261.

27 Ibid.

28 Moltmann, *Spirit of Life*, 42.

everything else."[29] Furthermore, the Spirit can also be construed as space because *ruach* is related to *rewah*, meaning breadth. In other words, God's Spirit also refers to God's Space, in which all living beings can grow and unfold (Ps 31:8; Job 36:16).[30] As both the Spirit of life and space, the Holy Spirit stays ubiquitous and interpenetrates all things.

In Taoism, *ch'i* (*qi* or *ki*) is also understood as "the life force, vital breath, [and] inner pneuma of all existence."[31] As the life force, *Ch'i* interpenetrates not only the living being but also all natural objects. Chapter 43 of the *Tao Te Ching* states, "The softest thing in the world dashes against and overcomes the hardest; that which has no (substantial) existence [*ch'i*] enters where there is no crevice. I know hereby what advantage belongs to doing nothing (with a purpose)."[32] The formless, unsubstantial *ch'i* penetrates into all existing entities. Moreover, this *ch'i* sustains the structure of the universe.[33]

Ch'i is inherent in all four areas of life: the body, nature, the sky, and society, which equally stems from the true all-encompassing *Tao*. There is no structural difference between *ch'i* in humans and *ch'i* in nature. *Ch'i* existing in the four areas of life varies with different density and velocity. *Ch'i* can be either too thick or too thin; it can also flow too fast or too slow. Traditional Chinese medicine specified the movements of *ch'i* in the body. The *yin* and *yang* system expatiates on various activities of *ch'i*.[34]

Any entity, including a human being can deviate from its inherent harmony given by the *Tao*. Typically, one's excessive activity causes this deviation. For example, physical over-exercise can cause harm to one's body because she did it too much. Greed, fear, and even earthquakes are engendered by the derailment of *ch'i*. When the flow of *ch'i* is blocked, it results in irregularity and disharmony in oneself and nature. One needs to reopen this blockage by acupuncture, moxibustion, mediation, and prayer.[35]

In addition to the universal presence of the Spirit, both Moltmann and Taoism also accept the continuity between the Spirit of God (the

[29] Ibid., 42.

[30] Ibid., 43.

[31] Livia Kohn, "Chinese Religion," in *The Human Condition*, ed. Robert Neville (Albany: State University of New York Press, 2001) 23.

[32] *The Sacred Books of China: The Texts of Taoism*, trans. James Legge (New York: Dover, 1962) 87.

[33] Paul Chung elaborates further on *Ch'i* in chapter 15 of this volume, "The Mystery of God and *Tao* in the Jewish-Christian-Taoist Context."

[34] Kohn, "Chinese Religion," 24.

[35] Ibid., 24–26.

Primordial *Ch'i*) and the spirit (*ch'i*) of existent things. In contrast to most modern Protestant theologians (including Karl Barth) who separated the two, Moltmann teaches the continuity between the two. It is the same Spirit of God who is present in humans, living creatures, and nature. God's Spirit of Creation and God's Spirit of redemption are the one and the same.

Each force (*ch'i*) exemplifies a manifestation of the *Tao* without an active break from the pure, shapeless *Tao*. *The Primordial ch'i* (*yuanqi*) was part of the *Tao* before creation (substantial existence). According to chapter 42 of the *Tao Te Ching*, the *Tao* is the One! The One produces Two; Two produces Three; Three produced all things.[36] All things originated from the *Tao*, which is one, and all things endeavor to return to the origin. In the philosophical framework of Taoism, there is a clear continuity between the *Tao* and the manifested *ch'i.*

The theology of the *Donghak* movement in Korea also found a continuity between the "Utmost Energy" (God) and the spirit in a human body. Jae Woo Choi (C.E. 1824–1864), the key leader of the *Donghak* Movement, promulgated the notion that the "Utmost Energy" represents the creative energy that is pantheistically immanent in human bodies as well as cosmos-nature. The *Donghak* incantation, which functioned like the Lord's Prayer in Christianity remarks,

> Oh Utmost Energy, I'm praying for your advent here and now. Wait on God and everything goes well. Don't forget God at any time and you get to know All. To wait on means that *the divine spirit is inside the body,* the energization is outside the body, and everyone knows the truth which cannot be relocated.[37]

This active energy of the Spirit is not only inherent in the human body, it can also provide harmony and peace in the cosmos as well as physical healing and prophecy.

The Spirit's Discontinuity in Barth's Theology

Many theologians and philosophers of modern Europe overemphasized the transcendental aspect of the Holy Spirit at the expense of the Spirit's immanent side. One step further, they insisted on the discontinuity between God's Spirit and human spirit. Karl Barth is a prime example of

[36] *The Sacred Books of China*, 85.

[37] Kyoung-Jae Kim, "The Cosmotheandric Vision in the Third Millennium," *Exchange* 28, no. 4 (October 1999) 351–63.

these thinkers, but Moltmann argues that the Spirit is both the Spirit of creation and the Spirit of the church. As Stanley Samartha points out previously, the Scriptures do not ask Christians to control or restrict the presence and work of the Spirit, but ask them to discern the Spirit(s).

Karl Barth speaks of discontinuity between the Holy Spirit and human spirit. In his lecture "The Holy Spirit and Christian Life" (1929), Barth points out the radical difference between God's Spirit and human spirit because there is no continuity between Creator and creatures.[38] In several places in *Church Dogmatics*, even though Karl Barth accepts the fact that the Holy Spirit dwells in believers, he repeatedly underscores that the divine Spirit always remain distinct from human spirits. Barth reiterates the difference between the two in *Evangelical Theology*:

> There are also *other* spirits, those created good by God, such as the spirit natural to man. Moreover, there are demonic, erring, and disruptive spirits of annihilation which deserve nothing else than to be driven out. *But none of these are the sovereign power of which we speak.* Of none of them, not even of the best among them, can it be said that where they are, there is freedom.[39]

The Spirit's Presence in Other Faiths

In view of the pneumatologies of Jürgen Moltmann and Stanley Samartha, it would be very hard to refute the presence of the Holy Spirit in people of other faiths. In terms of exterior criteria, these people meliorate ethical virtues such as love, kindness, and generosity through their religious practices. In terms of interior criteria, they find inner peace, serenity and restfulness in their religious devotion. In terms of social dimensions, Samartha points out that these people of other faiths also promote renewed communities that go beyond prejudice and limitation of each religious tradition so that they can perceive peace between religions. These people of other faiths, moreover, exhibit ecological sensitivity by revering the whole nature that includes both spiritual and material entities.

Even in the Hebrew Bible, God's Spirit not only came upon Israelites but also non-Israelites. Balak, a Moabite ruler, asked Balaam to anathematize the Israelites, but Balaam instead blessed the Israelites according to Yahweh's order. The Book of Numbers 24:2 remarks, "Balaam looked

[38] Moltmann, *Spirit of Life*, 6.

[39] Karl Barth, *Evangelical Theology: An Introduction* (Grand Rapids: Eerdmans, 1963) 53. Emphasis is mine.

up and saw Israel camping tribe by tribe. Then *the spirit of God came upon him*."[40] Balaam was neither an Israelite nor a Moabite, but God's Spirit came upon him. Hence, he saw visions and made prophetic utterances.[41]

In the New Testament, God also worked with Cornelius prior to his conversion in Acts 10. That he received a vision and utterance antecedently should be accepted as the preparatory work of the Holy Spirit. In terms of a narrow definition of Christian, Cornelius was a non-Christian when he received the vision from the Spirit in Acts 10.[42] Moreover, in Acts 10:44, the Holy Spirit came upon the Gentile audience at Cornelius' house in the middle of Peter's sermon. It is logical to think that the Gentiles at that time underwent neither conversion nor (water) baptism (Acts 10:47). From a sacramentalist standpoint, the Spirit had come upon them even before they became Christians. On the basis of the previous verses, one may conclude that the Holy Spirit is also present and active in non-Christians.

Although it would be hard to negate the presence and activity of the Spirit in other faiths, one should still raise questions concerning the degree and purity of the Spirit's presence. As Taoists mention the deviated *Ch'i*, Christians also speak of evil/demonic spirits, which bring about estrangement and destruction, instead of bringing and preserving peace, unity, harmony and life. Despite the fact that discerning the spirits appears very challenging, it is still possible by focusing on the interiority, exteriority, and sociality of the Spirit as Samartha engaged in this task throughout his life.

Toward a Holistic Pneumatology

Modern European theologies in general have endeavored to comprehend God from a christological (or even christomonistic) perspective, so that the role of the Holy Spirit in salvation and the ubiquity of the Spirit in creation have been unrelated. They also tended to be rationalistic and reductionistic by leaving out experiential, emotive, and abductive aspects of a human being. The conscious, rational construal of human self and subjectivity excluded the unconscious and emotive sides of religion; as a result, religion became unduly dry and intellectual.

[40] Emphasis is mine.

[41] Cf. Michael Welker, *God the Spirit*, trans. John Hoffmeyer (Minneapolis: Fortress, 1994) 96–98.

[42] Cf. Clark H. Pinnock, *Flame of Love: A Theology of the Holy Spirit* (Downers Grove, IL: InterVarsity, 1996) 201.

Against this reductionistic, rational orientation, theologians like Jürgen Moltmann and Donald Gelpi along with the author invoke a *holistic* pneumatology, which shies way from previous narrow pneumatological understandings that limited the Holy Spirit to the Christian church only. These previous pneumatologies undermined freedom and spontaneity of the Spirit, which resulted in dissipation of exuberant charisms in the mainstream modern European churches. To some degree, the 20th century Pentecostal movement retrieved the experiential and emotive aspects of the Christian faith, so pneumatologies became more holistic.

Nowadays churches long for a pneumatology that embraces both the Spirit of redemption and creation, as well as the Spirit of mind (*Geist*), the Spirit of heart (emotion), and the Spirit of nature (physicality). Christians today call for a pneumatology which includes both transcendental and immanent dimensions of the Holy Spirit. God is not merely the "Wholly Other" but also the "God with us and in us." At the beginning of the third millennium, we long to see, touch, and feel the presence of the Divine Spirit. Come, Holy Spirit!

11

The Christian Witness to Buddhists

John B. Cobb, Jr.

Buddhist Universalism

GAUTAMA sought the salvation of all sentient beings. He did so by explaining the cause of suffering and showing the way to gain freedom from suffering. He proposed a way that did not require superhuman austerities. Nevertheless, others, including those most closely associated with him, found his path extremely difficult.

Standard Buddhist teaching in the Theravada tradition pictured the way to salvation as requiring many lifetimes. Over a period of thousands of years the rare soul could move from the ordinary human condition to that freedom from all attachment that is the life of the saint. Such a soul could then enter Nirvana.

Other Buddhists were disturbed by the elitist character of this doctrine that removed the ordinary Buddhist so far from enlightenment. They dubbed this teaching Hinayana, the lesser vehicle, and they proposed that the true Buddhist position was Mahayana, the greater vehicle. Here there is emphasis on enlightenment in this life, and hence on understanding how it can be obtained. It was in its Mahayana form that Buddhism moved into China, Korea, and Japan.

The primary interest in Mahayana has been on meditational methods that enable the meditator to realize truth. These have been highly varied, but all are quite demanding. They require time and personal discipline, and many who have tried them have still not received enlightenment.

From very early times many Buddhists felt themselves quite unable to attain enlightenment by their own efforts. They looked for help to the Buddhas. Legends grew up about Bodhisattvas, those who are spiritually ready for Buddhahood but who, out of their great compassion for the multitude, vowed not to enter Nirvana unless all sentient beings could be saved. This salvation they effected by creating worlds, called Pure Lands, to which people could go when they died. A Pure Land is not Nirvana, but unlike the present world, a Pure Land makes it easy to attain enlightenment. And whereas the requirements for attaining enlightenment in this life are still very difficult to fulfill, the requirements specified by the Bodhisattvas for entering the Pure Land on death were quite practical. They usually included the avoidance of gross immorality and calling on the name of the Buddha with sincere faith.

One such legend gained preeminence. It was said that an Indian prince by the name of Dharmakara vastly excelled all the others, creating a Pure Land which subsumed them all and simplifying the requirements for entering it to the greatest extent possible. This prince then became the Buddha Amida. For the Pure Land tradition it is Amida who is the true savior.

The general Buddhist understanding in China was that the primary and most appropriate way in which one should seek salvation was through the monastic life with its meditational disciplines. But for those who could not or would not submit to this pattern of life, a second, lower, possibility was acknowledged. It was this to which many ordinary lay people turned as their only hope. Hence the Pure Land tradition in Mahayana Buddhism was important as the expression of its concern for the universality of salvation.

In Japan in the twelfth century, two developments occurred. First Honen and his disciples came to the conclusion that although in past epochs self-salvation through discipline had been possible, in this evil time it is not. The merciful vow of Amida, far from providing an inferior alternative to the superior self-salvation, offered the only possible way of salvation. And second, especially in the formulations of Shinran, faith was declared to be the *only* requirement for receiving the grace through which alone salvation was possible, and this faith as well was understood to be the gift of Amida. With great insight Shinran understood that if salvation is for all it may not depend on any human merit but solely on the grace of Amida.

Whereas Shinran was correct that the universal compassion of Buddhism could best come to expression through his doctrine of salvation by grace through faith alone, he was not inclusive in other respects. In this, he resembled Luther. When Luther understood that monastic disciplines were irrelevant to justification, he opposed monasteries. Similarly Honen and Shinran opposed the disciplines and meditational practices of other Buddhist schools.

But this exclusiveness is not necessary. Christians today know that although they are justified apart from special spiritual disciplines, they are free to practice those disciplines. The disciplines they are free to practice include Buddhist as well as traditional ones. They practice them not in order to be justified but because they want the depth and spiritual maturity that such disciplines can help to provide. There is nothing in Pure Land Buddhism to prevent its encouragement of the important and effective disciplines developed in other schools such as Zen. What is important is that salvation not be understood in such a way that people are *driven* into these disciplines. The Pure Land Buddhist or the Christian is free to practice Zen meditation or not to practice it. There is no obligation. Understood in this way, Pure Land thought and practice can rightly see themselves as the fulfillment of the Buddhist quest for universality.[1]

Amida as Christ

Christians sometimes use "Christ" as a proper name for Jesus. This is misleading. At the very least it should be distinguished as a title given to Jesus because of his redemptive work. The Christian knows Jesus *as* the Christ. Similarly it is possible to use "Amida" as a proper name for the Indian prince Dharmakara, but this too is misleading. It is only as this human being became a Buddha that he acquired the name Amida. There is some parallelism here, but it is far from perfect, and in this usage "Christ" and "Amida" do not refer to the same reality. Amida is not Christ in this sense.

But the meanings of Amida and Christ have not remained at this level. Christ could be thought of as the preexistent one who took on human form in Jesus and then returned to the right hand of the Father, with or without his human body. Amida is the Buddha who is now in Nirvana. Both Christ and Amida are divine beings, but they are quite different. This Christ is a supernatural being subordinate to God and most naturally conceived along Arian lines. Amida is one Buddha among others, however great. There are similarities, but this Christ is not Amida and this Amida is not Christ.

The early church, however, repudiated Arian subordinationism. Christ is not a creature, however exalted. Christ is God. But when we

[1] This, of course, is a claim made by some Jodoshinshu Buddhists, for example, by Prof. Yoshifumi Ueda.

say Christ, we are not simply referring to God in general but speaking of God as everlasting Word, creatively and redemptively working in the world. This is the Truth that opens us to all truths. Similarly, in Pure Land Buddhist reflection, Amida did not remain one Buddha among others. Amida came to name instead the reality that is incarnate in all Buddhas. This raises the question whether Amida as that which is incarnate in all Buddhas and Christ as the creative and redemptive activity of God in the world name the same reality. I believe they do, but this must be shown.

When pressed along the lines indicated, Pure Land teaching can lose much of its distinctiveness. What is incarnate in all Buddhas, it is generally understood, is Emptiness or Nirvana. Amida can then become another name for Emptiness without altering the meaning of Emptiness. If this path is followed, then again Amida is not Christ.

Nevertheless, there is an important distinction which preserves Pure Land's distinctive teaching. It can best be made in relation to the traditional Buddhist teaching about the Buddha body. In this teaching ultimate reality, understood as that which is embodied by each Buddha, is called the Body of Dharma or *Dharmakaya*. The form taken by *Dharmakaya* in individual human beings when they become Buddhas is the Manifest Body or *Nirmanakaya*. The form taken by *Dharmakaya* in the Buddhas who rule over their Pure Lands is the Body of Bliss or *Sambhogakaya*. Amida is not the *Dharmakaya* as such but rather the *Sambhogakaya*.

The true character of the *Sambhogakaya* is manifest in the vows of the Bodhisattvas and especially in the vow of Dharmakara. But in the deepest understanding, Amida is not simply the new and glorified form of Dharmakara as he rules over his Pure Land. Amida is the *Sambhogakaya* itself which is perfectly embodied or incarnate in the vow of *Dharmakara*. What is there manifest is wisdom and compassion, the essential characteristics of the *Sambhogakaya*.

In most schools of Buddhist thought, even when Amida is understood in this view, he is subordinate to the *Dharmakaya*. This is because the *Dharmakaya*, ultimate reality as such, is beyond and above the other manifestations of the Buddha body. Amida as the *Sambhogakaya* still has a distinct character, the character of wisdom and compassion. The *Dharmakaya* as such is beyond all forms. Ultimate reality assumes the form of *Sambhogakaya* for the sake of those who cannot realize ultimate reality as such, but this is a concession to human weakness and should not be taken as the ultimate truth. In this view, the deepest and purest achievement of enlightenment can bypass the *Sambhogakaya* and realize the *Dharmakaya* itself.

Even among Jodoshinshu believers this relativization of Amida and his subordination to the *Dharmakaya* is sometimes accepted. This is easy for Christians to understand because similar tendencies were present in the early church where the Logos was often regarded as subordinate to the Father and sometimes even as a creature. But Christians recognized that faith in Christ can be existentially ultimate only if Christ is truly God. Insofar as anything else is regarded as superior to Amida, Amida cannot name for Buddhists what Christ names for Christians.

The conceptual and traditional pressure on Pure Land Buddhists to acknowledge the subordination of Amida to the *Dharmakaya* is greater than the analogous pressure on Christians to subordinate Christ to the Father. But in Shinran himself this pressure is strongly resisted, at least so far as religion is concerned. In our concrete situation, Amida is ultimate. Amida is ultimate reality *for us*, because ultimate reality for us *is* wise and compassionate.

Here as elsewhere, I have found the conceptuality of Alfred North Whitehead useful in the understanding of Buddhism. Elsewhere I followed the Western tradition in calling ultimate reality *esse*, being, or *Sein*. Whitehead's term is creativity. He, too, recognizes that ultimate reality as creativity is beyond all forms since in principle it is susceptible of any form whatever. In many respects his analysis of creativity corresponds to some Buddhist accounts of the *Dharmakaya*, especially as *Dharmakaya* is explained in terms of dependent origination.

But Whitehead believes that in actuality, although creativity is completely without any character of its own, it is never experienced apart from a primordial ordering of the infinite array of the forms or pure possibilities. This ordering is directed to the realization of novel intensities of feeling in the actual instances of creativity, that is, in such creatures as ourselves. Thus what is wholly without character in itself has been primordially characterized by a decision that ordered what is possible for the sake of all creatures. Whitehead calls this character of creativity the Primordial Nature of God.[2] There is no creativity not characterized by this Nature.

Pure Land Buddhism has come to its formulations in quite a different way, but they are remarkably congruous with Whitehead's. In Amida the *Dharmakaya* has a primordial character. This character is fully revealed in the vow of Dharmakara as the aim to save all sentient beings. There is

[2] "The primordial nature of God is the acquirement by creativity of a primordial character." Alfred North Whitehead, *Process and Reality*, corrected edition, eds. David Ray Griffin and Donald W. Sherburne (New York: Free Press, 1978) 344.

for Shinran no access to an ultimate reality that is not characterized by the primordial vow.

Viewed in this way, the tendency to subordinate ultimate reality as primordially characterized to ultimate reality apart from any character appears arbitrary. All that could ever be *actually* experienced or realized is ultimate reality *with* its primordial character. To regard ultimate reality in abstraction from this character as superior to ultimate reality as thus characterized seems to express an unnecessary prejudice.

There are at least two Buddhist reasons for opposing the view I am presenting. The first is that we can have no advance notion of enlightenment, even that it will realize wisdom and compassion. To assert that enlightenment will be characterized in this way implies some pre-established pattern to which it must conform. This is precisely the way of thinking which must be abandoned if enlightenment is to be attained.

However, this objection does not apply in relation to Whitehead's understanding. The primordial ordering of forms for the sake of promoting intensities in the creatures does not make possible prediction of what specific forms will be relevant. On the contrary, it is precisely this ordering that is the basis for creative novelty and appropriate spontaneity in the world. That the act performed by the Enlightened One expresses wise compassion may be recognized when it is performed, but the anticipation that the act will be one of wise compassion does not afford any way of predicting its particular form. Wise compassion is always spontaneous.

A second Buddhist reason for opposing this view is the claim that people can realize the *Dharmakaya* as such apart from all forms. But this claim is not evidently established by history or present experience. All Buddhists expect that Buddhas will be wise and compassionate. In standard Buddhist teaching this wisdom and compassion express their full realization of ultimate reality. There is no apparent evidence of a higher state in which wisdom and compassion are left behind. Hence it is not clear how this attainment can be used to argue for the superiority of the *Dharmakaya* as such to the *Dharmakaya* as characterized by wisdom and compassion, that is, to the *Sambhogakaya* or Amida.

It is sometimes held that the teaching of the wisdom and compassion of ultimate reality as *Sambhogakaya* is *upaya*, that is, skilful means for drawing people toward the realization of an ultimate reality that has no character whatsoever. But is it not equally possible that the teaching that ultimate reality can be realized apart from any character whatsoever is skillful means for encouraging the withdrawal of attention from all forms, including the most attractive ones? It may well be that in order to realize ultimate reality with its wisdom and compassion through Zen discipline, for example, one must detach oneself completely from any concern about wisdom and compassion. But this provides no support for any ultimate subordination of Amida to the *Dharmakaya* as such.

Whitehead's account of the Primordial Nature of God addresses the same feature of reality as that spoken of by Shinran as the primal vow of Amida. Both of these are remarkably analogous to the Johannine and patristic accounts of the Word of God or Logos or Truth which is Christ. That, too, is a primordial character apart from which nothing exists. It is a creative-redemptive character.

The conclusion from the above is that Amida is Christ. That is, the feature of the totality of reality to which Pure Land Buddhists refer when they speak of Amida is the same as that to which Christians refer when we speak of Christ. This does not mean that Buddhists are completely accurate in their account of this reality—nor that Christians are. It does mean that Christians can gain further knowledge about Christ by studying what Buddhists have learned about Amida. It means also that Buddhists can gain further knowledge about Amida by studying what Christians have learned about Christ. Indeed, we should be able to reflect together about many questions of concern to both of us. But truly joint work is still in our future. For the present we consider in partial separation what each can learn from the other.

What Buddhists Can Learn from Christians

The preceding has dealt in general terms with what Christians can appropriate from Buddhism and included some discussion for the specific contribution of Pure Land Buddhists. For example, Christians can learn that Christ's concern is for all sentient creatures and not for human beings alone. Also we can more clearly perceive that much of what we have regarded until now as faith in Christ is idolatrous. That is, Christ is too often understood as a feature of reality bound to particular times and places and yet is treated as absolute. Such faith is a form of clinging from which reflection about Amida can help to set us free. It correlates with Arian heresy rather than Christian orthodoxy. Christ is God and not anything more limited.

Even when it is recognized that Christ is God, faith in Christ can still be a kind of clinging. One may cling to some past manifestation of Christ or identify faith in Christ with particular beliefs and practices. Against this the church at its best has taught that Christ is Truth itself and not a particular truth. To have faith in Christ is to be open to all truth and to all reality—not to cling to one truth and one reality. To trust Christ is to abandon all prejudice, all defenses, and to receive all that can be received. The recognition that Christ is Amida will help us toward this faith.

But in this section our interest is primarily in what Buddhists can learn of Amida when they recognize that Amida *is* Christ. Two areas of investigation are potentially fruitful here: 1) The sense in which Amida is personal; and 2) The sense in which Amida is ethical.

1. The view of Amida as ultimate reality characterized by wisdom and compassion is the most fully demythologized form of the understanding of Amida. But in this form Amida is somewhat less personal than is Christ in the dominant forms of Christian thought. Since the question of the sense in which God is personal is important, we will consider somewhat further the relation of Christian thinking about Christ to Shinran's understanding of Amida.

From one point of view the personal element is just as strong in the teaching concerning Amida as in the idea of the Christian God. Amida is Dharmakara, a legendary human being who has become a Buddha. As *a* Buddha he certainly retains personal characteristics even though he is now radically trans-human. But since this suggests that Amida is simply one Buddha among others, I did not emphasize this approach above when arguing that Amida is recognizable as Christ or the Word of God.

Still, we can see in Pure Land Buddhism, as in Christianity, the effort to hold together the universal and the personal in that to which faith is directed. Amida is that Buddha in whom the intentions of all Buddhas are fulfilled. In a sense Amida includes all other Buddhas without ceasing to be a personal being. As the Body of Bliss or *Sambhogakaya* assumed by Dharmakara, he is also the *Sambhogakaya* as such.

The point here is not to suggest that Pure Land Buddhism has solved the problem of holding together the personal and the universal elements in the understanding of Amida. The point is only that, as in Christianity, both elements are present and prized. To whatever extent Christian theology has succeeded in attaining a doctrine of God that does justice to both elements in a coherent manner, this can be of help to Pure Land Buddhism, too.

There is another sense of the personal, however, which is important for many Christians but runs counter to the mainstream of Pure Land teaching. This is the element of interaction between God and human beings. Christian prayer is ordinarily experienced as presupposing that God "hears" us. That means that God takes account of contingent human acts as they occur. Biblical language suggests that God rejoices when a sinner repents and knows when even a sparrow dies. What we do to the least of our brothers and sisters we do also to Christ. It even seems that God's activity is adjusted to changing circumstances.

This imagery has been in tension with that orthodox philosophical theology which has insisted upon divine immutability. The implications of this doctrine are that while God acts upon us, we can in no way affect God's experience. God's action expresses perfect love, but this is a purely active love, not one of receptivity or empathy. In the twentieth century there has been extensive theological critique of this understanding of divine immutability. There has been an effort to give less qualified affirmation to the biblical imagery of personal interaction between God and human beings. Philosophical theologians influenced by Whitehead have long argued against the monopolar prejudice of traditional theism in favor of a dipolarity of activity and receptivity in God.

Whitehead's formulation of this dipolarity is in terms of the Primordial and the Consequent Natures of God. It is the Primordial nature which qualifies creativity in a way so strikingly similar to the qualification of the *Dharmakaya* by the primal vow. Just as the Primordial Nature of God is the primordial decision for the sake of all creatures, even more clearly the primal vow is made for the sake of all sentient beings. But there is no sense among Buddhists that we can contribute anything to Amida. There is no encouragement of prayers of petition or intercession, no idea that Amida "hears" our prayers. There is, in other words, nothing comparable to what Whitehead calls the Consequent Nature of God.

Much of traditional Christian theology also lacks this element, but in actual Christian piety, based on biblical imagery and Christian experience, the sense of personal interaction with God has been so strong that it is worth considering whether Buddhists can extend their understanding of Amida to include this aspect of what Christians have found in Christ.

For many Buddhists there is a sharp contrast between Samsara as the world of dependent origination (*pratitya-samutpada* or *engi*) and Nirvana as the perfect world of the enlightened. Given such a contrast there would be strong reason to deny that the Enlightened One could be affected by events in the world of *pratitya-samutpada*. The Enlightened One might exert a gracious influence in this sphere, but there could be no reciprocal effect.

However, Nagarjuna, and much of Mahayana Buddhism following him, rejected this idea of two worlds. There is no world beyond the world of *pratitya-samutpada.* It is in the true realization of *that* world that enlightenment lies. In this case the Buddhas are not outside this world; they are the perfect realization of this world. That means that they are perfectly affected by everything we do at the same time that we are affected by them. The Buddha unites perfect receptivity to perfect activity.

What now of the *Sambhogakaya* which is incarnated in each Buddha? Should it not have the same duality of relations? At least in Christian experience and teaching it has seemed appropriate to believe that the One that gives gracious character to ultimate reality also responds perfectly to all that happens in the world. It is hard to see that anything of worth would be lost to Buddhists if they assimilated from the Christian knowledge of Christ the conviction that our lives are in this way of importance to Amida.

2. What Christians most miss in Buddhism is often referred to as the ethical and especially the social-ethical emphasis. Some Buddhists have acknowledged that in this area they have something to learn from Christianity. And there are already movements among Japanese Buddhists seeking to fill this lacuna. Especially in the area of activity for peace have Buddhists given leadership.

Nevertheless, the basic difference between Christians and Buddhists remains quite marked. The difficulty is in stating this accurately and fairly, for sweeping statements to the effect that Buddhism is not an ethical religion or lacks a social ethic can be extremely misleading. It is well, first, to state what is *not* lacking.

The point is not that Buddhist cultures fail to do a good job of socialization. They have well-developed structures of society with clear understanding of socially desirable behavior patterns, and their members conform to social needs and expectations with a minimum of coercion. On the whole, Buddhist societies probably function better than Christian ones, and could well be said to be more moral.

Secondly, Buddhism tends to make the mores of a society more humane. It discourages violence and greed. It works against exploitation of the weak. Its opposition to the caste system in India reflects this basic humanism. Buddhists societies have also, on the whole, been more pacific than Christian ones. One would not expect wars to be fought for the sake of Buddha as Christians have fought for the sake of Christ. Buddhist societies tend to be more tolerant religiously.

Third, there is no lack of personal kindness and generosity in Buddhist societies. Buddhism encourages these virtues as much as Christianity and perhaps inhibits them less. They are directly related to the quest for enlightenment and especially to its attainment. They may even be expressed in heroic ways. Buddhists are as likely as Christians to sacrifice themselves for the good of the community.

Fourth, Buddhists shoulder their responsibilities within the community with as much fortitude and discipline as do Christians. Buddhism encourages its adherents to work faithfully and diligently at the assigned tasks, not seeking recognition or reward. In this respect also the level of morality in Buddhist societies is high.

What seems to the Christian to be missing, then, is not virtue or goodness. What is lacking is a trans-social norm by virtue of which society is judged. Even this must be stated with care. Buddhist humanism does provide a check against the tendency to value people only in terms of their social role or relationship to others. Human beings do count as such, and hence their welfare does stand as a norm against existing social structure and behavior. But this potential principle of leverage is rarely thematically developed. On the whole, Buddhism does not encourage attention by its adherents to critical evaluation of social and political programs or exhort them to be in the forefront of movements of social protest. This seems to be because the mode of the relation of individuals to trans-social reality, namely, to Emptiness or to Amida, does not direct them to a judgment of social structures and their historical roles.

Initially at least, these comments should be taken as descriptive rather than as negative criticism. Christians are deeply divided as to whether the socially critical aspect of our heritage is of central importance or whether our faith, like Buddhism, relates primarily to our inwardness. Some converts to Buddhism find its freedom from this struggle and from the guilt associated with it profoundly attractive and santisfying. Buddhists may point to the extremely ambiguous effects of Christian efforts to shape history and argue that the results for all will be better if those efforts are abandoned.

But from the Christian point of view, this lack *is* a flaw. Many Christians look at the global situation historically and are appalled by the danger that human beings may bring upon themselves—unparalleled disaster and suffering if not actual extinction. Even if the human race muddles through these threats, we find intolerable the level of suffering inflicted on the world's poor and on our fellow nonhuman creatures through wrongly conceived programs of so-called "development." It seems of utmost importance that humane people guide in re-directing us away from our destructive political course. Any form of Christianity or of Buddhism that turns the attention and energy of humane people away from these global problems is inadequate.

The question, then, is whether Buddhists could discover from the Christian experience of Christ those aspects of Amida which would strengthen their critical orientation to the socio-historical world. That question can be approached through consideration of the characteristics of biblical and Western ethics that have functioned in this way.

In the Bible God is often conceived as lawgiver and judge. Although Jewish society in part embodies these laws and is thereby sanctioned by this view of God, God's commands are frequently experienced as judging the society. Certainly God stands beyond society as a trans-social source of norms whose commands have direct social relevance. The question as to whether society is functioning rightly is constantly renewed.

There is no doubt that this biblical view directs attention to issues of social justice, but it has its own problems. First, it has a strongly mythological cast, which can lead to the attribution to God of almost any command. Second, it produces a legalistic structure of life and self-understanding, against which Christianity is constantly struggling and which has driven many of its most sensitive children from its fold. Thirdly, it can work against the growth of creative imagination and sensitivity, which are so badly needed if problems are to be dealt with wisely.

The first can be removed by going from a mythological deity to categorical imperatives, which can be worked out in a fully rational system. But this does little to overcome the other objections. Living by categorical imperatives is even more legalistic than living in obedience to divine commands. The fact that the source of one's principles is one's own reason adds arrogance to the problematic. And these principles are likely to interfere with intelligent responsiveness to the actual needs of people and institutions.

Even if Christians could endorse the theory of divine commands or categorical imperatives, we could not recommend them as a possible development of Buddhist thought. Buddhism offers a way to escape from the too-structured world into freedom and spontaneity. To propose that it adopt legalism as part of its goal would be too ad hoc and distasteful to be relevant at all.

The Bible offers other images of God's relation to the world more appropriate to Christ. Deeper than the image of the one who commands is that of the one who offers and calls. This image is in greater continuity with that of Amida and yet extends it in the direction that seems important to me.

The call of Christ can be understood as mythically as the command of God. But it can be demythologized without reducing the actual role of Christ. The call consists in introducing into our existence, moment by moment, possibilities for our self-actualization that lead to good for ourselves and for others. These involve a tension between what simply is and what might be and should be. They involve some urge or impulse to the realization of desirable possibilities. By doing so, they introduce a space for human freedom. We are free to create ourselves in relation both to the actual world from which we come and to these new possibilities for our existence. The effective working of these liberating and challenging possibilities is the presence of the creative and redemptive Christ. Christ is present as the life-giving call to be more than we have been both for our own sake and for the sake of others.

The relation between traditional Buddhism and Christianity can be clarified by attention again to *pratitya-samutpada*, dependent origination. This is the coalescence of the world into the new experience. That world includes both what is actual and what is possible. Christian spirituality has concentrated on discerning the possibilities, determining which constitute God's call, and responding appropriately thereto. Buddhist disciplines have concentrated on the realization that what is occurring is just this coalescence in which there is finally no dualism of subject and object. Attention has been directed to the actual world as it coalesces rather than to novel possibilities.

Buddhist disciplines have been far more refined and effective than Christian ones, partly because the latter have not overcome the illusions of substance and dualism. Further, the openness attained by the Buddhist is in fact an openness to the possibilities of each situation as well as to the actualities that constitute it. But because Buddhism does not encourage attention to this side of the coalescence and does not thematize what is involved, the Christians misses in Buddhism the ethics which arise from the core experience of Christ.

For the Pure Land Buddhist who recognizes that Amida is Christ it may be possible to expand the understanding and experience of Amida's grace. Amida's vow may be understood to give us freedom, to invite us quite specifically to achieve what can be achieved by freedom in each moment, and to make possible the response to that invitation. To extend the understanding of Amida in that way need not violate what the Buddhist has come to know of Amida in the past.

If the call of Amida is to be understood as more than immediate and private, if it is to be experienced as having social and world-historical meaning, then other changes in traditional Buddhism will also be needed. Buddhism has concentrated on liberating us from our false conceptualizations. These include the ways in which we understand society and history, and ourselves as participants in these. We are sorely in need of such liberation. But this freedom should be used to arrive at better concepts and theories. If we are called to live for others as well as for ourselves, we are also called to think in such a way that our decisions will truly benefit others rather than worsen their lot. Pure spontaneity works well in immediate human relations, but it is a poor basis for public policy. Yet that policy will be immensely benefited if those who have freed themselves from the illusion of a substantial self and from the attachments that go with that illusion can help to correct the illusions which are so deeply built into our social and economic theories. A Christianized Buddhism has much to contribute.

The Centrality of Christ

It is not uncommon for Christians to recognize that outside of explicit Christian faith, people can in some way know and trust Christ. Indeed, the development of the Logos doctrine in the early church was partly for the sake of understanding how wise and virtuous pagans were oriented in their lives to the same truth as that which Christians know in Jesus. Hence to use the same doctrine today to show that some Buddhists also put their faith in the one Logos which Christians know as incarnate in Jesus is simply to continue an ancient Christian tradition.

But Christians also recognize the incarnation of that Logos in a particular historical figure, Jesus of Nazareth. Is there any reason internal to Buddhism to affirm this Christian teaching about Jesus? In particular, are there inner characteristics of Jodoshinshu which impel it, precisely for the sake of its own adequate development, to appropriate biblical history and the centrality of Jesus within that history? Clearly this would be a major development in the history of religions, but the shifts involved would be no greater than those proposed for Christianity in the preceding chapter. Let us consider how such a development might come about.

Internal to Jodoshinshu teaching are certain tensions. Shinran did not ask people to put their total faith in Amida on his own authority or on the basis of clear empirical evidence of Amida's graciousness. He called for faith on the basis of what was presented in the tradition as an event in the remote past—the vow of an Indian prince, Dharmakara, and his creation of a Pure Land. Shinran presupposed the general Buddhist confidence that a Bodhisattva had the ability and the compassion to act in this way for the salvation of others. Much of the effectiveness of Pure Land teaching has been derived from the power of this story to evoke grateful belief and to convince the hearer of the reality of the Pure Land.

Until recently Japanese Buddhists have felt little compulsion to discriminate historical fact from legends and myths. The point of all stories was to lead to present realization of truth rather than to provide factual information about past occurrences. The story of Dharmakara could provide confidence in the salvific power of the vow without raising clearly focused questions about historical factuality. This is still true for many Buddhists.

Today, however, historical consciousness and critical historical methods increasingly characterize the mentality of thoughtful Japanese. The question of truth and falsity does arise with respect to traditional Buddhist stories as it does in the West with respect to biblical stories. When this happens, Gautama appears as a historical person, and efforts can be made to distinguish his original teaching from latter attributions. But Dharmakara can only be seen as a mythical figure.

Pure Land Buddhists have several options. They may insist that a mythical story is just as good as a historical one since the point is the encouragement of present faith. When this option is chosen, belief in the gracious character of ultimate reality loses its grounding in such other Buddhist doctrines as the saving power of the vow of a Boddhisattva. One may continue to argue that the believing state of mind associated with the repetition of Amida's name is an effective way of attaining enlightenment here and now, and such an assertion may or may not be true. This is a different religious world from that of salvation by grace through faith.

A second option is to take the authority of the historical Gautama as the basis of confidence in the Other Power. The Dharmakara story can then be seen as a way of emphasizing essential features of Gautama's own teaching. But this proves difficult to sustain in the light of historical research.

A third option is to direct trust to Shinran himself. This is probably the most common response among the followers of Jodoshinshu. It is before the statue of Shinran that they keel most often, and it is his teachings to which they are most likely to listen in confidence. In him they find a clearly historical ground for their faith.

Nevertheless, this option, too, has its problems. Whereas the authority of a Zen master may be his own experience, Shinran did not present himself in this way. He pointed away from himself to that Other Power in which he placed his faith on the basis of authoritative tradition. To take Shinran seriously from an historical point of view, one must examine the validity of the tradition to which he appeals and the accuracy of his interpretation. Such a critical historical investigation is bound to raise problems for believers.

Consider the matter in general terms. Belief in the graciousness of reality is bound up with beliefs about the actual course of events. Equally, beliefs about the actual course of events are bound up with beliefs about reality. In the Pure Land traditions, belief about reality may play the primary role, whereas in Christianity beliefs about the actual course of events may be primary. But in both cases we deal with a circle in which both aspects are needed. Both circles center in the graciousness that characterizes ultimate reality, and both have depended for their convincing power on recounting stories believed to be true.

Two hundreds years ago, the Christian account of events had become highly doubtful. As it lost its convincing power, the beliefs about God and the world that were associated with it also eroded. Christians fought back in various ways. One of the most important was by leading the effort to replace the mythical history we had been telling by an historically accurate one. That task will never be finished, but it has gone far enough now that little doubt remains that there *is* an historical story to tell and that its deepest meaning can be understood as just as supportive of belief in the graciousness of God as the mythical story could ever have been.

The new story relates to the totality of world history in new ways. What is learned from this story can illumine and be illumined by the entirety of the natural-historical processes that have brought us to where we now are. As Christianity more and more fully extricates itself from its mythical and parochial past and comes to live out of the inclusive history to which it can give meaning and direction, its long period of decline may come to an end. In that inclusive history the history of Buddhism must play an important role. In an earlier work I indicated some of the deep changes still needed if Christianity in this way is to become a universal faith.

Jodoshinshu has not yet worked through the crisis of the relation of history to faith. If this crisis must be faced, then in some respects its problems are more acute even than those faced by Christianity, for its basis is still further removed from the actual course of history. It can indeed find in Gautama himself and in the history of Buddhism much to support it, but its most distinctive teaching is the one that is least adequately supported in this tradition prior to Shinran himself. However, there is nothing about Buddhist self-understanding that leads to the necessity of finding the requisite history solely in India and East Asia. On the contrary, Buddhism intends universality. It, too, needs an inclusive view of all things, and today such a view must include world history. World history includes the history of Israel and the event of Jesus. The history that supports the Christian understanding of the graciousness of God supports equally the Jodoshinshu understanding of the wisdom and compassion that characterize ultimate reality. It provides also the grounds for a desirable expansion of the Pure Land Buddhist understanding of Amida.

Until the attitude of mutual suspicion and defensiveness between Christians and Buddhists is fully overcome, it is inconceivable that Jodoshinshu would appeal heavily to Christian history for its support. But once that attitude is truly superseded, there is no reason in principle why Buddhists cannot internalize the Palestinian as well as the Indian past. It is in Palestine, rather than in India, that history, when it is read as centering in Jesus, provides the strongest basis for believing that we are saved by grace through faith.

Conclusion

It is my conviction that Christians need to be open to truth wherever we can find it and engage in the hard work of incorporating it into our theology. We also need to witness to the truth with which we have been entrusted through our own history. We know that too often in the past we have confused accidental cultural accretions with that truth and have idolatrously identified that truth with our own opinions. We also know that we have usually spoken without listening. For all of this we must repent. But to repent of past mistakes does not entail abandoning our witness. It means learning to witness aright. And the goal of that witness is to lead the other to attend to what we believe to be truth and to be transformed by it.

That is evangelism, the announcement as we understand it of the gospel of Jesus Christ. That is not the recitation of set formulae. Such are too often experienced as bad news by the hearers, who feel badgered and beaten by them, forced to accept or reject ambiguous claims without the refinement and development they need. Our word is good news only if it reveals possibilities which are truly positive ones for the hearers. We cannot engage in true evangelism today except as we first listen and learn and transform ourselves in light of what we have learned. But when we have been attentive to the ambiguities in the situation of others, when we have been transformed by the truth they can teach us, then it is also time to try to show them how faith in Jesus Christ can creatively transform their traditions in such a way as to free them from bondage. This chapter has illustrated what this kind of evangelism might be in relation to some segments of Mahayana Buddhism.

Our question now is how such a transformed Buddhism would be related to a transformed Christianity. Clearly these will be far closer than any now existing forms of Christianity and Buddhism. Yet there would continue to be differences rooted in the profoundly different roads they have traveled. To what extent these differences would disappear as each appropriated more fully the history and truth of the other, only time can tell. It is not clear that this would matter very much. From the Christian point of view, if Buddhists realize the rich meaning of faith in Jesus Christ, there is no reason to hope that they would also become like us in those many ways that are determined by our dominantly Western historical experience. Why should they become Roman Catholics, Southern Baptists, or Missouri Synod Lutherans, become members of the United Church of Christ in Japan, or join the nonchurch Christian movement there? Similarly, if Christians can realize the truth of the Buddhist doctrine of Nirvana, no essential Buddhist concern is served by the Easternization of Christianity in ways that are only accidentally related to that realization. A Buddhized Christianity and a Christianized Buddhism may continue to enrich each other and human culture generally through their differences.

This vision clearly has implications for the Christian mission. I suggest that in relation to other religious Ways today this has two main features neither of which has been prominent in missiology in the past. First, it is the mission of Christianity to *become* a universal faith in the sense of taking into itself the alien truths that others have realized. This is no mere matter of addition. It is instead a matter of creative transformation. An untransformed Christianity, that is, a Christianity limited to its own parochial traditions, cannot fulfill its mission of realizing the universal meaning of Jesus Christ. It can only continue to offer its fragment alongside the offerings of other traditions. When it appeals for total commitment to so fragmentary a realization of Christ, it is idolatrous. When, to avoid idolatry, it asks for only fragmentary commitment to the fragment of truth it offers, it ceases to express the ultimacy of the claim of Christ and continues its inevitable decay. Only as, in faithfulness to Christ, it opens itself to transformation can it ask people to participate wholeheartedly. Thus the most pressing Christian mission is the mission of self-transformation.

Second, it is the mission of a self-transforming Christianity to invite other religious traditions to undergo self-transformation as well. There is nothing wrong with opening our doors to individual converts from other traditions. Indeed, if we begin seriously to undergo self-transformation we will need the help of those who have known other truths from within other traditions. But more important than the conversion of individual Buddhists, Hindus, or Muslims is the conversion of Buddhism, Hinduism, and Islam. I have tried to indicate what that might mean in the case of Mahayana Buddhism. Equally concrete descriptions are possible in other cases. Our mission is to display the universal meaning of Christ freed from our past compulsion to contradict the truths known in other traditions. As long as we present Christ as the opponent of something that others know to be true, they will not be open to hearing what Christ has to say to them. But once we allow Christ to speak apart from the impediments we have placed in the way, Christ will carry out the authentic Christian mission. Christ as Truth will transform the truths of all other traditions even as they transform ours.

PART III

Asian Contextual Theology in Dialogue with Judaism

12

Why the Talmud Interests Me as a Christian*

Friedrich-Wilhelm Marquardt

I

"THEREUPON Jesus addressed the crowd of people and his disciples and said, 'The Scribes and the Pharisees sit in the Chair of Moses. Do and obey everything which they say to you!'" (Matt 23:1–3). This is one of the sayings of Jesus of which we are perhaps least conscious, and still less have Christians obeyed it. The very names "Scribes and Pharisees" have called forth all kinds of instinctive defensive reactions among us Christians. One believes to remember that these are the bitterest enemies of Jesus, and, at the end, the driving forces behind his death. The solidity of this view is, to be sure, seriously called into question by such a saying as this one, and therefore perhaps preaching, theology, and Christian consciousness have simply suppressed it. Nevertheless, it is in our New Testament, in the first Gospel, and we ought to at least think about it.

The "Chair of Moses" is a teaching chair in a synagogue. It is said that God built a teaching chair for Moses on Mount Sinai, so that he (Moses) could teach the people from there the lessons he had received on the mountain heights. Rabbinic Judaism traces its lineage as a succession from this teaching of Moses in the following chain: "Moses received the Torah from Sinai and delivered it to Joshua, Joshua passed it on to the Elders, the Elders to the Prophets, and the Prophets passed it on to the men of the Great Synagogue (*knesset ha gedolah*)" (Avot I:1). And in these schools and teachings, the Mishna, came into being, the basic text of the Talmud. And

* Paper presented at the 25th German "Day of the Church" (Kirchentag), Munich, June 10, 1993. Translated from the German by Don McCord and edited by Andreas Pangritz.

this was discussed and commented upon in the two Talmudim and passed on from generation to generation. The institution of the "Chair of Moses" in the rooms of the synagogues continues this chain of teaching. Though one reads from the Bible *standing*, the commentary and exposition and teaching occur *sitting down*, from the teaching chair.

Now Jesus says, the Scribes and Pharisees sit in the Chair of Moses. He says this without any overtones, just stating the fact: this is right and proper, this is where they belong; since the times of Ezra (which was, at the time of Jesus, more than 400 years earlier!) they belong there. They are the ones who protect the oral teachings of Moses. They pass them on and develop them further, so that they might be bound in every generation fresh and new with contemporary questions, and so continue as a living oral tradition.

[By the way, this is also how Martin Luther viewed the relationship between Scripture and proclamation; not the written letters of the Bible, but the spirit of the *viva vox evangelii*, the living voice of the Gospel—that is truly the Word of God. And Luther had determined that it was also the relationship between the New and the Old Testament. Actually, he claimed that the Old Testament alone was the Bible; that it was basically a misunderstanding to add a written New Testament to it, for the message that we today have in the New Testament Scriptures is essentially only to be understood as an "oral cry," "good news." And this should properly be sung and spoken and called out, but not really become Scripture! Here Luther shares, though it is seldom noted and thought about, the Jewish Rabbinic point of view: Scripture is the Tanakh—everything else is essentially to be passed on orally. Only so, from mouth to mouth does it remain relevant, does it remain "new!"] [1]

Jesus spoke "to the crowd of people and to his disciples" about this oral teachings of Moses. Only in one other place in the New Testament, at the Sermon on the Mount, do we have this combination, "the crowd of people and his disciples." To both, Jesus addressed the Sermon on the Mount and this saying with which we are concerned today. One might think: Good! Jesus says to the crowd of people, "hold fast to the Jewish tradition; it is something with which you have long been familiar, keep it!" And we might think: But he surely would not have counseled that to his disciples and followers: Remain Jews and keep yourselves in the Jewish tradition! This is exactly what Jesus advised both the crowd and his closest

[1] This paragraph was part of an earlier presentation in December 1992. It was omitted in the later Kirchentag version (1993), which Marquardt authorized for publication.

friends: "Everything now they tell you, hear and do!" That is: Jesus asks his followers to learn not only from the teachers of Scripture, but also from the teachers of the oral tradition, and to learn and live the Torah as it is also passed on and developed further in the teachings of the Mishna and the Talmud. Jesus does not want to pull his followers out of Judaism, but seeks to lead them into the very heart of the Pharisaic and Rabbinic Judaism of the day. (Whoever has ears to hear should hear!)

This puts Christians in a difficult position. It is precisely the opposite of what we think we have heard up to now from Paul and the other disciples of Jesus! How shall we deal with this?

Perhaps, one thought, this might be something from the "pre-Easter world," possibly something from the "historical Jesus," and nothing essential, something historically relative, replaced by the Easter events, through which Jesus has been elevated to a larger human dimension, out of the narrow confines of Judaism.

But, with the image of an "historical Jesus," that's not so simple. We cannot get around a lot of arbitrary decisions. And even if we were able to prove that here in Matt 23:1–3 we are concerned "only" with something from the "historical Jesus," the question as to why the first evangelist saved this saying and wove it into the story of Jesus. The author of the first Gospel possibly belongs to the second or third generations of Christians—why would he place his readers and hearers still under this old instruction of Jesus?

The commentators on Matthew's Gospel suggest that the first evangelist might perhaps have been influenced by a Christian community in Syria, somewhere still strongly influenced by Jewish thought, but perhaps in a strong dispute with the synagogue congregation about the right to claim the Jewish heritage and tradition for themselves, and perhaps to claim the right to be "the True Israel." In that way, this saying of Jesus would be explained as follows: Christians wanted to connect to Judaism and understand this connection as an instruction of their Risen Lord. But here, too, we cannot be so sure: this is only an academic theory.

Then, however, we have to face the fact that one or two generations later the Christians who then gathered a New Testament from many fragments and sections did not lay a hand on this text but gave it to the Christians of their own time as an instruction of Jesus. We are there already very much in the churches of the middle of the 2nd century C.E., who for a long time no longer stemmed from Judaism, but from "the gentiles." And gentile Christians also are to give heed: "The Scribes and the Pharisees sit in the chair of Moses; therefore do what they tell you (also you gentile

Christians!); pay attention to their words." There is also a Christian line of tradition. With the Jews, there is continuity from Moses on Mt. Sinai to the teachers of the Great Synagogue and those of the Talmud. So also (perhaps) with the Christians, there is continuity from the historical Jesus through the Jesus raised from the dead to the Jesus of the second or third generation of Christians to the world-wide church of the time in which the biblical Canon was formed and a New Testament was gathered and added to the Old. Christians also formed their chains of tradition and sought in this way to keep their traditions fresh and new. If we would follow the way of the church today, then the instruction of Jesus reaches us also saying, "Everything that you can learn from the oral Torah of Israel, give attention to it and follow it. Jesus counsels you so."

II

However, against this teaching there is an incorporated mistrust, which has prevailed through two thousand years of Christendom. I am deeply moved by the report of a Dutch colleague (W. Dekker), which he shared for the first time publicly not long ago. According to this report, the great Dutch theologian K. H. Miskotte is supposed to have encouraged Karl Barth, several times, to read some of the works of contemporary Judaism, such as, for example, Franz Rosenzweig's *Star of Redemption.* Barth rejected the advice later just as he did in 1935, after Miskotte's important book was published about *The Essence of the Jewish Religion: Contributions to the Knowledge of Jewish Spiritual Life.* At that time, Barth reacted to Miskotte's book with the following words: "What are you trying to prove then with this thick book? Do you think perhaps that we have to learn from the Jews about how to read the Scriptures?" Thus it was also my teacher Karl Barth, who in resistance to National Socialism stood the test of the time and contributed to the saving of the Jews more than other theologians, but who also found it unthinkable that a Christian theologian or preacher might be able to learn something of a better understanding of the Bible from the Jews. Barth was still speaking with the voice of two thousand years of Christian thought: it was simply presupposed that there was nothing a Christian could learn from a Jew. My teacher from Basel was not aware that thereby a commandment of Jesus was being rejected!

That statement of his had as a theological basis the presupposition that the context for the proper understanding of the Bible was for 2000 years only the story of the incarnation of the eternal Word in Jesus Christ, the narrative of his death and his resurrection from the dead for the salvation of all humankind. The Old Testament, too, could be read, was to be read, and should be read, only in this context, through the filter of the New Testament. The possibility that there might be for both parts of the Christian Bible—the Tanakh of the so-called Old Testament and the Jesus writings of the so-called New Testament—another context in the existence and history of the whole Jewish people, from which Jesus came, was set aside as theologically irrelevant. It seemed to be merely something superficial, which could have no meaning for theological understanding, because God is in reality suprahistorical, and is not to be sought or found in historical and temporal comings and goings. Something like this was the position of Christian dogmaticians. And the theological historians and Biblical scholars weren't any better.

For generations they had the idea that it would be better to understand the Bible from the point of view of pagan backgrounds than from Judaism, and that the New Testament, too, was easier to understand from pagan Gnosticism, the philosophical school of the Stoa, and other pagan perspectives than from the Tanakh and the teachings of the Jewish people. Nevertheless, one did look at sources of Jewish teachings in order to understand the New Testament. But how was that done? One made use of—and still does today!—a collection (very commendable at the time) of Jewish parallel sayings to almost all the sayings, sentences, and thoughts of the New Testament: the five-volume collection by Strack-Billerbeck, *Aus Talmud und Midrasch* (From the Talmud and Midrash). But the Jewish texts are chosen there according to the dictate of the New Testament texts, simply according to the NT understandings and order, without any regard for their own relationship to one another or their meaning in their own sources, i.e., their Jewish roots and the Talmud from which they were taken. The texts are here only for a heap of fragments, gathered to suit a Christian purpose and need. There is nothing here to be gleaned from their internal Jewish connections and meanings. And so it is no wonder that the use which Christian scholars made of the texts confused things all the more. For generations this collection of Jewish material, split as though by a nuclear fission, misled theologians to present the smallest units as something which could not be compared with the Christian material, rather than as something comparable. After one had broken the Jewish material out of its own context and relationships, it was easy to claim the spiritual and religious superiority of the New Testament, as was clear to see *vis a vis* materials from the Mishna, Talmud and Midrash. Among theological historians, as well as among Christian dogmaticians, Judaism was used merely as a negative foil against which one could more easily bring the greater heights or deeper spiritual depths of the Christian material into the spotlight. This eclectic and arbitrary manner of considering Judaism was and is still today methodical anti-Judaism in academic theology, and shows very clearly that Karl Barth was not alone in his question to Miskotte: "Do you think we have anything to learn from the Jews about how Scripture is to be read?"

III

Jewish instruction was rejected because for a long time one had no longer seen any theological sense in the existence and history of the Jewish people. "Christ is the end of the Law," (Rom 10:4) Paul had said, and for more than two thousand years Christianity stubbornly insisted on understanding this text like: Until the coming and activity of Jesus of Nazareth, the Torah was a good gift of God that was given at Sinai. The Jewish people sought through faith and unfaith to live out of this gift and to lift it up among the people. But then came One who with combined divine and human power fulfilled the law, and God accepted that on behalf of all humankind, Jews and Non-Jews. As a result of the fulfillment of the requirements of the law by this One, God decided no longer to require the fulfillment of the law by any human being, any single woman or any single man. God declared God's readiness to love and praise humankind without any works of the law. If they would lay claim to Jesus and his obedience to God, reminding God of Jesus and his achievements on humankind's behalf, that would be sufficient for God's benevolence. With this, of course, the Jewish people had already fulfilled their duty. Even if they continued to exist, the loss of the Jewish state, the destruction of the Temple in Jerusalem, and the dispersion among the nations of the world sufficed as evidence that the Jewish people had played out and ended their role in the history of salvation. Christ was "the end of the Law," and at one and the same time, the end of the history of Israel. And there are to this day important Christian theologians who see in this the end of history itself. Only in our inner, spiritual life can anything good develop. There is in the external sphere, in social life and in world history nothing more to expect from God. Nothing more concrete is commanded, except to behave in all things with love and especially to let love "carry" all that torments and all that is lacking for us in the world. As a result, a question emerges: How should we, after Christ, still have anything important to learn from the Jews who have now become "a people without a history"? They have, along with their lost world-historical identity, also lost their appearance as the People of God which they once enjoyed in the Bible. Therefore all the more: What is there still for us to learn from a group of people who have lost the biblical form they once had?

Is this view frightening or is it still familiar to you? I learned it after 1945 from my teachers of Protestant theology: Rudolf Bultmann and Karl Barth. They determined the horizons of consciousness for my generation. Today, I can only repeat this view with dismay, because the Jewish people have reported back to the stage of world history with a claim and conviction that the Bible speaks, in fact, of their history and their obligation to God. So a Christian today, who truly holds to the Bible, can do nothing other than take it seriously and consider the connection between the self-witness of the Jewish people and the biblical witness of God about this people. Our task consists of recognizing two thousand years of disdain of the Jewish people and our neglect of their life and their ways with God, and belatedly critically reappraising this neglect. We must do this in order to become contemporary with Judaism today and to be able to live with our Jewish neighbors today. The decisive thing laid upon us today, after Auschwitz, is to live with Israel *now*, to understand *now*, and to intervene for the Jewish people *now*—Shalom for Israel, *achschav*, now.

In order to do this, we must deconstruct two thousand years of religious enmity and the understandings of Judaism which have been only caricatures we Christians have built for ourselves with the help of biblical materials. We will never accomplish this with books and academic theology alone. Theology and scholarly research have always been corruptible by anti-Jewish prejudices. Therefore, if we are sincere, we will have *to learn from Jewish self-understandings* and let our texts be corrected from that position, because we have written down much too much historical nonsense and theological untruth about the Jewish people into them.

The Judaism that we do not know has its focus in the Mishna and the Talmud. The conversation of the teachers in the Talmud held this people together spiritually and practically through the thousands of years of their dispersion.[2] And the two Talmudim are today still the identity centers not only for orthodox Jews, but also for the conservative and liberal, and in part also for secular Jews who know that they can connect to biblical Israel only when they pass on the oral Torah from mouth to mouth, from person to person, through the generations, and develop and live that understanding further.

[2] [Editor's note: "Zerstörung" in the German text is probably mistaken; it should be replaced by "Zerstreuung."]

I have consciously spoken first about the *task of contemporaneity*, the necessity that Christians today must become contemporaries of Jews, and therefore, for example, must have a catch-up course in the Talmud, but then also in the Cabbala, Jewish philosophy, and Jewish Haskala. In a time when we, in Germany, are letting ourselves be driven back into a time of national self-satisfaction, back into the ghetto of our Christian identity, this is a most important instruction: Learn with all your might to enter into a world which appears to you to be alien. Expose yourself to the task of learning to adjust yourselves spiritually, mentally, morally, politically and socially to the culture and religion of others, not in order to deny yourselves by so doing, but in order to give yourselves a chance to change, to remain alive in progressive transformation, flexible, and not locked into a narrow fundamentalism. Ben Bag-bag said: "Stir around in the Torah and stir in it, because everything is there (the whole world); look deeply into it and become old and used up in it and do not retreat from it, because there is nothing better than the Torah" (Avot V 25).

But now we must immediately add something more. *It is worth* listening to the Talmud, listening to the conversation of the teachers of Israel about the life of a people of God who live in constant danger, from within and from without! It is valuable for us, for our understanding of the Bible and for our self-understanding as Christians, in short, for our Christian identity.

IV

We will come to know Jesus in a new way! Up until now we have learned to know him from God's-side—as God's eternal Son, as "one essence with the Father," pre-existent in the eternal majesty of God. This Son then humbled himself and came into our humanity, and as the time was fulfilled, God raised the man Jesus of Nazareth from Galilee into life and community with Godself, so that this man from then on not only gave witness of God's word and will, but also was God's very word and will in person! From his superior understanding of God he preached the kingdom of God; from the healing powers of God he healed the sick; in the power of God which is mighty in the weak, he lived, suffered and died, totally obedient to God. And then God awakened him from the dead, called him home into his high, and set him at his right hand where he pleads and intercedes for us, in order to turn everything for us with God to the best end. And God will give him the last judgment and complete all things, natural and historical, in him. That's how we know and confess Jesus as the only begotten, uniquely from God.

But is that really the picture that the New Testament paints of him? Is that the *whole* picture? Isn't a great deal of the New Testament set aside in such a picture? Is it the *right* picture? For centuries doubts have been expressed. Some gave in their doubts and began a search for "the historical Jesus," who was supposed to be just the opposite of the man who came from God, a man only according to the measure of what we know to be genuinely human, quite apart from all things divine, which cannot be grasped historically, and the essence of which can only be seen with the eyes of one's personal faith. We still find ourselves in the midst of this movement. We project one picture after the other onto the man Jesus, today: a man in solidarity with the poor, the New Man, the outsider, the post-modern exotic, the pacifist, and who knows which Jesus will be next in our midst. Certainly there will be one after another! Perhaps this human Jesus is less satisfying than the divine Jesus of our traditional theologies. Personally I can no longer, with good conscience, follow the one or the other, since I have begun to get to know Jesus the Jew.

As a *Jew* he is not exchangeable, and he baulks at any further projections of ours; for there he stands in the midst of his people, which, today, thank God, is no longer available for whatever pagan fantasies we might concoct of what a "true Jew" might be, or what a "true Israel" might be either—either something terrible or something very great! I am seriously of the opinion that the contemporary Judaism, so conscious of its own identity, protects Jesus from being made again and again into a target of whatever the latest human pious fantasies might make of him, even the most noble or socially important! Conversely, Jesus the Jew needs no other form of nearness to God than that which the Jewish people live in their survival and in their daily wrestling with the hearing and doing of God's will. Jesus is as much the "son of God," as God has spoken of the whole people of Israel as "God's son," making them certain of his eternal loyalty and fellowship. Jesus needs nothing more than to be understood as every other, woman or man, every child of his people. He is the "light of the world" precisely as, and insofar as, God has called the whole Jewish people to be *or goyim*, a light to the nations. This One lives out, perhaps in a concentrated form, the life of his people, but he does so in the commission of his people. For this reason Paul has called him "the fulfillment of the law" (Rom 10:4).

If this is so (and these are not our phantasies, but biblical proclamations), if Jesus is from God for us what his whole people is from God for us, then we very much need to let ourselves be taught by this people, from the wellsprings of their knowledge about God, their *daat Elohim.* If we can do this, then we will learn to know Jesus with other eyes and discover in the New Testament things which up until now have not seemed so important.

Paul said he was "born of woman and under the Law" (Gal 4:4). Only one who knows his way around the Talmud knows that with these two designations Jesus is designated a Jew through and through. For according to the laws of Jewish religion, one is a Jew who has a Jewish mother (simply put: because in doubtful cases, it is easier to prove maternity than paternity!). That Jesus' father in the New Testament so clearly steps back behind his mother Mary shows also how it is his mother who gives him his Jewish identity. Only recently this was also very important in the Nazi era, as "German Christians" sought to make Jesus into a Galilean Aryan and Non-Jew, taking their Mother-cult from Mary. And yet it was precisely his mother who was the guarantee of his Jewishness—being "born of a Jewish mother," in Bethlehem, in the land of Judea. He was born a Jew; educated as a Jew—that is the meaning of "born under the law," i.e. instructed in the Torah, and that was the source of his life and his prayers until his very last breath. But not only his parents, God also placed him under the Torah. This is what Paul knew and said of him.

Appropriately, Jesus was *circumcised* as a Jewish male child and received therewith on his body the sign of the covenant—as commanded by the law (Luke 2:21ff.). Then, again according to good Jewish order, he became *Bar Mitzvah,* "Son of the Commandment," and was called forth in the synagogue service to read from the Torah and to enter the company of Jewish adults. The story of the twelve-year-old Jesus in the temple in Jerusalem underlines this. Still today, when possible *Bar Mitzvah* is celebrated at the foot of the Western Wall. From that moment on, Jesus could complete the *Minyan,* the number of Jewish men necessary to be assembled before the worship service could begin. I experienced Yehoshua Amir once on a Sabbath evening, as the time for the service of worship had come, walking around worried, trying to get the men to come out of their houses for his service in the Synagogue *Emet ve Emuna.* Since that time I know how good it is, that also with Jesus a Jewish service of worship could begin. He became and remained an adult Jew! He "fulfilled the law!" (Matt 5:17).

In the *first place* (and we cannot impress that firmly enough into our consciousness!): He *prayed the Shema Yisrael* along with everyone of his people! (Mark 12:29). He too, as with all Jews until the present moment, considered it to be the most important commandment (Mark 12:31). It is, it seems, really questionable that we are right in naming the "Our Father" the "Lord's Prayer." At least the *Shema Yisrael* is it as well. Jesus also wore the *appropriate clothing for a Jewish service of worship*. We know this from the story about his healing the woman with the flow of blood. The text says, she touched "the hem of his garment." That is really the *Zizit*, the blue-white tassels on the four corners of the *Arba Kamfot*, the small prayer shawl which belongs to the everyday clothing of every practicing orthodox Jew.

According to John's Gospel, Jesus was a passionate *pilgrim* to Jerusalem where, according to the instructions of the Torah, a Jew should appear three times a year—for Pesach [Passover], Shevuot, and the Feast of Booths, or Tabernacles. John has him in Jerusalem five times, and above all, naturally, at Pesach, the memorial feast of the liberation of his people from Egyptian slavery. He celebrated it with wine and bread and a sacrificial lamb.

He *learned and learned*—and thereby forgot his family. And when he taught later, he referred first of all, in proper Jewish teaching form, to what is written in Scripture, and then to that which was heard from "of old," and then he spoke of his own experience. The form for the Sermon on the Mount is exactly that of Jewish teaching: "You have heard . . . " (this and that biblical quotation), then that which you have heard from "of old . . . ," and "now I, Jesus, say to you . . . " (teaching this and that). Precisely in the Sermon on the Mount, where he allegedly distinguishes himself so radically from Judaism, he observed, as any good Pharisee, the teachings of the *Knesset ha gedolah* and erected *a fence around the Torah* (Avot 1 1). Moses set the Torah out before the Jewish people for life or death (Deut 30:15ff.), but he intended for the people to use the Torah for life and not for death! (That's why it was even commanded to break the Sabbath when life was threatened. It would have been foolish to follow the commandments for life come hell or high water, and thereby bring someone into life-threatening circumstances! This was *not* something new or original with Jesus, but a rabbinical teaching, that the Sabbath was made for humankind and not the other way round (Mark 2:27f.; cf. bYoma 85b). But so that humankind would not even approach the death zone of the Torah, both rabbinic Judaism *and* Jesus created an ante-room before the really dangerous words of the Torah. Already at that point one can keep the commandment, in order that one might not even come into the danger of transgressing it. So that you don't even come into the danger zone of the 5th commandment, "Thou shalt not kill," I say to you that you ought to get along better with your brother, before something happens, even if he is your enemy. So that you do not even come close to committing adultery, I give you advice for your heart and your eye. So that you do not come close to the danger of false oaths, I create an ante-room there for you—don't swear at all! And so forth. The Jesus of the Sermon on the Mount is not teaching anything originally Jesus-like, he rather teaches as a good rabbi.

In hundreds of details, we learn today that Jesus drew completely from the streams which had begun to gather in the Mishna and were further discussed in the two Talmudim. Jesus belongs to this conversation.

But decisive in our context is this: with eyes sharpened by the Talmud, we observe Jesus throughout his life living according to the instructions of the Torah which is alive in his people. He lives his life as a member of his people which God has called to hallow God's name, and to be made holy; to complete all the movements of life, inwardly and outwardly, as service to God (worship), allowing God to come near and to come near to God. Or, expressed in a Jewish manner, to become one with God over and over again and to become reconciled with oneself. All of life is to become reconciled, at-one with God! Here is a picture of Jesus' reality that in any case tells me more than some Christological determination about a unity of two natures—one human, one divine—in Jesus. Jesus' oneness with God is the eternal history of Israel in him. [It reveals] how God and his people, his people and God try again and again to be practically unified. That is how Jesus lives, that is how Jesus helps. When he heals the sick and forgives sin, then he does this always with the intention that they may once again be able to be a part of the worshipping assembly: "Go and show yourself to the priest!" (Matt 8:4).

V

We also learn to know ourselves differently! The portrait of humankind into which we are educated as Christians teaches us what sin is. Martin Luther said that it is the first thing the Gospel does with us, it makes us sinners so that we have no illusions about ourselves and desire the help of Jesus. Adult Christians have to learn to understand themselves as beings of two worlds. Somehow they must have a clear understanding of being before God, "both a sinner and justified." But above all, they must learn that they cannot help themselves. How differently the Mishna and the Talmud perceive humanity before God! While we Christians are always taught to look beyond ourselves to God and to see and judge ourselves through the eyes of God, Rabbinic Judaism teaches humankind to live according to God's will in their human relationships. Humankind does not need to look up to God because God looks down into our situations.

Let us look quickly through the six orders, *Sedarim*, of the Mishna and the Talmud. According to the first order, *Serayim*, "Seeds," *a person belongs to the land*. We are farmers, tillers of the field, of the trees, vineyards, plants. The poor also live from the produce of the fields. We are obligated to care for the poor, to leave something in the corners of the fields for the poor to harvest. And for the priests and Levites something must be offered. In this way the care of the land takes on a quality of service to God, worship, not because the earth has anything mythological or divine about it, but because it is the land which God has promised and has given to God's people. It is no wonder that Zionism could emerge in the Judaism of our time! This is the first instruction of humankind in the tradition of the Talmud which views persons on the surface of the field (and, therefore, in the face of God), and views Israel as people of the Land.

According to the second order of Mishna and Talmud, *Moed*, "Feast Days," a person is essentially human in his or her *experience of times*. A person's experience of time is not primarily determined by the dates at the edge of life, from the secrets of birth and the puzzles and anxieties of death, but rather by the middle of life, by the feasts of life. The first experience of time is the *Sabbath*. Then, for the people there is the most important experience, Passover [*Pesach*], the feast of the liberation of Israel. Then there is *Yom Kippur*, the day on which humankind appears before God and in the midst of the congregation as a sinner. Then there is the Feast of Booths or Tabernacles [*Sukkot*], a remembrance of the fact that the people are on a journey, on the way; and then *Rosh Hashanah*, the memory or remembrance of a new beginning. There are, of course, times of fasting as well including a prayer that God might send rain upon the thirsty land. The ecological question is a question of time. There are times of pilgrimage that separate human life into sections: the journey to Jerusalem—not a children's game (German children play, "We are traveling to Jerusalem!") but the goal of life!

Then we are considered as *women and men* in the third Seder, *Naschim*, "Women." So that no name is lost in Israel a man is to marry his sister-in-law when her husband dies. Husband and wife are to be bound in legal covenant to each other, for marriages which are only based on romantic love or attraction cannot last. Above all, women are to have legal rights, and men should know what awaits them when they forcibly rape women. Vows and promises are also legally binding. Adultery is a bad thing. To be sure, there are divorces and they are to be regulated. However, the most important thing is the betrothal, *Kidduschin*: here husbands and wives are brought together, whether through payments of money, letters of betrothal, sleeping together, etc.

These persons are *citizens*, usually in sensitive tension with other citizens. The concept of "the neighbor" is seldom something ideal. The fourth Seder is *Nezikin*, "Torts," which characterizes us as citizens. We are hurtful to each other, and therefore, we would do well to relate to one another through laws. All the things we can do to one another are recognized here in advance—what we can steal, how we can defraud one another, what we can destroy, how we can take somebody for a ride, beat one another up, do one another bodily harm. But also there is thought for how we do business with one another, how we set prices and wages, make house and land deals, bear witness for one another. For this reason the *Sanhedrin* is so important, the court of judgment, and a well-developed sense that human rights and laws are crucially important for life together. There is no room anymore for anarchistic strands and impulses which Martin Buber saw at work in very early Israel, where God alone should be king. Norms of justice and punishment belong to humanity. Beatings are more humane than extinction and expulsion out of the fellowship. The problem of the oath plays a role questioning our reliability in relationship to one another. And then also the *avodah zarah*, idolatry, belongs here. It is a civil problem because idols call into question the identity of Israel.

Then, in the fifth Seder, *Kodashim*, "Sacred Things," *a person worships and serves God*. This deals with what and how offerings are to be made and on what occasions—after births and transgressions—and how priests are to behave. This is something which concerns all; the priests have no secrets! This also deals with the times for temple observance—morning, evening, night—and how they fit together. The service of God, worship, is as important for humanity as a civil responsibility. There is nothing of a "two kingdoms" distinction!

And, finally, sixth, *the person is one who keeps purity*, who hallows and purifies him/herself: Seder *Tohorot*, "Cleanness." This is related also to the service of worship. Not just anyone can enter there and participate. For whoever has touched something dead cannot enter, since the world of God is the world of life, and whoever touches death is foreign to God. Also whatever has to do with bodily fluids, which actually serve life, but without serving hang on us, for example, the semen of the man, menstrual blood of the woman, cause one to need cleansing. Purity of body, clothing, things, furniture, walls have also to do with hygiene. But hygiene serves not only health; it is also theology. God desires to see in the services of worship his image in integrity, and purity laws can be understood as instruction in the symbolism of the divine image. A person is to appear before God, in both the literal and symbolic sense, washed and with clean hands (*Yadayim*).

A person of the land, a person in his/her different time periods, but above all a person of the feasts, a person as a citizen, a person as a worshipper, a person who is fit for the presence of God: this is the concrete way in which the Rabbis portray us as God's humanity. Much of this can be gleaned from the life of Jesus, but unfortunately much of it comes to us without touching or obligating us. We have removed ourselves theologically from Jesus' concrete understanding of humanity and thereby from the practical understanding of human life in general. What we *think* about God, the world, and other human beings is more important to us than how we are to live as human beings before God! The Talmud interests me also because of the 613 *mitzvoth* which are contained there, but it is still of more interest to me because it speaks of what it really means to exist as a human being, and to be a human being in existence with God!

VI

Now, finally, one very last item: *We get to know God more closely, more in God's own humanity.* God reigns, judges, and loves in many more forms than are outlined in the New Testament. God cries from pain and anguish. God roars like a lion, and makes self-accusations. God admits to being wrong, and gives human beings credit for being right! God rejoices over being bested in debate, and asks for blessing from human beings. There is a treatise in the Talmud about the laughter of God (Avoda zara 3b). God even prays that divine love will overcome divine justice! God can and wants to be saved, redeemed along with Israel from the power of the Goyim, and therefore God is a One who needs salvation! Christians often smirk at such Haggadoth. Ironically, I am always moved that *we* speak about God taking on human form, yet in the Talmud God appears much more human than we can possibly imagine theologically!

And I confess, last of all, that the Talmud interests me because it makes me consider what corresponds more to God—our Christian language about God taking on human form or the Jewish knowledge about the humanity of God. "The Scribes and Pharisees sit in the Chair of Moses. Do and obey everything which they say to you!"

Now I hear Jesus going on, "But do not do according to what they do, for they say it but do not do it" (Matt 23:3b). Is Jesus negating that which he has just taught us, and denigrating the Pharisees and warning us about them? Unfortunately that is what most of the Christian theologians think to this day, and many church members think they can hereby save themselves from Jesus' Jewish demands which are so disconcerting to us.

But no, this is *not* what Jesus means! He says we need to learn the Torah as the Jews did, along with the Pharisees. Every Jew knows from earliest times, learning alone is not enough; we must do what we have learned! There has been a continuing controversy among the rabbinical teachers: what is more important, learning or doing? One says one thing, and another says the other. There is no one in Judaism who can make this decision, no Pope, no global catechism, no synod and no church board! Jesus holds the scale in his hand. First he says, "learn, learn, learn!" Then he says, "do, do, do!" And thereby to do it better than many of the Pharisees, if you could, if only you could!

13

Recent Developments in the Jewish-Christian Relationship in Europe after the Shoah *

Andreas Pangritz

For almost forty years, the major European churches have undertaken far-reaching revisions in their theological teaching on the Jews, revisions that have brought about a considerable improvement in the Jewish-Christian relationship.

For centuries the Christian attitude towards the Jews had been characterized by a teaching of contempt. The Jews were blamed for allegedly having killed Jesus Christ, God's son. In the context of this Christian teaching, the people of Israel, God's chosen people according to the Bible, were described as disobedient. They therefore had been rejected by God and replaced by the Church, who maintained to be the "new Israel." The legal discrimination and persecution of the Jews within the Christian West was regarded as justified punishment imposed by God himself.

It is widely accepted that the traditional Christian teachings of contempt over against the Jews must be counted among the roots of modern Western antisemitism culminating in the "shoah" [Hebrew: catastrophe, destruction], the extermination of European Jewry in the Nazi death camps during World War II. It was only after the war that the Christian churches changed their attitude towards the Jews. More precisely: With the exception of some individual initiatives it took another post-war gen-

* I avoid the term "holocaust" with respect to the destruction or extermination of the European Jews, because it has problematic theological connotations: In biblical language "holocaust" originally means the sacrifice of an animal by slaughtering and burning it (cf. Gen 22); if applied to the killing of the Jews, the term would provide a kind of religious meaning or even legitimation.

eration until the churches officially adopted resolutions declaring that they had failed in the past and that they were ready to change their way and to revise their teaching. Meanwhile these revisions have received grateful Jewish responses.

"Nostra Aetate," Vatican Council II (1965)

Within the Roman-Catholic Church, it was the important Vatican Council II in the Sixties, which on October 28, 1965, adopted a "Declaration on the Relation of the Church to non-Christian Religions," known by its first words in Latin as "Nostra Aetate" ["In our time"], which contains, among others, a chapter on the Jewish-Christian relationship.[1]

If one wants to understand the revolutionary content of this declaration, it is important to recall some characteristics of the former Christian doctrine on the Jews or the people of Israel. According to traditional Christian teachings, Jesus Christ had fulfilled the Old Testament law and abolished the old covenant by his blood. Therefore the Christian church had replaced the Jews as God's chosen people. This doctrine cannot be found in the New Testament. It has its origin in the teachings of the Church fathers of the first centuries of the Christian era.[2] And their teaching was not a theoretical concept only but it had practical consequences within the Catholic liturgy and within the attitude of Christians towards the Jews in everyday life. In the prayer of Good Friday, the day of the crucifixion of Jesus Christ, the traditional Catholic liturgy included a prayer "pro perfidis Judaeis" (Latin: "for the unbelieving" or "disloyal Jews" with the connotation of "perfidious, mean, nasty, contemptuous"). For centuries Christians had left the services on Good Friday with feelings of revenge against the Jews, who allegedly had killed their Lord, and it happened more than once that Christians organized pogroms against their Jewish neighbors on Good Friday.

It was Pope John XXIII, who immediately after his election in 1959 cancelled the term "perfidious" within the prayer for the Jews on Good Friday and convoked a great council of the Roman-Catholic Church, Vatican Council II, which had the task to adapt the church to modern

[1] "Nostra Aetate" is quoted according to the "traditional translation" in: http://www.jcrelations.com > Statements > Roman Catholic > 2552 > traditional translation.—For the revised English translation see *The Basic Sixteen Documents. Vatican Council II: Constitutions, Decrees, Declarations,* ed. Austin Flannery, O.P. (Northport, Dublin: Costello, Dominican, 1996).

[2] Cf. for instance, an influential Easter sermon by Melito of Sardes (towards the end of the second century).

times including a revision of the theological teaching with respect to the Jews. There was no other topic on the agenda of Vatican Council II that received such an amount of controversial discussion as the document on the Christian relation to the Jews. Christians from Arab countries, for instance, feared that a paper on the Jewish-Christian relationship might be understood as political support in favor of the state of Israel. The declaration that was finally adopted is the result of a compromise.

Some observers have regretted that the declaration on the Christian relation to the Jews finally was integrated into a declaration on the relation of the church to non-Christian religions in general. In fact, the decision of Vatican Council II to deal with the Jewish-Christian relationship under the headline of the relation to non-Christian religions suppresses the evidence of a special relationship between Christians and Jews, based on the fact that the first part of the Bible, the so-called Old Testament, is common to Christians and Jews, and on the other fact that Jesus Christ was a Jew. However, the text of the "Declaration on the Relation of the Church to non-Christian Religions" (*Nostra Aetate*) moves forward in concentric circles, starting with the relationship of the Christian church towards other religions in general (1),[3] via the relationship of the Church towards "religions that are bound up with an advanced culture," especially Hinduism and Buddhism (2),[4] via the Christian-Muslim relationship (3)[5] to the Jewish-Christian relationship (4), which in fact forms the inner circle of the relationships of the church towards non-Christian religions. That means: Jews are non-Christians, but compared with other non-Christian religions they are regarded as the closest neighbors of the church.

The chapter on the Jewish-Christian relationship starts by emphasizing "the bond that spiritually ties the people of the New Covenant to Abraham's stock," that is the Jewish people. The church "acknowledges" according to that chapter that "the beginnings of her faith and her election" are found already among the people of Israel in the times of the Old Testament.

[3] In the first chapter, every religion is acknowledged in so far as it asks questions shared with the whole human race, such as: "Whence do we come, and where are we going?"

[4] In the second chapter, the document expresses the "sincere reverence," by which the Catholic Church regards the "ways of conduct and of life" and the "precepts and teachings" of Hinduism and Buddhism, "which, though differing in many aspects from the ones she holds and sets forth, nonetheless often reflect a ray of that Truth which enlightens" all human beings. It therefore "exhorts" the Christians to enter into "dialogue and collaboration with followers of other religions."

[5] The third chapter expresses the Christian estimation for the Muslims, because they, too, "adore the one God," "revere" Jesus "as a prophet" and "honor Mary."

> She professes that all who believe in Christ—Abraham's sons according to faith (Gal 3:7)—are included in the same Patriarch's call, and likewise that the salvation of the Church is mysteriously foreshadowed by the chosen people's exodus from the land of bondage. The Church, therefore, cannot forget that she received the revelation of the Old Testament through the people with whom God in God's inexpressible mercy concluded the Ancient Covenant. Nor can she forget that she draws sustenance from the root of that well-cultivated olive tree onto which have been grafted the wild shoots, the Gentiles (Rom 11:17–24). Indeed, the Church believes that by His cross Christ, Our Peace, reconciled Jews and Gentiles, making both one in Himself (Eph 2:14–16).

Moreover, the church, according to this chapter, "keeps ever in mind the words of the Apostle about his kinsmen: 'theirs is the sonship and the glory and the covenants and the law and the worship and the promises; theirs are the fathers and from them is the Christ according to the flesh' (Rom 9:4–5). . . . She also recalls that the Apostles . . . sprang from the Jewish people."

After having expressed the deep obligation and solidarity of the church with the Jewish people the chapter continues by mentioning that most Jews did not "accept the Gospel" in the time of Jesus. Nevertheless, the Vatican declaration emphasizes that God "does not repent of the gifts He makes or of the calls He issues (Rom 11:28–29)." The declaration recalls that "the Jewish authorities and those who followed their lead" had "pressed for the death of Christ" (John 19:6). However, it emphasizes that, "what happened in His passion cannot be charged against all the Jews, without distinction, then alive, nor against the Jews of today." Besides, as the document stresses towards the end of this chapter: "Christ underwent His passion and death freely, because of the sins of men and out of infinite love, in order that all may reach salvation."

The declaration deals also with the Jewish-Christian relationship in present times—that is, with the relationship of the church to the great majority of the Jews who do not accept the Christian message. It seems that the attitude of the Roman Catholic Church is still ambiguous. On the one hand, the document recommends "mutual understanding and respect" and pleas for "fraternal dialogues." On the other hand, it expresses the hope that one day "all peoples will address the Lord in a single voice," that means that the Jews, too, will accept Jesus as their Lord. The declaration maintains that "the Church is the new people of God"; nevertheless it emphasizes that "the Jews should not be presented as rejected or accursed by God." The Church "decries hatred, persecutions, displays of anti-Semitism, directed against Jews at any time and by anyone."

"Nostra Aetete" represents a revolutionary breakthrough in the attitude of the Roman Catholic Church to the Jews. However, there are some shortcomings to be mentioned. Still, the attitude of the church is somehow paternalistic: The Jews participate in the truth, but it is only the church who possesses the truth completely. Therefore the church cannot give up her intention to convert the Jews and to make them Christians. The document does not mention Christian co-responsibility and guilt with respect to the extermination of European Jewry during the Nazi era. And the question is not reflected on whether the foundation of the state of Israel in 1948 has meaning for Christians.

Meanwhile during the last forty years the Roman Catholic Church has taken further steps in order to improve its relationship with the Jewish people. It has been particularly Pope John Paul II who showed a personal commitment in Jewish—Christian relations, visiting for instance, for the first time as a head of the Catholic Church, the synagogue in Rome in 1986, establishing diplomatic relations between the Vatican state and Israel in 1994, and visiting the state of Israel, including the Holocaust memorial Yad va-Shem in Jerusalem, in 2000.

In 1998, the Catholic commission for the religious relationship with the Jews published a document entitled "We remember: A reflection on the Shoah," which on the other hand demonstrates that certain ambiguities continue to characterize the attitude of the Roman Catholic Church towards the Jews. The document "We remember" admits that some "sons and daughters of the Church" have failed during the Nazi era. In a sense it can be regarded, therefore, as a kind of confession of guilt. On the other hand, the document is careful to avoid any mention of guilt of the church as such. Instead, the positive exceptions of bishops who acted in solidarity with the Jews are praised. It seems that the Catholic understanding of the nature of the church still has prevented the authors to admit that the church has failed. As long as the church is conceived as the bride of Christ and associated with Mary in her virginity, she must be characterized as religiously "pure," without any "blots and wrinkles" (cf. Eph 5:27).

"Towards Renovation of the Relationship of Christians and Jews," Evangelical Church of the Rhineland, Germany (1980)

The Protestant understanding of the church has always included the knowledge that the communion of saints consists of justified sinners. Therefore, in contrast to the Catholic doctrine on the nature of the church, Protestant theology can admit failures and guilt of the church as such. However, German Protestants, who traditionally had been closely linked to the nationalist German ideology and in parts even to the Nazi party, hesitated to confess their co-responsibility and guilt after World War II. Most Protestant confessions of guilt from the time immediately after the war do not mention the persecution and extermination of the Jews. They prefer more general and vague expressions which can be interpreted in different ways. Another reason which caused a lot of hesitations within the Protestant churches has been the sharp contrast of (New Testament) gospel and (Old Testament) law traditionally emphasized in evangelical, particularly Lutheran teaching. In this context the Jews were blamed for clinging to a law which had been abolished by Christ.

It took one generation after the war until one of the most important regional Protestant churches in Germany dared to proclaim a new start. It was the Synod of the Evangelical Church of the Rhineland, which, in January 1980, adopted a resolution "Towards Renovation of the Relationship of Christians and Jews." During the last 25 years, this has become the model for a great number of similar resolutions of other Protestant churches.

The Rhineland resolution,[6] acknowledging the fact that the church originally is rooted in Judaism,[7] "accepts the historical necessity of attaining a new relationship of the church to the Jewish people." It mentions "four factors" which have brought the church to this new insight: "1) The recognition of Christian co-responsibility and guilt for the Holocaust—the defamation, persecution and murder of the Jews in the Third Reich. 2) The new biblical insights concerning the continuing significance of the Jewish people within the history of God (e.g., Rom 9–11), which have been attained in connection with the struggle of the Confessing Church"

[6] "Towards Renovation of the Relationship of Christians and Jews" is quoted according to the English translation by F. Littell, revised by R. Rendtorff, in: http://www.jcrelations.com > Statements > Protestant > 1005.

[7] The resolution has as its motto "Thou bearest not the root, but the root thee" (Rom 11:18b).

(the oppositional stream of the Protestant church during the Nazi period). "3) The insight that the continuing existence of the Jewish people, its return to the Land of Promise, and also the foundation of the state of Israel, are signs of the faithfulness of God towards his people," and "4) The readiness of Jews, in spite of the Holocaust, to (engage in) encounter, common study and cooperation" with Christians.

In consequence the Rhineland synod declares: "1) We confess with dismay the co-responsibility and guilt of German Christendom for the Holocaust." It is remarkable that—in contrast to Catholic documents and former Protestant documents—the Rhineland resolution from 1980 starts with the confession of the "co-responsibility and guilt" of the church for the extermination of the Jews. In a series of "Theses on the Renewal of the Relationship of Christians and Jews" expounding the resolution, the synod even admits that the church has "no answer" with respect to Jewish questions referring to Christian responsibility.

The Rhineland synod continues: "2) We confess thankfully the 'Scriptures' . . . our Old Testament, to be the common foundation for the faith and work of Jews and Christians. . . . 3) We confess Jesus Christ the Jew, who as the Messiah of Israel is the Savior of the world and binds the peoples of the world to the people of God." The intention of this third sentence was to emphasize the close link between the church and the Jewish people. However, the fact that Jesus Christ is called in this phrasing the "Messiah of Israel" has received some critical remarks from Jewish commentators. More recent resolutions on the Jewish-Christian relationship by other Protestant churches consequently have avoided this expression and sought for alternative formulations.

The Rhineland synod continues: "4) We believe the permanent election of the Jewish people as the people of God and realize that through Jesus Christ the church is taken into the covenant of God with his people. . . . 5) We believe with the Jews that the unity of righteousness and love characterizes God's work of salvation in history. We believe with the Jews that righteousness and love are the commands of God for our whole life. As Christians we see both rooted and grounded in the work of God with Israel and in the work of God through Jesus Christ. . . . 6) We believe that in their respective calling Jews and Christians are witnesses of God before the world and before each other. Therefore we are convinced that the church may not express its witness towards the Jewish people as it does its mission to the peoples of the world." With good reason this last sentence has been understood by most commentators as the definitive renunciation of the Evangelical Church of the Rhineland to proselytize among Jews and to convert them to Christianity.

The Rhineland synod continues:

> 7) . . . Throughout centuries the word 'new' has been used in biblical exegesis against the Jewish people: the new covenant was understood in contrast to the old covenant, the new people of God as replacement of the old people of God. This disrespect to the permanent election of the Jewish people and its condemnation to non-existence marked Christian theology, the preaching and work of the church again and again right to the present day. Thereby we have made ourselves guilty also of the physical elimination of the Jewish people. Therefore, we want to perceive the unbreakable connection of the New Testament with the Old Testament in a new way, and learn to understand the relationship of the 'old' and 'new' from the standpoint of the promise: in the framework of the given promise, the fulfilled promise and the confirmed promise. 'New' means therefore no replacement of the 'old'. Hence we deny that the people Israel has been rejected by God or that it has been superseded by the church. 8) As we repent and convert we begin to discover the common confession and witness of Christians and Jews: We both confess and witness God as the creator of heaven and earth, and know that we live our everyday life in the world blessed by the same God by means of the blessing of Aaron. We both confess and witness the common hope in a new heaven and a new earth and the spiritual power of this messianic hope for the witness and work of Christians and Jews for justice and peace in the world.

Finally the Rhineland synod gives some practical recommendations for the future: For instance, the proposal to constitute a permanent committee "Christians and Jews" in order to "to advise the church leadership in all questions concerning the relationship of the church and Jewry and to assist the congregations and church districts towards a deeper understanding of the new standpoint in the relationship of Jews and Christians."

The Rhineland resolution "Towards Renovation of the Relationship of Christians and Jews" received controversial comments at the time when it was adopted by the synod. For instance, the great majority of professors at the Faculty of Protestant Theology in Bonn, Rhineland, adopted a document that disputed a great deal of the statements of the resolution. They could not accept the confession of guilt, because they maintained that the Nazi government had not only been antisemitic, but it was anti-Christian as well. In addition, they insisted that the mission of the church refers to every human being and that the church therefore could not renounce the task to convert Jews to Christianity.

However, 25 years after the Rhineland synod adopted the resolution "Towards Renovation of the Relationship of Christians and Jews" it can be said that most of the statements of the resolution represent more or less a consensus within European Protestantism. On June 24, 2001, the assembly of the "Community of Protestant Churches in Europe" (CPCE), an umbrella organization comprising the great majority of the Protestant churches in Europe, adopted a voluminous document entitled "Church and Israel,"[8] which in general follows the line of the Rhineland resolution.

Moreover, in the year 2000, a group of American Jewish scholars published a document entitled "Dabru Emet" (Hebrew: Speak Truth), which acknowledges the fact that "in recent years, there has been a dramatic and unprecedented shift in Jewish and Christian relations." The document mentions that "an increasing number of official church bodies, both Roman Catholic and Protestant, have made public statements of their remorse about Christian mistreatment of Jews and Judaism." And it realizes that "these statements have declared . . . that Christian teaching and preaching can and must be reformed so that they acknowledge God's enduring covenant with the Jewish people and celebrate the contribution of Judaism to world civilization and to Christian faith itself." The authors "believe that these changes merit a thoughtful Jewish response." They "believe it is time for Jews to learn about the efforts of Christians to honor Judaism," and they "believe it is time for Jews to reflect on what Judaism may now say about Christianity."[9]

[8] Cf. Leuenberg Church Fellowship, "Church and Israel: A Contribution from the Reformation Churches in Europe to the Relationship between Christians and Jews," 24 June 2001, in: http://www.jcrelations.com > Statements > Protestant > 1009.

[9] National Jewish Scholars Project, "Dabru Emet—A Jewish Statement on Christians and Christianity," in: http://www.jcrelations.com > Statements > Jewish > 1014. See also: *Christianity in Jewish Terms*, ed. Tikva Frymer-Kensky et al., (Boulder, CO: Westview, 2000) xv.

14

Jewish and Christian Theology

The Essence of Christian Theology from the Perspective of the Aggadic Tradition of Judaism *

Choi In-Sik

In this article I shall make an attempt to suggest a theological response to the crisis of Christian identity in pluralistic contexts in terms of relevancies between Judaism and Christianity. This task is related to understanding the essence and tradition of Judaism in relation to early Christianity.

In fact, Jesus Christ and his community, which are the basis for the identity of Christian theology, did not reject the tradition of Judaism in order to found a brand-new religion. Rather, Jesus Christ and his community stood in the tradition of Judaism, while moving beyond it, and proposed a new interpretation of Torah in view of the Talmud. In other words, the community of Jesus Christ understood the life of Jesus Christ on the basis of the Mosaic Torah, especially the Passover *Ha-aggadah*, which was the crux of the Aggadic tradition. Hence it transmitted the narratives of Jesus Christ through the Aggadic tradition. Finally, it shaped the Gospels, the foundation of Christian theology, which in my opinion, can be understood as *Passover Aggadic Midrash*.

Therefore, I argue that Christian theology needs to actualize such a principle of hermeneutics regarding the postmodern situation today. The interpretation of the words and deeds of Jesus Christ can be undertaken in light of the Passover Aggadah of the Exodus of Israel. Christian theology confirms its identity within the *Aggadic Midrash* tradition of the community of Jesus Christ. At this juncture, Jesus Christ may be understood as

* Translated from the Korean by Jong-In Lee and edited by Paul S. Chung.

"Embodied Torah" so that the essential message of the Gospel narratives will be deepened as Passover Aggadah.

Protestant Theology in Critical Situation

First, there has been an identity crisis in Protestant theology. The basis of Protestant theology is Jesus Christ, the Holy Scripture, and the creeds. But Protestant tradition regarding them has failed to sustain harmony and integrity because there has been a variety of voices reconsidering and reconstructing them. The positivistic-dogmatic explication, which attempts to establish theological identity upon the ground of 'objective' history, faces limitations, resulting in a dominant tendency of theological skepticism. The result is theological subjectivism. A subjective hermeneutic prevails in this context. But since the context which humans experience is not singular, but multi-contextual, a contextual theology aggravates the confusion of theological identity.

Second, there has been a lack of a theological position in dealing with the pluralism that has driven postmodern culture. Protestant theology has merely availed itself of it, not giving it enough reflection. It failed to face up to many accommodations to the paradigm of plural cultures. Therefore Christian theology has come to arm itself with a firm fundamentalism, or to retreat to relativism in the face of the postmodern challenge. In our present day, we can neither seek a culture state (*Kulturstaat*) in terms of the theological ideal of the Ritschlians in 19th century Germany, nor aim at the church state (*Kirchentum*) of the Lutheran Orthodox school.

Third, there recently has been a slowdown in Protestant churches that have focused on evangelism. Due to inflexible paradigms of both theology and ministry, both conservative and liberal churches have been dwindling, except for some evangelistic or Pentecostal churches. With the help of capitalism and individualism, the Protestant church in South Korea especially has grown. However, it has been losing its essential commitment to the Gospel, falling into ever growing secularization.

Fourth, there has been theological parochialism. Protestant theologies have concentrated on specific theological movements after the Reformation in order to construct their own various theological identities while competing with each other based upon denominationalism. In seeking a theological distinctiveness over against other denominations, and emphasizing their own denominational theologies, Protestant theologies have failed to secure a theological integrity and ecumenicity; hence, there is no concord of ecumenical or catholic theology. At this juncture, we perceive in the Korean context a general tendency toward indifference to and exclusion of Catholic theology, which is the womb of Protestant theology. Furthermore, anti-Judaism is smuggled into the internal context of Protestant theology,[1] bringing forth a chaotic situation in Protestant theology. Thus Protestant theology, far from conversing with the tradition of Jewish theology or Catholic theology, ends up rejecting them by opposing their rich historical-theological legacies.

Fifth, Protestant theology has been recognized as having caused much suffering to the human community and all the creatures of the earth. Theology begins as the salvific answer to suffering. This is the existential rationale of theology. But the 20th century experienced terrible moments, culminating in the Holocaust committed by Germany, a Christian state. Similarly, the atomic bombings of Hiroshima and Nagasaki were perpetrated by the U.S., also basically, if not officially, a Christian state. We are aware of the series of massacres around the world between Christianity and other religious communities. This experience seriously brings into question the nature of humanity and religion. Even though Protestant theology is not entirely responsible for such horrible disasters, it has failed to address the cause of these sufferings, and to engage these problems in a responsible way.

Need for the Study of Judaism

First, the study of Judaism is needed because of the worldwide impact of Jews. Jews have exercised strong cultural leadership, which has influenced politics, economics, the sciences and the arts, and culture in general, with values rooted in Judaism. In addition, Jewish-Islamic relations have assumed a politically serious character.

Second, it is needed for dialogue between religions. It is indispensable to understand and dialogue with Jewish religion.[2] If Christianity is required to engage in dialogue with other religions, a dialogue with the Jewish religion has a priority because of its special relationship with Christianity.

Third, dialogue is needed for theological reflection on the suffering of humankind. We can hardly find other peoples in history who have gone through sufferings like Shoa. The Jewish history of suffering is deeply connected with Christian anti-Semitism in the West. At this juncture, it is

[1] Rosemary R. Reuter, *Faith and Fratricide: The Theological Roots of Anti-Semitism* (New York: Seabury, 1974).

[2] Here, I do not refer to 'Judaism' as 'Jewish religion.' I think Judaism is better understood as designating Jewish thoughts and culture in general, including Jewish religion.

worthwhile to explore the Jewish understanding of God and the Hebrew Bible in order to grasp their unique theology.

Fourth, dialogue is needed to understand the formation of the Old Testament and the New Testament, and to deepen the characteristics of Christian interpretations of Scriptures alongside of Jewish interpretations. Especially for studying the Second Temple Era, it is important to grasp the historical understanding of Jesus Christ and early Christianity which is central and basic to Christian identity. It should be remembered that Jesus Christ was a Jew and the authors of the Bible lived in the Jewish tradition.[3] The Kingdom of Heaven that Jesus preached can only be understood properly in the context of early Judaism. In other words, we gain a more solid ground for understanding Jesus' message through the lens of early Judaism.[4]

Fifth, dialogue is needed to restore the right biblical tradition and legacy of Christian theology in conversation with Judaism. Judaism begins with Torah, and through *Tanakh, Talmud, Zohar, Midrash and Kabbalah*, returns again to Torah. All of these are mixed with the Aggadic and Halakhic forms of Judaism. What is more relevant for Christianity lies in the Jewish paradigms of Aggadah and Halakhah.

Characteristics of Judaism

First, Judaism is about the ethical relationship between God and humanity. Judaism includes all dimensions of thought and practice as ways of knowing God. The beginning and the fulfillment of Judaism is possible only through God. Knowing God is the primary goal of Judaism. Judaism, as the way of knowing God through thought and practice, takes place in earthly life, here and now, not beyond this world. Therefore, Judaism is basically a love toward God which is practiced in the present.[5]

To grasp such an essence of Judaism, it is of utmost importance to understand the prophets. What made Israel "Israel," was the spiritual struggle of the prophets through many centuries. It was the prophets who expressed the peculiar spiritual orientation of Judaism. The most characteristic of the vision of the prophets was the intuition and the practice of

[3] Brad H. Young, *Jesus the Jewish Theologian* (Peabody, MA: Hendrikson, 1995).

[4] J. Neusner and Bruce D. Chilton, *God in the World* (Harrisburg: Trinity Press International, 1997) 131. See Bruce D. Chilton, *The Kingdom of God in the Teaching of Jesus* (London: SPCK, Philadelphia: Fortress, 1984); "The Kingdom of God in Recent Discussion," in *Studying the Historical Jesus*, ed. Bruce D. Chilton and C. A. Evans (Leiden: Brill, 1994).

[5] Leo Baeck, *The Essence of Judaism* (New York: Schocken, 1948) 35–37.

the word of God. The ethical demand was the most crucial element in their thought.[6]

Thus, priority belongs to the prophets' personalities rather than to their words. Knowledge of God was not to be gained by intellectual reflection. Rather, they affirmed that God should be conveyed through their personalities after they experienced God. They thought that the attempt to prove the existence of God was a sign of unbelief, which was clear proof of losing God or of being denied by God. Therefore, they tried to show the presence of God through their lives and to demonstrate that a religion could be vividly alive only in the hearts of people.[7]

In connection with this, it should be noted that in Judaism, discord between faith and life is basically impossible since faith can be grasped only through life according to the teachings of Torah and the prophets. That is, faith is not proved by knowledge, and does not belong to the realm of knowledge. Thus, a discord between faith and life is inconceivable.

Another characteristic of the prophets is that they are immersed in the presence of God in relation to the world and human life rather than being immersed in speculation on the nature of God. They concentrate on preaching the relationship between God and the world rather than elucidating the mystery of Being.[8] In this way, God and the life of the human being are connected. Judaism is defined by life, and life is fulfilled through Judaism in this sort of practical structure of religion and life. There is no place for fanatics or equivocal attitudes. The prophets show a new way of religious life rather than trying to demonstrate a new philosophical concept about the world.

Since Jews could retain their religious autonomy in this way, they were not undermined by natural philosophy or Gnosticism. They understood the ontological mystery of the universe in the observant religious life, not in metaphysical assumptions. Hence, they saw the reality of life shaped by an ethical life.

If we expound such characteristics of Judaism in this regard, it can be said that Judaism provides the answer of divine revelation regarding the appeal of human needs. What is needed for the human being to live? How does God answer that question? To work out that kind of question is a practical assignment for Judaism. The structure of Judaism was formed in the course of finding an answer for such a question. The basic theological

6 Ibid., 31.

7 Ibid., 34.

8 Ibid., 35

structure is well articulated in the following statement: "The world is the world of God, and God is the God of human life."[9]

Second, Judaism is not a hierarchical system. Every religion has proponents of ecclesiasticism. In this regard, Judaism is no exception. But the Jewish religion can be distinguished from Judaism. Judaism is a tradition forged by a continuing group of rabbis, not a system of structural authority. If there are incidents of trying to form structural authority, they faded away sooner or later. And it is not given to Judaism to decide matters of faith. Even if there is a need for the formation of dogma, there is no authority to confirm it in Judaism.[10]

Judaism is understood as the continuing process of formation by masters, not by a compilation of dogmas, or by a certain person, or a founder. Judaism cannot be a finished system since it is not a system of dogma but the outcome of the continuing teachings of teachers. It is identical with the characteristic of *Tanakh* (Scripture) which is the basis of Judaism. *Tanakh* is fragmentary, not dogmatic, not a succession of conclusions, not formulas, not a system. *Tanakh* is full of questions, unfinished like a human being. It is replete with complicated questions that resist analysis. It is a treasury of authentic personal life. It is a sign of youth. Its real meaning can be communicated not by lips, but only by the heart.[11] As we can see from *Tanakh,* which is the foundation of Judaism, Judaism is an open organism, not an authoritative system.

Third, Judaism can be understood as the relationship between God, Israel, and Torah. Torah is definitive for understand Judaism. All of Judaism lies in Torah. In Judaism there is a firm belief that Torah is the revelation of God. "Torah came from God."[12] The faith that this Torah (which came from God) was given by Moses became the foundation of Judaism. Unlike other prophets, because Moses could see all things through a transparent glass, the divine revelation of Torah given to Moses was solid and secure. Therefore, it has worked as a major premise of Judaism.[13] Based on Torah as the revelation of God, Judaism does not become an authoritative creedal system. Rather it is consistently open toward the future, and therefore ever reinforcing itself. It has been believed that God does not close God's

[9] Ibid., 39.

[10] Ibid., 15.

[11] Ibid., 42.

[12] Mishnah, *Sanhedrin* 10, 1.

[13] Jacob J. Petuchowski, "Zur rabbinischen Interpretation des Offenbarungsglaubens," *Offenbarung in jüdischen und christlichen Glaubensverstaendis,* ed. Jacob J. Petuchowski and Walter Strolz (Freiburg: Herder, 1981) 77.

revelation through the written Torah given to Moses at Sinai, but has continuously revealed Godself. With the so-called Moses' Pentateuch, orally transmitted Torah through the continuing prophets and teachers has also been accepted as the revelation of God.[14]

The Two Hermeneutical Traditions of Judaism: The Halakhic Tradition and the Aggadic Tradition

Torah is not law, but much more than that. Torah itself is the revelation.[15] Translating Torah as law, brings about difficulty in understanding Torah properly and rightfully. Torah is the law for all Israel to observe the divine plan at the outset of creation, and cosmic wisdom simultaneously. In short, God created the cosmos with Torah. Thus, the theology of creation should come from Torah. Without Torah, the world is doomed to return to the chaos of before creation.[16] Paul Van Buren summarizes it in the following statement: "Torah precedes the creation."[17] Therefore, Torah is the revelation of the presence of God, *gilluj schekhina*.[18]

Mishnah and *Midrash* had concrete hermeneutical and realistic intentions and principles in editing and compiling Torah, *Tanakh,* and other traditions. According to those principles, they were minutely classified and constituted, becoming hermeneutical traditions within Judaism, the Halakhic tradition and the Aggadic tradition.

Halakhah (walking) is the law, the regulations, and the rules which govern the whole life of Jews. It deals with not only religion, but also every human relationship that derives from society, politics, family, and the economy. Jewish religion has been divided into Orthodox, Reformed, and Conservative according to attitudes toward Halakhah.

The Orthodox thoroughly observe the articles of Halakhah, permitting no change. The Reformed freely applies new interpretations and dis-

14 Ibid., 81.

15 Markus N. A. Bockmuehl, *Revelation and Mystery in Ancient Judaism and Pauline Christianity* (Tübingen: Mohr, 1990) 13, 28. D. S. Russell, *The Method and Message of Jewish Apocalyptic: 200 BC-AD 100* (London: SCM, 1964) 26: "To the apocalyptists every bit as much as to the Pharisees the written Torah was the revelation of God to his people."

16 Petuchowski, "Zur rabbinischen Interpretation," 82.

17 Paul M. Van Buren, *A Theology of the Jewish-Christian Reality II: A Christian Theology of the People Israel* (NY: Seabury, 1983) 54.

18 Arnold M. Godberg, *Untersuchungen ueber die Vorstellung von der Schekhinah in der fruehen rabbinischen Literatur* (Berlin: De Gruyter, 1969). Petuchowski, "Zur rabbinischen Interpretation," 85.

cards traditional articles of practice. The Conservatives abide by tradition while attempting to change organically.

Aggadah is a kind of story that tries to comfort, teach, and enlighten people with historical events, unofficial histories, legends, folktales, and some edifying lessons which do not intend to directly handle legal issues.[19] Etymologically, Aggadah has two characteristics in broad perspective.[20] First, it has a strong emphasis on an educational goal, which relies heavily upon the text itself, frequently citing "the text says" (*magid hakatuv*). Thus, it appears as an exegetical Aggadah.[21] Second, it functions as media, which orally conveys transmitted stories, based upon the phrase, "Tell your son," (*vahigadeta lebinka*: Ex 13:8).[22]

Now we have arrived at the very heart of Judaism. The reality of dynamism and rigidity, toughness and softness in Judaism arises in the tension, conflict, and harmony between Halakhah and Aggadah Judaism in practical life. Characteristics of Halakhah and Aggadah are poetically described through analysis and comparison by Hayyim Nahman Bialik (1873–1934), a renowned Hebrew poet of the early 20th century.[23] He articulated his these characteristics so finely that his writing has attained the status of textbook.[24]

Halakhah is dark, narrow, heavy, fixed, tenacious, straight, stable, and linear while Aggadah is bright, open, airy, flexible, floating, pliable, shaky, and curved. Halakhah stands for righteousness, formality; it regards visible body, and is active, impassible, colorless, and one-dimensional. Aggadah gives priority to mercy, is concerned with content, looks upon the invis-

[19] In general, the Jewish encyclopedia differentiates Aggadah from Haggadah. The latter designates the Passover Haggadah, while the former is used as a contrasting concept. Louis Jacobs, *The Jewish Religion: A Companion* (New York: Oxford University Press, 1995); *The Encyclopedia of the Jewish Religion*, ed. R. J. Zwi Werblowsky et al. (New York: Adama, 1986) 15; Philip Birnbaum, *Encyclopedia of Jewish Concepts* (New York: Hebrew, 1993) 16: "The Aggadah penetrates deeply into the spirit of the Bible by means of its broad interpretations of the text."

[20] The root of aggadah is 'ngd,' 'to tell,' or 'to relate.' It implies the verbal communication of tradition from one generation to the next.

[21] Wilhelm Bacher, "Origin of the Word Haggadah (Aggadah)," *Jewish Quarterly Review 4* (1892) 406–29. D. Ben-Amos, op. cit., 2.

[22] Leopold Zunz, *Die Gottesdienstlichen Vorträge der Juden Historisch Entwickelt*, trans. M.A. Jack, ed. H. Albeck (Jerusalem: Mosad Bialik, 1954) 250, note 1.

[23] Hayyim N. Bialik and Y. H. Ravnitzky, ed., *The Book of Legends Sefer Ha-Aggadah: Legends from the Talmud and Midrash* (New York: Schocken, 1992).

[24] H. N. Bialik, "Halacha and Aggada," in *Modern Jewish Thought: A Source Reader*, ed. N. N. Glatzer (New York: Schocken, 1977) 56–61.

ible heart, seeks novelty, and is colorful and multi-dimensional. Halakhah demands obedience, expresses itself prosaically, pursues a definite style, gives priority to intelligence and the sustains tension, while Aggadah gives priority to freedom, expresses itself poetically, does not repress emotion, and is indeterminate and loose. Halakhah is firm and fixed like ice while Aggadah is soft and unfixed like water. Figuratively speaking, Halakhah is a solid rock while Aggadah is an open sky.

These seemingly contrasting traditions of Halakhah and Aggadah constitute the magnificent organic structure of Judaism. When Judaism is dynamic, Aggadah confers to Halakhah spirit and content, while Halakhah gives Aggadah practice and method. Aggadah bestows freedom on Halakhah, while Halakhah presents concrete reality to Aggadah for resolute practice. In other words, Aggadah without Halakhah is an empty dream of animated emotion, while Halakhah without Aggadah is an endless, rigid, and lifeless obligation. We can find a balanced wholeness of Halakhah and Aggadah in the healthy mature individual or community.[25]

When we examine the history of Israel, we find that it has committed fatal errors in ignoring the Aggadic tradition unilaterally by clinging to Halakhah. As a result, we can hardly ever find dynamic Judaism. In the Orthodox tradition, Halakhah is usually divinized and literalized as the essence of Torah while Aggadah is depreciated as merely entertaining or irrational stories. Aggadah does not see the poetic splendor in Halakhah, nor does Halakhah realize the essence of truth hidden in Aggadah.[26]

Aggadic Judaism and Christian Theology

The interpretation of Torah in the early days was very simple. It was called '*Midrash-Torah*', or simply *Midrash.* It meant a homiletic exposition of, broadly, the Hebrew Bible, and narrowly, of the Torah, which worked in a central role in Judaism's Aggadic tradition. *Aggadic Midrash* was composed of biblical texts and their interpretations from which they developed new insights. Such a tradition of Aggadah enabled Jews to experience heaven and undertook the role of leading them to heaven, by which it glorified God and comforted Jews.

Addadic Midrash deals with religious truth, moral maxims, divine judgment, and the spiritual enlightenment of the law. It demonstrates the greatness of Israel in history and in the future, the tradition of Jewish his-

[25] Ibid., 61.

[26] Ibid., 62.

tory, praise of the holy land, and encouraging stories of consolation and invigoration. The rise and fall of Israel, the experience of suffering during times of oppression, the hope for perfect salvation, and new ideas produced through the response against invaders and encounters with other cultures, in turn, made the Aggadah tradition rich. In order to provide spiritual nourishment, stories, proverbs, philosophical allegories, and even various forms of science and literature were utilized to interpret the Hebrew Bible.[27]

Aggadah was divided into two parts. One was made up of stories, ethical lessons, proverbs, and wisdom for practical life. It was formed and well-known before the fall of the Second Temple. The other was always related to the interpretation of the Hebrew Bible. It was consistently developed through the homilies in synagogue at each Sabbath and feasts.[28]

Aggadah has constantly reminded Israel that the power of God has always been with her from the start. Even in the times of captivity, God has never forgotten Israel. Through the teaching of Jewish virtues, Israel was encouraged to have a religious consciousness of being chosen for special ministry, and to understand the manifestation of important events in Jewish history. Among them, Aggadah related especially to suffering.

On the one hand, it taught the sufferings of Israel as the punishment for sin. On the other hand, it described them as a means of future reward. Above all, Aggadah splendidly depicted the glory of the day of the Messiah. One of the characteristics of the day of the Messiah is that the material and the spiritual would not be differentiated, but rather understood as one reality. Such a tradition of Aggadah provided living water to Jews in captivity, gave consolation and inspiration at times of struggle, and nourished Jewish children with infinite poetic imagination and creativity.[29]

In the early days of the Hebrew Bible, Aggadah was used in *Midrash* in a limited way outside the Halakhic tradition. Most of the contents transmitted stories and theological, ethical lessons, rooted in the Hebrew Bible. This tradition was changed in the late days of the Hebrew Bible when even non-factual, fabricated stories were incorporated into the Aggadah tradition. Some were transmitted as having an ethical value; *Talmudic Midrashic* narratives belongs to this category.[30] To put it simply, *Mishnah* has more of the characteristics of Halakhah, and *Midrash* more of Aggadah. If seen

[27] Samuel Umen, *Pharisaism and Jesus* (New York: Philosophical Library, 1963) 28–29.

[28] Ibid., 30.

[29] Ibid., 32.

[30] D. Ben-Amos, op. cit., 3.

chronologically, *Midrash* was complied during 6–11th century. *Mishna* was complied in the 3rd century. We may say that it was a great contribution to the balanced development of Judaism. In other words, the Aggadic tradition was the fruit of an unceasing movement toward the restoration of authentic Judaism when the Halakhic tradition was dominating.

Although *Midrash* was compiled after the 6th century, the *Midrashic Aggadic* tradition already was there at the time of the Hebrew Bible and early Judaism. With these presuppositions in mind, I deal with Jesus and the New Testament, whose backgrounds were rooted in early Judaism. As discussed above, Palestinian Jews had to go through extreme suffering after the Babylonian captivity and under the Hellenistic Empire.

Under the Roman Empire, they experienced the fall of the Second Temple, thus losing both the holy land and the Temple, and beginning a life of wandering. That era, when Israel faced the issue of revival or annihilation seriously and acutely, was, in short, "chaotic." In such a time, transition and standardization were urgently needed.[31] After Pompey made a triumphal (albeit tragic for Israel) entry into Palestine in 63 B.C.E., the self-understanding and the pride of the Jewish tradition were devastated tragically and decisively.

Numerous prophetic and apocalyptic writings kept Israel from discerning what the standard was. Politically, there seemed to be no future after the surrender of the Hasmon dynasty to the Roman Empire. From a cultural perspective, after the conquest of Palestine by Alexander the Great, there was a drastic influx of alien cultures, such that people of Israel, especially young intellectuals, were exposed defenselessly to global Hellenistic cultures, which caused confusion in their sense of values.[32] Most Jews came to be under the impression that they should prepare for the imminent future, possessing an apocalyptic, eschatological worldview (*Weltanschauung*), rather than engaging in Torah.[33]

For them, the conviction that Jerusalem is the center of the world had evaporated. The thought that God was no longer with them, unlike how God had been with Abraham, prevailed.[34] In such a time of tension and

[31] James H. Charlesworth, "Hillel and Jesus: Why Comparisons Are Important," in *Hillel and Jesus: Comparative Studies of Two Major Religious Leaders*, ed. J. H. Charlesworth and Loren L. Johns (Minneapolis: Fortress, 1997) 12.

[32] Charlesworth, "Hillel and Jesus," 16. James H. Charlesworth, "Greek, Persian, Roman, Syrian, and Egyptian Influences in Early Jewish Theology: A Study of the History of the Rechabites," in *Hellenica et Judaica: Hommage à Valentin Nikiprowetzky*, ed. A. Caquot et al. (Leuven-Paris, 1986) 219–43.

[33] Flavius Josephus, *The Wars of the Jews*, Book I, chap. 347.

[34] Charlesworth, "Hillel and Jesus," 16.

crisis, Jesus of Nazareth interpreted the Torah in a new way and taught the people of Israel, preaching the imminent Kingdom of God, healing the sick, and performing miracles. In so doing, the Jesus movement began.

At this point, we should ask in which tradition of early Judaism Jesus and early Christianity sought their identity and found their answer. At that time of chaos, there were many religious sects. According to Flavius Josephus, Sadducees, Pharisees, and Essenes were the most influential.[35] Whence did the difference between Jesus' community and other Jews come? It depends on how and to what extent Halakhah was applied to practical life.[36] How and to what extent was an Aggadic interpretation of content applied to Halakhah practice?[37] It is evident that the Pharisaic community and Jesus' community demonstrated very different positions regarding Halakhic rulings. I think *the Jesus community interpreted and practiced the Halakhic tradition on the basis of Aggadic Judaism to a greater extent than others.*

There is an aristocratic quality in the Halakhic practices of the ordinances of the Pharisaic Jews who held onto Orthodox Judaism. It is because they had at least the economic status of the middle class, which enabled them to observe the law without economic restraint. The demands of the law could hardly be observed by the people who did not have the luxury of wealth, intelligence, and social status like the Pharisees. But for the community of Jesus, since most of them belonged to the lower classes (*ochlos*-minjung), the rigorous practices of the Halakhic tradition were almost impossible. In fact, such rigid demands contradicted the spirit of Torah. Against this, Jesus approached the law differently from the Pharisees. I argue that the extensive practice of Aggadic Judaism by Jesus and his community gave them a new and distinctive flexibility.

To prove the validity of such an argument, it is necessary to follow a meticulous biblical analysis of the Gospels. Jesus' community never ignored the Halakhic tradition of Judaism. Rather, by restoring the Aggadic tradition, which was not observed at that time, Jesus' community tried

35 Flavius Josephus, *The Wars of the Jews*, Book II, chap. 119–166, Ant 18, 12–22; B. Pixner, "Jesus and His Community: Between Essenes and Pharisees," in *Hillel and Jesus: Comparative Study of Two Major Religious Leaders*, ed. James H. Charlesworth and Loren L. Johns (Minneapolis: Fortress, 1997) 193.

36 Pixner, "Jesus and His Community," 194. "The heart of their differences lay in the halakhah: how the Law should be observed in practical life."

37 Marc Gellman, "Law and Story in Judaism and Christianity," in *Fireball and the Lotus*, by Ron Miller and Jim Kenny (Santa Fe: Bear, 1987) 65.

to achieve the genuine goal of Halakhah, that is, *zekhut*.[38] In fact, Jesus' community did not arbitrarily cast aside the Halakhic tradition for the sake of the Aggadic tradition.[39] In other words, it is evident that Jesus and his community made certain that the ethics of Aggadah affected the kernel of Halakhah, so that Aggadah could truly reveal the rationality behind Halakhah. For Jesus and his community, Halakhah was understood through Aggadah.[40]

In Judaism, the prototype of the Aggadic tradition is the Passover Ha-aggadah.[41] The heart of Torah, which commands Israel to tell the power and love of God who saved Israel from the suffering of slavery, is Haggadah. The central figure of Haggadah is Moses, who guided Israel from Egypt and proclaimed Torah at Sinai. Torah becomes the story of God's salvation through Haggadah. All of the following Aggadah is reinterpreted through the Passover Haggadah, which is the prototype, resulting in the Halakhic tradition. Thus, in Torah Judaism, Aggadah always precedes Halakhah.

Jesus' community heard, saw, and experienced bodily "Jesus Haggadah." Jesus was embodied Torah, in his being and doing, prior to Halakhah.[42] Accordingly, it can be said the Church of the New Testament era rediscovered Torah, which was centered upon Passover Haggadah in Jesus, and wrote the Gospels as *Christological Midrashic Aggadah*. The reason that all the Aggadic narratives of the Gospels culminate in the Passover Aggadah of Jesus is that the writers of the Gospels came to re-appreciate the Passover in Moses' Torah, which is the prototype of Torah revelation.

38 Thomas Kazen, *Jesus and Purity Halakhah: Was Jesus Indifferent to Impurity?* (Stockholm: Amqvist & Wiksell, 2002) 338. According to Kazen, regarding the Halakhah practice against impurity, Jesus, through divine exorcism, practiced Halakhah essentially by expel the impure spirits which caused impurity.

39 Pixner, "Jesus and His Community," 213. Pixner says that Jesus' family was deeply involved in the Essenes movement. But "he distanced himself from it, coming closer to the Pharisees during his stay Capernaum, but *he developed his own halakhah*." (italics are mine).

40 Umen, *Pharisaism and Jesus*, 68. Umen rightfully explains the relationship between Aggadah and Halakhah. "The ethics of the Haggadah (aggadah) condition the heart of the Halacha. It sheds light on the reasoning behind the Halacha. The Halacha becomes understandable through the Haggadah."

41 Generally speaking, Haggadah (ha-aggadah) designates inherently Passover Ha-aggadah. Judah Goldin, "The Freedom and Restraint of Haggadah," *Midrash and Literature* (New Haven: Yale University Press, 1986) 56–57.

42 John Corbett, "The Pharisaic Revolution and Jesus as Embodied Torah," *Studies of Religion/Science Religieuses* 15 (1986) 375–91.

Thereby they interpreted the Passion of Jesus as embodied Torah. In other words, Gospel writers came to grasp the authentic meaning of Passover Ha-aggadah that they had already known through the Passover Aggadah of Jesus. It consists of the Lord's Supper, his suffering on the Cross, and the Resurrection.[43] Consequently, it is plausible that the Gospel of Mark should be called *Midrash* since it is widely believed to be the groundwork for the Gospels of Matthew and Luke.[44]

As regards the Haggadic meaning of Mark, John Bowman claims that not only can Passover Ha-aggadah be compared to the Lord's Supper, but it provides the whole pattern of Mark. Mark has more characteristics of the peculiar style of orally-transmitted literature in Judaism than Moses' Passover Ha-aggadah. It contains the story of the Messiah, for whom Israel longed, in its form. And it renders, in the form of *Midrashic Aggadah*, the powerful words and deeds of the redeemer who saved Israel from Egypt.[45]

Above all, we notice that the Lord's Supper is exactly the Passover Order of Israel. Just as the Passover Order is a commemoration of salvation from Egypt, which God carried out with mighty power and miracle, so is the order of the Lord's Supper. Passover Order was remembered by the first Christians to commemorate Jesus and his work of salvation, that is, Passover Haggadah.[46] For this reason, we might say that Gospel of Mark is a Christian Passover Haggadah, agreeing with Bowman.[47]

In this manner, it becomes possible to re-appreciate the essence of Christian theology in the context of Aggadic Judaism. We confirm in Torah and Jesus Haggadah that the theme of Christian theology is to tell the sin of humankind, the reality of suffering, and the salvation of humanity from that sin and suffering. Wherever and whenever Israel went through suffering, the Passover Haggdah was narrated and reinterpreted, leading to a renewal of faith in the God who hears and saves. That Passover Haggadah has been finished in Passover Haggadah of Jesus. Therefore, the primary task of Christian theology encourages everyone who suffers to hear Jesus' Haggadah, and to ever renew and reinterpret it in the context of one's

[43] J. Duncan Derret, "Haggadah and the Account of the Passion," *Downside Review 97* (1979) 308–15.

[44] Dale Miller and Patricia Miller, *The Gospel of Mark as Midrash on Earlier Jewish and New Testament Literature* (Lewiston: Edwin Mellen, 1990). J. Duncan Derret, "Good Shepherd: St. John's Use of Jewish Halakhah and Haggadah," *Studia Theologica 27* (1973) 25–50.

[45] John Bowman, *The Gospel of Mark: The New Christian Jewish Passover Haggadah* (Leiden: Brill, 1965) xiv.

[46] Ibid., 91.

[47] Ibid., 102.

own suffering. In the postmodern pluralistic context, Jesus Haggadah as the Gospel, which is beyond the Passover Haggdah of the Jews, proclaims that God fulfills the salvation of every nation and every generation from sin and suffering.

Conclusion: The Task of Aggadic Theology

Just as Judaism finds its central story in the Mosaic Passover Haggadah, so does Christian theology begin with Jesus Haggadah. Every Halakhic tradition and practice should seek its spirit and meaning in Jesus Haggadah. This means that the entirety of Christian theology should be evaluated rightfully in the light of Jesus Haggadah. If this were to happen, what would be the concrete task of Jesus Haggadah?

First, the task is to restore the identity of Christian theology drifting into crisis, in terms of Jesus' Haggadah tradition. The disastrous separation of the historical Jesus from the Christ of faith, which is the product of the struggle with modern science, must be overcome and integrated into One Jesus Christ in the light of Jesus Haggadah. Jesus Haggadah is a Haggadah of the *Shekinah* of God's hand. God's salvation performed the miracle of the Resurrection from the event of Cross and reaches its culmination favorably for humanity in regards to its sin and suffering. The Jesus community transmits ("You shall tell your child." Ex 13:8) this Jesus Haggadah in order to proclaim the presence of God, who desires to save humankind. Such proclamation would enable people who listen to the Jesus Haggadah to approach Jesus Christ historically and *faith*-fully at the same time.

Second, by accommodating religious pluralism and postmodernism, Asian contextual theology successfully attacks the exclusivism of Christianity that settled down comfortably in modernism.[48] But it tends to lose its identity by being entrapped in a relativism which demands the compromise or renunciation of faith in the uniqueness of Jesus Christ, which is the foundation of Christian identity.

48 Here, the reason why I point out modernity as the cause of Christian exclusivism is that by rooting on modernity, Christianity has developed itself toward exclusivism. As is known in general, modernity is related to Cartesian dualism, and professes Western cultural progressivism. Cartesian dualism supports the primacy of spirit over against body. And Western cultural progressivism sets the standard of culture on Western culture, hence presses what is not Western into what is Western. By adopting such modernity, Christianity has championed exclusivism which has oppressed non-Western, non-spiritual. This Christian exclusivism has come to lose its legitimacy by the fall of modernity through the emergence of postmodernism.

In this situation the Jesus Haggadah has the task of presenting the hope of salvation from sin and suffering to all humankind, without running into exclusivism or relativism. In fact, the Jesus Haggadah has been collected from the narratives of the Cross and of Jesus' life, which were fused with various traditions of Haggadah from Mesopotamia, Egypt, Canaan, Persia, Greece, and Rome. Diverse understandings of Christ have been developed from Jesus who is the "Delta Point."[49]

Though Jesus Haggadah adopted the narrow way of Jesus only, it nevertheless has a universality of salvation for all. The Jesus Haggadah was formed during the days of the Greco-Roman world, which deeply influenced Judaism in terms of politics, culture, and religion. This complexity helps us to understand the richness and flexibility of the Jesus Haggadah by constructively interpreting the effects of the Greco-Roman world on Judaism. As a result, this allows us to overcome the debates of the past that sought the origin of Christianity only in an Israel-alone model. By positing the origin of Christianity not only in a Jewish context but also in a Greco-Roman context, the kernel of the Jesus Haggadah can be revealed with much more depth and complexity in terms of its universal relevance.[50]

Finally, the Jesus Haggadah has the task of promoting active dialogue not only with diverse traditions of Protestant theology but also with Catholicism, Orthodox Christianity, and various traditions of Judaism. For example, each of the Protestant denominations, Catholic Christianity, and the Jewish religion have their own Halakhah for the practice of their religious convictions. They all have assumptions that an intimate dialogue with other religions would threaten their own Halakhic practice. Since they equate defending their own Halakhah with preserving their own identity, they reject dialogue with other religions which, in their opinion, would jeopardize the practice of their own Halakhah.

Be that as it may, if the Jesus Haggadah grants authentic theological meaning to each tradition's own Halakhic tradition,—accepting that the diversity of Halakhah among various religious traditions becomes possible,—it can lead to true dialogue in the Christian tradition. The Jesus Haggadah poses a task also for Asian contextual theology to develop its contextuality without falling into antisemitism.

[49] "Delta Point" is the place where all the rivers converge. From here, many tributary streams are newly formed and flow in various direction, and finally run to the sea. Likewise, various hermeneutical traditions converge at one point and new hermeneutical traditions are generated from there, the "Delta Point."

[50] Gregory J. Riley, *The River of God: A New History of Christian Origins* (San Francisco: HarperSanFrancisco, 2001) 10.

15

The Mystery of God and *Tao* in Jewish–Christian–Taoist Context

Paul S. Chung

It is not a matter of course that a Christian reads and interprets Taoist philosophy for its relevance to Christian theology. The wisdom of *Tao-te-ching* was already available in a Western Latin translation in the sixteenth century. In this translation, which was accomplished by Jesuit missionaries in China and presented to the British Royal Society in 1788, translators wrote that "the Mysteries of the Most Holy Trinity and of the Incarnate God were anciently known to the Chinese nation."[1]

Some Western scholars concerned themselves with attempting to extend and utilize the Chinese concept of the organic naturalism of the interconnectedness of all as a corrective to the customary dualistic and mechanistic pattern of thought in the West in which God was found to be only a *machina* (*Deus ex machina*). Others attempted to interpret the *Tao-te-ching* in such a way as to make it an antidote to cure the sick and vulnerable Western society. In addition, there was an attempt to articulate the continuity between the *Tao-te-ching* and religious Taoism within a Chinese cultural system and framework.[2]

Recently, Jürgen Moltmann initiated, from his own theological perspective, a daring conversation with "Tao: the Chinese Mystery of the World," seen through Western theological eyes.[3] What I find intriguing in

[1] James Legge, *The Texts of Taoism*, vol.1 (New York: Dover, 1962) xiii.

[2] Julia M. Hardy, "Influential Western Interpretations of the Tao-te-ching," in *Lao-tzu and the Tao-te-ching*, ed. Livia Kohn and Michael LaFargue (New York: State University of New York Press, 1998) 165–85.

[3] Jürgen Moltmann, *Science and Wisdom*, trans. Margaret Kohl (Minneapolis: Fortress, 2003) 172–93.

Moltmann's dialogue is his attempt at reading and discussing *Tao-te-ching* from a Jewish-Christian standpoint. Sharing Moltmann's vision of *Tao* in a Jewish-Christian way, I concern myself with discovering the wisdom of *Tao-te-ching* for a Jewish-Christian concept of the God of Israel, Jesus Christ and the Spirit.

What is *Tao-te-ching* in Taoism? Before attending to the point of my dialogue with *Tao-te-ching*, let me explain the background of Taoism to facilitate increased readability and understandability. The history of Taoism can be conveniently divided into four periods: proto-Taoism, classical Taoism, modern Taoism and contemporary Taoism.[4] The first period, proto-Taoism spans from antiquity to the second century C.E. *Tao-te-ching* is often understood as having first appeared during the period of the Warring States (479–221 B.C.E.).

The person most revered in Taoism is known simply by the epithet Lao Tzu, which can be translated as "Old Master." According to the cultural legend, Lao Tzu was regarded as an elder contemporary of Confucius (551–479 B.C.E.). The earliest biography of the Old Master is contained in the *Shih-Chi* (*Records of the Historian* dated 90 B.C.E) by the great Han dynasty historian Ssu-ma Ch'ien (145–86 B.C.E).

According to this record, which admits uncertainty regarding the historicity of Lao Tzu, he was said to have been born in the state of Ch'u, where he later became an archivist at the royal Chou court under the name Lao Tan. He cultivated *Tao* and its virtue and he taught without fame in the world. He was consulted by Confucius. After he had lived in Chou for a long time, he realized that the Chou dynasty was in decline. Retiring from the court, he set off to emigrate across the pass toward the west. In the western frontier, he was asked by *Yin Hsi*, the guardian of the pass, to compose a text outlining his philosophy of *Tao*. The result was the text known as *Tao-te-ching* (The Scripture of *The Way and Its Power*), the content of which is presented in two sections that deal with the *Tao* and with its virtue [*te*].[5] This book remains the basic text of Taoist thought to this day.

Apart from Ssu-ma Ch'ien's biography, we have little historical information about Lao Tzu in his original person. Furthermore, this biography

4 Cf. James Miller, *Daoism: A Short Introduction* (Oxford: Oneworld, 2003) 4–15.

5 Chapter 63 of the Shi-chi. Cf. Fung Yu-Lan, *A Short History of Chinese Philosophy* (New York: Macmillan, 1964) 93–94.

of Lao Tzu is qualified by its own confession that no materials existed at all for such a biography.[6]

The *Tao-te-ching* is a compilation of terse aphorisms about the *Tao* and its power. The text exists in a standardized edition made by the commentator Wang Pi (226–49 C.E.). Of all the commentaries on the *Tao-te-ching,* the most important ones are those of Ho-Shang-Kung (probably second century C.E.) and Wang Pi. The text in the first chapter speaks of *Tao* as the formless and ineffable Way that is the wellspring of creative power for a universe of constant transformation. The *Tao* is the mother of heaven and earth, the spontaneously self-generating life of the universe.

Tao as the Source of Life and Its Nature

The root meaning of *Tao,* around which everything in *Tao-te-ching* revolves, is path or way. When used as a verb, the same word means to direct, to guide or to establish communication. The Way, which by definition cannot be spoken of and cannot be named, is the wondrous beginning of the ten thousand things. The Way gives them birth, and its power [*te*] brings them up, nourishes them, makes them secure and perfect, giving to each its strength. "That's why the ten thousand things always honor Way and treasure Integrity" (ch. 51).[7]

The Way in its formlessness and namelessness originates and completes the ten thousand things. The transcendence of *Tao* in its formlessness and ineffability is conceived of as both the initial beginning and the source of life in relation to all living sentient creatures. Its occurrence happens of itself perennially. "It was always and of itself so." The *Tao* is called "the mysterious power," or "dark-enigma Integrity" (ch. 51).

[6] Arthur Waley, *The Way and Its Power: A Study of TAO TE Ching and Its Place in Chinese Thought* (New York: Grove, 1978) 108. In the Chinese view the dating and evaluation of Lao Tzu is as an elder contemporary of Confucius in the sixth century B.C.E. Against this, the Western view places Lao Tzu in the fourth or third century B.C.E. even after the completion of Chuang Tzu. Cf. A.C. Graham, *Chang-tzu: The Seven Inner Chapters and Other Writings from the Book of Chang-tzu* (London: Allen & Unwin, 1981).

5. Graham claims Chuang Tzu to be a compilation of works of different schools, while Fung Yu-lan conceives of it as an anthology of Taoism. Against the view of Graham, Liu Xiaogan rejects the hypothesis of the completion of Lao Tzu after the time of Chang Tzu. Cf. Liu Xiaogan, *Classifying the* Zhuangzi *Chapters* (Michigan: University of Michigan Press, 1994) 172, 184.

[7] Chapter number in parenthesis in the text refers to *Tao-te-ching,* the two different texts which are used. *Lao Tzu, Tao Te Ching*, trans. David Hinton (Washington D.C.: Counterpoint, 2000). Arthur Walley, *The Way and Its Power: A Study of the Tao Te Ching and Its Place in Chinese Thought* (New York: Grove, 1978).

Tao eludes all human conceptual thinking because it is beyond what can be affirmed or negated. In the *I Ching* (*Book of Changes*), one of the Confucian classics, *Tao* is explained as the constantly self-renewing and creating energy of life as it moves. *Yin* and *yang*, in mutual interaction, are fundamental categories of this system. *Tao* creates all that is created through a continuous interaction of *yin* and *yang*.

Te is usually translated as virtue. To Confucius, *te* was a quality acquired by living nobly in cultured company. The virtues preached by the Confucianists are, however, in the eye of Taoism, attacked as an utter degradation of the *Tao*. In *Tao-te-ching* we read that when the great Way was abandoned and fell into disuse, the virtues of human heartedness and morality (righteousness) arose. When intelligence and knowledge emerged, great artifices and deceptions began. When family discord is rife, the duty of obedience and kindness come forth. When the State falls into disorder and misrule, loyal subjects appear (ch. 18). Human heartedness (*jen*) and righteousness (*i*) are the supreme virtues of Confucianism, the principles of which became the foundations of the ethical code of the nobility for Mencius.

In Lao Tzu's view, however, *te* is the realization or expression of the *Tao* in actual and natural living. *Te* is what happens by the natural way of *Tao* as distinct from human striving. It does not imply any supernatural intervention in the course of nature. "A noble official is never warlike, and a noble warrior is never angered. A noble conqueror never faces an enemy, and a noble leader stays below the people he wields" (ch. 68). It is this aspect which is called the *te*. It arises not out of contending with the people, but out of wielding the people. According to Lao Tzu, even the best will in the world, when forced, achieves nothing. The best righteousness, when forced, achieves nothing.

The *te* (the greatest power) is available to those who do not seek power and who do not use force. The person of highest power does not act. "Therefore the Sage relies on actionless activity, carries on wordless teaching" (ch. 2). Though one acts, one is regarded in this way. Perhaps it would be beneficial to draw a parallel with the *Bhagavad Gita,* the so-called Hindu "New Testament," and its concept of action without concern for results.

In contrast to the Confucian idea of morality, in Taoism the *te* can be attained when the *Tao* is attained. *Te* is obtained by adopting a policy of non-action. Each thing has *te* to grow and develop, so long as it is properly nourished and looked after. The *te* lies and abides in the *Tao*. Therefore, *te* is itself the manifestation of the *Tao*. The life-style based on *te* is characterized by production without possession, action without self-assertion and development without domination. Therefore, *te* is in harmony with the *Tao* by following the *Tao* by which it is directed.

What then is *Tao*? *Tao* is born before heaven and Earth. We may think of it as the Mother of this world. We do not know its name. It is the Immense, nameless. The ineffability of the *Tao* is affirmed in the very first chapter of the *Tao-te-ching*: A *Tao* that can be told of is not the Permanent *Tao*. Rather than maintaining "the religious art of mystical silence,"[8] the ineffable *Tao* points to profound knowledge, according to which the *Tao,* though incomprehensible in human languages, is the source of all meaning for living creatures.

Hence Taoist mysticism, unlike Western mysticism, becomes possible without the presupposition of the personal-mystical union with a metaphysical reality of the Absolute. Taoist thinking centers around "where is the Way?" not "what is the Truth?" In this spontaneous way of life the mystical experience aims at transforming body and soul.[9]

However, this *Tao* does not refer to the metaphysical principle of transcendence in the sense of qualitative difference or dualism. It refers instead to the ground or womb from which all life springs and after which all life follows and to which all life finally returns. This carries a sense of non-duality or relationality. Of all great things, surely *Tao* is the greatest. But its ineffability remains still the mystery of all mysteries. "Those who know do not speak; Those who speak do not know" (ch. 56). *Tao* transcends space and time and is yet simultaneously within space and time. In other words, *Tao* is transcendentally immanent and immanently transcendental. The immanence of *Tao* refers to the way of the universe which is the driving force in flux of all life and nature. It is called the Mother of the world in terms of giving life to all living sentient creatures.

Mystical Elements and Principle of Mutual Interconnection

The unnamed is the origin of heaven and earth. Naming is the mother of ten thousand things. Whenever there is no desire, one beholds the mysterious way and power of *Tao*. Whenever there is desire, one beholds its manifestations in the universe. Its identity is *hsuan hsun* beyond *hsun*, all

[8] Moltmann, *Science and Wisdom*, 173.

[9] Hardy, "Western Interpretations," 178.

mystery's gate (ch. 1). The chaotic and obscure state of *hsuan*, the dark-enigma, is the nature of the world before any distinction has been made.

This is the identity principle between mystery and manifestation from which one distinction has been made between *te* and *ch'i* or *yin* and *yang* or non-being and being. God's aseity (or God *in se*) exists by and through itself *sui generis*. The *Tao* operates mysteriously and secretly. In addition to the *Tao* which is incomprehensible silence, there is the *Tao* which is speakable or nameable. Lao Tzu envisioned a speaking about the unspeakable. The silence and void before heaven and earth pervades all things. Lao Tzu calls the mother of the world *Tao*, always in motion and returning (ch. 25).

The thought of *Tao-te-ching* may be a form of mysticism, though not in a theistic sense. The Taoist mystical experience does not center on an ontological union between human self and ultimate reality. Lao Tzu uses the word *ming* (light) on several occasions to mean the sage's characteristic insight into the mystery. Going to the origin of all things characterizes the main idea of Taoist mysticism. The Taoist mystics abolish time by identifying themselves with an eternal now. Lao Tzu is more concerned with how to make the best of our life in this world than with a hope in expectations of a better future. Everything comes from God, and everything goes to God.

At this point, we see similarities to Meister Eckhart's metaphysics of flow. In this there is a dynamic reciprocity and movement of flowing-forth (*exitus-emanatio*) of all things from the hidden ground of God, and a flowing-back (*reditus-restoratio*) of the universe into identity with God. The *reditus* of all things to God corresponds to the *exitus* of all things from God.[10] So the future of God is to be realized and grasped in this "to-and-fro" movement.

In Chinese thought, the two poles of cosmic energy are *yang* (positive) and *yin* (negative), and their conventional signs are respectively [–] and [--]. The ideograms are associated with the masculine and the feminine, the firm and the yielding, the strong and the weak, the light and the dark, the rising and the falling, heaven and earth. The male individual must not neglect his female component, nor the female her male. Thus Lao Tzu says: "Knowing the male but keeping the female, one becomes a universal stream. Becoming a universal stream, one is not separated from eternal virtue" (ch. 28). The Taoist metaphor of the feminine in the biological-

[10] Bernard McGinn, *The Mystical Thought of Meister Eckhart: The Man from Whom God Hid Nothing* (New York: Crossroad, 2001) 71.

generative sense affirms nature. Taoist mysticism affirms and connects the world of nature to its source of life in which the feminine functions as the symbol of non-action and spontaneity.

The key to the relationship between *yin* and *yang* is called *hsian sheng*, mutual arising or inseparability. As Lao Tzu puts it,

> when everyone knows beauty as beautiful, there is already ugliness. When everyone knows good as goodness, there is already evil. "For truly Being and Not-being grow out of one another. Difficult and easy complete one another. Long and short test one another. Pitch and mode give sequence to one another. Front and back give sequence to one another (ch. 2).

Everything and everybody are in mutual sequence. The permanent *Tao* and its manifestation of *te* are in mutual arising. In this regard Lao Tzu contradicts the Confucian idea of rectification of name, according to which a father in the family must be a good father in accordance with the name of the father. In the same way a son must be a good son in relation to his father and other members accordingly. This establishes order in human relations.

However, *Tao* cannot be expressed fully even in terms of rectification of name. *Tao* is effective in the world by non-action. *Tao*, as non-existence, is the beginning of Heaven and Earth, while existence is the mother of all being. From enmeshment with the excessive development of Confucian rationality based on rectification of names, one must return to non-conceptual simplicity, non-discriminating mutual relationship, non-action, and the way of watercourse. According to chapter 42 in *Tao-te-ching,* we read,

> Tao generates the One. The One generates the Two. The Two generate the Three. Three generate the ten thousand things. The ten thousand things carry Yin and embrace Yang. They achieve harmony by combining these forces.

The *yin-yang* view of the world was later developed in connection with the theory of the five elements or energies (*wu hsing*), whose first celebrated advocate was Tsou Yen (350 to 270 B.C.E.).[11]

The forces are so interdependent that no one can exist without all the others, just as there can be no *yang* without *yin*. This is similar to the Buddhist principle of dependent origination (*pratitya samutpada*). Dependent origination, which is based on the *sunyata*, has been developed

[11] Cf. Yu-Lan, *Short History,* 135.

and expanded in the direction of a fusion of horizons with *sunyata* as absolute nothingness in Buddhism and as the wondrous being of nonexistence in Taoism. If non-being and being are in mutual arising, the Taoist idea of cosmogenesis is inclined to the naturalistic panentheism of *Tao* rather than pointing to the basic law of cause and effect.

In the *yin-yang* and *wu hsing*, the organic and relational view of the world is implicit, but it becomes explicit in Lao Tzu and in Chuang Tzu. We do not find it stressed in Confucian thought until the Neo-Confucianism of Chu Hsi (1131–1200) in which all the compatible threads of Confucianism, Taoism, and Buddhism are woven together. Perhaps the greatest advocate of this organic view was the Buddhist Fa-tsang (643–712) of the Mahayanist Hua-yen school, whose image of the universe was a multidimensional network of jewels, each one containing the reflections of all the others *ad infinitum*. Each jewel was a *shih,* or a thing-event. His principle of *shi shi wu ai* (between one thing-event and another there is no obstruction) expounded the mutual interpenetration and interdependence of everything happening in the universe. In other words, the whole cosmos is implicit in every member of it, and every point in it may be regarded as its center.[12]

The Feminine Side of *Tao* and Its Watercourse

The *Tao* can also be symbolized by the female side. The valley spirit never dies; it is called the mysterious female. The gate of the mysterious female is the origin from which heaven and earth sprang (ch. 6).The feminine, as the symbol of the origin of life and the principle of non-action and spontaneity (*tzu-jan*), is linked to the symbol of the valley characterized by its empty space and its passive receptivity. *Tao* personified as mother is not only tolerant and life-giving but also ruthless and inhumane in response to attempts to artificially manipulate it (ch. 5).

In Lao Tzu, the idea of mother—the female, the mystical womb—is closely associated with that of emptiness. This void is none other than non-being. It is efficacious because, like bellows, it is capable of producing breath at will. As Lao Tzu says, the *Tao* principle happens of itself (*tzu-yan*). *Tao* is the ultimate reality and energy of the universe; it is the Ground of being and non-being. *Tao* does nothing, but nothing is left undone (ch. 37).

[12] Alan Watts, *TAO: The Watercourse Way* (New York: Pantheon, 1975) 35. Cf. Paul Williams, *Mahayana Buddhism: The Doctrinal Foundations* (New York: Routledge, 1989) 130–32.

It loves and nourishes all things but does not lord it over them. *Creatio ex nihilo,* in a Taoist sense, can be conceptualized as a way of emerging and happening of itself. It refers to the character of the void. One models after the earth; earth models after heaven; heaven models after *Tao*; *Tao* models after the naturally-so, abiding by occurrence appearing of itself (ch. 25).

Modeling after *Tao* does not mean acting contrary to nature. *Tzu-jan* is a term that expresses the ultimate movement after one another. According to Lao Tzu, all beings come into existence by the virtue of having obtained primal unity. "Valleys realized primal unity and so came to fullness. The ten thousand things realized primal unity and so came to life" (ch. 39).

Unsurprisingly, Lao Tzu's exaltation of femininity went dead against all the conventional thinking of his contemporaries, a fact which witnesses to the subversive and even revolutionary component in the *Tao-te-ching*. Lying low in stillness, the female overcomes the male (ch. 61). Lao Tzu uses the flow of water as the principal metaphor of *Tao*. It is called the Watercourse Way, the process of nature. In Lao Tzu's favorite image of *Tao*, water is the essence of life.

> THE HIGHEST good is like that of water. The goodness of water is that it benefits the ten thousand creatures; yet itself does not scramble, but is content with the places that all men disdain. It is this that makes water so near to the Way (ch. 8).

But *Tao* cannot be defined in words and is not an idea or concept. Water is an eloquent and extraordinary metaphor in portraying *Tao* as the flowing course of nature. The term *tzu-yan*, translated as nature, means the spontaneous, that which is so of itself. But it is also basic to the Taoist view of the world that every thing-event is what it is only in relation to all others. Therefore, the principle is that if everything is allowed to go its own way, the harmony of the universe will be established since every process in the world can do its own thing only in relation to all other things. Because of the mutual interdependence of all beings, harmony will emerge *tzu-yan*, of itself, without external compulsion. Therefore, *Tao* is esteemed and virtue is honored without anyone's order. They always come naturally.

Christian Reflection of *Tao-Te-Ching*

Tao *and Creation*

In his reading of *Tao-te-ching* in the context of Christian theology, Moltmann pays special attention to the Taoist idea of nature as "the highest reality of not-doing."[13] For him, *tzu-yan* spontaneity corresponds, as a matter of course, to the self-forgetting, delighted play of Wisdom as seen in Israel's Wisdom literature. According to this tradition, the indwelling of God in creation becomes efficacious in terms of God's Spirit (*ruach*) and Wisdom (*hokma*) (cf. Proverbs 8.22ff). Regarding the biblical story of creation, Moltmann discerns a similarity between the concept of *tzimtzum* in the Kabbalah and the Taoist idea of the Way.[14]

At the level of absolute truth, the statement of the permanent *Tao* in the first chapter of *Tao-te-ching* can reflect on *Ehyeh*, or "I shall be" (Ex 3:14), yet without implying the idea of a personified God. "I shall be" is the answer to Moses' question "what is your name?" It could mean: I am nameless because I cannot be conceived of in terms of human languages. To look at it from another perspective, the word H-W-Y-H means existence. The universe exists entirely within God, but God is more than it. Y-H-W-H as *Eyn Sof* (that which has no end), or *Makom*, is greater and more comprehensive than H-W-Y-H.[15]

Likewise, the *Tao* as the way of ultimate mystery cannot be perceived or clearly conceived of by human rationality. The *Tao* as the Great Void is greater and more comprehensive than the universe. The fact that the *Tao* cannot be named or clearly conceived of is due to its character of mystery and freedom. At the level of relative truth, however, the *Tao* is frequently referred to as the mother of all creatures. This is an aspect of the named *Tao*. In chapter 1, the *Tao*, considered in terms of its named or perceptible aspects, is called the mother of the ten thousand creatures. When the *Tao* causes all creatures to be born, *te* nourishes them and makes them grow. This *te* function of the *Tao* comes into play when the principle has form and name.

In chapter 1, the supreme *Tao* produces heaven and earth and then the ten thousand creatures. In chapter 42, *Tao* gives birth to the One; the One gives birth to two and three things, successively up to ten thousand creatures. Everything shoulders *yin* and embraces *yang*, blending *ch'i* to establish harmony. The concepts of *te* and *ch'i* are analogously correlated to the Jewish-Christian concepts of wisdom and Spirit.

In the Jewish tradition of Kabbalah, *En Sof*, God as an endless, limitless, incomprehensible reality reveals Godself as the ten *sefirot* within the

13 Jürgen Moltmann, *Science and Wisdom*, trans. Margaret Kohl (Minneapolis: Fortress, 2003) 185.

14 Ibid., 184–85.

15 Arthur Green, *EHYEH: a Kabbalah for Tomorrow* (Woodstock, VT: Jewish Lights, 2003) 1.

cosmic structure. *Keter,* which represents the first undefined intent toward movement within *En Sof,* has no specific content in itself. It can be described as Nothing. The spiritual journey to and from the Nothing is continual. *Keter*, devoid of content, is a locus of pure compassion. In its very emptiness, *keter* is the point of departure of the cosmic process accepts the future movement. It may be depicted as a state of divine openness *ad extra*.

With *keter* understood as a crown or circle, the *sefirot* is a great circle in which the end is connected with the beginning, and the beginning with the end. Out of *keter* arises *hokhmah* (wisdom). The movement from *keter* to *hokhmah,* which is the first step in the primal process, is a transition from Nothingness to being. In Job 28:12, "Wisdom comes from Nothingness." As *hokhmah* arises out of Nothingness, it brings forth its own mate, *binah* (contemplation). *Hokhmah* and *binah,* as primal pair of *yin* and *yang*, are in mutual connection with each other. The energy radiating from *hokhmah* is described metaphorically as flowing light and water. These three, *keter*, *hokhmah,* and *binah*, are the first three *sefirot*. The energy of *hokhmah* fills the womb of *binah* which in turn gives birth to the seven lower *sefirot.*

Isaac Luria (1534–72) transformed kabbalistic speculation about creation. For him, creation was a negative event, whereas in the literature of early kabbalists, creation was understood as a positive act. The *Eyn Sof* had to bring into being an empty space in which creation could take place. This was accomplished by the process of *tzimtzum*, God's self-contraction. By going into exile, God allowed for empty space so that the process of creation could be initiated.

According to Taoist cosmogony (reflection on how the world came into being), *Tao* above and within is the source of the mystery that is life. From the *Tao* above we see the mystery of Nothingness, while seeing the appearance from the *Tao* within. Non-being gives birth to being. The *Tao,* in utter silence and mystery, revealed itself in mutual relationship and mutual permeation with all that exists through the *te* and the *ch'i* to establish harmony among all. It is called the gateway of all mystery. The principle of mutual interconnection between non-being and being, or *yin* and *yang*, presupposes the other side of the *Tao*, namely *te* and *ch'i*. Therefore, there is no difference between the triadic self-evolution of the *Tao* in the manifestation of *te* and *ch'i* and the emergence of the ten thousand things. Taoist theogony proceeds and evolves in the cosmogony of every living organism.

The permanent *Tao* describes the eternity of the *Tao* in the manifestation of *te* and *ch'i*. Speaking in Taoist fashion, creation comes from *Tao*, not out of *nihilo*. There is no void, nothing outside the *Tao* to underline and evolve everything. The *Tao* underlines and sustains everything which flows forth from it. Because of this, the Biblical idea of *creatio ex nihilo* is not sufficient to describe the Taoist idea that there is no name outside the *Tao*. The self-movement of the *Tao* refers to its self-evolving emanation from the hidden mystery to the world of form and appearance. In this regard there is a parallel between Taoist cosmogenesis and the Jewish idea of *tzimtzum*. God as holy Nothingness, or *Tao,* underlies *En Sof* (non-being) and *sefirot* (*te* and *ch'i* including the ten thousand things). God accomplished creation by contraction in the same way *Tao* caused being through emptying the void.

The Christian idea of creation depicts a more personal dimension of the divine act of creation in presupposing the existence of 'nothing' outside God. *Tao* cosmogenesis, on the other hand, refers to the natural and self-evolving way of impersonal and hidden *Tao* in which creation *ex nihilo* is to be understood as *creatio ex 'the Way' (Tao)* of the great void. *Tao* embraces being, non-being, and nothingness, one and all. This unseen is neither personal nor trans-personal. Rather, it is understood as the all-inclusive Way of the self-emptying void, the living source of life.

If *creatio ex nihilo* is understood as *creatio ex* the Way (*Tao*), in which, out of God's mystery, God paves God's Way of openness to grant life and freedom to all, then a personality centered theology of God in the Western tradition could be enriched in a way that incorporates the all-inclusive living and dynamic side of God.

Lao Tzu speaks of the *Tao* that is not the permanent and constant *Tao*. This is a double play on words since the term *Tao* is also a verb, "to speak." The Chinese word *Tao* is an equivalent of both the Greek word *logos* and the Greek word *hodos*, the Way. *Tao* is God's speech, logos, and way. This understanding of the meaning of these words has been used in translations of St. John's Prologue—"In the beginning was the *Tao*"—and contains, therefore, echoes of the line, "I am the Way, the Truth, and the Life." This is a Christian appropriation of Taoist philosophy in China and Korea in each Bible translation. God's speech remains still a mystery in its manifestation of *te*, the embodiment of Jesus Christ.

Tao *and Jesus Christ*

Tao, as God's speech, became flesh. This parallels the Taoist idea of immanence through *te* and *ch'i*. This idea corresponds to the Jewish notion of divine contraction or the self-limitation of *En Sof* (*tzimtzum*). Withdrawing or holding itself back from Godself, God as *En Sof* allows non-God to exist. This does not mean merely a once-and-for all action but a continuing divine action to allow room for the other to exist. God's creation out of God's own self and God's ongoing revelation of the divine act of creation has a parallel in structure with the Taoist notion of creation out of the Way and of radical immanence within all that exists through the virtue of *te* and spontaneity of *ch'i*.

All creatures issue from the *Tao*; they are its children. But they must return to its womb. Progressing and returning is the movement of the *Tao*. All creatures in this world are born from the seen; the seen is born from the unseen. They move from *Tao* to *Tao* in the great cycle of *yin* and *yang*. "[All things emerge together And I see them return again]. They grow and flourish and then return to the source. Returning to the source is stillness. [Stillness means returning to what is destined.] Returning to what is destined means to be [enlightened]. To know the eternal means enlightenment" (ch. 16).[16]

The *Tao* to which all things return is the root and origin in which they find eternal rest. This homecoming is what is destined for all. The circulation of emergence and return articulates the movement or companion of *Tao*, issuing out of itself into the life of the ten thousand things, and together with them returning to itself. This return to the root is called stillness, a submission to fate which has become part of the always-so. Those who know the always-so have room in one for everything. *Tao* is forever and not destroyed (ch. 14). Richard Rubenstein, a Jewish thinker, writes of a

> Holy Nothingness, known to mystics of all ages, out of which we have come and to which we shall ultimately return....The limitations of finitude can be overcome only when we return to the Nothingness out of which we have been thrust. In the final analysis, omnipotent Nothingness is Lord of all creation.[17]

The person who possesses perfect virtue participates in the life-giving efficacy of the *Tao*. Lao Tzu calls this person by the name *sheng jen*, the sage. This person is illumined and enlightened. In terms of self-cultivation in a naturally spontaneous way, the holy person is illumined to know that

[16] Cited from Lao Tsu, *Tao Te Ching*, trans. Gia-Fu Feng and Jane English (London: Wildwood House, 1973). Cf. Moltmann, *Science and Wisdom*, 187.

[17] Richard L. Rubenstein, *After Auschwitz* (Indianapolis: Bobbs Merrill), 154.

everything comes from *Tao* to *Tao* in harmony with the eternal *Tao*. The sage follows after the Way, the non-action of *tzu-yan* and spontaneity.

For Taoists, the Christian idea of future must be interconnected with past (origin) and present (way of life in non-action). This perspective points to Jesus as the figure of *tzimtzum*, a model of going off to a far country and of coming home. In Jesus' farewell sermon to his disciples, we see a Jesus who comes from the Father to the world, and who returns to the Father, leaving the world to prepare a place for it (John 14:2; 16:28). Jesus mirrors the way of *tzimtzum*, going into the exile of the cross to allow for a space for the people. Jesus does not find a place on earth (Lk 9:58), because his place is *Makom*.[18] The locus of creation exists in Christ rather than existing in the universe. The idea of *Makom* in Jesus' saying is related to his spontaneous submission to the will of God and his way of non-violence. This offers a basis for extending Christ's way to the Taoist ideas of non-action and sagehood.

Jesus Christ as the embodiment of *Tao* becomes the ideal holy person in realizing and fulfilling God's virtue and Torah. Meekness, compassion, and non-violence in the life of Jesus provide a parallel to the Taoist idea of sagehood. However, God remains mystery even in embodiment. The words of Jesus Christ are not in competition with God, nor do they replace God.

Jesus Christ and Sagehood

The sage is the one who is of childlike spontaneity (*tzu-yan*) and non-action. This is one who returns to infancy by knowing the masculine and nurturing the feminine. This is one who becomes like a river of all in abiding by perennial integrity. This is the one who is like the valley of all and returns to the boundless by knowing the white and nurturing the black. This is one who, like "a true minister for the great governing blade, craves nothing" and "returns to the simplicity of uncarved wood" (ch. 28).

Jesus' feminine compassion can be seen in his exhortation of the simplicity of a child: "Unless you become like children, you will never enter the kingdom of God. Anyone who receives one such child in my name receives me" (Matt 18:5). "I praise Thee, O Father, Lord of heaven and earth, that Thou didst hide these things from the wise and intelligent and didst reveal them to babes" (Matt 11:25). Likewise, Taoist anthropology of

[18] Cf. *The Talmud*, Selected Writings, trans. Ben Zion Bokser (Mahwah: Paulist, 1989) 16.

sagehood does not recommend unilateral patriarchy (*yang*) or matriarchy (*yin*) but proposes childlike simplicity in harmony with both of them.

Jesus Christ, in this light, means a perfect harmony between Jesus as a Jewish man and Christ as the Eternal Logos. Jesus lives in perfect harmony with the Supreme *Tao* (Father) of his origin in fellowship with the Spirit rather than in the ontological state of *homoousios*. He is the cardinal way of incarnating, embodying and practicing the Way of God. In other words, he is God's *te*. The Christian idea of the preexistent Christ can be understood in accordance with Jesus' saying: "Truly, truly, I say to you, before Abraham was born, I am" (John 8: 58). "For if you believed Moses, you would believe me; for he wrote of me" (John 5: 46). Moses bore witness to Jesus Christ who IS before Abraham was born. Essentially Jesus Christ belongs to the world of Torah, which as a companion of life leads to life, not to death. At this juncture we see a correspondence between Jesus and Moses (cf. Deut 18: 15.18).

In the Jewish tradition, Torah is not just the message given by God to Moses on Sinai but the Eternal Word of God. Torah existed before the foundation of the world. In Christianity, the Torah as the eternal Word of God is identified with the incarnation of Jesus Christ while in Judaism it remains forever the Word. The primordial Torah is seen in relation to *hokhmah* which speaks in the verses of the Books of Proverbs and Job. She was with God from the beginning and is the beginning of God's way. Jesus as the embodied (or incarnated) Torah means he has the broadest scope and dimension in the universe because all was and is created through it. From the *Zohar*'s statement we read. "There is *nothing* that is not referred to in Torah."[19]

However, Torah is not fixed, or final, but dynamic. Prophetic inspiration has evidence in the lives of such non-Israelites as Balaam and his father, and Job and his four friends. Because of the limitations of human understanding, Moses and the prophets could not see or understand the fullness of God's mystery. For the sake of comprehensibility and communication, the Torah speaks of God in terms of analogy. In Talmudic discussion, there is no sharp distinction between *halakha* (law) and *haggadah* (or aggadah, the nonlegal teaching). As such, it calls for human imagination, exercising initiative in reinterpreting and reconstructing the Torah to each particular life context (Deut 17:8–12). Commitment to Torah becomes

[19] Zohar 3:221a. Cf. *Zohar: The Book of Enlightenment*, trans. Daniel Chananmatt (New Jersey: Paulist, 1983).

meaningful in a living and dynamic interpretation of the texts in a contextual way.[20]

Jesus, the incarnated Torah, can be seen as the embodiment of God's Way in terms of *te* and through *ch'i*. In this he represents the ideal of sagehood in a Taoist sense, and he appears to be childlike and living water, a figure inclusive of the knowing mother and of the children (ch. 52). "Look at the birds of the air, that they do not sow, neither do they reap, nor gather into barns.... Observe how the lilies of the field grow; they do not toil nor do they spin" (Matt 6:26–28).

Nature for Jesus implies God's Way of being present, sustaining, and nurturing. Jesus' self-description as living water (John 4:10), given for us to drink, provides a striking example of the Taoist source of living water. Those who drink the living water of Jesus abide in the source which gives water that is eternal life. "From their innermost being shall flow rivers of living water" (John 7:38). This refers to the indwelling of the Spirit.

Jesus embodies the spirit of valley and follows God's Way of emptiness. In chapter 76 of *Tao-te-ching*, we read a striking example of the Taoist ideal of sagehood in continuity with the suffering Servant in Isaiah 53 and with Jesus' beatitudes.

> WHEN HE is born, man is soft and weak; in death he becomes stiff and hard. The ten thousand creatures and all plants and trees while they are alive are supple and soft, but when they are dead they become brittle and dry. Truly, what is stiff and hard is a "companion of death"; what is soft and weak is a "companion of life." Therefore "the weapon that is too hard will be broken, the tree that has the hardest wood will be cut down." Truly, the hard and mighty are cast down; the soft and week set on high.

Likewise Jesus says, "blessed are the poor in spirit for theirs is the kingdom of heaven. Blessed are the pure in heart, for they shall see God. Blessed are the meek, for they shall inherit the earth. Blessed are the peacemakers, who will be called children of God" (Matt 5:3, 5, 8).

According to Talmudists, a sage is a peace-lover and peace-maker. The ways of peace are mentioned in Psalm 15: Walking with integrity, pursuing righteousness, speaking the truth in the heart, no slandering with the tongue, committing no evil against a fellow-human, bringing no shame to a neighbor, despising a vile person, honoring those revering God. In Micah, these ways are reduced to three: to do justly, to love mercy, and to walk humbly with your God (Mic 6:8). In Isaiah, keeping justice and

[20] *The Talmud*, 11.

doing righteousness (Isa 56:1) are the two cardinal paths to peace. Amos reduced them to one, "Seek me and live" (Amos 5: 6), or, Habbakuk reduced them to one, "The righteous shall live by his faith" (Hab 2:4; B.T. Makkot 23b-24a).

In Ex 18:30, the path people are to walk in refers to the law, but the work they are to do refers to acts of sagehood, beyond the measure of the law. Ethical conduct does not mean a soulless formalism. Even in messianic times of liberation and enlightenment, human spontaneity leads to the right action in every situation without a need of the law. In the hereafter the laws will become obsolete.[21] As R. Yohanan said, "Jerusalem was destroyed because her people hewed strictly to the letter of the Torah."[22]

The Taoists considered all social values to be prejudices, but prejudices form and shape our tradition, language, culture, and society. Human beings live in the world of prejudices. The *Cogito* principle (*I think*) is captive in the world of contradiction and opposition. The point is to get out of the vicious circle of contradiction and opposition by transcending or overcoming it. Transcending might be referred to as the Taoist logic of embrace and harmony rather than the Buddhist logic of neither-nor.

No matter how hostile and sinful people are, the *Tao* may not deny them. The Taoist logic of embrace and harmony constitutes and regulates the way of human life, as well as creaturely life in nature for harmony and peace. In the *Tao* all contradiction and opposition is reconciled and canceled out from the life source of *Tao*. The *Tao* is a source of life, of peace-harmony, and of salvation, even for the wicked. The *Tao* rejects no one. No one is really good or really wicked. "The Holy man is a good savior of humans and rejects nobody." The life of a holy person represents and embodies the Way, Truth, and Life of *Tao* in a universal-spontaneous manner.

Heavenly *Tao* conquers without striving. *Wu-wei* and non-violence are the most effective means of getting power and holding on to it. *Wu-wei* is not pure passivity. The holy man, when acting, expects no reward for his actions. Once the good deed has been done, he does not bask in his merit. The holy person who performs great achievements dies, not abiding in his or her merits (ch. 2). This is a Taoist's understanding of God's grace and human attitude. "A good tree cannot produce bad fruit, nor can a bad tree produce good fruit" (Matt 7:18). The sanctified person does not abide in his or her achievement, because it comes in a natural-spontaneous way

[21] Ibid., 55.

[22] Ibid., 49.

rather than out of human striving. God's grace does not oppose God's way of nature but is efficacious in the web of complementarity. Likewise, love of God and of fellow-humans is to be done only for the sake of love rather than for the sake of merit and reward.

Spirit and *Ch'i*

The *Tao* emits the vital energy [*ch'i*] and gives rise to change. Consequently, heaven and earth came into being. In turn, they produced the ten thousand things, namely, all beings. Like a mother (chs. 1, 25, 52), the *Tao* creates the world and also nourishes it with its powerful energy. The claim of transcendence is balanced by the idea of the *Tao*'s creative power. The former aspect, which refers to nothingness or emptiness, is not an absolute absence in a nihilistic fashion.

The *Tao* as nameless is without shape or form. The cosmic energy which emanates from *Tao* brings forth all forms of life in primal unity with the *Tao* in the circular balance of *yin* and *yang*. The emptiness of the *Tao*, properly understood, is no less than a way of affirming the fullness of the vital energy. The void of non-being is no less than the Whole or the wondrous being which causes all to live.

The cosmos is constituted and sustained by vital *ch'i* energy which pervades all levels of existence. In *Tao-te-ching*'s cosmogeny (ch. 42), the *Tao* as the emptying void produced the One which in turn generated *yin* and *yang*. These two gave birth to the harmonious, the clear and the turbid. These three forms of energy are differentiated to form heaven, earth, and human beings, which together produced the ten thousand things.[23] All existence depends on the vital essence of *Tao* in virtue of the vital essence. At this point, we may understand the One as life-giving virtue or energy.[24] The Taoist idea of *Tao*, in the manifestation of the vital energy of

[23] The Taoist trinity can be found in chapter 42 of the *Tao-te-ching*; "The Tao gives birth to One; One gives birth to Two; Two gives birth to Three; Three gives birth to the myriad things." By the time of T'ang dynasty, the Taoist trinity had become well established. By then, Nestorian Christianity was also active and well known in China. Certainly, there was contact and interaction between the two religions. The primal celestial one, controlling the past, has been likened to God the Father. The precious celestial one, controlling the present, has been compared to God the Son, and the Way-and Its Power celestial one, controlling the future, has been compared to God the Holy Spirit.

[24] In contrast to an interpretation of the One as the vital essence in the tradition of Ho Shang Kung, Wang Pi took the One to be that of non-being as a negative concept. From non-being and because of non-being comes the One. Cf. Alan K.L. Chan, "A Tale of Two Commentaries: Ho-shang-kung and Wang Pi on the Lao-tzu," in *Lao-tzu and the Tao-te-ching*, ed. Livia Kohn and Michael LaFargue (New York: State University of New York

ch'i and *te,* balances a relation between *Tao* in utter silence and emptiness, and *Tao* as the life source of all in terms of the all-pervading movement of *ch'i*.

In the tradition of Neo-Confucianism, Chang Tsai (Chang Heng-chu, 1020–77), stressed particularly the underlying unity of *ch'i*. Inspired by his study of the *Book of Changes,*[25] Chang said that the Great Harmony (or the Supreme Ultimate) known as the *Tao* is a name for the *ch'i,* or "wandering air" in its entirety of the dynamic movement of the *yin* and the *yang*. The universe originates in *ch'i,* which is both the source of the universe and the driving force of endless changes.

In the beginning, there existed *ch'i* without form, and it was called the Great Void. Because of the void of *ch'i*, there is neither non-existence nor emptiness in the Buddhist sense. All things in the universe are based and formed on one and the same *ch'i* which is no less than the *Tao*. This *ch'i* then begins to contract and consolidate, because of the interaction between *yin* and *yang*, that from which heaven and earth emerged.

All creatures are constituted by consolidated *ch'i,* which has various shapes, and all creatures return to unconsolidated, or dissolved *ch'i*, which has no shape. The great ultimate produced the two forms (*yin* and *yang*) in the Great Void which is none other than *ch'i* or the material forces. Since *ch'i* is everywhere, its constituents, *yin* and *yang*, are also active everywhere. Thus the eternal process of change and transformation takes place in the universe.

In Jewish tradition, especially Hasidic sources, *Shekhinah,* regarded as the tenth *sefirah,* is God who is fully immanent within the natural and physical world. The whole earth is filled with God's glory. In kabbalistic teaching, *Shekhinah* is *malkut*, the kingdom in which perfect harmony and fulfillment are found. The image of *Shekhinah* is portrayed in feminine terms or in aspects of natural elements linked to femininity. This *yin* of God is the symbolism which balances her relationship with other masculine *sefirot* in the divine sphere. *Shekhinah* is the flow of creative energies throughout the universe. Energy runs forward through the *sefirotic* channels and into *Shekhinah*, back from the outer world, into *Shekhinah* and up through the *sefirot*, reaching back toward *keter*.

In the *Zohar*, *Shekhinah* is likened to the holy Sabbath, the day that is the source of blessing for all the others. All the upper *sefirot* are to be

---

Press, 1998) 105.

[25] In Appendix III of the *Book of Changes* it is stated: "In the *Yi* there is the Supreme Ultimate which produces the Two Forms [i.e. the *Yin* and *Yang*]." Quoted from Yu-Lan, *Short History*, 279.

found with *Shekhinah*, which represents the final letter of God's name. Human access to the Divine always begins through *Shekhinah*. From this standpoint, the transcendence of God is affirmed as immanent in the universe without taking away human freedom and responsibility regarding the reality of evil. Already in the rabbinic period, the doctrine of the *Shekhinah* was formulated to denote the indwelling divine presence within the universe.

In the Talmud (*Meg.* 29a), we read:

> Come and see how beloved Israel is before God, for wherever they went into exile the *Shekhinah* went with them; in Babylon, the *Shekhinah* was with them and in the future, when Israel will be redeemed, the *Shekhinah* will be with them.[26]

From the biblical perspective, God's Spirit (*ruach*) is the breath of God's life. In the Genesis account of creation, the Spirit is present, hovering above chaos with its vibrating field of energy before the foundation of the world (Gen. 1:2). As the *ruach* is the breath of the eternal God and vitality of created beings, so *ch'i* is an emanating spirit of *Tao*, a principle that gives life to all that exists. The Spirit in the Bible is not only active in human redemption, but also as the Creator of all life in a proleptically new creation and consummation. The work of the Spirit in creation and the Spirit's presence in the life of the church and believers are interconnected with the phenomenon of life in all its breadth. All living things are created, preserved, and renewed in the continual flow of *ruach* and its presence within them.

Ruach is the cosmic Spirit. If God hides God's face, every living thing is dismayed. When God takes away the breath of divine life, they die and return to dust. When God sends forth God's breath, God renews the face of the earth and every living thing that is created (Ps 104:29ff; Job 34:14). The breath of God's life fills the world and holds together all things (Isa 34:16).

Therefore, the Psalmist asks: "Where can I go from Thy Spirit? Or where can I flee from Thy presence? If I ascend to heaven, Thou art there: If I make my bed in Sheol, behold, Thou art there" (Ps 139:7–8). The spirit of life constitutes the connection and cohesion of all living creatures. All living things are mutually dependent in symbiosis within each other. In Isaiah 32:15f, we read the "ecology of God's Spirit."[27] God's Spirit fills

[26] Cf. Dan Cohn-Sherbok, *Judaism: History, Belief and Practice* (New York: Routledge, 2003) 350.

[27] Jürgen Moltmann, *The Source of Life: The Holy Spirit and the Theology of Life*, trans.

the earth, which in turn, as our mother, brings forth plants, trees and animals, and a human life within its atmosphere and biosphere.

Today's environmental problems are the result of nature being more and more subject to domination and exploitation by human civilization and technology. Creation in bondage (Rom 8: 22) is captive to "the companion of death" (ch. 76). In the groaning of creation, the Spirit intercedes with sighs or groans. The Spirit is the Mother who gives life, the companion of life, and she is present in the life process of all living creatures. The presence of God is immanent in the world and present in all things. God's Spirit is present everywhere, sustaining, nourishing, and quickening all things in heaven and on earth. The earth is the place of God's indwelling of all. All living creatures are invited, through the power of God's *ch'i,* to become God's house. In using Luther's metaphor, creatures are *larva Dei*, and mummery of God.[28]

In a scientific discussion of energy, we see that the function and role of the Spirit is related to the external, invisible, and incomprehensible field of force. In understanding the Spirit as the Creator Spirit, the life-giver, Christian theology perceives the presence of the Spirit at work in natural processes and in a spiritual and unifying force. The Spirit, as the third Person of the Trinity, participates in the original creation of the past, in the on-going creation of the present, and in the final consummation of the future.

When we meet the Taoist metaphor of life-giving water, we find a striking parallel in the Bible to the Spirit of life. The power of the life-giving water characterizes the direction of Christian discipleship in terms of nonviolence and spontaneity. In the context of Ezekiel (31:4), the water with its rivers continually extends all around its planting place. Furthermore, the creative and providential work of God is portrayed in terms of wisdom which is seen as a personified agent of God (Prov 3:19; Jer 10:12; Matt 11:19). The concept of wisdom (Sophia) plays a double role in terms of the Logos as well as the Spirit.[29] Both are universal in scope in the embodiment of divine action.

When Asian contextual theology encounters the *ch'i* of Taoism and its spirituality, it expands the dimension of the Spirit toward the cosmic-natural process of living organisms for the multi-religious mystical experi-

Margaret Kohl (Minneapolis: Fortress, 1997) 25.

28 *WA*, 17 II, 192, 28–31. Cf. Bernhard Lohse, *Martin Luther's Theology: Its Historical and Systematic Development*, trans. and ed. Roy A. Harrisville (Minneapolis: Fortress, 1999) 213.

29 C.F.D. Moule, *The Holy Spirit* (Grand Rapids: Eerdmans, 1978) 20.

ence of human life. Although the Spirit in Christianity is not equated with an immanent and impersonal force, Jesus does say, "the wind blows where it wishes and you hear the sound of it, but do not know where it comes from and where it is going" (John 3:8).

Christian theology has lost, by and large, the universal function of the Spirit in respect to the cosmic process in natural life due to its overemphasis on the sacraments of the church and on the subjectivistic-mystical experience. The Spirit needs to be reinterpreted within the wider and broader horizon of all sentient creatures.

After his work of systematic theology, Tillich expressed his perspectives on this topic in close affinity to *The Phenomenon of Man* by Teilhard de Chardin. In emphasizing the tendency toward self-transcendence in life, both of them share the same basic idea.[30] However, Teilhard does not discern a relationship between the divine Spirit and spirit as a dimension of life in the way that Tillich does.

According to the former, there is only one spirit which permeates and activates all the material processes. It urges them beyond themselves toward progressive spiritualization and converges in unification toward a center of perfect unity. This center marks the end of the evolutionary process and turns out to be its true dynamic origin. In so doing, the created spirit can participate in the dynamics of the spirit which is the animating power of the entire process of evolution.

At this juncture, Teilhard spoke of a spiritual inside of every material phenomenon. All energy is spiritual in character. In the manifestation of the energy, a distinction is made between a tangible energy or force and a radical energy. However, Pannenberg takes issue with how the idea of an energetic field is ignored in Teilhard's thought. An autonomous idea of energy can be conceived of as a field. In utilizing Einstein's theory of relativity in which matter is understood as a function of space, Pannenberg takes energy as the primary reality for transcending the body. Energy, as the animating subject, manifests itself through the body.

However, for Teilhard, energy is not conceived of in terms of a field, but in terms of the inside reality of bodies. At this juncture, Pannenberg perceives that confusion would occur as to which idea dominates the entire process of evolution, referring to Teilhard's idea of Omega point or the evolving entities. In revising Teilhard's idea of radical energy with a field of energy, Pannenberg maintains that field energy manifests itself in the

30 Paul Tillich, *Systematic Theology*, vol. 3. (Chicago: University of Chicago Press, 1963) 5.

self-transcendence of the living organism and thereby shapes the process of evolution.

Therefore, the term "spirit" is applied to interpret, in a border context, the self-transcending activity of organic life in the process of evolution, and also to include the results of its self-creative and self-integrative activity, which anticipates the final goal of the evolutionary process.[31] Insofar as God is understood as the all-determining reality, the divine spirit is also the unifying ground of the whole universe active in the natural world. In utilizing the notion of a dynamic field to describe the working of the Spirit, spirit would be equated with a force field.

However, the Taoist idea of *ch'i* is not merely a source of self-transcendence in terms of field energy. But it also allows for a principle of complementarity in unifying and sustaining harmony at the subatomic level. If the Christian idea of creation through the Word and mediation through the Spirit can be understood in terms of the principle of complementarity in quantum physics,[32] then the Taoist idea of *ch'i* can be understood as the underlining principle of mediating and unifying a wavelike dimension to a particlelike one in a complementary way. Without the vital power of *ch'i,* the harmonious and complementary balance between *yin* and *yang* would collapse into a pure *yang* or pure *yin* dichotomy.

The Taoist triadic idea of *Tao*, *te* and *ch'i* attests that God's *ruach* in the Genesis account is present, hovering above chaos with its vibrating field of energy. *Tao* is both eternal and temporal in terms of *te* and *ch'i*. *Creatio ex nihilo* is also seen as an evolution *ex the Way* of *Tao* in naturalistic-spontaneous fashion in which *ch'i* as the spirit of life penetrates and pervades all living sentient creatures. The action of *Tao* happens in natural spontaneity. It reigns, but does not rule. A relationality between the Great Void of *ch'i* and its manifestation in *te* put into balance the transcendental side and the immanental side of *Tao* in utter silence, yet ready to change.

From this perspective, the concept of divine interaction with the cosmic process can be consonant with the activity of *ch'i* inside all. We find God in the process of on-going creation, not in any gaps. In the Taoist framework, there is no need to distinguish God revealed in Jesus Christ

[31] Wohlfart Pannenberg, *Toward a Theology of Nature: Essays on Science and Faith*, ed. Ted Peters (Louisville: Westminster/John Knox, 1993) 132–37.

[32] Moltmann, *Science and Wisdom*, 192. For the relation between Taoist thought and modern physics, Kapra holds the opinion that the subatomic world of modern physics is strikingly in accord with the description of Eastern thought. Fritjof Capra, *The Tao of Physics* (Berkeley: Shambhala, 1975). For further reading, see Matthieu Ricard and Trinh Xuan Thuan, *The Quantum and the Lotus* (New York: Crown, 2001).

from God manifest in us, which embraces a panentheistic approach of assimilating the divine and the cosmic to one another.

Nevertheless, the otherness of the incomprehensible and ineffable God remains in the realm of mystery rather than the realm of qualified dualism. However, biblically speaking, there is more Spirit than *ch'i*. The work and efficacy of Spirit is hidden and veiled within the flow of the life process, but the personhood of the Trinity is not assimilated into the immanence of nature, nor does it amount to a total identification of God with nature.

Conclusion

Theology is ectypal, assuming the character of a pilgrimage in God's Way. Theology as *theologia viatorum* is always on the way to learning from God's mystery manifested in the wisdom of world religions. There are similarities and differences between Christianity and Taoist wisdom. The Bible and the *Tao-te-ching* have, however, much in common when understood as witnessing to the mystery of God which manifests itself as the life-giver for all that exists.

Like God, *Tao* produces creatures, and nourishes and accompanies them until their return to their origin of eternal life. Unlike Christianity, Taoist philosophy would be hesitant to accept the Christian idea of naming and reducing God in a merely personified sense or in its overemphasis on the grace of God over nature, the locus in which the *ch'i* indwells.

The difference is not a barrier but an opportunity for Christians to reflect and deepen their own tradition in respect to God as the creator of the universe through the Word and through the mediation of the Spirit in encounters with other wisdoms. Wisdom can be conceived of and accepted as a free and extraordinary way of divine communication for Christians.

In crossing over the terrain of other wisdoms and returning to Christianity, the Taoist self-understanding of the way of life in the universe and of the human attitude of non-action and spontaneity is not an enemy but a friend in helping Christians actualize and renew another side of God, for enriching the good news of God in Jesus Christ through the Spirit for all. Therefore, we believe in "one God and Father of all who is over all and through all and in all" (Eph 4:6).

PART IV

Asian Contextual Theology in a Multi-Religious Tapestry

16

Christianity and the Religious World of East Asians

*The Principle of Three Religions as One**

Chung Dai-Wi

KOREAN "national religion" puzzled and embarrassed the early Western visitors to the Korean peninsula, who wanted to find what in the Korean religion had a counterpart in organized Western religion. Their opinions were diverse, "from those who think that Koreans have no religion, to those who would say . . . that they are very religious. If you were to ask the average non-Christian Korean about his religion, he would say no-religion."[1]

> He [a Korean] personally takes his own education from Confucius; he sends his wife to Buddha to pray for an offspring; and in the ills of life he willingly pays toll to Shamanist "Mudang" [sorceress].[2] As a general thing, we may say that the all-round Korean will be a Confucianist when he is in society, a Buddhist when he philosophizes, and a spirit worshipper when he is in trouble.[3] Korea has a strange religion, a mixing of ancestor worship with Buddhism, Taoism, spirit cults, divination, magic, geomancy, astrology, and fetishism. Dragons play a part, devils of natural gods are abundant; "tokgabi" (elves, imps, goblins) are legion.[4]

* Translated and edited by Paul S. Chung.

[1] Harry A. Rhodes, ed., *History of the Korea Mission, Presbyterian Church USA 1884–1934* (Seoul: Chosen Mission Presbyterian Church, 1934) 47.

[2] G. H. Jones, "The Spirit Worship of the Koreans" in *Transactions of the Korea Branch of the Royal Asiatic Society*, Vol. II, Part II (Seoul: Branch, 1901) 39.

[3] Horner B. Hulbert, *The Passing of Korea* (New York: Doubleday, 1906) 403.

[4] J. S.Gale, *Korea in Transition* (New York: Laymen's Missionary Movement, 1909) 70.

Given this fact, the Western missionary attempted to name this "religion" "Shingyo," or teaching of the gods.[5] This phenomenon of religious syncretism seems to have left a strong impression on Western visitors who observed this "religion without a name," as it is evidenced in their numerous writings.[6]

Let us single out a typical case from among the many bizarre practices. For instance, at a funeral service, Confucianism instructs the mourners to dress in sackcloth while a Buddhist monk recites and chants the sutra in order for the departed to enter into the pure land, a Buddhist paradise. Besides this, a Shaman has a role in the funeral service of exorcizing the evil spirits that may annoy or harm the departed on the journey after death. Taoist geomancers are involved in advising the mourners to dig the grave on the site that is regarded to be the best location.

In case of a funeral service, each religion is in strange harmony in spite of their different characteristics. Confucianism provides the religious etiquette. Mahayana Buddhism offers its ritual and vision of future life. Taoism ensures the safe journey of the departed to the spiritual world, while promising prosperity to the bereaved who conduct the rites. A Shaman is necessary to call directly on the souls of the dead. It is no wonder, therefore, that Western observers were confused when confronted with the syncretistic phenomena having such complicated purposes and characters. They were at a loss for how to understand it.

Obviously, there were independent organizations of religion, such as Confucianism, Buddhism, and Taoism. They functioned separately in the society. Although Shamanists did not belong to any type of religious organization, Shamanism was also regarded as a religious institution. However, if we think that religious attitudes among Korean people toward other religions are fundamentally indifferent, this would be definitely erroneous, especially after Confucianism became the state religion in the early years of the Choson Dynasty. It persecuted, without hesitation, other faiths as "superstitions," "abominable deeds to embroil heretic sacrifice," or "evil-causing heresies."

This Confucian persecution of other religions happened because of the fact that Confucianism itself was monopolized by the *yangban* class. Women, as well as commoners, were excluded from Confucian rituals. On the other hand, the suppressed religions did not remain entirely silent, but

[5] H. G. Underwood, *The Religions of Eastern Asia* (New York, 1910) 94.

[6] Cf. H. G. Underwood, "A Partial Bibliography of Occidental Literatures on Korea from Early Times to 1939," *TKBRAS* 24 (1935).

arose in protest. It is not surprising to find that the revolts of Hong Kyong-Rae (1811), the Paek Kon-Dang of Chinju (1863), and the *Donghak* (1894) were all colored with Taoist and Buddhist beliefs, although they were basically the movements of the minjung against the ruling class.

Hong Kyong-Rae, the leader of one of the revolts, assumed the role of a Taoist mystical general who was believed to possess supernatural powers. Five years after his death, following the failure of the revolt, some of his followers believed that he was still alive, and, based on this faith, they attempted to organize another revolt. The *Donghak* movement in later years definitely took the course of a religious war against the ruling class. Chondogyo and a host of similar indigenous religious sects, which are located within the group of Chondogyo, are the offshoots of this movement.

The most outstanding feature in all these complexities is that the prototypical Korean could always give allegiance to all of these religions at the same time. Regarding this situation, an observer from Uppsala stated definitively: "Die Religion Koreas ist synkretitisch" [The religion of Korea is syncretistic].[7]

Korea's religion is syncretistic; but in what sense? What is the structure of this version of syncretism? Seen in the historical sense, the Korean syncretistic attitude has been going on for a long time. Ch'oe Ch'i-Won, the great scholar of the ninth century Silla dynasty, wrote about the national religion of his age, which "embraced the three religions of Confucianism, Buddhism and Taoism, grafting them to its own body and nourishing the divergent understandings therefore in harmony."[8] This clearly shows that already in Ch'oe's century "the principle of three religions as one," inherited from the Chinese, was rooted deeply in the Korean cultural soil.

The Tangun myth about the foundation of Korea itself has a syncretistic background. This is the foundation myth of Korea, which tells that the nation was founded by Tangun, the descendent of the heavenly deity Hanunim or Hwanin. Later, the Koryo dynasty's version of this myth in the thirteenth century, which is recorded in *Sam Kuk Yu Sa* and *Che Wang Un Gi,* is colored greatly with Taoist and Buddhist mythologies and terminologies.

7 Peter Beyerhaus, *Die Selbständigkeit der Jungen Kirchen als Missionarisches Problem* (Wuppertal-Barmen: Verlag der Rheinischen Missions-Gesellschaft, 1959) 216.

8 His "Preface to the Nanllang Inscription" is recorded in *Samguksagi*, vol. 4.

If we accept the hypothesis of Kim Che-Won regarding the highly controversial problem of the origin of the Tangun myth,[9] then Tangun mythology might have been already set in a syncretistic framework, with a strong Taoist influence, at the time when it was recorded on the stone slabs of Wu Liang Tzu of the Chinese Han dynasty. If Kim is right, the Han dynasty stone-slab version could be obviously dated from around the second century C.E. Prior to this date, the northern part of the peninsula was under the dominion of the Han.[10]

If we apply to the Korean myth the time-depth measurement of *Kulturkreise-methode* (culture circle-method), proposed by Wilhelm Schmidt, an Austrian anthropologist, then the origin of syncretistic tendency could be dated back much farther. According to the myth, Hwan Ung, the son of a primitive monotheistic deity Hwanin, or Hanunim, was married to a bear-woman, Kom, which is an animal deity widely worshipped by the North Asiatic tribes in Manchuria and Siberia.[11]

This marriage meant a hybrid of two societies with different cultural and religious backgrounds (one is patriarchal and nomadic with a monotheistic male deity; the other is matriarchal and agricultural with a totemic female deity). We may trace the lost memory of the people into the realm of prehistory through the Tangun myth. Even in this stage, which was free from Taoist and Buddhist influences, we may infer without difficulty, that the myth was also syncretistic in form, with the marriage of the two deities.

Although each opinion is a hypothesis, one thing is clear: Korean religious attitudes have been syncretistic for a long time. In what sense and in what character and structure is this so? Kraemer introduces oriental syncretism in the pre-Christian era as an adequate example of his thesis. According to him, the relativism of Eastern religions is based on their "inherent natural monism."[12] As he observes,

> the religious allegiance of the average (Chinese) is not related to one of the three religions. He does not belong to a confession or

[9] Kim Che-Won, "Han Dynasty Mythology and the Korean Legend of Tan-gun," in *Archives of the Chinese Art Society of America* 3 (1948–49) 43–48.

[10] Wilhelm Schmidt, *Handbuch der Vergleichenden Religionsgeschichte* (Munster: Aschendorf, 1930) 213–43. W. Schmidt, *Ursprung der Gottesidee*, vol. 1 (Munster: Aschendorf, 1926) 752–66.

[11] *Gom* in Korean might be a derivative of the common root between *Kamui* in the Inu tribe and *Kami* in Japan.

[12] Hendrik Kraemer, *The Christian Message in a Non-Christian World* (New York: Harper, 1947) 156.

> a creed. He participates, unconcerned, as to any apparent lack of consistency, alternately in Buddhist, Taoist, or Confucian rites. He is, by nature, a religious pragmatist. Religiously speaking, we find him *prenent son bien où il le trouve* (taking his good will from wherever he finds it). . . . We are repeatedly told, especially of the Chinese and Japanese, that they have a deep-rooted indifference towards dogma and doctrinal differences.[13]

However, in examining the religiously complex situation more carefully, Kraemer's interpretation is not right in several ways. First, "average" East Asians, including Koreans, are not "relativists." It is certain that they do not think from the standpoint of absolutes, but they believe that they know the absolute norm to which they are to be conformed. They do not develop dogma regarding revelation. Nevertheless, if they believe that something belongs to the will of God, they do indeed afford this norm the absolute highest importance. This is understood as the voice of God, which was heard through their most revered sages. They are, by no means, progressive-minded relativists. On the contrary, they are conservative absolutists in their orientation toward archaism.

Second, religiously speaking, they are not pragmatists. Although they are committed and pious to religious devotion, they are biased against other religions. "Seek where there is benefit"– this attitude contradicts, psychologically speaking, the idol worshipper. If not, why was Christianity not accepted without undergoing tragic persecution? The reason for persecution was not related to their hatred of Westerners. The persecution was really a persecution of foreign religion. De Groot gives a more convincing explanation of this problem. According to him,

> the three religions are actually branches of a common trunk which has existed since ancient times; this trunk is the religion of universism (Universismus). . . . Universism, as I will call it is one single religion of China; the three religions are simply its integrating components. This is the reason why the Chinese feel equally at home in all three of them without being burdened by conflicting and incompatible dogmas.[14]

The religious system of China is universistic (universistisch) animism (which is to say, the universe including the *yin-yang* and the five

[13] Ibid., 201–2.

[14] J. J. M. de Groot, *Religion in China: Universism, A Key to the Study of Taoism and Confucianism* (New York: Putnam's, 1912).

elements).[15] Looking at it superficially, the principle of "Three Religions as One" appears to be a chaotic conglomeration of heterogeneous and bizarre elements. However, it is, in fact, a coherent system. The following historical facts support this interpretation. Confucianism and Taoism have maintained a close kinship throughout the history of China, despite their very much exaggerated differences of doctrine. Regardless of their antithetical ontological theories of the universe and their ethical positions, and also regardless of their rootedness in different social strata, they are inseparably united with each other in that they share the same animistic ideologies, as well as identical religious vocabularies. It is very interesting to note that the *Chung-yung*, which has been believed to be one of the most important writings in Confucianism, has been thoroughly analyzed recently by competent scholars who attribute *Chung-yung* to be of Taoist origin.[16]

It is well known that Buddhism is a foreign religion in China. It was accepted into Chinese society by being acculturated successfully through the various stages of interaction and accommodation. The term 'Chinese Buddhism' refers to a branch of Buddhism with a peculiar Chinese character. To be more precise, Mahayana Buddhism in China came to play an integral part in the religious life of the Chinese people through the syncretistic process. I think that an investigation of the process of syncretistic integration would contribute to understanding the hidden structure of the principle of three religions as one. When Buddhism was introduced to China, it was accepted because it was seen as identical with Taoism. The Chinese version of Buddhism, as was accepted in the later Han dynasty, was like a Taoist religion with occultism and magic.

There are a lot of opinions about when Buddhism was introduced to China. Some argue that Confucius himself knew the Buddha. In the book *Lieh-tzu*, there is a dialogue between a high official Pi and Confucius.

> Who is the Saint? Fu-tzu [Confucius] solemnized his expression and kept a reverent silence for a while and spoke: Ch'iu [Confucius], that is, heard that in the West there is a Saint who does not rule, and the world is not rebellious. He does not inculcate, but the people believe in him. He does not propagate, yet the people gladly follow him.

[15] Ibid., 12.

[16] Carsun Chang, *The Development of Neo-Confucian Thought* (New York: Bookman, 1957) 48.

However, this statement in *Lieh-tzu* was a later fabrication of a Confucian-Buddhist in either the Wei or the Chin dynasty.[17] The early accounts of the mysterious introduction of Buddhism into China are bewildering. The related documents could be classified according to the degree of their exaggerations.[18] But they all seem to agree that Buddha revealed himself (c.63 C.E.) to emperor Ming of the Han dynasty in a dream, as a luminous golden deity who could fly over the emperor's court freely. In this account, this Chinese Buddha seems to have embodied all the magical power that the Taoists at that time were desiring.

The documentary evidence shows that most of these accounts were the later additions of overzealous Buddhists. This is not what we are concerned about. Buddha was deliberately made to be a Taoist deity. It is not surprising at all, under such circumstances, that the myth of Lao Tzu's visit to India, namely, *hua-hu-shuo*, appeared and was strongly attractive in its age.

By 166 C.E. Hsiang-chieh reported to Emperor Huan saying, "Some people say that Lao Tzu went to the barbarian country and became Buddha." In *T'ai-p'ing-ching* it was only mentioned that Lao Tzu went to the West and stayed for eighty years and lived through the Yin and Chu Dynasties. But another Taoist-Buddhist document, *Hua-hu-ching*, amplified it and mentioned:

> Lao Tzu . . . was made an official to the Government during the reign of Yü-wang. But again with Yin-his he went to the Western country and became Buddha. He gave the King of the barbarian country *Hua-hu-ching,* consisting of 640,000 words. After he came back to China, he wrote the *T'ai-p'ing-ching.*[19]

The first royal convert to Buddhism was Prince Ying of Ch'u, who was definitely syncretistic. Emperor Ming himself testified that Prince Ch'u believed in the mysteries of the Emperor Hwang-ti and Lao Tzu and worshiped Buddha and had mystical union with gods. Lao Tzu and Buddha together might have shared the altar in the reign of Emperor Huan. According to one record, Emperor Huan worshipped Lao Tzu at a Buddhist temple called Yo-lung-ko in 166 C.E. The Leaping Dragon Hall, with the Taoist name Yo-lung-ko, was reported to have been renamed pri-

[17] Tang Yongtong zhuan, *Han Wei liang Jin Nan Bei chao fo jiao shi.*, vol.1 (Beijing: Zhonghua shu ju,1955) 4f.

[18] Ibid., 16.

[19] *Hua-hu-ching*, 72. [Editor's note: a Chinese source]

or to the Emperor's worship a Taoist-Buddhist name: the Temple of the Admiration for Nothingness.[20]

Such Taoist-Buddhist syncretism seems to have been approved not only by the prince and the emperor, but also by the average general attitude of the devout Buddhists of that age. In *The Biographies of the Eminent Monks* by Hui-chiao of the Liang dynasty, An-Shik-Kao (Lokottamer), the missionary from Parthia who translated the Buddhist texts, was made a highly competent Taoist occultist. The famous monks of the Wu Dynasty, K'ang-seng-hui and Wei Chih-nan, and the Wei Dynasty's T'an-k'o-chio-lo were among those who were depicted as accomplished Taoist magicians. The composite picture of Buddha himself during the Han Dynasty and the Three Kingdoms period which was found in the biographical literatures of that period was definitely a Ta-hsien, or the Great (Taoist) Immortal from India. This is how equivalence has taken its place of syncretistic phenomenon in the Chinese setting.

In the process of translating Buddhist literature into Chinese, this syncretistic phenomenon emerged gradually. Anyone who is familiar with the Taoist literature and the Chinese Buddhist texts in the early period can indicate, without serious difficulty, how many identical words are used on both sides with different meanings. A careful comparative study on this problem is beyond the scope of this chapter. Nevertheless, we are able to pick up a few fundamental common words that had distinctly different semantic features from the view of the respective religions. One is *Tao.* The second is *wu.*

Tao, in the earliest Buddhist texts, was the translation of *Bodhi*. A keen observer is aware of the fundamental disagreement between the two terms, which were parsimoniously joined. *Tao*, for the Taoist, is the principle of inaction (*wu-wei*), naturalness, or *tzu-jan*, while *Bodhi* is an inspiration and the goal of inspiration. One may return to *Tao*, while striving toward *Bodhi*. Hsüan-tsang gave new meaning to the translations. *Marga* was translated as *Tao*, and *Bodhi* was translated as enlightenment. *Wu,* in the early Buddhist texts, is the translation of nirvana. *Wu* is an absolute negation, while Bodhi is the principle of ultimate reality.

At any rate, under such linguistic limitations and ambiguity which involved symbolic communications, Taoism and Buddhism were approximated in the early years of their contact with each other and were made into religions of the same principle. A syncretistic author says the following:

[20] Cf. Tokiwa Daijo, *Shina ni Okeru Bukkyo to Jukyo, Dokyo* (Tokyo: Tokyo, 1930) 512f.

> The Tao of *yin* and *yang* created with their harmony everything in the world. Tao [Lao Tzu], being born in the East, became the tree (Lao Tzu's family name is Li, an apricot tree) of *yang*. Fu [Buddha], being born in the West, became the Golden *yin*. Tao is the father; Fu is the mother. Tao is heaven; Fu is the earth. Tao leads one to live peacefully; Fu leads one to die peacefully. Tao's causality and Fu's corollary are like the *yin* and *yang* and could not be, therefore, separated.[21]

The benefits of this interaction ran in both directions. Buddhism found a secure place in Chinese society through this process, while Taoism was provided with a newly introduced doctrinal, ritual, and institutional refinement of Buddhism. As its position became more and more secure in the society, Buddhism expanded itself as a collaborator of syncretism. The effort to purify Buddhism from a syncretistic amalgam was the business of the experts or specialists whose works affected only their faithful followers. The *religio publico* of China remained, in fact, unchanged despite the unceasing efforts of the leaders from both camps who tried to clarify their respective positions.

This is also true of the relation between Confucianism and Buddhism. In this encounter, mutual influence is more interesting, following the initial translation period. It started with equivalence and ended with a consensus. It is natural that the spirit of fraternity had appeared from the Buddhist side. Its early representative was Sun Ch'o, who identified the seven Buddhist *Tao-jen* [sages] with the seven Confucian Worthies in the Bamboo forest, in his conciliatory *Tao-hsien-lun*. In his other thesis, *Yü-hsien-lun*, he solemnized the unity of the two religions, saying,

> Confucius of Chou is Buddha. And Buddha himself is Confucius of Chou. For these two names are nothing but the foreign and native names of one and the same person. Confucius saves [humanity] from the ultimate calamities while Buddha enlightens and teaches the ultimate causes. They are the beginning and the end. Their fundamental truth is not inconsistent. . . . Therefore, a radical inquirer may find them to be two, but a man of comprehensive understanding finds them not to be two.[22]

There were only a few in the Confucian camp proper who were willing to embrace the conciliatory spirit. They did not bother to mention explicitly their indebtedness to Buddhist doctrines. What they tried to

[21] Cf. Wen-shih-ch'uan. [Editor's note: the reference is to an ancient Chinese text]

[22] Quoted in *Hung–ming-chi*, III. [Editor's note: a Chinese source]

do was to show the Confucian contextual equivalence with Buddhism. In Buddhist dogma regarding emotions and desire, which are understood as defilement, there is a strong contradiction to the traditional Confucianism. Li Ao, for instance, maintained that the essence of human nature is tranquility, and evil comes from the disturbance of emotions.

Li Ao's terminology, as well as concept, has its origin in the traditional Confucian texts. But the more important thing to note is that such expressions and ideas were newly taken from the contexts that had been neglected until that point and revived in meaning under the new stimulus of Buddhism. This kind of contextual equation became clearer with the Neo-Confucians of the Sung dynasty. They were supposedly anti-Buddhist. But it is not too much of an exaggeration to say that "if there were no Buddhism, there would be no Sung Learning [neo-Confucianism]."[23]

The founders of Neo-Confucianism ruled the minds of the intellectuals during the following six centuries until the end of the Ch'ing dynasty. They established a school mainly with their counterproposal to Buddhism. In other words, it was Buddhism that provided Neo-Confucianism with its doctrinal framework. The Sung philosophers attempted to fill this Buddhist framework with material drawn from ancient sources and some fresh interpretations of their own. Their interpretations were what Matteo Ricci and Leibniz ran up against because, according to them, it was a serious materialistic deviation from pure Confucianism under the influence of Buddhism.[24]

Regardless of the anti-Buddhist attitude of the Neo-Confucianists, Chou Tun-I (the founder of the Southern branch of the Neo-Confucian school) and Chang Tsai (the founder of the northern branch of the school) developed their teachings of *T'ai-chi* (Supreme Ultimate) and *T'ai-ho* (the Great Harmony), respectively, by establishing a Confucian equivalence to the idea of emptiness (*sunyata*) in Buddhism. Chou Tun-I's *T'ung-shu* especially reflected on the traces of the influence of Ch'an (Zen) Buddhism in its ideas and vocabulary.

Regardless of the fact that Chang T'sai's *Chen-meng* posed a radical criticism to the Buddhist doctrine, it was also full of counterproposals to the Buddhist doctrine. This book was, in its real content, a Confucian reflection on a Buddhist teaching. His *T'ai-ho*, which nourished the principle of action and inaction as well as their reciprocal harmony, seems to

23 Cho Yu-t'ung, *Chu Hsi*, Shanghai, 5. [Editor's note: a Chinese source]

24 Cf. Johannes Bettray, *Die Akkommodationsmethode des P. Matteo Ricci S.J. in China* (Rome: Gregorian University, 1955). David Chung, "The Problem of Analogy Between Christianity and Confucianism," *Korean Quarterly* 1, no. 2 (1959) 115–30.

have been made equivalent to the Buddhist idea of One Mind. This includes two aspects, *sui-yüan* (result from conditioning causes) and *pu-mieh* (anirodha: immortality). His "Great Void" and "Temperamental Energy" seem to reflect equally on the relationship between the *chen-ju* (bhutatathata: the True Self) and *alaya-vijnana* (store house consciousness)[25] of Buddhism.

The vehement critic of Buddhism, Chu His, attacked Buddhism for several reasons, but especially because of Buddhism's resemblance to Confucianism and Taoism in its doctrines. He enumerated the resemblances and insisted that it was due to Buddhists' borrowing and stealing of the wisdom of Chinese religions.[26] Chu His and his followers made an effort to emphasize, to some extent, several distinctive features of Confucianism in contrast to the contextual equivalences or counterparts of Buddhism. What they actually accomplished in the public mind was not the idea of Confucianism as the absolute religion; rather, it was the relative validation of Buddhism in light of the traditional truth in China. The consensus, namely the "Three Religions as One" principle, gradually crystallized itself and took its permanent place in the religious life of the Chinese people.

Given what has been described, the whole complicated process took place in the capillary system of the society. The following took place on the part of the giver: 1) The effective challenge that is suitable to stimulate an eager native response (precondition); 2) The ability to voluntarily or involuntarily compromise the environment to produce the effectiveness of the challenge (selectivity in action). On the part of the receiver the following took place: 1) The keen receptivity to the particular challenge; 2) The ability to actively participate with its own resources to exploit the maximum benefit from the alien stimulus by acclimatizing or acculturating it (selectivity in action).

The whole thing looks as if it were a partial absorption or assimilation of the encountered religions in terms of metamorphosis made, to some extent, on both sides. Hence Buddhism was accepted by the Chinese public to be an integral component of their national religion. This is the general picture of the Eastern tapestry, the principle of three religions as one.

The same process can be applied to the introduction of Christianity into East Asia. Christianity is a religion with an absolute truth claim and with well-systematized doctrines and militant organization. To illustrate

[25] [Editor's note: *alaya-vijnana* is the Yogacara Buddhist understanding of *sunyata*, which is identical with the existence of non-existence (mind only), and stands in contrast to Nagarajuna's middle way of understanding *sunyata* in a negative way.]

[26] Tokiwa Daijo, *Shina ni okeru Bukkyo to Jukyo, Dokyo*, 374–76.

the syncretistic process of Christianity in the East Asian societies, we take three examples from China, Japan, and Korea.

On the grand scale, we have an important example in China's T'ai-p'ing Rebellion (1851–1864). In this shocking incident, there were many aspects involved: political, economic, and religious. It was the Han people's movement in revolt against the ruling Manchus, first of all. The Communist press reported that this movement was the first organized movement of the Chinese proletariat against the ruling class. But the battle was fought in the name of Christianity as "a bizarre syncretism of misunderstood Christianity and native beliefs" or "a strange compound of Christianity and Chinese beliefs and practices."[27]

The victorious army occupied Nanjing by Christian banners. Hung Hsiu-chüan, the leader, who fanatically believed himself to be the brother of Jesus, ruled his Heavenly Kingdom of Great Peace like a Heavenly King with a strong legalistic administration based on the Holy Bible.

The special feature that interests us in this movement is the rebels' understanding of Christianity. The T'ai–p'ings "declared that their doctrine was not new but that the ancient classics had taught it in part and later generations had departed from it."[28] This claim is in perfect concordance with what the Riccian Jesuit missionaries announced in seventeenth century China.

However, the T'ai-p'ing religion was still not Christianity in all accounts. Along with Latourette, we conclude that

> [H]ad it had the immediate contact through missionaries with Christian communities in other lands, it is possible that in time, it might have developed into a movement which, while preserving many peculiarly Chinese features, would have caught the meaning of Jesus and have become a church which would have deserved both the adjectives of Chinese and Christian. As it was, it was quite clear that even the leaders had never really understood the Christian message.[29]

Let us next turn to Japan. As Buddhism once was a stimulus in China for making Taoism and Confucianism develop their own organized systematic forms, Jesuitism was the stimulus in Japan for awakening Shintoism

[27] Kenneth Scott Latourette, *The Chinese: Their History and Culture* (New York: Macmillan, 1946) 356.

[28] Kenneth Scott Latourette, *A History of Christian Missions in China* (New York: Russel & Russell, 1967) 190.

[29] Ibid., 285–86.

to develop its own independence against its long-term partner in Ryubu Shinto-Buddhism. As has been observed above, the ingenuity of the neo-Shinto theologians successfully accommodated Riccian Christianity into its own doctrinal system. Ryubu Shinto was an exemplary case of syncretism. The arbitrary identification of Shinto and Buddhist deities was an inevitable step in the process for Japanese society to make itself a real adherent to Buddhism. It was only the Shingon sect that explicitly attempted to bring out the essential features of the native religious responses. The average Buddhist or Shintoist in Japan did not hesitate to pay due respect to the *Hotoke* or *kami* in the temples or shrines, regardless of their religious distinctions.

Hirata's theological contribution lay in making the three creator gods of Shinto mythology into the transcendental God of the Judeo-Christian pattern. In addition, he accepted the doctrines of paradise and the hell, so that the departed were classified according to their earthly deeds. He invented a story between the Chinese and Hirata by utilizing Ricci's *The True Meaning of the Lord of Heaven* in which Ricci also converses with Chinese scholars. Hirata placed himself in the seat of Ricci and reported that what Ricci told was his own. The following is an interesting example of transformation: "Blessed are those who endure persecution for righteousness. The kingdom of Heaven is theirs. They will not die. This is the mystery of Shintoism beyond human wisdom." This case indicates that there was in Japan a fraternal connection between Christianity and Shintoism.

Unfortunately, a disastrous event happened to Francis Xavier, the father of the Jesuit Oriental mission. He preached the *Dainichi* as he arrived on the Japanese islands. He misunderstood this term to be an appropriate Japanese term, equivalent to God in a Christian sense. He had been misinformed by a *Yajiro*, or *Nanjiro*, a Japanese with little education and an escapee to India. He believed that the term *Dainichi* could designate the Deity in the Japanese language. However, this term was completely inappropriate since it entails other meanings. Xavier came to believe that it signified the 'primal substance', or the Great Sun or its divinity, or a nick name *Mahavairocana* . . . it means instead the human sexual organs! As soon as the scandalized people informed him of it, he returned to the various places where he had preached before, shouting, "Do not pray to Dainichi!"[30]

[30] Georg Schurhammer, *Das Kirchliche Sprachproblem in der Japanischen Jesuitmission des 16. und 17. Jahrhunderts* (New York: Johnson Reprint, 1965) 25–33.

The Jesuits in Japan hastily initiated the direct transliteration of Portuguese terms, producing a bizarre series of remarkable Christian terminology. Accordingly, Dainichi was replaced by *Deusu*, originating from *Dios* or *Deus*. If a supplementary explanation was not given to the created vocabularies, it would not have been helpful for spreading the Gospel. In the absence of a supplementary account, the term *Deusu* would not mean anything at all. Jesuit missionaries had a difficult experience in converting Japanese people to Christianity.[31]

Nevertheless, the native syncretistic elements soon crept in, just at the same moment when the influence of the missionaries began to ebb under persecution (1587–1873). This permitted the tropical jungle to reclaim the abandoned city. The jungle-like results are still seen among the Kirishitan remnants who have totally alienated themselves from the Catholic church.[32] This group chanted the Ave Maria in a bizarre Japanized Latin formulation. This phenomenon is an indication of the painful syncretism which really took place.

Longobardo's opposition to the Riccian approach was actually because of this hasty policy of the Jesuits in Japan and thus initiated the long-lasting futile "rites controversy." Yi Kyugyong introduced Longobardo's transliteration of Christian terms into Korea. According to this, Ricci's *Shang-ti* was substituted with *Tou-ssu* (Deus) and *T'ian-ch'in* with *Ju-te-ya* (Judea), etc. However, the introduction fortunately came after Riccian Christianity had already set roots in the soil. It had no negative effect on the development of Catholicism in Korea. In Korean society, Christianity gave a subsidiary impetus to the syncretistic religion Ch'ondogyo, the religion of the Heavenly Ways, which placed itself in an artificial opposition to Christianity.

The founder of Ch'ondogyo, Choi Jae-Woo, declared Eastern teachings or Eastern religion contradictory to Western learning or Western religion. In his biographical confession we read:

> I heard about the Western Christians who were willing to give up wealth and reputation to follow Heaven's will. Last April I felt cool to my heart all of sudden, and trembled in my body. Nobody knew what disease it was, and my pain was beyond measure. As I was frightened with pain, a mysterious word came to me. Surprised, I

[31] Cf. Walbert Bühlmann, *Die Christliche Terminologie als Missionmethodologische Problem* (Schoeneck-Beckenreid, Switzerland: Administration der Neuen Zeitschrift für Missionswissenschaft, 1950).

[32] Cf. Koya Tagita, "Transformation of Christianity in a Japanese Farming Village," in *The Japanese Journal of Ethnology* 18, no. 3 (1953).

> woke up from my bed, and looked around. "Don't be afraid, don't panic. People call me Shang-ti. Chinese Christians used the same word to express Heaven. Don't you know who I, Shang-ti, am?" After answering the question, I asked the reason for the sudden visit. Shang-ti said, "I will send you to the world to teach the Tao. Don't doubt it!" And I asked, "Do I have to teach people with Western religion?" The voice said, "No!"[33]

Ch'ondogyo acquired its theological framework from Christianity, as well as its institutional aspect. Hanunim or Hanalim or Chun Ju or Shang-ti are worshipped by Korean Christians as well as by the people of Ch'ondogyo. No doubt that the terminologies of Eastern religion were influenced directly, to some degree, by the literature of Western religion. Hence, it is not erroneous to insist that a large number of Korean Christian converts came from this syncretistic stock. Through historical cases, we can perceive the nature of the principle of three religions as one in the Far East.

[33] Cf. David Chung, *Shamanism: The Religious Context of Christian Beginnings in Korea* (Albany: SUNY, 2001) 103.

17

A Conception of an Ecological Theology of Spirit and *Ch'i* *

Kim Kyoung-Jae

THIS paper will critically examine the traditional Western view of nature in light of the theology of creation (for instance, with regard to Paul Tillich and Jürgen Moltmann) and then bring this theology into dialogue with the Asian religious view of nature, especially the philosophy of nature in Hua-yen Buddhism and in Neo-Confucianism. As such, it includes a typological study of the comparison between the Christian faith and the East Asian religious belief system regarding ultimate reality.

To be more concrete, the purpose of this paper is to actualize a dialogue between pneumatology in Western Christianity and the philosophy of *ch'i* in East Asian philosophy. It will propose a dialogue between a creational view of nature in Western Christianity and an emergent or self-producing view of nature in East Asian religions. Finally, I will attempt to bring forth a comparison between the future-oriented and eschatological view of reality in Christianity and the present-centered and cosmic view of reality in East Asian religions.

My motivation comes from today's ecological crisis, a crisis of civilization and a destruction of nature. In this context, we need to understand that nature is a womb and residence of human life. For this purpose, it is significant to reexamine critically theological patterns that focus unilaterally on a history-oriented salvation and an anthropocentric understanding of creation. In so doing, I intend to trace the significance of natural science and expand the horizons of pneumatology toward the source power of life in the universe.

* Translated and edited by Paul S. Chung.

In retrospect, when a theology of nature mysticism disappeared and modern society began, the history of Christianity developed in the direction of eradicating the category of nature from theological subject-matters and placing at the center a history-centered theology, namely a theology of salvation-centrism, ecclesiology, and a theology of the Word of God, a theology of Enlightenment.

We discern this trend generally in Protestant theology rather than in Roman Catholicism. Epistemologically, or methodologically speaking, it is possible to distinguish the realm of nature from the supernatural realm. However, it is impossible to divide the entire creation of reality dualistically into the realm of nature and the supernatural realm, or the realm of value and that of fact, or phenomenon and essence.

At any rate, following this dualistic pattern of division, Christian theologians were committed to exploring and securing the supernatural realm by limiting natural science to the scientist's investigation. As a result, mechanistic and dualistic views of nature in a Newtonian-Cartesian framework became the dominant paradigm in the interpretation of nature. Christian theology has subsequently developed in the direction of reflecting on and practicing this mechanistic view.

Today we see the Newtonian-Cartesian paradigm deeply challenged, and shifting to an emerging postmodern idea. Likewise, theology has shifted, calling for clarification of pneumatology through a theology of creation that faces the emergence of a new natural science.

The Understanding of Nature in Western Theology

First, let us begin with Paul Tillich. The idea of mystical participation in nature comes from the influence of nature mysticism and philosophical Romanticism. Theologically, he stands in the Lutheran tradition of *finitum capax infiniti*, and philosophically, he was influenced by the philosophy of Schelling.[1]

According to Tillich, the basic theological question relates to the question of God; therefore, he defines God in a more comprehensive way as the answer to the human existential question.[2] In criticizing transcendental philosophy or theology, Tillich insists that the question of the structure presupposes a subject-object structure of the human being. From this

[1] Paul Tillich, "Autobiographical Reflection" in *Theology of Paul Tillich*, eds. C. W. Kegley and R. W. Bretall (New York: Macmillan, 1952) 33–41.

[2] Paul Tillich, *Systematic Theology*, vol.1 (Chicago: University of Chicago Press, 1951) 163.

standpoint, the spirit cannot exist as the subject ego, the self autonomously existing as one, at all. A being in the world cannot exist without a hermeneutical, ontological reference to the world.[3] As for the basic structure of being, Tillich lays out the following threefold symmetrical structure: individuality and universality, dynamics and form, freedom and destiny.[4]

These polar pairs co-exist and have meaning in operating dynamically. Individuality, dynamics and freedom refer to the self-relation of being, while universality, form, and destiny refer to the belongingness of being. The self-relation of being implies the tendency of the concrete individual to retain self-affirmation, self-character, and self-identity, while the belongingness of being expresses the organic relationality of every creature and its ontological interdependence and limitation. In other words, individuality and universality mean individualization and participation.

In order for a human being to have self-consciousness and self-identity as the unity of soul and body, one must be physically in an on-going material exchange with nature and in participatory communion with the environmental world. Spiritually, one is capable of individualization by means of communication and participation in the world (as cultural tradition and structure of meaning). Individuation is an attainable process of exchange with the environmental world, externally by participation in nature and internally by communication with tradition, language, and culture.

Think about dynamics and form. The concept of form includes external form as well as the inner structure and rationality of all that exists. The dynamics shape and constitute a form, and conversely they operate in and within the form. Dynamics and form can be compared to the relation between *li* (principle) and *ch'i* (natural force) in the Neo-Confucian framework. In Neo-Confucianism, a relation between *li* and *ch'i,* which is non-dual and non-separable, functions as the ontological structure for all that exists. The dynamics and form of human life are not operative within a closed system but become possible only in an open system that includes universe. Henceforth, dynamics and form are related organically to nature.

We read Tillich's concern about nature and the universe in the following statement:

> Long after I had written the sections on life and its ambiguities, I happened to read Pierre Teilhard de Chardin's book, *The*

[3] Ibid., 164.

[4] Ibid., 165.

> *Phenomenon of Man*. It encouraged me greatly to know that an acknowledged scientist had developed ideas about the dimensions and processes of life so similar to my own. Although I cannot share his rather optimistic vision of the future, I am convinced by his description of the evolutionary processes in nature. Of course, theology cannot rest on scientific theory. But it must relate its understanding of man to an understanding of universal nature, for man is a part of nature and statements about nature underlie every statement about him.[5]

From this statement we see that Tillich understands the human being as a part of nature and connects every human life inseparably to the human understanding of nature. Furthermore, he shares with Teilhard the idea that there are diverse dimensions of life in the universe, and that they arise and emerge in a process of evolution and stand in organic inter-relationality. There can be mutual interference in each of the dimensions of life, like the sphere of material life, the animal-vegetarian dimension, and the spiritual dimension, etc. According to Tillich, nature mysticism reminds us that there is correspondence and mutual communion between the sighs of nature, humans, and the Spirit.

Like Teilhard, for Tillich, creation and evolution are not in contradiction with one another, but the latter is integrated into the former. Tillich's symbolic understanding of the Genesis account in the Scriptures finds it meaningful to understand creation in a way in which the original possibility of life existed latently and potentially in God as Being itself. In order for the potentiality of life to realize itself, its condition and constellation of structure must presuppose God's directing creativity, namely divine providence. And it precedes into the ontological structure of human beings, that is, freedom and destiny. Let me quote Tillich's statement regarding this:

> The appearance of a new dimension of life is dependent on a constellation of conditions in the conditioning dimension. Constellations of conditions make it possible for the organic to appear in the inorganic realm. Constellations in the inorganic realm make it possible for the dimension of self-awareness to become actual, and in the same way constellations under the predominance of the psychological dimension make it possible for the dimension of the spirit to become actual. The phrases "make it possible" and "provides for the conditions" for a dimension to become actual are crucial in these statements. The question is not how the condi-

[5] Paul Tillich, *Systematic Theology*, vol. 3 (Chicago: University of Chicago Press, 1963) 5.

> tions are provided; this is a matter of the interplay of freedom and destiny under the directing creativity of God, i.e., under the divine providence. The question is rather how the actualization of the potential follows from the constellation of conditions.[6]

In addition to Tillich, we see also Moltmann's theology of creation in which he tries to overcome the dichotomy between revealed theology and natural theology. The problem of natural theology and creation in our century was basically related to the problem of the knowability of God in creation. During the 30s, theological confrontation was about a religious or political ideology of blood and land, race and people, capitalism and socialism, secularism and optimism.

However, for Moltmann, the theological task of today is to construct a pneumatological concept of creation or an ecological concept of it in the face of the destruction of nature, ecological crisis, and destruction of the integration of creation. What is at issue in this regard is not the transcendence of God, but the constructing of the integration of immanence and creation in the Spirit and through the Spirit. The essence of a theology of creation is an understanding of the whole universe of creatures as Immanuel and as the shalom in glory through God's self-limitation (*tzimtzum*) and Shechina. Let me summarize Moltmann's groundbreaking thesis of ecological pneumatology.

1) If the traditional understanding of the Trinity emphasizes the unity between the subject and the transcendence of three Persons, an ecological theology of creation articulates fellowship, mutual penetration, and communion; participation in suffering, and the glory of creation in terms of divine life and its relationality within the created world. Theology of the Word of God (Karl Barth), or existential theology (Rudolf Bultmann) describe God as the transcendental subject, and unilaterally emphasize that the world is a mere object of salvation. Moltmann takes issue critically with this condescending, authoritative structure of dialectical theology which prevailed in the 20th century.

2) According to Moltmann's ecological theology of creation, the ultimate purpose of creation consists, in a way, in the struggle and liberation of the cross toward the cosmic rest and divine glory in which all creatures will participate. The *telos* of creation is the Sabbath, which is the fulfillment and inner aim of creation. Creation proceeds not only toward mutual fellowship and interpenetration among creatures, but also

[6] Ibid., 25.

finally toward the eschatological fulfillment of creation, so that God the creator will be all in all and dwell in all, and God's glory will be present in humans and on earth. Moltmann's theology of eschatology is directed toward healing the wound of history and nature.

In it, all living things are liberated from crying and alienation, and participate in the great feast of eschatological joy. Given this fact, Moltmann does not accept a theological anthropocentrism, according to which humans are exalted as the crown of creation, seen from a genuine biblical tradition. God's creation of the world is done for God's glory and the crown of creation is the Sabbath, not humans.

3) Moltmann takes issue with the grounding thesis of Karl Barth. According to Barth, creation is the external ground of the covenant and the covenant is the inner ground of creation.[7]Moltmann formulates, in light of his eschatological, pnuematological theology of creation, the thesis that grace does not complete nature but prepares it for the eternal glory of God. Therefore, grace is not the completion of nature but the messianic preparation of the world toward the kingdom of God.[8]

   Critical of Barth's framework of covenant and creation, Moltmann insists that it is not the historical covenant of God, but that the coming kingdom of God in glory, which is promised and guaranteed by the historical covenant and the inner ground of creation.[9] However, when it comes to the relation between creation and covenant, Barth speaks primarily of the eternal covenant of grace, or the eternal gracious election of Jesus Christ, in a supralapsarian sense, and then of the historical dimension of the covenant between God and Israel. Although Moltmann's critique does not hit the mark, his intention is rather to speak of nature itself in expectation of its participation in the great feast of cosmic messianic glory and rest.

4) The pneumatological Trinity offers a theological basis for an ecological theology of creation. In it, the presence of God the Creator assumes a panentheistic character that embraces the transcendental and immanent relation of God in the Spirit of creation. This avoids transcendental theism or immanentalist pantheism. Moltmann accepts Calvin's

[7] Karl Barth, *Church Dogmatics* III/1, eds G. W. Bromiley and T. F. Torrance, trans. T. F. Torrance (Edinburgh: T & T Clark, 1949) 45.

[8] Jürgen Moltmann, *God in Creation: A New Theology of Creation and the Spirit of God*, trans. Margaret Kohl (San Francisco: Harper & Row, 1985) 21.

[9] Ibid., 22

statement that the Holy Spirit is present everywhere and sustains, nourishes, and quickens every life.[10]

Every reality in the universe is unified together and experiences the unity of communion and fellowship in the divine Spirit. The presence of the world and the presence of God are not separated from each other, though also not confused with each other either. At this juncture, there is a parallel between Moltmann's theology of creation and the panentheism of process philosophy from Whitehead.[11]

5) From the perspective of "God in creation," creation and evolution are not in contradiction but in complementarity. The creation of the world is a creative evolution because it is directed toward the kingdom of glory and transcends the present. It is also an evolving creation because the Spirit of God does not work without being incarnated through the matter of the world. For Moltmann's theology of ecological creation, an alternative, either creation or evolution, is meaningless. The Spirit operates in organizing, and forms the open system of nature and rides with it.

   Where there is Spirit, there occurs openness, freedom, self-transcendence, revival, and the expanding of horizons toward a higher spiritual level, and finally, the unity of cosmic consciousness and divine consciousness. We perceive such a unity in Jesus' saying, "I am in Father, and Father is in me" (John 14:11). Or, "The Father and I are one" (John 10:30). For Moltmann, such an experience of Jesus is based on the perichoretic fellowship of Father, Son, and Spirit in the Trinitarian life.

6) From the perspective of an ecological theology of creation, Moltmann rejects asymmetrical structure between heaven and earth, or man and woman, which corresponds to a relation between God the Creator and the world in a hierarchical manner. According to Karl Barth, heaven has priority over earth, and this concept forms his point of departure for the doctrine of creation. The Barthian structure of hierarchy, which is based on the sovereignty of God, is criticized by Moltmann and by feminist theologians under the patriarchal principle. The principle of ecological creation is directed toward the mutual permeation, interaction, and circulation of all that exists.

[10] John Calvin, *Institutes of the Christian Religion* I.13.14.

[11] Cf. Alfred N. Whitehead, *Process and Reality*, eds. David R. Griffin and Donald W. Sherburne (New York: Free, 1978) 348.

7) The ecological proposal of a new theology of nature, which Moltmann develops, protests the one-sided tendency of salvation history that restricts biblical faith to the internal side of the human being. Not only humans but also nature are conceived of as subjects, and there is concern for the naturalization of humans. When theology is only concerned with the internal side of humans and the salvation of their souls, the physicality of the earth in which "the Word became flesh" is violated and abandoned.

   At this juncture, Moltmann finds Ernst Bloch's concept of the nature subject to be legitimate. Because creation is a comprehensive concept of God's all-creating activities, God's creation includes a threefold dimension, namely *creatio originalis*, *creatio continua*, and *creatio nova*, which are interconnected with one another. From this standpoint, Moltmann interprets Barth's rejection of natural theology in a positive way, saying that revealed theology includes and integrates natural theology. Moltmann agrees with Ian Babour, who maintains that nature is a part of the divine drama, and it participates directly in the salvation drama of God for the world of creation.

8) Ecological theology of creation is concerned with the time of creation, as well as the space of creation. By distinguishing heaven from the kingdom of God, Moltmann interprets heaven to be energy, the possibilities and potentialities of God. Luther identifies heaven with the presence of God. In the Lutheran tradition, heaven was identified with the almightiness, omnipresence, and glory of God. However, for Moltmann, heaven and earth should not be confused or identified with one another, but should inseparably exist in mutual permeation, reciprocal fellowship and communion.

9) According to Moltmann, *imago Dei* is a sign of divine sovereignty, agency, and glory. As Sabbath is the ultimate purpose of creation, so the glory of God is humanity (Irenaeus). Corporeality is the end of all God's works (F. Oetinger). Moltmann is critical of Barth's Christological anthropology in which there is a primacy of soul over body unilaterally. Conversely, the body has primacy over soul. Humans do not possess souls, but they are themselves living souls.

10) Sabbath is the celebration of creation, completion, and glory. The genuine final rest appears at the eschaton of all things. God's glory will dwell in all, and all creatures will be in communion with each other. At the final rest, God does not reign over the world, but feels and

experiences it. If Exodus means external freedom and liberation from external oppression, Sabbath means internal freedom and liberation, a homecoming.

The Religious-Philosophical Understanding of Nature in East North Asian Civilization

The circle of East North Asian civilization, which is described here, refers to a society of civilization that includes and unifies China, Korea, and Japan, as Toynbee once defined it in his study of history. In this civilization circle, the cultures of Buddhism and Confucianism constitute the leading paradigm for people who live there. My concern is for the philosophy of nature in Mahayana Buddhism and Confucianism.

The Understanding of Nature in Mahayana Buddhism

Generally speaking, the understanding of nature in Mahayana Buddhism relates to cosmology in a narrow sense. However, I am concerned with analyzing and expanding the doctrine of dependent co-arising, which is fundamental to Theravada and Mahayana Buddhism. The doctrine of dependent co-arising does not merely refer to Buddhist epistemology, but to the substantial view of reality that makes Buddhism exist as such. Without it, it is impossible to understand the Buddhist notion of truth and to explain nature in an objectified sense. The four noble truths, which articulate the core principles of Buddhism, are also based on the teaching of dependent co-arising.

Based on it, the four noble truths are a teaching of means (*upaya*), which explains the nature of things, expounds the cause of suffering in human existence and then presents the way to Enlightenment. In fact, Gautama Siddarta's becoming the Buddha under the Bo tree is due to the fact that he penetrated the reality of dependent co-arising and was enlightened with this truth. Therefore, "anyone who sees dependent co-arising sees the dharma (the Truth). And anyone who sees the dharma sees me."

The teaching of dependent co-arising, which is a translation of *pratitya samutpada,* denotes that there is no such thing among all as a substance that exists independently. It refers to a view of reality wherein everybody and everything exist in mutual dependence, mutual inter-being, and reciprocal organic relation. Because this exists, that exists. Because this arises, that arises. From a sutra we read a definition of this teaching. "Because of this, that exists. Because of that arising, this arises."[12]

Nothing in the universe is a substantiated independent reality. Material nature, disposition, and spiritual capacity and quality, spiritual power, and function in the universe arise through the connections of dependent co-arising. At this point, we should not misunderstand the teaching of dependent co-arising merely as the law of cause and effect in the sense of modern science. The scientific law of cause and effect presupposes the irreversibility of time and space and the unchangeable substance of matter. It speaks of the initial conditions of the physical world and its relation to expectation resulting through probability.

The Buddhist teaching of dependent co-arising points in a different direction. Instead of expressing the absolute concept of time and space, or the invariable nature of matter as an independent reality of substance, it teaches that all in the universe arises temporal-spatially in the relational web of simultaneity, mutual interdependence, and reciprocal co-existence.

In the teaching of dependent co-arising, there is a threefold sense of accounting for the phenomenon of reality. The first teaching is based on the karma of Hinduism. According to the teaching of karma, the act, will, and thinking each leave behind and produce a corresponding influence upon human life. Merit and the power of karma are left behind, and accordingly, all living sentient creatures are produced and influenced by it.

They are impartial and harvested without discrimination according to the extent of the sowing of the seed. The harvested seed, in turn, produces all things according to the law of cause and effect. Let's take my physical existence for an example. My physical health condition and some important parts of my physical function were transmitted to me or inherited, by and large, from the genetics of my biological ancestors. Besides this, my environmental condition—water, air, sun, weather, geographical climate, nutrition, and hygienic condition—co-participate in producing my physical existence. My spiritual life is constituted through the disposition of my ancestor's genetics, my cultural heritage, educational influence, studying, and mediation.

The second teaching is based on *alayavijnana* (literally "storehouse consciousness"), which in Sanskrit denotes imperishable, non-extinguishable consciousness or mind; in other words, the substratum of consciousness. It is a Buddhist theory concerning in which the power and merit of

[12] Cf. Kogen Mizuno, *Essentials of Buddhism: Basic Terminology and Concepts of Buddhist Philosophy and Practice* (Tokyo: Kosei, 1996) 135–50.

karma remain as the genesis potential of all and how one overcomes such a problem. Hsüan-tsang, in China, translated it as the womb of consciousness. *Alayavijnana* belongs to the 8th consciousness, which has to do with *tathagatagarbha* (Buddha-essence/ Buddha-nature).

This consciousness is likened to the sea or the state of mind in which the possibility and potentiality of every power and merit of karma exist. When this power and merit of karma come into contact passively with a certain objective relation and condition, or produce positive relationality, the phenomenon of all that exists arises. *Alayatijnana* is the sum of the possibility and potentiality of every power and merit of karma between the good and the evil, while *tathagatgarbha* refers to the potentiality of the truth, the good, and the beauty, and the arsenal of their possibility. However, according to the Cittamatra (Mind Only) tradition, only certain people possess seeds for full Buddhahood.

The third teaching is about a dependent co-arising of the true self (*tathata*) which is directed toward overcoming the subjective trend of *Alayavijnana* in the Cittamatra tradition. This teaching is central to the Hua-yen (the Flower Garland) doctrine of Mahayana Buddhism in China. *Tathata* is the expression of the free and endless creative power of the Truth and its reality, which cannot be conceived of in human language. In other words, it is God, Dharma, the Truth, and the noumenon in unity with phenomenon.

According to *Awakening of Faith in the Mahayana,*[13] *tathata*, *dharmadhatu* (the world as seen by the Buddha) and dharma are the original womb of the mind of all, the essence of every thing and every body and the reality of setting them in motion. In the *Awakening of Faith,* we see the Buddha-essence doctrine as a cosmological theory that explains the true nature of the cosmos. The Buddha-essence exists within all sentient beings and enables all beings to become enlightened. The principle is the Mind of all sentient beings, the one that includes in itself all states of being in the phenomenal and the transcendental world.

According to the commentary of Fa-tsang (643–712), this One Mind is no less than the *tathagatagarba*, which is the essence of *samsara* and *nirvana*. Therefore, the gate to the true nature and the gate to the world of life and death are two in one, and one in two. They are not distinguished,

[13] It is *Ta-ch'eng ch'-hsin lun* (Sanskrit title: *Mahayanasaddhotpada sastra*) whose authorship is attributed to Asvaghosa. For a study of East Asian Buddha-essence theory, *Fo-hsing lun* (given the Sanskrit title of *Buddhagotra sastra*), attributed to Vasubandhu, and the aforementioned sutra are regarded as the two most important exegetical treatises. Cf. Paul Williams, *Mahayana Buddhism* (New York: Routledge, 1989) 109.

yet they are inseparable from one another.[14] Similarly, in the *Avatsamsaka* sutra, we see the *dharmadhata*, the Dharma-realm, which is the universe of the *Avatsamsaka* sutra. In it, the Buddha is the all-penetrating, all-transforming awareness and principle.

The threefold sense of the Buddhist doctrine of dependent co-arising attests that all exists and arises in mutual organic penetration and interdependence and is preserved and changed in circulation. In dust or a grain of rice, all is included. From the perspective of Hua-yen's cosmology, the Western anthropocentric view, in which humans have the privilege to dominate nature and all living creatures, is denounced as ignorance, attachment, and greed.

Ch'i philosophical View of Nature in Neo-Confucianism

Nobody doubts that Taoism is one of the important world religions, next to Buddhism and Confucianism, in East Asia. Confucianism and Taoism, as the indigenous philosophies in China, encountered Buddhism from India, such that Confucianism and Taoism had mutual interaction with Buddhism. This encounter exercised a great impact upon spiritual and religious culture in China, Korea, and Japan. Confucianism, the moral philosophy that represents Chinese culture, deeply influenced the development of Confucianism in Korea.

Especially Neo-Confucianism in the Song dynasty, influenced by Mahayana Buddhism, developed original Confucian ethics and morality in its practical intent, and moved in the direction of a religious-philosophical ontology in which a doctrine of the human mind was fully affirmed.

Wang Shou-Jen (1472–1528), the master of Yang-ming, developed a way of mediation for the training the mind and nature. This way of meditation showed his influence clearly under Ch'an Buddhism and, without doubt, Lu Chiu-Yüan's concept of the Mind as *Li* was developed on the soil of the Buddhist doctrine of the Mind only and the *yogacara* tradition. Even the father of Neo-Confucianism in the Song dynasty, Chu Hsi (1130–1200), held a concept of the *Li-Ch'i* relation that can be understood as his creative response to the challenge of Buddhism at this time.

In the preface to *Chu Hsi's Philosophy of Nature*, we know from Yamada Kagy that Chu Hsi's philosophy of nature began from Lao Tzu and Chuang Tzu's thought during the warring states period and finally

[14] Cf. Asvaghosa, *The Awakening of Faith: The Classic Exposition of Mahayana Buddhism*, trans. Teitaro Suzuki (Mineola: Dover, 2003).

was based on the philosophy of *ch'i* in Chang Tsai (1020–1077). It arose on the basis of science and technology, which were at their height during the Song and Won periods. It refers to the existence of matter, in a more strict sense, a basic concept of matter that consists of the natural world. It is a comprehensive concept of existence grasped in terms of the three categories of one *ch'i, yin-yang*, and *Wu Hsing* (the Five Elements or Agents).

Throughout the long history of China, the concept of *ch'i* seems to expand and deepen its meaning and horizon. Let me summarize the philosophy of *ch'i*, which appears in the thought of ancient China.

A. The root of *ch'i*, which is based on ancient Chinese characters, has something to do with wind, breath and earth. *Ch'i* is full and prevailing in the universe and also full in the human body. It originally denotes one and manifests itself as *ch'i* of *yin* and *ch'i* of *yang*, *ch'i* of heaven, *ch'i* of earth and *ch'i* of humans.

B. In Chuang Tzu, human life is depicted as the consolidation of *ch'i*, while death is its dispersion. *Ch'i* is changeable and operative in matter, and related to the phenomenon of life. *Ch'i* is also related to the will and the mind. If *ch'i* is controlled and taken properly, the human mind becomes clear and bright, and the body becomes strong and self-increasing.

C. Although human *ch'i* is expressed as the *ch'i* of brightness or divine spirit, essentially human *ch'i* is equated with the *ch'i* of heaven and that of earth. The humans, like all living things, have *ch'i* as their constituting element. Light, *ch'i,* and spirit are interpenetrating and essentially various manifestations of *ch'i*, pure and bright and transparent.

D. According to Mencius, *ch'i* can become great, right, and strong along with righteousness and *Tao*. The principle of nurturing human nature through *ch'i* refers to fostering greatness and strength, namely righteousness.

E. According to the *I Ching*'s idea of heaven, earth, and humans, the way of heaven is called *yin* and *yang*. The law of earth is soft and descending, while the way of humans is heartedness and righteousness. There is change in accordance with the interaction of *yin* and *yang*; therefore, change appears in the pairing of strength and softness. Heaven, earth and humans correspond and are interconnected with one another.

F. According to Chuang Tzu, human diseases take place when the *ch'i* of *yin* and the *ch'i* of *yang* do harm to each other. In other words, their balance is lost. Therefore, the reason for disease is an abnormal relation between *yin ch'i* and *yang ch'i*.

G. *Huau Nam Tzu* states that the geographical condition of all living creatures, including human beings, is closely connected with the sexuality, physical type, temper, character and intellectual ability of human beings. In East Asian philosophy, as a rule, the doctrine of *ch'i* is directly linked to metaphysical ontology and cosmology as well as to the problem of medicine and medical treatment. In the oriental world of medicine, five levers and six parts inside the physical body are not independent objects of biological or pathological anatomy, but functionally complex symptoms of various *ch'i*. Because the blood line corresponds to the stream of *ch'i* in nature and the universe, oriental medicine takes into account life, balance, harmony, circulation, complementarity, and relationality.

H. Original *ch'i* refers to the state of origin of *ch'i*. The original *ch'i* means the essence of *ch'i* before it divides into *yin* and *yang*. The human being receives the original *ch'i* from heaven and, in the original *ch'i*, the physical shape and type and life. When one is born by receiving the original *ch'i* replete with heaven and earth, one takes earth *ch'i* (*yin*) as body to form *pack* and heaven *ch'i* (*yang*) as body to form *hon*, so that one is equipped with *hon pack*. The function of *hon* is called spirit or spirit *ch'i*. Therefore, *ch'i* is the basis for the function and operation of all.

I. *Ch'i* thought in China became complete in the Song period. According to Neo-Confucianism, *ch'i* is the source of matter and, at the same time, the source of life and vitality. Heaven and earth and all that exists are made up of *ch'i*. *Ch'i* is the subject of change and movement and the basis for causing and vitalizing the changing movement. Both human beings and all other living things are made by *ch'i*.

J. Zhou Dunyi (1017–1073), known as the first of the Neo-Confucian philosophers, is considered to be the founder of Song Learning. In *An Explanation of the Diagram of the Supreme Ultimate*, Zhou established the supreme Ultimate, *yin* and *yang*, and genetic cosmology. Zhang Zai (1020–1077) explained death and life in terms of the consolidation and dispersion of *ch'i* and called the Great Void *ch'i*. Chu His, whose thought represents the culmination of Neo-Confucianism, considered the Supreme Ultimate as principle (*Li*), *yin* and *yang* as *ch'i*, and the five elements as quality.

K. In *li*/*ch'i* philosophy, what makes *ch'i* original and essential is the position of *ch'i* philosophy. There are various positions of the primary *ch'i* doctrine and the *ch'i* only doctrine. Wang Pu-Chi (1619–1692) and Lee Yul-Gok (1536–84), in the Cho Sun dynasty of Korea, were representatives of the primary *ch'i* doctrine. The former said that there was no independent principle (*li*), while the latter said that the principle increased in accordance with the operation of *ch'i*.[15] According to the idea of material force in China, *ch'i* is considered to be the original *ch'i* equipped with the creative and productive life force and vitality rather than the remaining material energy. Therefore, *ch'i* enables existence to appear, in material and spiritual phenomena, as various forms and modes of being. Spirit *ch'i,* or spirit soul, is more the manifestation of the pure and wondrous function and operation of the original *ch'i* rather than supernatural transcendence.

A Pneumatological Understanding of Faith in Creation in Dialogue with *Ch'i* Philosophy

Given the various ideas and understandings of *ch'i* mentioned above, I attempt to make convergence and divergence between the Biblical-Hebrew idea of the Spirit and the East Asian philosophy of *ch'i*. Prof. Kim Yong-Yok, in his *Essays on Ch'i Philosophy,* states the following:

> There was *ch'i* in the beginning. *Ch'i* exists together with space and time. *Ch'i* includes every possibility. *Ch'i* evolves. The evolution of *ch'i* is the consolidation and dispersion of it, which can have a direction. The beginning is simply understood as the *ch'i* event taking place between balance and unbalance. This is the event in which the middle way of *ch'i* changed into its excessive or less state. We can realize that the perfect middle of *ch'i* was the beginning of all. The dynamic of *ch'i* is inherent to *ch'i* as such. Therefore, Li En Si said that the great ultimate was the movement the produced *yang*. That which is the subject of the movement is no less than

[15] Korean neo-Confucian Learning reached a climax in two great scholars: Yi Hwang (or T'oegye, 1501–1570) and Yi I (Yulgok, 1536–1584), who elaborated on Zhang Zai and Zhou Dunyi, but found some disparities in Chu His' theories regarding the relation between principle and material force. These different understandings led to heavy debates. Xinzhong Yao, *An Introduction to Confucianism* (Cambridge: Cambridge University Press, 2000) 117–18.

> the great ultimate. The great ultimate is a moving. It is not moved. This view is different from the world view of Aristotle, which conceived of the great ultimate as the unmoved mover.[16]

This statement, breaking with the static framework of *li* / *ch'i* philosophy, shows the possibility in paving a way for converging *ch'i* philosophy with the Christian faith in God's creation. The beginning was the creative, or genesis, movement in which the original *ch'i* becomes the moving agent and is directed by means of unbalance, the interaction of *yin* and *yang* and excess-deficiency. Therefore, the beginning broke the balance of the original *ch'i* which had been complete and perfect and self-sufficient. Such an interpretation is in affinity with Moltmann's interpretation of creation in terms of God's self-emptiness and indwelling within the creatures.

The great ultimate in Neo-Confucianism refers to the creative Spirit, of which the Bible speaks. Christian theologians in the West are limited in positively understanding *ch'i* philosophy in East Asian culture because they tend to conceive of the great ultimate as an originally created force, or the beginning of the universe from chaos. Their understanding of the original *ch'i* overlooks its life force, vitality, prevailing omnipresence and fullness. Instead, it is captive to a way of thinking it as material force or energy. Likewise, Confucian philosophers also misunderstand by regarding *ch'i* only as material energy. A genuine understanding of the original *ch'i* helps to change traditional pneumatology within soteriology into a pneumatological theology of creation. In the Christian tradition, the doctrine of the Spirit has been confined to soteriology or ecclesiology, such that other comprehensive dimensions of the Spirit creator were suppressed.

Christian theology is eschatologically oriented. According to Moltmann, pneumatological faith in creation means that all living things proceed creatively in experience with the pain of laboring, in order to participate in God's eternal rest and finally to join the glory of God's eschaton in the power of the Spirit. Time consciousness takes the form of a linear and straight direction.

Time consciousness in Neo-Confucianism is a worldview that is grounded on *hic et nunc* and fills all fragments of the universe in every direction. At this point, Kim Yong-Ok is critical of the generalization that Oriental time consciousness is circular, while the Occidental one is linear. According to him, *ch'i* philosophy is more concerned with the shape than the directionality of time. The mode of shape is relevant to directionality as such. As a rule, it is an image portrayed according to the persistence of

[16] Kim Yong Ok, *Essays on Ch'i Philosophy*, 33–34.

a given direction. The picture of all temporality is the combination and configuration of a straight line and circle. For instance, the curve takes place in the combination of a straight line and a circle. The straight line and circle in time cannot be compartmentalized.

To recognize monistic totality, people in the East Asian world subject the straight line to the circle, while people in the West, as a rule, subject the circle to the straight line. In investigating human history, we are aware that the circle and straight line presuppose always the dynamic of an over-determined reality. Otherwise, we would fall into the error of superficial thinking by assigning and reducing a circular or linear way of thinking to each different worldview. Culturally dualistic typology, in its comparative study of East and West, was in error in this regard.[17]

Christian theology has misunderstood nature, circulation and the rhythm of the body as merely repetitive. Strictly speaking, there is no such thing as repetition in the time of life. Every moment is a new formation, and every year and every period is a new creative performance. However, in Christian theology, there is a tendency to ignore the present life in the overemphasis on the eschatological direction of future.

Whitehead, in his *Process and Reality,* understands that actual entities in all living things form an integral, whole and organic nexus of relational connection, and they evolve toward a more complex and over-determined organic society. They are conceived of as the universe continuing in an on-going process of concrescence. All things in this regard are understood with each small society. Similarly, according to Hua-yen philosophy, the world exists in mutual and organic interconnection and interdependence. Because of metaphysical creativity, eternal objects and God are interfused in the process of concrescence, and the process movement of these actual entities is not a mere complex of confusion or a boring repetition of the same thing.

Rather, it is the ontological place in which something new happens in an on-going way. According to Neo-Confucianism, the whole picture of actual reality is expressed in terms of *ch'i*, while creativity, eternal objects, and God are, put together, expressed as principle (*li*). In the tradition of primary *ch'i* philosophy, *ch'i* is conceived of as a productive source of reality, which essentially includes creativity, activity and life. At this point, *ch'i* philosophy forms a point of conversation with Trinitarian pneumatology in the Christian tradition.

[17] Ibid., 42, 44.

Toward Ecological Ethics

The human is a living being with a body that is incorporated and integrated by heaven and earth. The human body is connected organically with all other living things, and exists in a circular rhythm and a relation of complementarity. Therefore, an anthropocentric cosmology and worldview are not tenable.

Ecological ethics is an attitude of the mature person who is aware of the ontological structure and organic relationality surrounding human life. It is ethics according to which the mature person serves as the nerve web of the backbone and unfolds self-control, harmony, and ethical responsibility in complementarity, making self-sacrifice and commitment to the greater altar of life in favor of beauty, justice, and sincerity among all. Christian theology stands before a task of reinterpreting the Gospel in the global and universal horizon, going beyond Latin, Greek-orthodox, Anglo Saxon, and European frameworks.

Christian theology in East Asia should, first of all, take into account the Hebrew tradition of Christian faith. In order to enrich and deepen the biblical idea of redemption and faith in creation, it also needs to expand its horizons in profound conversation with Buddhism, Confucianism, and Taoism. A theology that is merely fixed to the Western paradigm of Christian theology cannot make a contribution to the dynamic development of the church and humanity in the future.

18

Mission and Inculturation in the Thought of Matteo Ricci

Paul S. Chung

When the Gospel is introduced to a non-Christian country, a problem occurs about how to deal with the cultural tradition in which the Gospel is to be shaped and understood. It is generally agreed upon that in the anthropological study of the relation between Gospel and culture, the understanding of the Gospel is culturally conditioned in every particular context. In the debate on Gospel and inculturation in the missiological field,[1] I am interested particularly in discussing Matteo Ricci, an Italian Jesuit missionary who arrived in China in 1582 and remained there until his death in 1610. His legacy of Chinese mission and his theory of accommodation offer insight for mapping the direction and content of Christian mission in our multicultural and global context.

The Jesuits went to China during the time of the high Renaissance in Europe. The Counter Reformation was energized by the Society of Jesus, founded in 1540 by the Spaniard, Ignatius of Loyola. The Society of Jesus was eager to spread Roman Catholicism to both India and China. Aided by Portuguese travelers and traders who were already in Japan in 1543, Francis Xavier (1506–1552), the father of the Jesuit Oriental mission, preached in India and Japan even without really knowing the native languages. Gaining people for the Catholic faith in Japan, Xavier was aware of the Japanese religious dependence on China and wished that Christianity would be spread to the intelligent Chinese. However, on 3 December 1552, he died on the small island of Shangchuan, which was

[1] David Bosch, *Transforming Mission: Paradigm Shifts in Theology of Mission* (Maryknoll: Orbis, 2004) 447–57.

used as a trading post between Chinese and Portuguese merchants, near Macau.

One of his successors in the Society of Jesus, Matteo Ricci, was born in Macerata on 16 October 1552. Although his father sent him to Rome to study law at the age of 17, upon feeling a religious vocation, he entered into the Order of the Feast of the Assumption on 15 August 1571. At that time, Father Alessandro Valignano was the acting novice master and later became the director of mission affairs for the Society of Jesus in India, Japan and China. Interested in foreign mission in the Society, Ricci was given the opportunity to join the India mission. Ricci arrived in Goa on 13 September 1578 and worked in India for four years.

Valignano, Xavier's successor and appointed as the papal visitor to the East, was successful in breaking free from the conquistador mission system. His model of mission, based on *il modo soave* (the sweet or gentle way), became the guideline for the Jesuit missionaries' profound study of the indigenous language, culture, and politics of China. This became instrumental in defending against the conquistador and *tabula rasa* mentalities of mission.[2]

Under the guidance of Valignano, before arriving in China, Ruggieri and Ricci studied for four years in India. In 1583, Ricci and Ruggieri were prohibited to reside in China without official approval. In 1598, Ricci and his companions were able to go to Beijing, the capital of the empire. In 1601, Ricci and three Jesuit companions returned to Beijing and received imperial permission to stay in the capital.

Ricci introduced the Chinese to valuable developments in the West through his scientific knowledge of sundials, mathematics, geometry, mapmaking, cartography, and astronomy. His knowledge of natural science was, despite his limitations, in the service of his mission.[3] Although the emperor and Ricci did not meet face to face, Ricci managed to have the presents he had prepared delivered to the emperor when he arrived in the capital in 1601. Ricci served as a repairman of clocks, which he

[2] Stephen B. Bevans and Roger P. Schroeder, *Constants in Context: A Theology of Mission for Today* (Maryknoll: Orbis, 2004) 186. Cf. Matteo Ricci, *The True Meaning of The Lord of Heaven (T'ien-chu Shih-i)*, trans. Douglas Lancashire and Peter Hu Kuo-chen. Ed. Edward J. Malatesta (St. Louis: Institute of Jesuit Sources, 1985) 4–5.

[3] Critics accused the Jesuits of misleading the Chinese through their introduction of the geocentric Ptolemaic and Aristotelian theories. In fact, the Chinese view of natural science was closer to the scientific truth than that of the Jesuits. Wolfgang Franke, *China and the West* (South Carolina: University of South Carolina Press, 1967) 45.

presented to the Wan Li emperor in Beijing, and he entered the emperor's palace at least four times each year.

Placing himself in the role of barbarians, Li Ma-tou (the Chinese name for Matteo Ricci) presented himself very humbly to the imperial court. In 1591 he was able to begin a translation of the four classical books of Confucianism (*The Confucian Analects*, *The Book of Mencius*, *The Great Learning*, and *The Doctrine of the Mean*) into Latin and transliterated the Chinese K'ung Fu-tzu as Confucius.[4]

When Ricci died on 11 May 1610, the emperor donated a site for his burial and for the erection of a new residence for the mission. He was buried on the outskirts of Beijing. He occupied an honored place in China for his immersion into the local culture and for his profound study of Confucian philosophy. These things led Ricci and his fellow Jesuits towards fulfilling an inculturation of their Christian mission. Its spirit is expressed through tolerance for local customs and through the incorporation of practices such as ceremonies to honor ancestors and Confucius. He is referred to in some Chinese histories as "the wise man from the West."

Alexandro Valignano, supervisor of Ricci and Ruggieri, was convinced that they could win people through "his principles of adaptation, equality and friendship with the governing class."[5] Influenced by Valignano, the attitude of Ricci was characterized by integrity, humility, and respect. His missionary goals laid in linking Chinese culture, and especially Confucian culture with Roman Catholicism. He developed an intensive knowledge of that culture and recognized its positive value in connection with Christianity.

Therefore, his missionary work raises an important issue in the history of culture and mission: how to effectively communicate between two cultural traditions with different backgrounds. This is the heart of the problem of inculturation. Most likely, he approached this agenda by adopting a positive attitude towards Confucian culture in terms of the natural theology of Roman Catholicism. How do we understand his hermeneutical strategy of linking Confucian philosophy to Christianity?

[4] Vincent Cronin, *The Wise Man From the West* (Glasgow: Collins, 1961) 103, 107.

[5] Ibid., 35.

The Transforming of Gospel and Culture in terms of Accommodation

Ricci and Rugierri obtained permission from the governor-general of Guangdong and Guangxi in 1582 to take up residence in the city of Zhaoqing. From there these two pioneers worked their way to Nanchang and Nanjing, finally gaining a permanent residence in Beijing by 1601.

After arriving in the southern Chinese town of Zhaoqing in 1583, Ricci believed that shrouding himself in the robes of a Buddhist monk would be deemed as holy. He saw a parallel between Christianity and Buddhism regarding the priestly robes, the chanting in their service, the espousal of celibacy and poverty, the temples, statues, and even some of the painted images. In a letter to his friend Fuligatti (24 November 1585) he wrote: "Would that you could see me as I am now: I have become a Chinaman. In our clothing, in our looks, in our manners and in everything external we have made ourselves Chinese."[6]

Ricci and his colleagues were equipped with missionary ways of accommodation. Encouraged by his superior Valignano, Ricci changed his soutanes into the cloak of the Buddhist bonze and shaved off his hair and beard. This was the first step taken toward external accommodation. Ricci's companion Michele Ruggieri said in a letter to his friend (17 February 1583) that "so, before long, we became Chinese to win China for Christ."[7]

Several years later, however, Ricci and his fellows came to the realization that in China, unlike Japan, Buddhist clergy belonged to the low social class. Based on the experience of the Jesuit missionaries in Japan, they had hoped to be accepted as honored Buddhist clergy in China with due social respect. In the summer of 1595 Ricci made a final break with the Buddhist dress, and adopted the special dress of the Confucian literati, as opposed to that of the bonze that he used to have. He was aware that there were three religions of major significance in China: Confucianism, Buddhism, and Taoism. Realizing that the Confucian literati were the most important, he gained an appreciation of the ethical values associated with the state and family, which underlie the heart of Confucianism.

In Ricci's view, the teaching of Confucius, in its monotheistic form, is more akin to Christianity. In his study of the *Analects*, Ricci became

6 Cited from Jonathan D. Spence, *The Memory of Palace of Matteo Ricci* (New York: Viking Penguin, 1984) 114.

7 Cited from David Chung, *Syncretism: The Religious Context of Christian Beginnings in Korea* (Albany: SUNY, 2001) 59.

convinced that Confucius had taught about a reverence for Heaven, apart from idolatry. Along with reverencing Heaven, Confucius also articulated an emphasis on human ethical morality, which is inherently good. However, reason is not enough for Confucius to know the nature of God or the reality of life after death.[8]

Many Confucians, retaining ambivalence toward the existence of an afterlife, belonged to one of the other two sects of Buddhism and Taoism along with their own. During the Ming dynasty (1368–1644), the three religions were in co-existence, fusing with each other. This led to the growth of religious syncretism. As Ricci states regarding the late Ming syncretism,

> [t]he commonest opinion held here among those who consider themselves the most wise is to say that all three of these sects come together as one, and that you can hold them all at once; in this they deceive themselves and others and lead to great disorder by its appearing to them that as far as religion is concerned the more ways of talking about religion there are, all the more benefit will that bring to the kingdom.[9]

Since the Wei-Jin period (220–420 C.E.), Confucianism lost its supremacy under the rapid spread of Taoism and the new doctrine of Buddhism. During the Sui and Tang dynasties (581–907 C.E.), Confucianism began to regain, gradually, some position of dominance, alongside Buddhism and Taoism, which were still popular among ordinary people and in the courts alike. In the Song (960–1279) and Ming (1368–1644) dynasties, Confucianism experienced its full renaissance in humanistic and rationalistic flavor. Great scholars such as Chang Tsai (1020–1077), Chu Hsi (1130–1200), Lu Jiuyuan (1139–1193), and Wang Shouren (1472–1529), stimulated by Buddhism, sought to systematically respond to what Buddhism and Taoism raised against Confucianism. Chu Hsi argued that the genuine understanding of Confucius' teaching had been lost since Mencius, but was rediscovered by eleventh century thinkers such as Chou Tun-yi, Chang Tsai, and the Ch'eng brothers.

The basic Neo-Confucian quest is oriented toward self-transcendence in the achievement of sagehood. Finding the world of metaphysics in the *Four Books* and *The Book of Changes,* Neo-Confucianists made an effort to transform Confucian doctrines by integrating an evolutionary cosmology, humanistic ethics and a rationalistic epistemology. "Without

[8] Cronin, *Wise Man from the West*, 56.

[9] Ibid.

the introduction of Buddhism into China there would have been no Neo-Confucianism."[10] Nevertheless, Neo-Confucianism did not succumb to the worldview of Buddhism or Taoism. Articulating the value of family and community, it stresses the understanding of life in this world in contradiction to the Buddhist doctrine of impermanence or the Taoist life style of non-action.[11]

While Matteo Ricci was active, Neo-Confucianism prevailed in the Ming Dynasty of China. Having a good command of the Chinese language, he knew a great deal about Chinese customs and etiquette. Not only did he dress in Confucian style with a square piece of cloth on his head and call himself a Western Confucian, but he also followed the etiquette of a Chinese scholar. He carefully studied ancient Chinese classics and records and regarded Confucius as a great man of wide knowledge.

In Ricci's observation, the Chinese greatly appreciated the principle of filial piety. They faithfully followed the natural law of ancient times. This nation did not simply worship any idols, although many of the lower classes confused the practice of ancestral rites with divine worship.

> Chinese books on morals are full of instructions relative to the respect that children should pay to parents and elders. Certainly if we look to an external display of filial piety, there is no people in the whole world who can compare with the Chinese.[12]

From this we know that Ricci studied very closely traditional culture, especially Confucian-Chinese culture. As in ancient society, China was dominated by the patriarchal clan system, and moral importance was attached to filial piety, which was based on the principle of blood relation. It was regarded as natural law. In China, worship of Heaven and Nature was also moral, and hence naturally reasonable. Being quite knowledgeable of Chinese culture, Ricci regarded Confucianism not as a kind of religion, but rather as natural law. Although the literati recognized one supreme deity, they did not erect special places or temples for worship. There were no public or private prayers or hymns in honor of a supreme deity.[13]

He saw that the idolatry in ancient Chinese culture was not like that of the Egyptians, Greeks, and Romans. Hence, ancient Chinese philoso-

---

[10] Carson Chang, *The Development of Neo-Confucian Thought* (London: Vision, 1958) 43.

[11] Xinzhong Yao, *An Introduction to Confucianism* (Cambridge: Cambridge University Press, 2000) 96–97. Cf. Julia Ching, *Chinese Religions* (Maryknoll: Orbis, 1993) 157–58.

[12] Matteo Ricci, *China in the Sixteenth Century: The Journals of Mathew Ricci: 1583–1610*, trans. Louis J. Gallagher, S.J. (New York: Random House, 1942) 72.

[13] Ibid., 95.

phy, in speaking of human nature and heavenly principles, was different from Western philosophy. As a Catholic, he attached great importance to opposing idolatry and advocating morality. Ricci was strongly against the idolatry of Buddhism and Taoism.[14]

When it came to connecting Christianity with Confucianism, Ricci took the following steps: 1) he utilized the Catholic doctrines as a complement to Confucianism, 2) in some respects, he interpreted the Catholic doctrines to transcend and transform the Confucian ones, and 3) he made some revisions of the Catholic doctrines and sought for concordance with the Confucian ones. In his important book *The True Meaning of The Lord of Heaven,*[15] we see those basic hermeneutical assumptions in operation.

Ricci's Hermeneutics in *The True Meaning of The Lord of Heaven*

The years 1601–1610 were years of climax for Ricci's missional achievements. During these years, Ricci earned the conversion of Hsü Kuang-ch'i (1562–1633), Li Chih-tsao (1565–1630), and Yang T'ing-yün (1562–1627), who were "three pillars of the early church" in China.[16] In November 1594, when he completed his translation of the *Four Books*, Ricci kept on studying the *Six Classics* and in 1596 Ricci completed his first draft of *The True Meaning of The Lord of Heaven.*

This book is composed of the dialogue between Matteo Ricci and his friends and Chinese scholars. What is the Lord of Heaven? It is God. It does exist. The edition of *The True Meaning of The Lord of Heaven* during the Ming dynasty often used the titles God (*Shang-ti*) and Heaven (*T'ien*) for the Lord of Heaven. However, in 1704 Pope Clement XI banned the use of the terms *T'ien* (Heaven) or *Shang-ti* (Sovereign on High) to designate God. Hence, in the present English edition "the Lord of Heaven" (*T'ien-chu*) is often used simply to replace the Confucian traditional terms.[17]

[14] Ibid., 99–105.

[15] Cf. Matteo Ricci, *The True Meaning of The Lord of Heaven*, trans. Douglas Lancashire and Peter Hu Kuo-chen. Ed. Edward J. Malatesta (St. Louis: Institute of Jesuit Sources, 1985).

[16] Ibid., 10.

[17] Ibid., 20. Cf. Translators' Introduction. 33–35. The first English translation by Douglas Lancashire and Peter Hu Kuo-chen is based on the first Chinese edition. In the present edition the term Lord of Heaven (*T'ien-chu*) is favored over the term *Shang-ti,* which Ricci freely employed with preference.

The Lord of Heaven and *Shang-ti* in Christianity and Confucianism

In the introduction to *The True Meaning of The Lord of Heaven*, Ricci grounds the Confucian principles of the Five Human Relationships (between king and minister, father and son, husband and wife, among brothers, and among friends) and the three Bonds (between king and minister, father and son, husband and wife) in terms of the Supremely Honored One who is not only worshiped but also mediated as the first Father and creator of all.[18]

As humans are created with the five basic virtues (humanity, righteousness, propriety, wisdom, and trustworthiness), Ricci argues that his universal teaching of the Lord of Heaven refers to the Lord of Heaven as the final and active cause, as well as the cause of our moral and virtuous life. In a scholastic framework, Ricci compares formal cause and material cause with the *yin* and *yang* principle. At this juncture, Ricci's hermeneutical strategy was to discover the early theism in ancient Chinese writings in the person of *Shang-ti*, or Lord on High.[19]

As to the question of how to understand the Lord of Heaven as the most universal and the most supreme cause, Ricci introduced a famous story of a Western Catholic sage, St Augustine, who met a child on the beach making a small pool in the ground. The child wanted to use a shell to scoop all the water from the sea to fill the pool. The sage questioned the silly child, but the child illumined him, saying that human understanding about the truth of Lord of Heaven is like the great, which cannot be drawn with a shell and a small pool cannot contain it.[20]

The Lord of Heaven transcends all categories, bringing in the material universe, and bringing in a *via negativa* (the apophatic way of God's truth). The human being, as a small and lowly vessel, cannot contain or investigate fully and adequately the great truth and mystery of the Lord of Heaven, who is the transcendental, unmoved One, the active cause of all movements, supreme source of all phenomena and source of goodness in creation. God the Creator is the God of providence who was revealed through the ancient Chinese canonical writings.[21]

The Confucian teaching of the Supreme Ultimate, according to which existence becomes the basic principle of all things, including sincerity (i.e.,

18 Ibid., 63.

19 Ibid., 85.

20 Ibid., 92–93.

21 Ibid., 97.

the subject of self-cultivation), was highly regarded and thought to be close to the teaching of the Lord of Heaven.[22] To the degree that Confucianism refutes void-ness or nothingness in Buddhism and Taoism, Ricci wanted to avoid the misunderstanding that the Lord of Heaven, the source of all, should be identified with nothingness. Ricci was aware that the Confucian term of the Supreme Ultimate, or reverence of the Sovereign on High, in ancient Chinese times, was related to the movement of *yin* and *yang* in the *Book of Changes* (*I Ching*).

Therefore, he was reluctant to harmonize the Supreme Ultimate (*T'ai-chi*) with the truth of the Lord of Heaven. The Supreme Ultimate, which is the first principle, is found in the appendices to the *Book of Changes*. All things emerge and are differentiated from the Supreme Ultimate.[23]

Chu-Hsi's thesis, in the *Commentary to the Diagrams of the Supreme Ultimate*, that "principle is not a thing," was not taken by Ricci to further a dialogue with his twofold understanding of the Lord of Heaven in terms of divine essence and divine attributes. If the divine essence or nature is not known and shared in all phenomenological aspects to us, Ricci should have paid attention to the Neo-Confucian idea—that the Supreme Ultimate is the Ultimateless—as more relevant to the apophatic dimension of divine nature in Christianity.[24]

It is certain that Confucius invoked Heaven in his time of distress. However, the notion of a deity in a personal sense had been transformed into the essence of human virtues in Confucian development. Citing Confucius in *Doctrine of the Mean* and several classics, Ricci affirmed that the Lord of Heaven is the Sovereign on High (*Shang-ti*) of the ancient Chinese writings. The Sovereign on High in Confucianism and the Lord of Heaven in Catholicism were the same; different for Ricci only in name.[25] Given this fact, Ricci's use of the ancient term *Shang-ti* would be exposed to total identification between Christianity and Confucianism.

22 Ibid., 99.

23 Ibid., 113. For instance, Chou Tun-yi (1017–1073) attempted to integrate into his Supreme reality the Taoist concept of Non-Being and the Buddhist idea of void-ness. He furthermore combined this with his theory of *Wu-hsing*, according to which the universe consists of five elements (metal, wood, water, fire, and earth). Against the Neo-Confucian framework, in which the Supreme Ultimate becomes ultimate-less or empty, Ricci argued that Neo-Confucianism had no difference from the teaching of Buddhism and Taoism.

24 Although Ricci agreed that there was profound reason concerning the teaching of the Supreme Ultimate and wanted to write another book for discussion, he was not able to do so. Ibid., 121.

25 Ibid., 125.

Catholic Theology of Virtue and Confucian Self-Cultivation

Ricci's hermeneutics in *The True Meaning of the Lord of Heaven* was to draw Confucianism close to Catholic Christianity and to repudiate Buddhism, Taoism and Neo-Confucianism. This functioned as a springboard for expounding the Confucian ideas of self-cultivation from his Catholic perspective.

In Confucian development, Mencius (supporter of the goodness of human nature) and Hsüan tzu (supporter of the badness of human nature) opposed each other diametrically on the issue of human nature. Although Confucius, in the *Analects,* used an important term, *T'ien-ming* (mandate of Heaven), with reverence and affirmed a personal God, Mencius articulated his understanding with emphasis on the human heart, in which Heaven is present within human nature, becoming the source and principle of ethical laws and values. In the writings of Hsüan-tzu, the existence of a supreme deity was denied. His attempt at demythologizing Heaven moved him closer to the *yin-yang* school or the Taoist-naturalistic stream.

In Ricci's interpretation, Confucianism recognized sincerity as the foundation for the rectification of the name, which is embedded with self-cultivation, the regulation of the family, the ordering of the state, and the bringing of peace to the world. The Confucian tradition affirms God's transcendence, as well as God's immanence in human morality. According to Neo-Confucianism, however, humanity, righteousness, decorum, and wisdom are essential characteristics of human nature, which comes from Heaven.

In siding with Mencius, Ricci stated that if the essence of human nature and feelings is produced by the Lord of Heaven and if reason is the master of them, then human beings are essentially good.[26] Ricci arranged humanity, righteousness, decorum, and wisdom as subsequent to the capacity to reason, while in Neo-Confucianism, *li,* the Absolute, is called *hsing* (nature) in human beings and *ming* (order, destiny, mandate of Heaven) in Heaven. The *li* is more than reason, although Ricci interpreted it as reason. Human beings have the capacity to reason as an innate ability to understand their existence.[27]

On the issue of evil, Ricci followed the Augustinian definition of "a lack of goodness" in the sense of "speaking of a lack of life."[28] Since

[26] Ibid., 351.

[27] Ibid., 351–53.

[28] Ibid., 353.

the Lord of Heaven bestowed this innate nature on human beings, one is capable of doing both good and evil. The true merit of virtue, when added to goodness, expresses this goodness. For Ricci it was important to distinguish between two kinds of goodness, that is, "innate goodness" and "acquired goodness." The former refers to the goodness of human nature while the latter to the goodness of virtue.[29] Merit is confined to acquired goodness, which humans accumulate through their own efforts.

According to Mencius, humanness (equated with humanity) is closely related to righteousness, which is taken up to the level of a cardinal virtue. Humanness and righteousness are essential ingredients of true humanity in that the former is the mind/heart of a human and the latter is its path. Therefore, humanness is rooted within the human mind/heart. Humans are by nature good. Evil comes from the formation of bad habits.

There are four beginnings (dispositions) in the human heart: a feeling of commiseration for others (the beginning of humanness), a feeling of shame and dislike of anything dishonorable (the beginning of righteousness), a feeling of modesty and yielding (the beginning of propriety), and a sense of right and wrong (the beginning of wisdom). People who were born with a good disposition, when cultivated like a shoot, "would grow up to be a beautiful blossoming tree" which is "full of expressed virtues."[30]

Relating the Mencius theory of the beginning to innate goodness, Ricci argued that meritorious virtues are granted to a person who does what is right. Ricci's strategy was to add the Catholic teachings of human nature and meritorious virtue, in a spiritual-habitual sense, to the Confucian teaching of superior man and self-cultivation. A virtue is "the precious adornment of the spirit," or the genuine treasures of the human inner spirit.[31] A person who cultivates virtue becomes more beautiful and sanctified, like a blossoming tree.

Ricci used the illustration of memory, intellect, and affection to clarify the virtue of the superior person, namely, humanity and righteousness. The intellect is to clarify what is right, while affection is based on humanity. This is because, for Ricci, "humanity is the essence of righteousness," or "the noblest of virtues."[32]

A person who is rich in humanity has to cultivate intellect through education or self-cultivation. At this juncture, Ricci inserted the Catholic

[29] Ibid., 357.

[30] Xinzhong Yao, *An Introduction to Confucianism*, 74–75.

[31] Ricci, *The True Meaning of the Lord of Heaven*, 357, 359.

[32] Ibid., 367.

teaching of sanctification or perfection, in accordance with the will of the Lord of Heaven, which means returning to one's origin.[33] The Confucian references to humanity and righteousness, in terms of loving others, were transformed into loving both the Lord of Heaven and humans.

The Lord of Heaven has engraved sage learning into the human mind. This statement refers to the Confucian teaching of the illustrious decrees of virtue and glory. The virtue is clouded by human selfish defilement and thus engulfed in darkness. People who learn to do good have to prepare themselves to cultivate and learn through all of life. The Jesuit's way of spiritual discipline combines spiritual learning and training with Confucian self-cultivation for increasing virtue.

Eventually the disciple attains the highest level of perfection and habitually has the Lord of Heaven in mind. This happens in the following way: feeling genuine and profound remorse over evil thoughts (contrition), purifying them from the mind, entering into harmony with the will of the Lord of Heaven, and, finally, being in union with the Lord of Heaven.[34] To explain this similarity between Catholic spiritual discipline and Confucian self-cultivation, Ricci quoted from the *Book of Changes*, in which the great and originating principle in the human being is called the first and chief quality of goodness.[35]

Ricci summed up his definition of humanity in terms of a biblical statement: love the Lord of Heaven and others as you love yourself on behalf of the Lord of Heaven (Matt 22:34–40, Mark 12:28–34, Luke 10:25–38).[36] Ricci interpreted this biblical statement to say that human charitable love makes the meritorious work of the Lord of Heaven known widely. Augustine's dictum serves as a good example: "Love the Lord of Heaven and do as you wish."[37]

With Christian love equated with Confucian humanity, Ricci fully appreciated the Confucian way of the virtuous life through self-cultivation toward the perfection of sagehood, in his Catholic sense. The Lord of Heaven makes use of rites and ceremonies as a means of bestowing grace, instructing people, strengthening faith, and being worshipped. This is the adoration and praising of the grace of the Sovereign on High.[38]

[33] Ibid., 369.

[34] Ibid., 375, 389.

[35] Ibid., 375.

[36] Ibid.

[37] Ibid., 383.

[38] Ibid., 389

In combining Catholic teaching with Confucian orthodox teaching, Ricci banned the Buddhist veneration of the image of the Buddha and Buddhist rituals as idolatry, since Taoism and Buddhism have no understanding of the Sovereign on High. Nevertheless, contrary to Ricci's judgment, the term Sovereign on High was used in religious Taoism to designate a popular deity.

What is interesting in his critique of Buddhism is Ricci's rejection of Amida faith, which is expounded in the *Mahayana Lotus Sutra of the Wonderful Law.* By overemphasizing the similarity between the Catholic teaching of meritorious virtue and the Confucian teaching of self-cultivation, Ricci misunderstood the universal compassion of Amida faith.[39]

Unlike Ricci's view, moral conduct in Amida Buddhism is not belittled, but done in gratitude to the gracious Other Power of Amida. Against the religious elite striving for higher morality, the Buddhist faith in Amida Buddha and in universal compassion for all has been preached in China since the 7th century.[40]

Given what has been discussed and analyzed, Ricci tried to attain the concordance between Lord of Heaven and *Shang-ti*, seeking the connecting point between Christianity and Confucianism, thus quoting the Chinese classics frequently for his mission purpose. For instance, where he dealt with the cultivation of virtue, he confirmed that the doctrine of Catholicism should be combined with that of Confucianism. Besides this, Ricci was quite aware of the existence of a supreme personal God, namely, the Sovereign of Heaven (*Shang-ti*) in ancient China. Therefore, he argued that the Lord of Heaven in Western Catholicism and God in China were identical, albeit with different names.

He criticized Chu Hsi's explanation of the Supreme Lord in terms of heaven and earth because Chu Hsi obscured the personal character of the Sovereign on High. In his Introduction to *The True Meaning of the Lord of Heaven,* Ricci noted that the ancient sage advised that the subject should be faithful to the ruler. Thus they cannot be faithful to two lords. According to the three Cardinal Guides, the ruler guides the subject. In

39 Ibid., 397–98.

40 Here a possible connection with Nestorian mission in China could be traced. Good works and religious practices come from faith in and gratitude for the primal promise of Amida Buddha. Francis Xavier recognized in the Japanese sect of Amida Buddhism the so-called "Lutheran heresy." Besides this, Karl Barth recognized in Amida Buddhism "a wholly providential disposition" to the Reformation. Karl Barth, *Church Dogmatics* 1.2: *The Doctrine of the Word of God*, trans. G. T. Thomson and Harold Knight (New York: T&T Clark, 2004) 340, 343.

his discussion of human nature, Ricci critically asked: how can heaven and earth have two lords?[41]

Ricci and Mission Strategy

From his missional strategy, we conclude that Ricci attempted to create a parallel between Catholicism and Confucianism as much as possible. When it came to complementing Confucianism, Ricci's strategy was to expel Buddhism, Taoism and Neo-Confucianism, then to complement Confucianism for the sake of Catholicism. That is to say, he wanted to expel the idols of Buddhism and Taoism and add something of Catholicism to the doctrine of Confucianism.

At this juncture, the differences between Catholicism and Confucian tradition were critiqued as Confucian shortcomings, wherein Confucianism should yield to Catholic teaching. Confucians talk about the retribution of good or evil only in terms of personal moral cultivation. Everyone should have self-cultivation or stick to morality only for the purpose of reaching one's inner moral fulfillment. In this sense, Confucian morality pursues a kind of inner transcendence without attachment to gain or loss. But what Catholics do for good is done, after all, for the Lord of Heaven, which is a kind of outer transcendence, and is based on reward merit.

In dealing with transcending and modifying Confucianism, Ricci argued that China's Confucianism should go back to its roots where its inner transcendence is connected with the theism of outer transcendence. The Confucian virtue of humanity is, in this regard, not to be properly understood without the love of the Sovereign on High. The Confucian teaching of the Five Cardinal Relationships is transformed and taken up in Ricci's strategy of the Love of the Lord of Heaven and others.

In Confucianism, one may reach the way of sagehood through one's own inner moral cultivation without the help of other powers on the outside. But for Ricci, one can hardly reach this culmination through one's own inner moral cultivation. One must be helped by the outer transcendent grace of God. Thus, it is necessary to believe in and worship God. Therefore, Ricci defended the doctrines of Catholicism over those of Confucianism.

Ricci found it necessary to make some revisions of Catholic doctrines to accommodate some of the Confucian ideas, in order to reach concordance with Confucian thought. The methods adopted by Ricci and his Chinese missionary group had already become an issue, argued both at

[41] Ricci, *True Meaning of the Lord of Heaven*, 391.

home and abroad. It was disputed with two objections. In practice, he was accused of paying too much attention to the Confucian elite instead of pushing the missionary cause forward. In theory, Ricci's positive evaluation of Confucianism ran the risk of sullying the purity of Christianity. Making the Christian Gospel dependent on Confucian culture could only be carried out by means of a hyphenated intercultural complementarity.

Ricci also made some revisions to the idea of sin, in order to more closely approach the idea of virtue in the Confucian tradition. As the idea of sin in Catholicism implies, human nature may be considered virtuous, which is not entirely different from the idea of human nature being virtuous in Confucian thought. Human nature is essentially good and cannot be destroyed after the fall. People who are determined to do good, turning from evil, have only to change their minds by exercising human will. The Lord of Heaven is sure to reward them through protection and support.[42]

Ricci's theology of will and merit fit into Gabriel Biel's nominalism: *Facere quod in se est* (Do what is in yourself). One's preparation for God's justification, apart from the aid of God's grace, can make the subsequent justification congruous or appropriate. On the basis of human good works, God is under obligation to reward those who do their best.

According to Biel, the *voluntas signi* is the declaration of God's will for creation, in which all human morality and justice consist in the will of God, which is known through God's *voluntas signi*. To the degree that *voluntas signi* is the ultimate and the rule for human moral behavior, natural law is the manifestation of God's eternal law.[43] Everyone, including the heathen, is by nature in a position to perform the first duty *facere quod in se est*. This moral act lies within the reach of natural human ability, apart from the aid of God's grace. The abhorrence of sin and the love of God is sufficient preparation for receiving God's grace, so that God's grace is the fruit of human moral action, not the root of it. This semi-merit also has to be accepted as worthy of its reward, like the full merit *de condigno*. Therefore, God rewards all who do their very best.[44]

Rather than Augustinian and Thomist frameworks of human will and grace, Ricci expounded on a nominalistic-semi-pelagian basis his theology of human motives and morality: 1) doing good to reach Heaven and to

[42] Ibid., 447.

[43] Heiko A.Oberman, *The Harvest of Medieval Theology: Gabriel Biel and Late Medieval Nominalism* (Cambridge: Harvard University Press, 1963) 104.

[44] Ibid., 140–41.

avoid Hell, 2) doing good to repay the Lord of Heaven, and 3) doing good to harmonize with the will of the Lord of Heaven.[45]

Preaching and adding the medieval scholastic theology of merit and reward to Confucian moral philosophy, Ricci invalidated the idea of a life-style based on grace and non-attachment in ancient Chinese wisdom. Confucian self-cultivation, which basically has nothing to do with reward and merit, was modified and transformed by Ricci into a theology of the heavenly Banker who rewards according to human deeds, and, finally, in terms of Heaven and Hell.[46]

Using the missiosnal strategy of accommodation, and coincidence, and transformation, Matteo Ricci preached the doctrines of Catholicism for the purpose of connecting Western Christianity with Confucianism. Regardless of whether his attempt was successful or not, he was the first Western missionary to make such a complementarity of hermeneutical and historical importance.

Matteo Ricci and The Rites and Terms Controversies: A Lesson from the Past

The concern for culture on the part of Christian mission is long-standing, as we see in Gregory I's instruction to Augustine of England in 596. The letter exchanged between the Pope and the pioneer missionary became a classic document concerning the issue of the necessity of contextualization of the Gospel. The pope advised not to destroy the good things of Anglo-Saxon culture, but to utilize the heathen temples for spreading the Gospel to England. It was recommended to adapt the temple for worshipping the true God. Appointing festivals for the people, the pope insisted that slaying cattle should be done in honor of God instead of honoring the devil. The mission strategy the pope endorsed is characterized by "go[ing] upward step by step and piece by piece."[47]

In the work of the first missionary to China (in 635) we see a creative, yet controversial synthesis (*panchia*) of Taoism and Buddhism into the Christian Gospel. From "The Stone Sutra," which was originally erected in 781 in honor of the Da Qin Luminous religion of Christianity throughout China, we read about a Christian attempt at appropriating the Taoist and

[45] Ricci, *True Meaning of the Lord of Heaven*, 313.

[46] Ibid., 297, 303, 313.

[47] Pope Gregory the Great, "Letter to Augustine," in Bede, *Ecclesiastical History of the English Nation* (601) 1:30; quoted in *Classic Texts in Mission & World Christianity*, ed. Norman E. Thomas (Maryknoll: Orbis,1995) 22.

Buddhist religious terms and content for the sake of Christian mission. It recounted the arrival of the monk Alopen, probably from Persia, during the T'ang Dynasty in China.[48] Its discovery in 1625 occurred during the sojourn of Matteo Ricci in China.

Matteo Ricci's mission strategy, together with Ruggieri, was to adapt to local habits, customs, cultural patterns of morality, and indigenous beliefs. It was natural for them to immerse themselves in the study of Chinese language and culture. In Ricci's model of evangelism, based on friendship, we are aware of how, intellectually, Ricci understood friendship as a chief virtue by taking it as a springboard for an effective presentation of the Gospel. In his first book, *A Treatise on Friendship,* the dialogue takes the form of the prince asking Ricci about the meaning of Western thought of friendship. Ricci responds to him with all that he knows about European philosophers and saints.[49]

His life is characterized according to the statement that he lived a life of friendship and died as a martyr of friendship.[50] Ricci's sensitivity to people of other cultures lay in his recognition of ancestral rites. When food was offered to the dead, the Chinese showed affection and gratitude in the same way that Europeans laid flowers at a grave. The dead had no power to smell and taste. Ricci's option for acculturation and friendship evangelism won some significant converts from the Confucian elite, including the famous three: Hsü Kuang-ch'i (Paul), who held the office of Grand Secretary, which was comparable to that of prime minister; Li Chih-tsao (Leo), Ricci's collaborator in several publications on religion and science; and Yang T'ing-yün (Michael).

Even the emperor K'ang-his (1662–1723), in the subsequent Ch'ing dynasty (1644–1911), studied Ricci's writing for six months and issued the edict of toleration in March 1692. It was accepted that the principles of Catholicism were compatible with the Confucian view of morality. The 16th century Sino-Western relationship, unlike later Western incursions, was mutually respectful and friendly. This was when the first Catholic mission in China was founded.

However, other Catholic orders (such as the Dominicans and the Franciscans) were strongly against such compromises. They walked through the streets holding up crucifixes, not hesitant to proclaim that all

48 Martin Palmer, *The Jesus Sutras: Recovering the Lost Scrolls of Taoist Christianity* (New York: Ballantine, 2001) 204–32.

49 Cronin, *The Wise Man from the West,* 122.

50 Ralpf R. Covell, *Confucius, The Buddha, and Christ: A History of the Gospel in Chinese* (Maryknoll: Orbis, 1986) 45.

Chinese emperors were burning in hell. Denouncing the Jesuit method of adaptation as protective mimicry, they complained to Rome. The veneration of Confucius and dead ancestors was declared superstitious without qualification. Even the homage paid to Confucius after graduation and offerings on the graves of the dead were denounced. Filial piety in Chinese culture was prohibited.[51]

Nicola Longobardi, Ricci's successor, opposed the mission policy of acculturation. The so-called Rites Controversy involved eight popes and leading universities in Europe for seventy years. Those who were more tolerant of Chinese rites favored greater cultural adaptation, declaring the rites to be non-religious. Others, who opposed such acculturation, denounced these rites as a practice of superstitious paganism. The Jesuits who were working with the Confucian elite opted for acculturation, while Franciscans or Dominicans, working by and large with peasants, opposed it.

Ricci's approval of the Chinese rite manifested his way of inculturating and incorporating Confucian respect for ancestors into the way of the Gospel, including liturgy and catechesis from Western categories. Concerning the veneration of figures like Confucius, Ricci took an accommodation approach in which he thought of the ancestral rite as a way of strengthening filial piety instead of promoting idol worship. Ricci utilized natural theology in terms of his dialogical strategy, in which the Christian idea of God was rendered as the Confucian idea of *Shang-ti*. However, the Rites and Terms Controversies remained a stumbling block to the survival and growth of Christianity in China.

Behind this controversy, there was the painful experience of Francis Xavier who reached India in 1542 and by 1549 had arrived in Japan. For him, Japanese mission was the springboard for the conversion of China to Roman Catholicism. The Jesuits in Japan were good at accommodating their Christian faith and ritual practice to the indigenous culture in Japan. Xavier's mistake of translating *Deus* as *Dainichi*[52] was instrumental in creating tension between the accommodation approach of the Jesuits and the *tabula rasa* approach of other missionary orders.

[51] Cronin, *Wise Man From the West*, 267–69.

[52] Francis Xavier preached the *Dainichi* upon his arrival on Japan. From a Yajiro, or Nanjiro, a Japanese escapee to India, with little education, Xavier was misinformed that *Dainichi* would be equivalent to the Christian idea of *Deus*. However, this term in the Japanese language signifies one of the local deities, the human sex organs! After scandalizing people, Xavier returned to places where he had preached before, shouting, "Do not pray to Dainichi." David Chung, *Syncretism*, 102.

Regarding the Terms Controversy, Ricci's strategy was to find, in the most ancient tradition of China, terms for God, *Shang-ti* (Sovereign on High) and *T'ien* (Heaven). Ricci's strategy encouraged the Confucians to go back to their ancient beliefs in God. This was Ricci's backbone of *ad fontes*, which was behind his theology of accommodation. We already observed that he called attention to *T'ien* and *Shang-ti*, which were used by Confucius and in the ancient Chinese classics.

However, given the historically fatal mistake of Xavier, who chose the Japanese *Dainichi* to translate the Latin *Deus*, a safer path between Ricci's associates and conservative missionaries was to use the term *T'ien chu* (The Lord of Heaven) to signify God. Although this term has roots in Taoism and Buddhism, *T'ien chu* (literally meaning Master of Heaven), compared with *T'ien* and *Shang-ti*, was preferred as the equivalent to the Christian term of God. For the more fundamentalist-minded, *Deusu* (Latin: *Deus*) was preferred in Japan. However, *Deusu* sounded like *dai-uso*, in Japanese, which means "big lie."[53]

The Jesuit's theology of probabilism, which is associated with a positive attitude toward human nature and culture, was seriously opposed by Jansenist theology, which retained its more negative attitude toward human nature and culture. This conflict became visible regarding the issue of God's name, participation in funerals, and ancestor veneration.[54]

As I have already pointed out, Ricci interpreted China's Confucian tradition in order to link Christianity and Chinese culture. Naturally, he knew clearly that there were many differences and dissimilarities between Confucianism and Catholicism. He probably would have dealt with these by complementing Confucianism and transcending and modifying Confucianism, as well as by transforming Christian ideas. Therefore, he had to make some revisions of Catholic doctrines in order to make Christianity more consonant with Chinese tradition.

In Ricci's books, there are many signs of the Catholic stance against idolatry; the criticism of Buddhist idolatry is particularly strong.[55] However,

53 Cf. Julia Ching, *Chinese Religions*, 193.

54 Stephen B. Bevans and Roger P. Schroeder, *Constants in Context,* 193. Jansenism, named after Cornelius Jansen, returned to the original and genuine Augustinian tradition against the Thomistic Dominicans, while the Jesuits opposed this movement on behalf of human freedom associated with probabilism, according to which human action is encouraged to follow the probable opinion, despite that the opposite opinion would be more probable. Cf. Paul Tillich, *A History of Christian Thought*, ed. Carl E. Braaten (Evanston: Harper & Row, 1968) 222–23.

55 Cf. Matteo Ricci, *China in the Sixteenth Century*, 99.

he never criticized Confucian offerings to the sage, nor did he criticize Chinese offerings to their ancestors. The veneration by the Confucian literati of a figure of Confucius in a grand Confucian temple and the literati's offering sacrifices to him four times every year were not regarded as idolatrous acts. Chinese rites were first of all instituted for the benefit of the living rather than for the dead. The practice of placing food on the graves of the dead seemed to be free from any superstition and beyond any charge of sacrilege. For the converts Ricci recommended "to replace this custom with alms for the poor and for the salvation of souls."[56]

However, the acculturation dispute was reported to the Pope in Rome. Clement XI. Maillard de Tournon, the Patriarch of Antioch, came to China as the Pope's envoy. As a conservative, he had already condemned the Malabar rites of India, which the Jesuit Robert de Nobili had supported. The Jesuits in China appealed to a written document from the Chinese emperor, K'ang-his, for proof.

As the emperor stated in it,

> Honors are paid to Confucius not as a petition for favors, intelligence or high office but as to a Master, because of the magnificent moral teaching that he has left to posterity. As for the ceremony in honor of dead ancestors, it originates in the desire to show filial piety. According to the customs observed by Confucians, this ceremony contains no request for help; it is practiced only to show filial respect to the dead. Souls of ancestors are not held to reside in the tablets; these are only symbols that serve to express gratitude and keep the dead in memory, as though they were actually present.[57]

Emperor K'ang-hsi granted an edict of toleration to Christians in China. After Ricci died in 1610, there were still about 2500 believers in China. There were 200,000 Catholics in China in 1700.[58] However, the Emperor was less impressed by Tournon's policy and quite insulted by the fact that the Pope in Rome regarded himself as an authority over Chinese matters. In a decree of 1704, Pope Clement XI banned the use of the terms *T'ien* and *Shang-ti* as designations for God. He gave orders that Chinese Catholics should not follow traditional Chinese rites that did not conform

[56] Ibid., 96.

[57] Cronin, *Wise Man from the West*, 268.

[58] Donald W. Treadgold, *The West in Russian and China: Religion and China: Religious and Secular Thought in Modern Times* (Cambridge: Cambridge University Press, 1973) chs.1–2.

to Catholicism. Obviously, offering sacrifices to Confucius, as well as to ancestors, was declared idolatry and superstition; Confucius himself was denounced as a public idolater and a private atheist.

In 1742 Pope Benedict XIV, in his decree *Ex quo singulari*, condemned the Chinese rite and opposed the Jesuits' mission of acculturation definitively. Against imperial Catholicism, an imperial edict in 1724 also banned Christianity from the country.[59]

After the Vatican dissolved the Society of Jesus, Protestant missionaries came to knock on the door of China. They did not catch up with the intellectual prowess and moral integrity of the Jesuit missionaries. The missionaries in the nineteenth and twentieth centuries could not match the intellectual quality and religious openness of the earlier missionaries. In 1939, during the Second World War, almost two centuries after *Ex quo singulari,* Pope Pius XII reversed the decision of 1742, authorizing Chinese rites for Chinese Christians.

Ricci was successful in opening the doors of China to Christianity. However, his legacy is talked about in a positive way as well as in a negative way. For evangelicals, Ricci is accused of diluting the meaning of the Gospel and is even indicted as the champion for Christian-Confucian syncretism. For progressively minded Asians, the Jesuit mission in China is seen even as trickery, deception and expedience.[60]

Although Ricci took a positive stance on ancestral rites, his hostile position against Buddhism and Taoism remains a problem. Establishing natural theology only for ancient Confucianism was related to his political strategy for gaining the powerful class of the Confucian literati. Hence, his accommodation principle remained paralyzed in matters of tolerating other religions, such as Buddhism and Taoism. How do we understand Ricci's attack upon Neo-Confucianism? He played classical Confucianism against Neo-Confucianism, wherein he opposed the pantheistic imprint of the Buddhist worldview.

However, it would be out of the question to separate Neo-Confucianism from earlier Confucianism. Chu Hsi's notion of the Great Ultimate (*T'ai-chi*), which functions like the Form of the Good in Platonism, demonstrated a possibility for conversing with the Christian concept of God.[61] Besides this, in Chu Hsi's thought, the Great Ultimate,

59 Julia Ching, *Chinese Religions*, 193–94.

60 Joseph Levenson, *Confucian China and Its Modern Fate* (London: Routledge and Kegan Paul, 1958) 121.

61 Julia Ching, *Chinese Religions*, 160.

called the Heavenly principle, possesses a personal character as "creator and organizer of the universe."[62]

According to Ricci, the Buddhists and the Taoists had corrupted the notion of the Supreme Being in ancient China. This corruption remained a problem in Neo-Confucianism. Ricci's evaluation incited many attacks from Neo-Confucianism and Buddhism. Because of his scholastic training and limitations, Ricci was not capable of adequately understanding the concepts of *T'ai-ch'i*, *Li*, and *Ch'i* in the Chu Hsi school of Neo-Confucianism, the Taoist notion of *Wu* as permanent *Tao*, or the Buddhist *Sunyata* (Emptiness) as the non-dual principle. Nevertheless, Ricci's legacy will remain a springboard for his followers to improve upon his limitations in terms of engaging the wisdom of other religions.

Conclusion

The question of how culture and the Gospel meet and interact includes intercultural tension. The culture that receives the Gospel is called to a profound transformation of its nature, as conversely the meaning of the Gospel is also expanded in the process of inculturation. A vision of God working in all things and in all cultures does not mean non-resistance to culture. Every culture, as a human achievement, is both a source of creativity and a means of imprisonment. The essential attitude is to call for a renewal of cultures in the light of God's reconciliation with the world in Jesus Christ.

What does an evangelizing strategy mean in terms of inculturation? It involves dialogue and recognition of a culture through the Gospel. In light of God's reconciliation, we are summoned to a profound, humble encounter with culture and life's depths from which we attentively listen to God's irregular grace in other wisdoms. Inculturation refers to Christian witness to the Gospel, both in terms of incarnating into and transforming a culture. The theological presupposition of the incarnation, that Christ assumes human flesh, becomes the basis for Christian witness to assume humanity in every culture. Nevertheless, Christ is not a prisoner of human culture.

Ricci's accommodation approach indicates that there is a dichotomy between natural theology in China and revealed theology in Europe. Gottfried Leibniz proposed an exchange of missionaries between Europe and China. As his suggestion we read that "Chinese missionaries should be

[62] Cf. Julia Ching, *The Religious Thought of Chu Hsi* (Oxford: Oxford University Press, 2000) 70.

sent to us to teach us the aim and practice of natural theology as we send missionaries to them to instruct them in the revealed religion."[63]

In the Catholic tradition, faith and reason were conceptualized in mutual dependence: a knowledge of God is found in creation, acquired by natural knowledge. God can be known through demonstrative arguments in terms of a relation of cause and effect.[64] God continues preservation in the life of creation because all things depend on God for their continued existence. Hence, this natural knowledge offers a foundation for the knowledge of God revealed in the Bible. The knowledge of God, in terms of natural reason, makes Christian faith intellectually possible.

However, in the context of National Socialism, we should not forget that natural theology, in consonance with German Nazi ideology, was severely distorted and misused toward genocide. Pope Pius XII's endorsement of an alliance between natural theology and the ideology of National Socialism generated a fatal mission against the Jews. The political danger of Christian natural theology must come to terms with the prevailing political status quo. The demarcation of natural theology from revealed theology makes and establishes human culture as the independent order of creation sanctioned by God.[65]

If Ricci believed that God revealed Godself through the name of *T'ien* or *Shang-ti* in ancient Chinese culture, should he not have taken more seriously God's universal reign for all, rather than sorting out wisdom and natural reason in Chinese classics as the independent points of connection for consonance with God? Instead of rationalizing Chinese Confucian philosophy as independent natural revelation, should he not have deemed such wisdom (together with Buddhism and Taoism!), more dynamically, as analogical witnesses to God in light of God's reconciliation in Jesus Christ with the world? Ricci's understanding of Jesus Christ reveals a dysfunctional view of mission, so that his attempt at accommodation centers only on theism in Christian-Confucian relations.[66]

63 Arnold Rowbotham, *Missionary and Mandarin* (New York: Russell and Russell, 1966) 252.

64 Cf. Thomas Aquinas, *Summa Theologiae*, Ia.2.2.

65 Hans Kung, *Does God Exist? ?: An Answer for Today* (Garden City, NY: Doubleday, 1980) 513–15. In the statement of the First Vatican Council in 1870 we read: " If anyone says that the one true God, our Creator and Lord, cannot be known with certainty by the natural light of reason from created things, he is to be condemned." Cited from Hans Kung, *Does God Exist?*, 510.

66 Ricci, *True Meaning of The Lord of Heaven*, 449–53.

If all creatures are masks of God, God definitely speaks to us through the wisdom of other religions and cultures. Theology of the cross does not negate God's universal reign but makes it more explicit and sober in matters of limitation and corruption in cultural life. Every attempt at evangelizing culture (in addition to preaching the Gospel to individuals) emphasizes communitarian aspects of mission. The word of God's reconciliation is capable of affecting and breaking into the human criteria of judgment, determining values, points of interest, and models of life that are in contrast to the Word of God. God's kenotic way in Jesus Christ, in which Jesus appears as a friend of sinners, is the hermeneutical criteria of discernment in analyzing cultural tradition in terms of emancipation.

In the process of inculturation, the Gospel brings a prophetic challenge to every culture to remove all those things that are in contrast to the justice of God's reign and partisanship with the poor. The Gospel is the internal basis for inculturation, as inculturation is the existential basis for dialogue between a living people and the living Gospel.

In East Asia particularly, cultures had been formed by other religions, such as Confucianism, Buddhism, Taoism and Shamanism. Any dialogue with culture in Asia would entail no less than a profound study of, dialogue with, and recognition of the other world religions, which have shaped and influenced the life and mindset of Asian people. In this exploration, we acknowledge the inseparability of the three realms of justice, culture, and inter-religious dialogue.

The Christian message is to be open to all cultures, bound to no single culture, and made accessible to every human person through the process of inculturation. Through this process, the Gospel introduces something new into the culture and the culture brings something new to the richness of the Gospel. The church's very mission is to embody the Gospel in different cultures, enriching thereby the culture, but also being enriched in the process. Jesus Christ, in the Gospel, is involved in on-going creation, assumption, renewal, and transformation in interaction with the world of human life. Hence the Gospel would be richer, and we would know more of it, if more Asians truly embraced it and brought a Confucian, Hindu, Buddhist, or Taoist lens to read it, as early Christians read it through the lens of Greco-Roman society. Christological treatment of the Gospel and culture does not run counter to an anthropological treatment but prevents it from anthropological reductionism.

As the Gospel content is encultured in the process of on-going incarnation, God's on-going involvement in the life of cultures (*creatio continua*) and God's reconciliation with the world through Jesus Christ provide a basis for inculturating the Gospel and evangelizing the culture. The model of "faith as a kernel and culture as a husk" can be renewed and transformed to the point where God's mission is engrafted into a particular culture, yet without violating its mysterious transcendence over culture. In other words, any particular culture cannot monopolize the Gospel, which comes from God who loves the world in freedom. God's on-going activity directs, transforms, and unifies cultural expressions of the Gospel toward the prolepsis of God. Culture is changing, creative, and dynamic, and it is in need of self-renewal for serving God's universal reign.

Inculturation finds its locus dynamically in relation to the eschatological tension of justification (*simul justus et peccator*), rather than remaining an accomplished fact. Western theologies, in which their understanding of the Gospel is also culturally conditioned, need the exchange of interculturation or a multilateral relationship with non-Western theologies, turning away from their Babylonian captivity of the past.[67]

God, in the Bible, is pleased to have blessed Abraham through Melchizedek. God wants to help Israel through Cyrus. As God likes to communicate Godself through Jesus Christ for the world, so God likes to communicate Godself through God's people outside the walls of the Christian church. From reconciliation toward consummation, the inculturation of the Gospel progresses in a dynamic and creative way. In so doing, it defends itself from the danger of the absolutism of contextualism.

[67] Cf. Bosch, *Transforming Mission*, 456.

19

The Korean Self-Understanding of God from the Perspective of *Donghak* and Its Thought of the God Experience*

Kim Kyoung-Jae

I propose an understanding of *Donghak*'s "God-experience," which is typical of Korean spirituality. Chon Do religion inherited the legacy of *Donghak*, and was proclaimed by Son Byung-Hee, who played a major role in renaming and restructuring *Donghak* as the Chon Do religion in 1905. It is worth noticing that *Donghak* thought highlights quintessential Korean religious thought and the Korean God-experience in a typical and unique way.

Seen from a religious-cultural perspective, Korea can be likened to a great lake, the final destination towards which the world religions stream. From the beginning, Korea was a religiously pluralistic society in which there was an influx of various religious thoughts in process of self-realization, which were in constant and endless interaction with each other. Hermeneutically speaking, Gadamer uses the term "fusion of horizons" to describe this. This fusion of horizons is not meant to be a phenomenon of religious syncretism. Rather, it presents itself as a kind of growth in which each religion maintains its respective unique character and essence. It is compared to the constant growth of tree, taking in the general environment around it and contributing fertilizing elements at the same time.

What determines the typological character of religion is related to how the religion understands its ultimate reality. From a Christian perspective, a doctrine or view of God is foundational. According to a great philosopher in South-Korea, Park-Jong Hong, "the backbone of *Donghak*

* Translated and edited by Paul S. Chung.

is a crystal in which the quintessence of all our traditional thoughts are united and are put into amalgam".[1] Therefore, God-understanding in *Donghak* does not merely stop at an exploration of Korean people's view of God. Rather, it means an investigation of the religious mindset and patterns of the God-experience toward which Korean people as a nation orient themselves.

As Gadamer suggests, the emergence of new creative thought is an individual's original idea and at the same time, a creative process emerging out of the consciousness of effective history (*Wirkungsgeschichte*), which influences the individual's existence. In this regard it is worth noting that in the God experience for Su Woon, the founder of *Donghak*, the view of God is his subjective and unique experience (*Erlebnis* rather than *Erfahrung* in German terminology), and simultaneously his God-experience is influenced by the effective consciousness of Korean religious history, regardless of whether or not he accepted it. Furthermore, God-experience is presented as a transforming idea, critically overcoming and denying tradition.

According to Gadamer, the concept of "consciousness of effective history" refers to human consciousness with humans functioning as both understanding subject and the creator. Every human spiritual activity of creation, from literature to the understanding of historical events, stands always under the influence of the tradition in which human beings live their lives.[2] Thus the Gadamerian concept of consciousness of effective history is more profound than the so-called historical consciousness of human beings. The former does not function possessively in the stage of awakening of human consciousness; rather, it functions in the formation of human consciousness, as the pre-understanding, so that it effects a person's values and goals in life.

When we take into consideration the elements of consciousness of effective history in constituting the God-understanding and experience of Choi Su-Woon, a founder of *Donghak* thought, it includes the various and complex religious traditions and ideas of Korea. For instance, the following are notable in Choi's God-experience: faith in God as foundational at the heart of the Korean people as a nation since ancient times, the spirit-wind spirituality of Pung Ryu Do, the Ch'i philosophy of Neo-Confucianism, the *yin-yang* way of cosmogenic destiny, the Hua-Yen Buddhist view of

1 Park-Jong Hong, "A Study of Choi Soo-Woon," *Festschrift in Honor of Choi Soo-Woon's 150th birthday*, (published by the Association of Korean thought) in *Korean Thought* 12 (November, 1974).

2 Hans-Georg Gadamer, *Truth and Method* (New York: Crossroad, 1982) 305–10.

reality in Mahayana Buddhism, and the Shamanistic technique of healing with and experience of descending spirits, etc.

However, *Donghak* does not mix all the above-mentioned elements in a religiously syncretistic way, to the point where there exists only an amalgamation without organic vitality. On the contrary, all these elements are sublimated as kinds of spiritual fertilizers in Choi-Su Woon's life and social experience. They, in turn, manifest themselves as vital forces and creative-emergent phenomena by being integrated into the embodiment of his living and subjective God-experience, revelation-experience, and ecstasy of religious experience. In what follows, I will deal with some characteristics of the God-experience in *Donghak*'s thought.

God's Indwelling in Human Body: The Principle of *Ch'i* in Terms of Monism and the Idea of Si Chun Ju (Waiting on the Indwelling of the Heavenly Lord)[3]

The core idea of *Donghak* consists in Choi Su-Woon's confession of his living God-experience. As for the first characteristic, which he experienced as the ultimate reality, it is not Heaven, the mandate of Heaven, the principle Law, *Tao*, or Dharma. Instead, it is experienced, evidenced, and confessed as God, the heavenly Lord, in a more personal sense. In his explanation of accepting and serving God with honor, Choi Su-Woon elaborated on this dimension in three moments: the existence of the God-spirit intra, the energizing of *ch'i* toward the extra, and everyone's knowing of the truth that cannot be replaced.

The existence of the God-spirit intra means that human beings, as subjects of the God-experience, bear God subjectively as the object, like a woman bears a baby in her womb. To take this a step further, it purports to be an experiential awareness in which divine power springs up from within and transforms individual life in fullness of God's spirit. In a Christian expression, it can be compared to the work of the Holy Spirit, bringing human life to fullness through the indwelling of the human body as its temple (1 Cor 6:18).

From the extra perspective, *ch'i* is externalized, which indicates divine force in its fullness. The life force of vitality in the human body is subjectively not captured in human life, so it is unlike divine "thingness" or

[3] [Editor's note: in recent ecumenical dialogue, theosis-justification between the Lutheran and Greek Orthodox churches converges in this technical term "indwelling." It seems to me that *Si Chun Ju* articulates God's dynamic indwelling in the human heart rather than the passive human "waiting on."]

something that is locally limited. Rather, the idea of the externalizing of *ch'i* connects human life to the whole cosmic network, and enables human beings to experience unity with everything that surrounds them. This is what Choi said about bearing God in the human body.

The God-experience, in this regard, is experienced by everyone who is awakened. Its meaning lies in realizing God as the source of life and creator of *ch'i*'s indwelling in the cosmos, so that human beings cannot separate God from life. In other words, God is not subjectively at human disposal nor does God become objective "thingness" under human manipulation. The God-experience which Choi Su-Woon kept in *Donghak* refers to the experience of God as an immanently transcendental reality, which he terms *Si Chun Ju*.[4] This refers to God who, as the divine force, enlivens and awakens human life as the body itself. Knowledge of *ch'i* and of God is different expressions of the same ultimate reality.

God as the Growing and Renewing One in the Experience of *Novum*: Panentheism and the Idea of the Fostering Heavenly Lord

The successor of *Donghak*, Choi Si-Hyung (1827–1898), inherited the tradition of faith in the God-experience. He radicalized his forerunner's ideas towards a more provocative idea of the 'Yang' of the heavenly Lord, namely the principle of fostering of the heavenly Lord. Thus his idea looks like panentheism, which would be closer to pantheism.[5] What is characteristic of panentheism lies in the understanding that God and the cosmos are interrelated, interdependent, inter-penetrating, and inter-complementary.

Although it is a characteristic of panentheism, like theism, to regard God as the ultimate reality, the object of faith and awe which must be revered, worshipped and praised, panentheism, unlike theism, denies a transcendental God who existed antecedently from the beginning beyond the cosmos. In other words, it does not identify the cosmos with God, nor believe that God exists transcendently apart from the cosmos. Furthermore,

[4] [Editor's note: it means literally "waiting on the indwelling of the heavenly Lord in the human heart."]

[5] [Editor's note: panentheism means a position of criticizing and sublimating both transcendental theism, which emphasizes God's transcendence, while pantheism identifies God with the cosmos for the sake of God's dynamic involvement with the world without losing God's transcendence over the world.]

God is not self-fulfilled, not a self-satisfying being *a se*, but enjoys and experiences the process of the *novum* of the cosmos.

The tenor of panentheism after Choi Si-Hyng is infused without constraint into the traditional God-experience of Korean people who have lived in harmony and unity with nature in terms of an agricultural mode of life and production. We can say that Choi Si-Hyung's idea of *Donghak* would belong—from the perspective of its form—to a similar category as the panentheism of Whiteheadian process philosophy.[6] On the basis of his forerunner's view of the God-experience, Choi Si-Hyung proclaimed an attitude of religious life in more practical way. With more of an emphasis on God's immanence in mind, he spoke of the idea of "one eating Heaven through Heaven."

In a sermon in 1885 he stated: "Therefore the universe is a spiritual being in an organic whole, and the spiritual being works in harmony. The living world is the actualizing manifestation of the living spirit, *Hananim* (the personal God in Korean terminology). Is it only human beings who wait on the indwelling of *Chun-ju* (the Heavenly Lord)? All the universe waits on the indwelling of *Chun-ju* as well. It is the principle of the universe, so that one eats *Chun* (Heaven) through *Chun* (Heaven). Therefore, if you hurt or injure a sentient living creature without reason, or do any harm to one living thing, it means that the heavenly Lord injures the heavenly Lord." [7]

From this statement, we know that Chun Do religion, by inheriting the principle of *Donghak*, promulgated publicly the idea of "humans are heaven" as quintessential. However, the idea of identifying humans with heaven is an expression of the third generation of the *Donghak* movement whose initiator was Son Byung-Hee, the third successor. In the canonical writings of *Donghak* and the *Yong Dam Narratives*, there appears no such term as identifying humans with heaven immediately. The idea of identifying humans with heaven can be rather a religious-philosophical expression regarding the idea of waiting on the indwelling of the heavenly Lord, or the fostering of the heavenly Lord in the cosmic web of all living life.

At this point, we can gingerly notice that the God-experience of the founding father, Choi, which was living and vivid, and included a dynamic experiential vitality of relation between the heavenly Lord and human beings, would be transformed, to the degree that the idea of identification

6 Alfred North Whitehead, *Process and Reality* (New York: Free Press, 1978) 342–51.

7 Choi Dong-Hee, *History of Korean Religious Thought, vol. 3: Chun Do Religion and Won-Buddhism* (Seoul: Yun Sei University Press, 1993) 54.

appears as a universal religious truth and principle. Metaphorically speaking, the early faith of Choi Su-Wun and his idea of "waiting on of indwelling of the heavenly Lord" became like the seed of tornado occurring in the midst of the Southern Pacific occident, and this was changed into a storm with a powerful tornado through an idea like "eating (or fostering) the heavenly Lord" and "embodying the heavenly lord" and "eating the heavenly lord through the heavenly lord."

Finally, by the time of the third generation of Son Byung-Hee's *Donghak*, this became institutionalized as the principle of the identification of humans with heaven in a religious-philosophical manner, in which its powerful and dynamic character was changed into low temperature air without the power of a tornado. It goes without saying that Son Byung-Hee did not deny the idea of waiting on of the indwelling of the heavenly Lord as the core principle of *Donghak*. Nevertheless, I would say that that the core and quintessence of *Donghak* is grounded in one's waiting on the indwelling of the heavenly Lord rather than on an idea of total identification.

Hananim as Sovereign Lord and the Principle As Such: Non-Action as Harmonization and the Principle of Non-Duality

In the last chapter of the canon of Dong Hak, Choi Su-Woon said the following about the non-duality principle.

> "Therefore, what is necessarily difficult is" our saying that it is "not" and what is easy to judge is 'saying that it is so'. Seen from a far distance, the thing is that it is not, not, not. But seen from the perspective of the creator, it is so, so, so.[8]

It would be a leap of logic, if I draw immediately a logic of "unity in contradiction" from a hermeneutical perspective. But in this principle of non-duality, as Choi Soo-Woon stated explicitly, there is a rational and intellectual dimension of "it is so," when it comes to the explanation of change and form in the universe by human sensible knowledge and by the judgmental capacity of human reason. However, a rational explanation would amount to a dead end, when it comes to critically asking about the source of life. This is the origin of maternal instinct, the origin of the heart in gratitude to mercy, the constant order of change in the weather, the on-

[8] Cf. For the teaching of non-duality, see *The Great Canon of Dong Hak*, a chapter of non-duality principle.

tological source of law and movement in all. From here it follows that "it is not so." This phenomenon of contradiction would lead to a great affirmation of unity in contradiction, seen from the viewpoint of the creator.

The logic of unity in contradiction comes from Nicholas Cusa (1401–1464), according to whom the *finitum* of human reason is *non capax infiniti*. Yet, insofar as human reason possesses finite consciousness, it paradoxically takes part in infinitude partially and indirectly. Because all finitude is based on and rooted in the ontological capacity of the infinite, finitude is reflective of the infinite. Therefore, the infinite manifests itself through finitude as a sacramental medium.[9]

According to *Donghak*, non-action leads to harmony in which the ultimate reality is to be seen as such. The ultimate realty as the creator means the personal Absolute, seen in terms of "waiting on the indwelling of the heavenly lord." In other words, creation and evolutionary emergence are not two, but one. Unity in contradiction is the logic of experiencing empirically and holistically that the infinite and the finite, the absolute and the relative, eternity and time, creator and the principle, *Hananim* and all, creation and evolution are paradoxically integrated into a monistic structure of two different polarities. This is a featured element in *Donghak*'s thought. This is true not only to *Donghak*, but also to the highest level of all religions, because religion is not merely a rational world, but a world of paradox and mystery.

If *Donghak* is a manifestation of the Korean religious mindset, a biblical witness to God who is one God and Father of all, and who is above all and through all and in all (Eph 4: 6) is not totally different from *Hananim*, as *Donghak* bears witness to it and experiences it. There is no sense on the part of Christianity to have a religiously exclusive attitude toward it. Nevertheless, it would be superfluous to identify a Christian understanding of God and *Donghak*'s understanding of *Hananim* without proviso. It would be much wiser to take the path of understanding each other's way and learning its respective way in terms of mutual respect and dialogue. Waiting on the indwelling of the heavenly Lord par excellence in *Donghak* offers a possible field of conversation as regards a pneumatological understanding of God in Christianity. Today's ecological crisis teaches

9 [Editor's note: in the author's view, western philosophy is not capable of overcoming a contradiction between *capax* and *non-capax* fully. This question remains at a cross roads, either for the sake of ontological participation or for the sake of the non-immanent transcendental aspect of God. Maybe in Dong Hak, or generally in a principle of Buddhism or Taoism, this contradiction between *capax* and *non-capax* can be resolved for the sake of "infinitum capax finitum" in which finitude fully takes part.]

how unilaterally a traditional Christian theology is oriented toward God's transcendence in a history-centered, anthropocentric paradigm. In such, a framework of understanding human life also remains superficial and one-sided in relation to God and other living creatures in universe.

20

Global Ethic for a New World Order

Hans Küng

It is with great pleasure and honor for me to speak here at Wongkwan University, the high place of Won Buddhist teaching and learning. I thank you very much for your kind invitation.

This visit is of special interest for me, because I realize that there are many affinities and concordances between the teachings of Won Buddhism and the project of a Global Ethic as it is laid down in the Declaration of the Parliament of the World's Religions in Chicago in 1993 and as it is being promoted through the activities of the Global Ethic Foundation in Tübingen, Germany, of which I am the president.

I was impressed when I read that your Founder, Sot'aesan, was an ardent advocate of human dignity: Based on the principle, "The Wise One as the Standard" he fought against various kinds of social and religious discrimination occurring in the society of his time and acknowledged implicitly the basic dignity of every human being. This dignity is reaffirmed by the Chicago Declaration when it emphasizes that, "every human being without distinction of age, sex, race, skin color, physical or mental ability, language, religion, political view, or national or social origin possesses an inalienable and untouchable dignity" and that therefore "every human being must be treated humanely."

I was even more surprised to see how Soe'tasan's successor, Chongsan, developed this further in his doctrine of Samdong Morality. Quite obviously its first principle, "All doctrines have the same origin" stimulates dialogue and peace among religions. Referring to the Global Ethic I would, however, like to note that we prefer not to focus on doctrines where we can see differences rather than unity but that we emphasize the common ground of religions in their shared ethical values, principles, and standards. Chongsan's second principle, "All living beings are related by the same force of life" reminds me again of the fundamental dignity of every human being and their interdependence. This is also expressed in the age-old ethical principle of reciprocity, the so-called Golden Rule, "What you wish done to yourself, do to others." Finally, the third principle, "All enterprises are for the same purpose," underlines the need for cooperation of all people of good will, in a coalition of religious and non-religious people, for the good of society and for peace for our whole planet. This is indeed the final goal of the search for a Global Ethic. Let me now elaborate more in detail on some aspects of this project.

Challenges and Responses

1. We live in a world and time where we observe new dangerous tensions and *polarizations between believers and non-believers,* religious people and agnostics, secularists, between clericals and anti-clericals—not only in Russia, and Europe, but also in Africa, in North-America, and in Asia too. To this challenge I respond: *There can be no survival of humanity without a coalition of believers and non-believers in mutual respect!*

   But many people tell me: Are we not living in a period of a new cultural confrontation? Indeed:

2. We live in a world and time, where humanity is menaced by a "clash of civilizations," e.g., between the Muslim civilization and the Western civilization. We are threatened not so much by a new world war, but by all sorts of conflicts in a specific country or in a city, a street or a school.

   To this challenge I respond: *There will be no peace among the civilizations without peace among the religions!*

   But many people will ask: Do not religions precisely often support and inspire hatred, enmity and war? Indeed:

3. We live in a world and time where peace in many countries is menaced by all sorts of *religious fundamentalism,* Christian, Muslim, Jewish, Hindu, Buddhist, often simply rooted in social misery, in reaction to western secularism and in the desire of a basic orientation in life.

   To this challenge I respond: *There will be no peace among the religions without dialogue between the religions!*

But many people will object: Are there not so many dogmatic differences and obstacles between the different faiths, which make real dialogue a naive illusion? Indeed:

4. We live in a world and time, where better relations between religions are blocked by all sort of *dogmatisms* which exist not only in the Roman Catholic Church, but in all churches, religions and ideologies.

   To this challenge I respond: *There will be no new world order without a world ethic*, a global ethic despite dogmatic differences.

New World Order and World Ethic

1. In *negative* terms: A better world order will *not* be introduced on the basis:

   a. solely of diplomatic offensives which all too often are unable to guarantee peace and stability in a certain region and which are often, as now in former Yugoslavia, characterized more by hypocrisy than by honesty;

   b. simply of humanitarian help which cannot replace political actions and solutions: The European powers, by substituting humanitarian aid in Bosnia for political action, put themselves in the power of the aggressors and became complicit in the crimes of war;

   c. primarily of military interventions: Of course an absolute pacifism would allow a new holocaust, a new genocide at the end of this "never again century." But indeed, the consequences of military interventions tend often to be more negative than positive;

   d. solely of international law, as long as such a law rests on the unlimited sovereignty of states and is focused more on the rights of states than on the peoples and individuals rights. If moral convictions and moral intentions do not back a law, armistice or treaty, powers are not even prepared to defend the principle that only peaceful and negotiated territorial change is acceptable in Europe.

2. In *positive terms*: A better world order will ultimately be *brought in only on the basis of*

    - common visions, ideals, values, aims and criteria;
    - heightened global responsibility on the part of peoples and their leaders;
    - a new binding and uniting ethic for all humankind, including states and those in power, which embraces cultures and religions. No new worl*d order without a new world ethic, a global ethic.*

3. What is the *function* of such a global ethic?

    - Global ethic is not a new ideology or superstructure;
    - it will not make the specific ethics of the different religions and philosophies superfluous;
    - it is therefore no substitute for the Torah, Sermon on the Mount, the Qur'an, the Bhagavadgita, the Discourses of the Buddha or the Sayings of Confucius.
    - Global ethic is nothing but the necessary minimum of common values, standards and basic attitudes. In other words:—a minimal basis consensus relating to binding values, irrevocable standards and moral attitudes, which can be affirmed by all religions despite their »dogmatic« differences and can also be supported *by non-believers.* But is this really possible?

Lack of Orientation

What should human beings hold on to—in all circumstances and everywhere? The *vacuum in orientation* is a global problem. This is obviously the case everywhere in the former *Soviet block* after the collapse of Communism and under the surface even in Communist *China*, still as oppressive as before. It is a problem not only for Russia and China but for all civilizations to cope with this moral and spiritual vacuum.

In *Europe*, after the murder of a two-year-old child by two ten-year-olds in Liverpool even liberal journals and columnists complained about the "orientation jungle" and a lack of taboos unprecedented in cultural history: "The youngest generation must cope with a confusion of values the extent of which is almost impossible to estimate. For them clear standards of right and wrong, good and evil, of the kind that were still being communicated by parents and schools, churches and sometimes even politicians in the 1950s and 1960s, are hardly recognizable any more."

But please do not misunderstand me: I am pleading for the rediscovery and reassessment of *ethics* in politics and economics. I am all for *morality* (in the positive sense). But at the same time I am *against moralism* (morality in the negative sense). For moralism and moralizing overvalue morality and ask too much of it. Why? Moralizers make morality the sole criterion for human action and ignore the relative independence of various spheres of life like economics, law and politics. As a result they tend to absolutize intrinsically justified norms and values (peace, justice, environment, life, love) and also to exploit them for the particular interests of an institution (e.g. a party, church or interest group). Moralism manifests itself in a one-sided and penetrating insistence on particular moral positions (for example, in questions of sexual behavior, contraception, abortion, euthanasia, and similar issues) which makes a rational dialogue with those of other convictions impossible. In other words: In speaking out for a few common ethical standards, I do not want to support fundamentalists of any kind nor opportunist politicians who practice the emotive language of today's therapeutic ethos and politicking.

If in a new world constellation, which is coming into being, humankind on our planet is going to have any further guarantee of survival, there is urgent need for a *universal basic consensus on humane convictions*. A question which is thousands of years old is also unavoidable in our time: Why should one *do good and not evil*? Why do human beings not stand "beyond good and evil?" Why are they not just obligated to their will to power, to success, riches, consumer goods, sex?

Elementary questions are often the most difficult of all. And all over the world much about morals, laws and customs that had been taken for granted down the centuries because it was backed by religious authority, is no longer automatically accepted. A worldwide dialogue, a *global dialogue*, has already been set in motion which should lead to a consensus on shared values, standards and basic attitudes, to a world ethic, a global ethic.

It should be evident that there is a fundamental problem here particularly for *modern democracy*. Given the way in which the free democratic state, which recognizes freedom of conscience and religion, understands itself, its worldview must be neutral. A modern democracy must tolerate different religions and denominations, philosophies and ideologies. And a democratic government is not supposed to decree a meaning to *life or a life-style*.

But is this not quite manifestly the basis of *the dilemma of any modern democratic state*, whether in Europe, America, India, or Japan? Dr. Carey, the Archbishop of Canterbury rightly said about Great Britain: "Whilst this country is still deeply marked by its Christian heritage and whilst a large majority retain a belief in God, we can find today no clearly defined or sharply focused system of values which binds our whole society together. Secularization, with its utilitarian bias, does not provide a robust value system—as we are discovering to our cost."

People are not always happy with this moral vacuum. People normally feel an unquenchable desire to hold on to something. They want to rely on something. In our technological world which has become so complex, and in the confusion of their private lives, they would like to have somewhere to stand, a line to follow; they would like to have criteria, a goal. In short, people feel an unquenchable desire to have something like a *basic ethical orientation*.

But all experiences show that human beings cannot be improved by more and more laws and precepts, nor of course can they be improved simply by psychology and sociology; most psychologists and sociologists probably will agree. Technological know how is not yet knowledge about meanings, as technicians know better than others. And specialists of cybernetics may probably agree that rules are not yet orientations. And so, I hope, lawyers would share my point of view: laws are not yet morals. In short, all reasonable people would probably not object: The *law needs a moral foundation!* And security in our cities and communities cannot be bought simply with money, nor with more police and prisons.

In other words: The ethical acceptance of laws (which provide the state with sanctions and can be imposed by force) is the presupposition of any political culture. What is the use to individual states or organizations, whether these be the EU, the USA or the United Nations, of constantly new laws, if a significant part of the population or powerful groups or individuals have no intention of observing them? If they constantly find enough ways and means of irresponsibly imposing their own or collective interests: *Quid leges sine moribus?* runs a Roman saying: what are laws without morals?

Towards a Binding Global Ethic

Certainly all states in the world have an economic and legal order, but in no state will this order function without an ethical consensus, without that ethical concern among its citizens by which the state with a democratic constitution lives. Already in the Parliament of the French Revolution nearly half of those who voted for the Declaration of Human Rights wanted to have the *human responsibilities* (*devoirs*) formulated alongside human rights. This remained an issue of continuing debate.

Now in our century, after two world wars, the international community has already created transnational, transcultural and transreligious legal structures (without which international treaties would in fact be sheer self-deception). But if a new world order is to exist, it needs a *minimum of common values, standards, and basic attitudes*, an ethic which, for all its time-conditioned nature, is binding in all senses of the word on the whole of humanity, in short a global ethic.

And this is of decisive importance precisely in the age of globalization: The globalization of the economy, technology and the media means also the globalization of problems: from financial and labor markets to the environment and organized crime! What is therefore also needed is the *globalization of ethic*. Again: not a uniform ethical system ("ethics"), but a necessary minimum of shared ethical values, basic attitudes and standards to which all regions, nations and interest groups can subscribe—in other words, a shared basic *ethic* for humankind. Indeed: There can be no new world order without a world ethic, a global ethic.

But is it at all possible to elaborate and formulate a *global* ethic? Are the ethical norms of the different nations, regions, cultures and religions not incompatible? Of course, they differ in many concrete questions from each other. But on the other hand I discovered that on the base all great ethical and religious traditions of humanity have very much in common.

I found my conviction confirmed by the fact that my book entitled *Global Responsibility: In Search of a New World Ethic*, published in German in 1990 and in Korean in 1992, has received widespread international backing in recent years. Two documents are of particular relevance:

- On 4 September 1993, for the first time in the history of religion, delegates to the Parliament of the World's Religions in Chicago adopted a "Declaration Toward a Global Ethic."

- On 1 September 1997, again for the first time, the InterAction Council of former presidents and prime ministers called for a global ethic and submitted to the United Nations a proposed "Universal Declaration of Human Responsibilities."

These two declarations are not isolated documents. They are responses to the urgent calls of influential international bodies for global ethical standards. An entire chapter is devoted to this issue in the 1995 reports of both the UN-Commission on Global Governance and the World Commission on Culture and Development. The same issues have been on the agenda for some time at the World Economic Forum in Davos and also in the new UNESCO Universal Ethics Project. They are also receiving increasing attention in Asia.

The proposed Universal Declaration of Human Responsibilities supports and underpins the Universal Declaration of Human Rights from an ethical angle, as announced in the preamble: "We . . . thus renew and reinforce commitments already proclaimed in the Universal Declaration of Human Rights: namely, the full acceptance of the dignity of all people; their inalienable freedom and equality, and their solidarity with one another." If human rights are not being asserted everywhere that they could be, this is usually for want of the necessary political and ethical will. Even the most fervent of human rights activists must acknowledge that "the rule of law and the promotion of human rights depend on the readiness of men and women to act justly."

Of course it would be wrong to suggest that the legal validity of human rights should be dependent on the actual fulfillment of human responsibilities. The idea of human rights as a reward for good behavior is absurd—for this would mean that only those who had shown themselves worthy of the community by fulfilling their responsibilities towards it would be entitled to enjoy such rights. This would clearly conflict with the notion of the unconditional dignity of the individual, which in turn is a pre-condition for both rights and responsibilities. No one is suggesting that certain human responsibilities must be fulfilled, by the individual or by a community, before any claim can be laid to human rights. The latter are part and parcel of the individual, who is always, however, the bearer of responsibilities as well as rights: All human rights are by definition directly bound up with the duty to respect them.

What then are the basic principles of both Declarations? I can only quote their very core: First: "Every human being must be treated humanely" and the Golden Rule, "What you do not wish to be done to yourself, do not do to others." In positive terms: "What you wish done to yourself, do to others!" Or as Buddhism knows it in the Udana-Varga (5.18): "Hurt not others in ways that you yourself would find hurtful!"

On this basis four irrevocable directives are developed, four imperatives of humanity (extensively in the Declaration of the Parliament of the

World's Religions, in a more condensed and juridical form in the proposal of the Inter Action Council):

1. "Have respect for all life!" The ancient precept, especially urgent in a time of children killing children: "You shall not kill!" That means today the responsibility for a culture of non-violence and respect for life.

2. "Deal honestly and fairly!" The very old commandment, important more than ever in the age of globalization: "You shall not steal!" That means today the responsibility for a culture of solidarity and a just economic order.

3. "Speak and act truthfully!" The ancient axiom, valid also for politicians and the media: "You shall not lie!" That means the responsibility for a culture of tolerance and a life of truthfulness.

4. "Respect and love one another!" The age-old directive, even more important in an age which seems to be without taboos: "You shall not abuse sexuality, not commit sexual immorality!" That means the responsibility for a culture of equal rights and partnership between men and women.

I am convinced that the new world order will only be a better order if it will result in a pluralistic world society characterized by partnership, which encourages peace and is nature-friendly and ecumenical.

Conclusion

Great were the hopes of humanity in 1899. The God of the 19th century was, as we today know, "Progress," and people were convinced that eternal, almighty progress would also bless the 20th century. But we experienced in our century two world wars, the Gulag archipelago, the Holocaust, the atomic bomb. . . . Will the 21st century be better?

In 1899 nobody thought that this "eternal" progress could be stopped, that leaders of reactionary movements would arise, decisive figures in a century which is now called a "century of extremisms."

In 1899 a young Russian intellectual, Uljanow, later called Lenin, still lived in exile in Siberia.

In 1899 the orthodox seminarian, Djugashvili, later called Stalin, lived still in the seminary in Tbilissi/Georgia and just got acquainted with revolutionary activity.

In 1899 in Italy a boy of sixteen, and in Austria another boy of ten had only dreams about their future. They were later to be known as: "il Duce" and "der Führer."

Indeed communism, fascism and Nazism were to become the determinant great reactionary ideologies of this »century of extremes« which ended in 1989—ten years ago. I ask myself, and I am asking you: This century had three opportunities for a new and better world-order:

- 1918 the new world order was announced by President Wilson, who was defeated by "European Realpolitik" in Versailles; instead of a new world order a real world chaos;
- 1945 the new world order was prepared by the Charter of the UN and was ruined by Stalins "Realpolitik"; instead of a new world order a division of the world;
- 1989 a new world order was announced by President Bush after the Gulf War who did not know what it meant. The question therefore: Shall humanity also miss this third opportunity of this century?

It cannot be the task of such a lecture to draw a complete vision of a new world order. But I tried to outline from my specific historical, philosophical, and theological angle certain dimensions which seem to me essential and decisive. To conclude, let me summarize my convictions for the new century:

- There will be no peace among nations without peace among the religions.
- There will be no peace among religions without dialogue among the religions.
- There will be no successful dialogue among religions without considering common ethical standards for our globe.
- There will therefore be no survival of our globe without a global ethic.

Bibliography

Hans Küng, *Global Responsibility. In Search of a New World Ethic* (London/Continuum, New York: SCM Press, 1991; Korean, Waegwan: Benedict Press, 1992).

Hans Küng, Karl-Josef Kuschel (Eds), *A Global Ethic: The Declaration of the Parliament of the World's Religions* (London/Continuum, New York: SCM Press, 1993).

Hans Küng (Ed), *Yes to a Global Ethic* (London/Continuum, New York: SCM Press, 1996).

Hans Küng, *A Global Ethic for Global Politics and Economics* (London: SCM Press, 1997/ New York: Oxford University Press, 1998).

Hans Küng, Helmut Schmidt (Eds), *A Global Ethic and Global Responsibilities. Two Declarations* (London: SCM Press, 1998).

Epilogue

Minjung Seen in the Fourth Eye: Theology from a New Continent

Craig L. Nessan

If Christendom is coming and has come to an end, then the theology of Christendom also is coming and has come to an end. What did the theology of Christendom look like? We know the answer from recent memory. Christendom's theology was characterized by systematic presentations of the loci of Christian doctrine, researched and authored by individual theologians of epic proportions—Schleiermacher, Barth, Tillich, Pannenberg. The names are all familiar as the teachers of our recent past. These were the theological giants, whose passing we mourn with longing and nostalgia—as for a golden age.

Christendom's theology was Euro-centered. The main figures and concepts were all rooted in European intellectual history. The plot lines and footnotes in the theological timeline of Christendom's theology were almost exclusively European. If an author from another context were acknowledged at all, it was because that theologian also had been trained in the ways of Europe. And the subject of Christendom's theology was privileged—holding an elite academic chair in the university, engaging the academic currents of the time, addressing the cultured despisers of religion. This was a theology, university born and bred. Its interlocutors were the other disciplines of the university and their realm of discourse. Furthermore, the figures are male. Both the voices of women and people from the developing world were absent.

How does one recount the demise of Christendom and its theology? It is not necessary again here to articulate the origins of Christendom in the 4th century beginning with the edict of Constantine, the Roman emperor. Suffice it to say that the tacit alignment of church and theology with

Western civilization persisted uninterrupted well into the 20th century. Was it in the trenches of Verdun that the solid earth of Christendom began to crack, as Karl Barth detected in his commentary on Romans when he took leave from his teachers? Surely the rift became a gulf at Auschwitz, as Dietrich Bonhoeffer and the leaders of the Confessing Church took up resistance against the German Christian state, tragically too little and too late to interrupt the Holocaust. Friedrich-Wilhelm Marquardt, whose essay (Chapter 12) is wisely included in this volume, is prophet of the end of Christendom as he tirelessly insisted that there can be no Christian theology in opposition to the Jews. For anti-Judaism and its bitter fruit, anti-Semitism, have been horrible consequences of Christendom's theology from the beginning. Clearly at the beginning of the 21st century—after Gandhi, after the Korean War, after the end of colonialism, after Viet Nam, after 1989, after 9/11—Christendom is over. The analyses of a postmodern world and the loss of all grand narratives (Lyotard) mean that this emerging global age is post-Christian. The bankruptcy of the church in its service to Western civilization and Western politics should be plain before our eyes. Christianity has been in continental drift away from its all too familiar homeland in the West.

Yet every future is constructed out of the fragments of the past. This is equally true for theology after Christendom. Some of the figures whose feet are planted in Christendom scouted the frontier landscape: Karl Barth by insisting on the revealing God, not culture, as the point of departure, as well as through his commitment to the way of religious socialism; and Dietrich Bonhoeffer by his excursions to the France of Lasserre's nonviolence, Abyssinian Baptist Church in Harlem, and the nascent ecumenical movement. These two provide orientation, a compass, for those setting out from Christendom toward the new continent, as evidenced throughout this book.

The theological work of others—Jürgen Moltmann and John Cobb—demonstrates intentional effort to bridge the span between Christendom and the emerging theology. Moltmann takes with utmost seriousness the need for theology to begin with the experience of the poor, the marginalized, women, and the earth itself as an ecosystem. Early and consistently, Moltmann has engaged minjung theology and been changed by it, as we witness in the essay included in this volume. Cobb also engages the perspective of the economically disenfranchised, but the bridge he seeks to build is even more unique in that he entertains Christian faith as creatively transformed by Asian religion, particularly Buddhism. In the writings of Moltmann (cf. Chapter 5) and Cobb (cf. Chapter 11), we view the theological landscape of the new continent through the lenses of trusted guides.

Yet to begin to understand this new theological territory, it requires us to look not only through the two eyes of Western visionaries and bridge builders, but through the third and fourth eyes of those native to the new terrain. Third eye theology (Suzuki, Song) refers to the eye that is opened to see after Buddhist enlightenment. Clearly, the theology we read in this book sees with a third eye of religious insight from Buddhist, Taoist, Confucian, and other Asian traditions. The new continent requires us to engage Jewish-Christian theological tradition in living encounter with the great religions of Asia and to be changed by them. What is striking about this encounter is that it arises from those whose lives are immersed in a culture where religious pluralism is the lived reality. We listen to a discourse in which *ch'i, yin-yang, dharma,* and *Tao* are more native concepts than grace, faith, justification, and Christ. Fourth eye theology (Paul Chung) sees the minjung from the perspective of the Bodhisattva praxis of compassion. This is a new term, introduced in this book, derived from the engaged Buddhism of Thic Nhat Hanh. It is the fourth eye that sees the *han* of the little ones and moves the heart in the direction of minjung theology.

This book is unique in documenting the development of minjung theology over the course of four generations of Korean theologians. In the various contributions, we witness the shift from a theology decisively shaped by the theology of Christendom, to a theology drawing its inspiration from Korean culture, to a theology in full interaction with the religions of Asia, to a theology insisting on engaged praxis growing out of the Korean context of oppression and religious pluralism. As we read and reflect on the various contributions, we see the emergence of a truly post-Christendom theology from Korean perspective.

The first generation documented in this book is represented in the essays by Kim Chai-Choon (Chapter 1 and 2) and Chung Dai-Wi (Chapter 16). These are representatives of Korean liberal theology and the teachers of those who emerged as the first minjung theologians. Kim Chai-Choon articulates the shift in post-Christendom theology toward the serious consideration of social location and introduces the necessity of dialogue between Christianity and Buddhism. Chung Dai-Wi, an expert in Chinese civilization and the mission history of Matteo Ricci, draws lessons for contemporary engagement with the major Asian religious traditions, especially from the legacy of Ricci. Together, these chapters reflect the work of theologians oriented toward the West, yet freshly engaging the East Asian religious and cultural milieu.

The second generation—and the first generation of minjung theologians—documented in this book includes Ahn Byung-Mu (Chapter 3) and Suh Nam-Dong (Chapter 4). These are the figures that developed the profound insight into Jesus' solidarity with the *ochlos* of the New Testament Gospels and identified the *ochlos* with the Korean minjung. In this book, we witness the brilliance of Ahn Byung-Mu, who exegetes Jesus' Galilean ministry in solidarity with the *am-ha'aretz*, thereby restoring the connection of Christianity with its Jewish origins and linking the plight of the New Testament *ochlos* sociologically with the Korean minjung. The kingdom of God was and is for the minjung. Suh Nam-Dong draws upon biblical texts, church history, and recent theologians to further broaden and deepen the relationship between *ochlos* and minjung. Furthermore, he introduces a political connection between the kingdom of God and minjung movements in Korean history, a provocative step that precipitated conflict with the political and theological power keepers of the time.

A third generation of Korean theologians—and second generation of minjung theologians—is represented in this volume by the work of Kim Kyoung-Jae (Chapters 9, 17, and 19). What is innovative about his work is its full investment in the intercultural development of minjung theology. Kim draws upon the correlation method of Tillich, the hermeneutical insights of Gadamer, and the process categories of Cobb to rethink mission theology in an East Asian context. He draws upon the rich concept of *ch'i* and the *Donghak* experience of God to enrich a Christian understanding of Korean spirituality. Kim is fully conversant with the intellectual and religious traditions that inform Korean culture and draws upon these naturally to reconceptualize Christian thought.

A fourth generation of theologians—and the third minjung generation—comes to expression in the essays by Choi In-Sik (Chapter 14), Koo D. Yun (Chapters 6 and 10) and Paul S. Chung (Chapters 8, 15, and 18). Here we see the emergence of diverse trends and concepts, all most fluently conversant with Korean culture and history, yet in vital dialogue with the old continent of the West. Choi In-Sik, consistent with the agenda of Marquardt, brings Korean theology into explicit encounter with its Jewish origins. This is one of the most important contributions of this entire project: that in the development of inter-religious dialogue and with the post-Christendom emergence of an inter-religious Christian theology that the Jewish ethos of Christianity not be lost but honored and explicitly incorporated. To this end the essay of Choi, along with the contributions of Marquardt and Pangritz (Chapter 13), is crucial.

Koo D. Yun further expands the ecumenical discussion by writing from the perspective of Pentecostalism. With the rapid growth of Christian Pentecostalism in Africa, South America, and Asia, and spreading from there also to the post-Christendom West, the theologies of the future will need to engage the contributions of this viewpoint as a matter of habit. Koo introduces the world of Asian Pentecostals into the dialogue and draws upon Asian notions of spirit to solidify the importance of including spirit as an organizing category for future theology. The essay by Kärkkäinen (Chapter 7) expands this viewpoint by mapping the relationship of minjung theology to other contemporary streams of thought, including the encounter with the world religions.

Finally, the essays by Paul S. Chung demonstrate the fullness of inter-religious encounter from the Korean perspective of minjung. Chung is highly conversant with the theology of Christendom (e.g., Barth and Bonhoeffer), yet in original ways develops a post-Christendom theology that reinterprets Christian thought from the insights of Asian religious traditions. Like Choi, Chung is committed to the recovery of Christianity's Jewish origins and makes this an integral theme for the future of theology. As a student and former assistant of Ahn, Chung dedicates Chapter 8, "Dietrich Bonhoeffer Seen from Asian Minjung Theology and the Fourth Eye of Socially Engaged Buddhism," to him. Also as a student of Chung Dai-Wi, Chung dedicates Chapter 18, "Mission and Inculturation in the Thought of Matteo Ricci," to his memory. The work of Chung opens a path for integrating the various generations of minjung theology into a creative synthesis.

What are the characteristics of the theology emerging from the new continent of post-Christendom as articulated from the Korean minjung perspective? This is a theology that is engaged in social and political praxis in solidarity with the minjung of the earth. It is a theology that is in the process of recovering, honoring, and intentionally thematizing its Jewish identity. It is a theology that is by nature inter-religious, conversant and creatively transformed by the reality of Buddhist, Confucian, Taoist, and indigenous religious traditions. And it is a theology attuned to the movement of the Spirit, blowing anew from an unexpected context. It is a theology in which the Christendom distinction between theology and ethics no longer holds. It is a theology that is already leading the Christian church toward a "new world order" and the urgently necessary global ethic (cf. Küng, Chapter 20) that are a prolepsis of the kingdom itself.

Contributors

Ahn Byung-Mu is a founding representative of Asian minjung theology. He earned a doctorate at the University of Heidelberg, Germany, and then worked as a Professor of the New Testament at Han Shin Seminary. He served as the director of Han Kuk Theology Institute.

Kim Chai-Choon is a founding father of the Presbyterian Church in the People's Republic of Korea (PROK). He is also a former dean at Hankuk Theological Seminary in South Korea, and a former chairperson of the Korean Committee of Amnesty International. After his death in 2002, he was granted the "National Medal of Mugunghwa" by the Korean government.

Paul S. Chung is an Assistant Professor at Wartburg Theological Seminary in Dubuque, Iowa. He earned his doctorate at the University of Basel, Switzerland (Dr. Theol), and finished his postdoctoral studies at the Graduate Theological Union, Berkeley, California. His books include *Karl Barth und die Hegelsche Linke* (1994), *Spirituality and Social Ethic in John Calvin* (2000), *Martin Luther and Buddhism: Aesthetics of Suffering* (2002), and numerous articles.

John B. Cobb, Jr. is a retired Professor from Claremont School of Theology and Claremont Graduate School. He continues to be active in the Center for Process Studies. He helped to initiate, along with Masao Abe, a series of international discussions between leading Buddhist and Christian thinkers. Among his books related to the topic of this volume, in addition to *Beyond Dialogue,* from which the essay included here is taken, are *Christ in a Pluralistic Age* and *Transforming Christianity and the World.*

Chung Dai-Wi is a former President of Kun Kuk University and Hanshin University, South Korea, and a former Professor of Religious Studies at Carleton University, Canada. He earned his Ph. D from Yale University Divinity School.

Choi In-Sik is a Professor of Systematic Theology at Seoul Theological University and Seminary in South Korea. He earned a doctorate at the University of Humboldt (*Kirchliche Hochschule* Berlin), Germany. His doctoral dissertation is *Die taologische Frage nach Gott: Paul Tillichs philosophischer Gottesbegriff des ‚Sein-Selbst' und sprachliche Verantwortung des Glaubens in Begegnung mit dem Taogedanken Laotzus* (Peter Lang, 1991). His major concern is about theology of culture and theology of Jesus. His books include *Church and Theology in the Pluralistic Culture, Church and Theology in the Age of Multimedia, and Jesus and Culture in the Cybernetic Culture.*

Veli-Matti Kärkkäinen is a Professor of Systematic Theology at Fuller Theological Seminary, Pasadena, California, and a Dozent of Ecumenics at the University of Helsinki, Finland. He earned his doctorate (Dr. Theol.) and finished his postdoctoral *Habilitationsschrift* from the University of Helsinki. His books include *An Introduction to the Theology of Religions* (2003), *Trinity and Religious Pluralism* (2004) and *Doctrine of God: A Global Perspective* (2004), among others.

Hans Küng is a Professor Emeritus of Ecumenical Theology at the University of Tübingen and also President of the Global Ethic Foundation in Germany and Switzerland. He is widely acknowledged to be one of the greatest theologians of the twentieth century.

Kim Kyoung-Jae is a Professor Emeritus of Systematic Theology and Cultural Studies at Han Shin Theological Seminary, Seoul, South Korea. He studied at Dubuque and Claremont. Finally he completed his doctorate at the University of Utrecht (Dr. Theol). He is a leading theologian of hermeneutical theology of culture and religions in South Korea. He is the author of *Christianity and the Encounter of Asian Religions* (1994), as well as numerous other books and articles. He served as the director of the Christian Academy in Korea, engaging passionately in interreligious dialogue and fraternal co-operation for justice, peace and ecology.

Friedrich-Wilhelm Marquardt is a Professor Emeritus of Systematic Theology at the Free University of Berlin, Germany. He is a pioneer of the renewal of Jewish-Christian relations in Germany. He is also the author of books and essays on the theology of Karl Barth (e.g. *Theologie und Sozialismus*, 1972) and of Dogmatics (7 volumes, 1988-1997), reflecting the situation of Christianity "after Auschwitz."

Jürgen Moltmann is a Professor Emeritus at the University of Tübingen, Germany. He is a world renowned ecumenical theologian. His books include *Theology of Hope* (1964), *The Crucified God* (1972), *The Trinity and the Kingdom of God* (1981), *God in Creation* (1985), *The Spirit of Life* (1991), and *The Coming of God* (1995), among others.

Suh Nam-Dong is another founding representative of Asian minjung theology. He was formerly a Professor of Systematic Theology at Han Shin Seminary and at the United Theological Seminary at Yun Sei University. To honor his theological achievements and his commitment to the human rights movement, he was granted an honorary doctorate from the University of Toronto.

Craig L. Nessan is the Academic Dean and Professor of Contextual Theology at Wartburg Theological Seminary in Dubuque, Iowa. Among his theological interests are liberation theology, Dietrich Bonhoeffer, and theological ethics. In addition to other articles, reviews, and books, Dr. Nessan is the author of *Many Members, Yet One Body: Committed Same-Gender Relationships and the Mission of the Church* (2004), *Give Us This Day: A Lutheran Proposal for Ending World Hunger* (2003), *The Air I Breathe is Wartburg Air: The Legacy of William H. Weiblen* (2003), *Beyond Maintenance to Mission: A Theology of the Congregation* (1999) and *Who Is Christ for Us?* (2002, edited with Renate Wind).

Andreas Pangritz is a Professor of Systematic Theology at the University of Bonn, Germany. He is the author of books and essays on the theology of Dietrich Bonhoeffer (*Karl Barth in the Theology of Dietrich Bonhoeffer*, 2000) and on the Jewish-Christian relationship.

Koo D. Yun is an Associate Professor of Systematic Theology at Bethany University, located in Santa Cruz, California. He earned his Ph.D. from the Graduate Theological Union after earning two master degrees (M. Div., M.S.T.) from Yale University Divinity School. Also, he is the author of *Baptism in the Holy Spirit: An Ecumenical Theology of Spirit Baptism* (2003).

Index

T

U

W

Y